MARX AND MILL

Two views of
social conflict and social harmony

MARX AND MILL

Two views of
social conflict and social harmony

GRAEME DUNCAN

Professor of Politics
University of East Anglia

CAMBRIDGE UNIVERSITY PRESS

CAMBRIDGE

LONDON · NEW YORK · MELBOURNE

Published by the Syndics of the Cambridge University Press
The Pitt Building, Trumpington Street, Cambridge CB2 1RP
Bentley House, 200 Euston Road, London NW1 2DB
32 East 57th Street, New York, N.Y. 10022, USA
296 Beaconsfield Parade, Middle Park, Melbourne 3206, Australia

© Cambridge University Press 1973

Library of Congress Catalogue Card Number: 73-80472

ISBN 0 521 20257 4 hard covers
ISBN 0 521 29130 5 paperback

First published 1973
First paperback edition 1977

First printed in Great Britain by
Western Printing Services Ltd, Bristol
Reprinted in Great Britain at the
University Printing House, Cambridge
(Euan Phillips, University Printer)

To Conny, Denise and Kirsten

Contents

Preface

In these pages I have tried to present, as clearly and generously as I can, the social theories of Marx and Mill, and to evaluate their claims and assumptions comparatively. Although I have tried to work out my own account of the two thinkers, I cannot pretend that my interpretation of either is novel or original. My account of Marx's views is based almost entirely on English translations of his works. Unimpressed by the current fashion of Engels-baiting, which normally rests upon an exaggeration of Marx's Hegelian background and a vulgarisation of Engels, I have treated Engels as a semi-Marx. I have used his writings to elaborate Marx's views, or fill in the gaps, where they seem compatible, or where Marx approved of them, though I have also separated them at many points. Engels was an inferior thinker to Marx, and more positivistic and mechanical, but the difference is not as great as some of Marx's contemporary rescuers suggest. I have also tried to treat the visions of Marx and Mill in their terms, rather than as they have seemed to later and different advocates, or to those who dismiss them because of the doctrines and the actions of many who claim to speak and act in their names.

I would like to thank several people for their comments on particular parts of the manuscript: Max Hartwell, George Rudé and Frank Wright (the historical background), Eugene Kamenka (Marx on human nature), and John McCloskey and Barry Smith (Mill). The whole manuscript was read in its doctoral form by Isaiah Berlin, who supervised it, and John Plamenatz, who examined it scrupulously, and in close to its final version by Jim Cotton, Alan Ryan and Hugh Stretton. Each offered useful criticisms and suggestions, and I am especially grateful to Hugh Stretton for encouraging me to persevere in what often seemed a futile exercise. Naturally, I have been taught a lot – though not enough – by students and colleagues who are too numerous to mention.

Several typists have suffered agonies of boredom with good humour, and I warmly thank Bronwen Newbold, Joy Smith, Sue Campbell, Edna Hawke, and particularly Gale Mead. I also thank Peter Flynn for preparing the index.

G.C.D.

Adelaide
July 1973

PART 1   PRELIMINARIES

Introduction

Karl Marx and John Stuart Mill were both strong critics of mid-nineteenth-century industrial society, but their concerns, their range and their large background assumptions and presuppositions – and hence their critiques and their prescriptions – differ substantially. They were contemporaries who, despite their significance as the theorists and organisers of very different schools and movements, paid little attention to each other. Mill was born in 1806 and died in 1873, while Marx was a dozen years younger, and died ten years after him. They were fellow Londoners for more than twenty years. Mill concentrated on England in his writings, as did Marx after the late forties, although both commented frequently on events in the United States, in Europe, especially France, and Asia, especially India. But they were Europe-centred thinkers, and their writings on Asia are not only asides, but treat that vast conglomerate as a backward realm, lacking an independent principle of movement, and hence properly subject to the advanced European powers, which were steadily – and, for Marx, savagely – drawing it into civilisation. While differing decisively over the character and impact of the intervening powers, each saw Europe and America as treading the path of the world's future, and thus remained children of their own times, despite their universalist pretensions and hopes.

Marx and Mill were not only the creators of the classical communist and liberal theories, in which they strove to make sense of contemporary experience and to generalise and predict beyond their own era, but they were deeply involved in practical political life, as pamphleteers and political organisers, though each at times expressed strong distaste for concrete political activity. Like most great social and political theorists, they believed that they lived during a period of social and cultural crisis, and that their theories and their actions could play some part in the process of change and eventual stabilisation. They wanted to enlighten others, to remove impediments to their vision so that they could see the truth and follow it, moving with the forces of history to destroy division, suffering and obscurantism. Each was anti-conservative, refusing, though in quite different ways, to take the existing society as sacrosanct. Their grand theories of human progress were

1

developed when English capitalism was at its most vigorous and triumphant, and each of them was very much concerned with current changes in the distribution of economic and political power, and the related social conflicts. Naturally theirs were not lone voices, as many of their contemporaries wrestled with the same problems and sometimes came up with similar answers. But Marx and Mill were generally, if not clearer and more precise, at least more profound and more imaginative thinkers than other theorists of industrial capitalism and liberal society at that time.

However, it may be denied that there is much point in attempting a comparative study. To take one instance, George Lichtheim has suggested that 'there is little purpose in contrasting Marx with some representative figure of nineteenth-century liberalism, J. S. Mill being the obvious example'.[1] Even were it possible to take Mill more seriously as a social theorist, continues Lichtheim, 'he cannot be said to have furnished modern liberalism with a working model for everyday political use, whereas "the union of theory and practice" is the most distinguishing trait of Marxism'.[2] According to the argument, Marx was both theorist and historical actor, in whose person system building and revolutionary social currents came together, and this signally failed to happen in the case of Mill. Later in his book, however, Lichtheim describes Mill as the crucial figure in the movement of thought towards collectivism in nineteenth-century England. 'The crucial figure in this process is John Stuart Mill – Marx's contemporary and in a sense his only serious rival, *insofar* as he is one of the ancestors of Fabianism and welfare socialism generally.'[3] These assertions contain no serious objection to a comparison of the two thinkers, and the last statement even seems to encourage it. Of course, there may be little purpose in some kinds of comparison between Marx and Mill, and certain particular efforts, consisting of the juxtaposition of a few simplified notions of each, have been artificial and misleading. But the enterprise is not absurd or pointless as such. Whether there is purpose to it or not depends on the purposes of the person doing it, and how it is done. Mill clearly did provide a working model – or a series of working models – for everyday political use, in the form of goals or political programmes to be implemented. Utilitarianism, the doctrine on which he was trained, and to which he remained half-loyal, was a doctrine which quite explicitly combined theory and practice, seeking to embody right reason in public policy, while often degenerating into a naive concern with improvement. Mill viewed his whole theoretical system as intimately related to politics and practical life. Again, there were significant non-revolutionary currents during the nineteenth century. One could say, using Lichtheim's terms, that system building and reforming social currents came together in the person of Mill, and it is this which made him a serious rival to Marx. But the rivalry does not depend solely on any shift towards welfare socialism. The conflict is between rival doctrines of political change and rival accounts of the realities of capitalism. Mill was the champion of a mode of change, including movement towards political democracy, to which the history of nineteenth-century England approximated. And he himself had a powerful influence on thought and action in England during the second half of the century. The serious – and successful – rivals to Marx's disciples and followers, who at this time were hardly serious rivals to anybody, were the middle-class radicals or liberals struggling for the extension of the franchise and for other political reforms. Preoccupation with revolutionary social currents easily blinds one to quieter social movements and less far-reaching social doctrines. However, to claim that Mill's views may be fruitfully examined against those of Marx does not imply that they were equal in political influence or intellectual power – one could, indeed, accept Marx's harsh verdict on Mill, and still undertake a comparative analysis – but only that these are two significant, striking and conflicting theoretical reflections of changing capitalist society, and instruments for its transformation.

FACTS AND THEORIES

Marx and Mill saw things from different perspectives or vantage points, and offered conflicting accounts of their situation. Even to speak of 'their situation' begs the question, as the situation was and is subject to significantly varying interpretations, and was altering all the time. They were not disinterested observers of the same facts, nor even persons who saw the same facts and valued them differently, but committed participants within a changing society, whose character and tendencies were understood according to conflicting criteria and valuations.

It is necessary to note, in passing, the complex structure of most political theories, and the complex relations between such theories and the facts. Conflicts within and between political theories take place at a number of levels, which are not immunised from each other, but intertwine, and influence each other in many ways. There are factual or descriptive or empirical components; logical, linguistic, epistemological and methodological assumptions and habits concerning, in part, beliefs about the appropriate methods of asking questions and finding out answers; moral elements, including standards, evaluations and prescriptions, which express views about man's distinctive excellence or achievement and the nature of the good life; and metaphysical theories, concerning man's relation to the world in general. These factors can be distinguished analytically, and broken into logically distinct propositions. But although we can distinguish descriptive and value statements, many terms and notions both appraise and describe – value terms often have a factual reference and factual terms a value connotation, within particular social contexts. And in social theories these elements merge and influence each other in subtle and complex ways.

At the centre of political theories and political outlooks there lie, often merely implicit, conceptions of human nature, conceptions of man's needs, wants, interests, purposes, goals and capacities, as they were, are, and ultimately will be. Political theories are necessarily impregnated by values from the very beginning – such questions as what is human and what inhuman, what degrades and what ennobles man, what is a failure and what an achievement, and what kind of social order can satisfy him, are not empirical questions, though empirical evidence certainly bears upon them. In the consideration of such questions, judgment or preference and description – what is seen – are intimately linked. Assessments of the character and of the value of different polities are connected in that accounts of men's motives and concerns, and explanations of why they are grouped together as they are, already embody both a selection and a valuation. Values are not added later, like sauce to a meal, but penetrate the factual analysis itself. To assume otherwise easily leads to grotesque simplifications of complex intellectual activities, as in Popper's account of Marx as a 'moral futurist',[4] a worshipper of future success or might, rather than an intensely committed revolutionary, whose vision of human liberation strongly influenced his picture of existing social divisions and the forces challenging them. Hence political theories do not differ simply over how existing societies, similarly described, are to be evaluated: differences are built into their explanatory schemes, even when they pose as neutral.[5] In terms of their hidden valuations, certain things are presented as given, and certain options are excluded. The choice of a framework of analysis, which makes certain alternatives seem more feasible or desirable than others, itself depends upon certain selections and values – whether or not the conclusions to which it leads support the preferences of its author. Perhaps the greatest difficulty comes with conceptions of human nature, which cannot be measured easily against the facts, or torn out of the broader theories in which they are set. The evidence which is relevant to them is often of a peculiar and complex kind, and they themselves may admit – at the very most – only of peculiar and elaborate confirmation or disconfirmation.

Social and political theories are related complexly to 'the world of reality' which the theorist tries to describe and evaluate, and perhaps to change. What is seen depends upon the goal and the conceptual system of the observer or observer–participant, and these in turn depend heavily on the culture and social environment of which he is part. The seemingly clear-cut and independent facts – 'reality', correspondence to which, or exact copies of which, are held sometimes to constitute truth – can be organised and arranged in a great variety of ways, to support different accounts and images of life. Observation is itself an activity, and 'part and parcel of the intention and conceptual world of the observer'.[6] Given that particular concepts and categories, rather than others, are used in the pursuit of intelligibility, each mode of consideration becomes, in Whitehead's phrase, 'a sort of searchlight'.[7] The material of experience is selected from and weighted in different ways. Certain factors or forces are regarded as being of crucial significance (or 'real' or 'basic' or 'essential') and in terms of these everything else falls, or is thrust, into place. They occupy the centre of the stage while other factors are pushed into the background or excluded altogether. What comprises 'the relevant facts', though not what comprises mere facts, depends upon a system of classification, conventional or otherwise. Stuart Hampshire has illustrated this point in his account of the different ways in which a liberal and a Marxist will classify and organise events.

> In argument with a Marxist, a liberal may be startled to find that actions of his, to which he had never thought to attach a political significance, in his sense of 'political', are given a political significance and intention by his opponent. His opponent distinguishes the domain of politics by a different criterion that reflects a wholly different way of thinking about practical questions. That which constitutes a situation requiring a political decision, the extent of the domain of politics, is different for the two men, and each of them, absorbed in his own way of singling out and identifying situations confronting him, will fail to divide correctly the conduct of the other, separating phases of action that constituted a unity in the mind of the agent, and combining into a single action activities that the agent had envisaged under different headings.[8]

Nature, like society, can be dissected in many different ways, or subordinated to a variety of ordering principles. In *The Structure of Scientific Revolutions*, a work which has encouraged the subjectivists and moralists of social theory, Thomas Kuhn has challenged the established, objective status of the natural sciences, primarily through a cogent historical analysis of scientific conflict, development and change. Kuhn stresses the crucial role of metaphysics or ideology in creative scientific research, and rejects the view of scientific growth as an accumulation of truths, with myths, errors and unscientific notions steadily thrown on the wayside as scientists advance inexorably towards more and more complete approximations to reality. Scientists try to force nature into particular, 'preformed and relatively inflexible', conceptual boxes; at certain stages distinct and incommensurable views of nature – each roughly compatible with the dictates of scientific observation and method – compete with each other; and each specifies the kinds of entities the universe contains and, indirectly, those which it does not. Each necessarily partial theoretical network which directs fact collection, excludes or fails to take account of a great mass of facts, which may later illuminate, or transform, the issues under consideration. 'Scientific fact and theory are not categorically separable, except perhaps within a single tradition of normal-scientific practice. That is why the unexpected discovery is not simply factual in its importance and why the scientist's world is qualitatively transformed as well as quantitatively enriched by fundamental novelties of either fact or theory.'[9] During its reign, however, the paradigm – or constellation of beliefs, values and techniques shared by members of a given community[10] – will be defended against anomalies and paradoxes by a variety of means, and especially, because of its high generality, by subsidiary and intermediate hypotheses and *ad hoc* elaborations. Thus an historical account of scientific enterprise leads Kuhn to stress the prime importance of theory and methodology, which precedes and is necessary to selection, evaluation and criticism, and to warn us against mistaking a firm research consensus for a body of verified truth.

Distinctions and selections which are familiar or natural to us may be to others – and, in some circumstances, to ourselves – useless or irrelevant or absurd. For example, to adequately describe the workings of a primitive society we ordinarily need different distinctions and causal assumptions, and perhaps different notions of rationality, from those prevalent in the developed Western world. Explanations and the giving of reasons make sense in relation to the agent's particular conception of the world. We simply reveal our provincialism when we uncritically classify or explain novel or strange behaviour in our own categories. Any system of classification may act as a straitjacket, limiting the possibilities of analysis and inhibiting the imagining or conceiving of new, or radically different, forms of social life. Language already contains or supports a particular world view, so that as the individual learns it, he tends to take one attitude rather than another to social reality. Consequently, many social critics complain of the conservative effects of language, which, they say, determines a priori the direction in which the thought process moves, and establishes meanings which are themselves tenacious and limiting social facts. The radical competes at a huge intellectual and emotional disadvantage because, with a language tied so closely to current and past beliefs, he cannot convey adequately or convincingly his vision of a new world. Systems of classification, aided by languages which tend to freeze the world at certain points, often pretend to a permanent and universal validity, although – outside its range – things may change remarkably. It is exceedingly hard to break free from accustomed or traditional modes of doing things, and to treat new problems and issues on their merits, so to speak. As the new is always seen first with old eyes, it is hardly surprising that all sorts of curious compromises, muddles and halfway houses emerge, and that after a theoretical break-through thinkers are amazed at what they had overlooked previously. As Marx wrote to Engels: 'Human history fares like palaeontology. Even the best minds absolutely fail to see – on principle, owing to a certain judicial blindness – things which lie in front of their noses. Later, when the moment has arrived, one is surprised to find traces everywhere of what one has failed to see.'[11]

The impossibility of distinguishing sharply between facts and interpretations, between the acts of perception, cognition and valuation, makes even the categorisation of the differences between rival social theories – let alone any resolution of differences – an extremely difficult task. But normally they are not divided from each other, or from the world with which they deal, by a fixed and impenetrable wall. The relationship between the facts and political categories, values and goals is ordinarily one of interaction, the precise character and extent of which requires investigation in each particular case. Awareness of the loading or bias inherent in a particular conceptual scheme will enable us to see how evidence is being used, or what is taken to be evidence, and how certain information is liable to be absorbed into the theory or dismissed by it. Such an awareness arises from observation of the different ways in which, for example, liberals, conservatives and socialists find, gather and use evidence. It cannot come from some objective position outside the world. Thus criticism of loading within a social theory is set, not against a norm of objectivity or completeness, but against the fact of diversity. The critic of the bias of others cannot himself claim to be outside the area of human subjectivity and selectivity – though he may be outside specific arenas of conflict – and must recognise that his own social theorising is characterised by the selective perception which he rightly observes in others. His ability to see this is heavily dependent upon the kind of society in which he lives.[12]

Because social facts can be interpreted in so many different ways, and because of the diversity of human goals, what is to one man an exceptional and passing case is, for another, a firm indication of things to come. The evidence given in support of radical expectations of change may seem extremely thin, as when an impressive vision of life is supported only by a few examples of kindness or of human solidarity as indications of its own feasibility. A person who values and advocates relationships for society as a whole which are as a matter of fact confined to small groups or communities will be dismissed quickly as utopian. But it remains open – as well as essential – for him to indicate why most people fall short of his standard, to offer an account of those obstinate and tenacious societal facts upon which the conservative leans so heavily, and to display the foundations and the levers of change. Many critical theorists present history and civilisation as a record of manipulation, repression and malformation, and try, by envisaging the replacement of bad influences and crippling circumstances, to establish the feasibility, and not merely the desirability, of their social visions. On the other hand, the selections, descriptions, explanations and evaluations of a conservative such as Burke differ immensely, presenting as solid achievements what opponents saw as empty and evil, and as proper safeguards of the common man what others dismissed as sources of repression.[13] What radicals saw as mere custom and contingency, which stood in the way of true or authentic man, was to Burke vital to men, so that its removal would be like tearing the skin from their flesh.

Apart from these differences over values and over what particular cases mean – actually, what they are particular cases of – differences arise over the area and the ways in which confirmation of a social theory is to be sought, and the degree to which it can properly conflict with existing facts. For some, proof is to be sought in measurement of the theory against certain facts which are regarded as static or constant (at least for purposes of analysis), e.g. in the manner in which classical democratic theory is frequently measured against the evidence from voting surveys, and found wanting. Such an approach easily leads to a rejection of the reforming or revolutionising aspect of critical social theory. Theories which are presented as themselves historical forces, elements in a process of change, are sometimes simply assessed against the reality which it is their function to help overturn. Marxism is a theory which is to be confirmed, i.e. realised historically, through political action which both embodies the theory and is assisted and directed by it. Its own existence is a crucial social fact, for it unmasks, it shows the world in a new way, and how the world is seen strongly affects how people act in it. Thus the unblinkered critic–activist, given access to a deeper reality to which the ordinary observer remains oblivious, rejects the existing situation as temporary and imperfect, discerns the grounds of change, and does not leave others as they were.

It is easy to show how Marx's general doctrines and beliefs influenced his perception of the facts, e.g. in his discovery of evidences of human potentialities in the present, which his vision of the future supported and which seemed in turn to confirm it, and in the impact of his general conception of the class struggle upon his conclusions about the English proletariat of his own day, and about the likelihood, at different times, of imminent social revolution. Given certain large assumptions about the world, it was easy to discover favourable 'signs', to depict a class battle as a source and symptom of profound social disintegration rather than as an accident or aberration. Similarly, the adherent of a teleological view of history, or of history as a succession of fixed stages, will discover evidence which appears to confirm it, and this is possible because what is evidence is decided largely in relation to that larger view. But the precise relationship between the metaphysical or more general doctrine and particular political doctrines remains to be defined.[14] We are rarely justified in treating the myth or metaphysic or wish as simple father to the 'fact', as Feuer tends to do in assaulting the Promethean Marx. 'The forecast of the proletarian dictatorship and the advent of a classless society rested on an extrapolation from the slenderest of empirical foundations, but the minimum of factual evidence was matched with a maximum of Promethean projection.'[15] Here Feuer simply invokes a selected version of past experience against a prognosis which rests upon a very different empirical foundation, and which specifies and recommends a certain kind of future action to confirm it. Future or alternative possibilities cannot be dismissed simply by demonstrating their differences from present fact. Indeed, what empirical evidence can be produced to support the forecast that class societies will continue endlessly into the future?

In accepting the common view that the facts of social life and of human nature do not exist clearly and unambiguously, and cannot be seized by a neutral science and organised to form the objective basis upon which prescriptive theory might then build, I am not supporting a principle of unlimited arbitrariness. In stressing that perception is subjective and selective – that, apart from trivial cases, facts enter theories already interpreted, and that only certain facts are relevant to, and perhaps compatible with, our particular purposes – I am not asserting that the facts altogether lack solidity. There is a radical and disquieting, though incoherent, metaphysical doctrine which holds that the world itself is ambiguous or indeterminate, and that the facts are formed or created or constituted by the theorist. Yet any process of verification or disconfirmation presupposes facts which are independent of or outside the particular thesis or theory in question. Otherwise its truth or falsity could never be established. It does not follow from the inevitability of preconception or organising principles that theories are untestable by facts, or by hypotheses dependent upon other facts. Kuhn's subversiveness does not extend this far, as paradigms are shattered precisely because of an inability to accommodate anomalies and puzzles, which emerge out of a continuing process of scientific observation. Even Marx, the pragmatic liberal's myth-maker par excellence, altered his views in some major respects because of the facts. Feuer's argument underrates the continuous interaction between 'myth' or 'Promethean projection' and the facts of experience. The situation being analysed sometimes challenged and altered Marx's beliefs, e.g. his recognition of the possibility of a peaceful change in England and elsewhere – though tactics and programmes do not follow unambiguously even from clear-cut analyses of the situation – and his provision of subsidiary hypotheses to explain why history had not matched up to his expectations. He was at least aware of the need to take account of developments which clashed with both his political preferences and predictions, even if his characteristic response was to provide special, *ad hoc* explanations of counter-instances to, or apparent divergences from, his general theory. There was no Damascus road to overturn his fundamental values. Much of the social observation which was hard to accommodate within the pre-existing theory lay half-assimilated in his writings, creating potential incoherences within the total doctrine, which eventually fell apart under analysis and under the strain of translation into historical practice.

The interaction, both ways, of facts and theories must be kept in mind. For many reasons – including their particular origins and backgrounds, their powers, goals, energy and imagination – men focus upon certain things, and this peculiar confinement of vision leaves many other things unseen. On the one hand, the lines are not sharply and permanently drawn, so that thinkers, constantly confronted by diverse evidence, as a matter of fact modify and even reject established or favoured theories, and doubt the feasibility of what they once considered possible. But on the other hand theories – and especially social theories – can rarely be disconfirmed simply, for apparently subversive facts hardly ever travel like a bullet to the victim. Evidence which appears to be damning can be accommodated in various ways, and its recalcitrance or anomalous character diminished – especially if the theory is of a high degree of generality, or if it contains elements of prophecy, for in these cases supplementary hypotheses are necessary and protective. For example, Marx's general prediction of the breakdown of capitalism is far less subject to counter-evidence – or to falsification – than his specific hypotheses about wage levels.

But such tolerance, such recognition of legitimate diversity, must end at some point. Acceptance of the resilience of social theory does not extend recognition to the sheer dogmatist or ideologist. They are sworn, unyielding enemies of intellectual regicide – deductions killed by facts – and often they bear political arms. The history of Marxism in the countries of its alleged triumph is in large part the history of the calculated subordination of theory and research – if it can be called that – to the demands of the state. Consequently, theory withered into apologetics, a collection of banalities and ritual formulae which were not open to investigation or criticism. The great truths were upheld by authority and were closed to discussion, and while freedom of research is no guarantee against dogmatism or obscurantism, it is at least a necessary condition of their avoidance.

Theoretical latitude may also come to an end with the lunatic, though this is an extraordinarily complex matter. Those who are categorised as mad, or as having 'a chronically impaired sense of reality', rarely believe solely in what are – from 'rational' or 'commonsense' standards – illusions or fantasies; they may be remarkably perceptive; and the classification of them as mad may be itself political.[16] As the first part of a rational enterprise we can examine the structure and means of validation of what appears to be a lunatic theory or view – what counts as facts and why, what the appropriate methods of investigation are, what, if anything, would be required to prove or disprove or change particular beliefs. We may then discover that there is no appeal from the belief to reason or evidence, and that it cannot be described as rational in terms either of its derivation or its content. If we do this, particular rational processes and beliefs are assumed, though not necessarily taken for granted. All of our beliefs and criteria, including our basic logical categories, are culture-dependent or contextual. We cannot do much about that, however, and we may reasonably prefer our own fundamental concepts of intelligibility or rationality to others with which we are acquainted, and may, indeed, require them if we are to retain our sense of identity and our grasp of things.

Norman Cohn's *Pursuit of the Millennium* provides an especially clear-cut example of the culturally conditioned character of our ordinary conceptions of rationality. He writes that certain aspects of Nazism and Communism are 'barely comprehensible, barely conceivable even, to those whose political assumptions and norms are provided by a liberal society, however imperfect'.[17] Cohn appeals blatantly to the standards of a particular culture against certain movements and doctrines which he regards, in essential respects, as chiliastic, millennial, apocalyptic, eschatological, mythical, and inspired by archaic 'phantasies'. He clearly finds these doctrines both factually wrong or unprovable and violently destructive, and hence to be put at the other end of the scale to a liberalism which is, by implication, fact-based and pragmatic. Confronted with beliefs which are, from our viewpoint, fantasies, we may appropriately focus our attention on the believer rather than on the validation of his views,[18] but it must remain quite clear what is being done – not the disproof of what are classified as fantasies or absurdities, but explanations of their origins, through placing them within some intelligible psychological or social context. Within that context, they may become amply meaningful, or sensible, or functional. Reductionism may become simply a form of abusively dismissing ideas that are disliked, as it has become amongst some of the epigoni of Marx and Freud. Cutting through the outward appearance of things to their essence, the liberated man discovers that it is more appropriate to classify opponents than to answer them, for to engage in intellectual disputation is to miss the origins of error, which is the product of perhaps inescapable psychological or social deficiencies.[19] It is pointless to try to alter a man's mind. What is necessary is to change the circumstances in which choices are made and things perceived.

However, reductionist theories can disclose the disguised and subtle, as well as the crude, connections between beliefs and social or psychological conditions and interests, and constructively challenge the claims that reason is autonomous and that salvation or truth lie with the 'free-floating intellectuals'. It stresses the systematically selective character of social perception and its appropriateness to the particular world in which it arises and, in its Marxist form, asserts the close links between the dominant ideology and language and the dominant social relations, institutions and interests. Conceptual disputes are, on this view, products of and weapons in social conflicts, and are not merely linguistic or intellectual matters. A paradigm arises in relation to particular social or scientific problems and is destroyed by events. It is not disembodied, leading a life of its own, but has close worldly links. According to this view of the life of ideas, the elimination of basic intellectual disputes, the true end of ideology, comes with the transformation of social conditions, when the imposing structures of thought which have dominated man, distorted 'reality', and hence helped isolate him from it, are seen as they truly are – not as universal and absolute, but as a succession of mythologies.

The Marxist view of ideology, along with the account of ideas which is associated with British empiricism, suggests that the mere existence of basic differences in the characterisation of 'reality' in no way establishes the uncertainty of 'reality', or the legitimacy of continuing differences about it. And it must be admitted at once that disagreement itself no more establishes that disagreement about the facts is legitimate and lasting than the existence of deep moral diversity establishes the truth of ethical relativism. For the Marxist, conflicting accounts of the world are appropriate both within and between different historical periods, but the vision of the future is one in which men see the world clearly and see it whole – and in basically the same way. For an empiricist such as Hume, it is indolence and carelessness, embodied above all in traditional ideas, which keep us from the facts. What is required to end conflict, about values or facts, is some kind of cleansing or purging operation, so that men can read the open and unambiguous books of Nature and – for some – Society. Certain contemporary thinkers have argued that this epistemological belief has been a great boon to authoritarians and fanatics – though its dangers in no way show that it is invalid.[20]

My own belief, which I can defend but not establish, is that it is impossible to produce a substantial social theory which is free of prejudice, and which does not rest upon a mass of anticipatory and excluding decisions at different stages along the way, including the beginning. There are many plausible and reasonable conflicting views of social life – views which compete with each other at particular times, and succeed each other over time. Kolakowski invokes, against the myth of complete objectivity in the social sciences, the fact that 'nearly every human generation rewrites the history of the world', and concludes that this means that 'the same, or nearly the same, stock of factual knowledge lends itself to a great number of well-founded and rationally justified – though radically different – interpretations'.[21] Doubting that men are, or can be, sufficiently disinterested and omniscient to see the world steadily and see it whole, I must admit nonetheless that it is conceivable that things will be different one day. But hitherto the world has looked strikingly different from the different places that men occupy in it. It looks different from a peasant's hut, a labourer's tenement, an executive's split-level house, a president's palace, a monk's cell, or from the various prisons which woman has occupied historically. These differences of vision, which are not related solely to wealth or social position, should be at least chastening to bullies and dogmatists and bureaucrats. And hitherto efforts to establish one true view of the world have not resulted from argument, persuasion and imaginative endeavour, but from the readiness of certain men – perhaps under the guidance of the gods, or of some political fantasy – to impose their will on the remainder.

MARX AND MILL

Many of the basic political categories, preferences and beliefs of Marx and Mill are widely divergent, but there is neither a complete opposition, covering all major issues of social and political theory, nor much direct disagreement with the views of the other. In addition, there are overlappings and agreements, often below the surface. The fact that they were not participating in a particular and recognised polemic or debate meant that they did not sharpen their weapons or endeavour to justify themselves against each other.[22] It is not impossible, though it is certainly unilluminating, to extract from their theories a number of discrete and contradictory propositions which can be set neatly against each other. The isolation of particular theses from the larger theories which give them meaning, leads inevitably to their desiccation and distortion. Although particular testable assertions can be drawn out from the theories, in general the parts can be understood only in relation to the larger conceptual framework.[23]

The inadequacies of presentations of this intellectual division as a simple and tidy one are increased by the facts that neither was fully consistent, and that their theories did not remain constant. They did not fall full-grown upon the world, but were modified, applied to varying circumstances and, in some respects, substantially changed. Marx went through a moralising and radical democratic phase in the early 1840s, and moved gradually towards a materialistic conception of history and, at least superficially, to a preoccupation with economics, while Mill shifted significantly in relation to utilitarianism, democracy and socialism. Each theory contains subtleties, cavils, brilliant side excursions and displays, internal tensions, ambiguities and unresolved paradoxes, and hence could be developed in markedly different ways. Marx, more than Mill, has been simplified, reinterpreted and remade by his disputatious heirs, who ignore or underrate what clashes with moral preferences or political necessities. Yet the man's theory comprises all his writings and views, though in estimating what is central we must note his own explicit disclaimers and any clear transcendence of old beliefs. We can identify substantial differences between Marx and Mill, but it is fair to ask, against some of the simpler theories of ideological conflict and division: which Marx is being contrasted with which Mill?

Nonetheless, it is often assumed that Marxism and liberalism are diametrically opposed theories, clashing fundamentally at all major points. In relation to Marx and Mill the differences may be held to include, not only the content of the theories, but the manner in which they were asserted, the intellectual temper of their exponents. In the words of one writer: 'Anyone who passes from the pages of Mill to those of Marx becomes acutely aware of a sudden change of intellectual climate. It is the change from tolerant, democratic liberalism to intolerant, authoritarian communism.'[24] There are obvious differences of temper and tone, reflecting their contrasting relations with the bourgeois world of which they were both products. Mill was flexible, generally charitable to opponents, worried whether his beliefs were true, yet a little complacent, prim and supercilious. Marx was tougher, more arrogant and aggressive, more dissatisfied, an outsider who never came close to English political life. He was bitterly opposed to the bourgeois world, and often wearied by what he called the 'filth' of his opponents and 'the pestiferous vapours of the democratic cesspool'.[25] Carl Schurz, who became Secretary of the Interior in President Grant's Cabinet, described the Marx of 1849 in words which show how his hatred of the bourgeoisie and his general intolerance came together. 'I shall never forget the scornful tone in which he uttered the word "bourgeois", as if he were spewing it out of his mouth; and he stigmatised as "bourgeois", by which he meant the embodiment of profound moral degradation, every one who ventured to contradict him.'[26] But contrasting personal qualities, background and intellectual styles do not necessarily produce, or go along with, conflicting theories. Were it true that Mill was a pragmatic and intellectually generous Englishman, and Marx an angry, dogmatic and bullying German, we could draw no conclusions about the nature of the theoretical differences between them, nor about their appropriateness to the world in which they emerged.

One influential analysis of the doctrinal clash between liberal and totalitarian views is that presented by J. L. Talmon,[27] who regards the conflict between these two streams of thought as the source of 'the present world crisis'. As Marx is sometimes treated as a totalitarian – as he is by Talmon – we may find useful clues to the nature of the differences between Marx and Mill in these two general types. Talmon's dichotomy, which is seriously misleading in its historical application,[28] represents totalitarian democracy as a species of political messianism, growing out of a yearning for salvation, 'the longing for a final resolution of all contradictions and conflicts into a state of total harmony'.[29] Its exclusive doctrine, whose absolute and universal validity is asserted, informs us of the imminence of a 'preordained, harmonious and perfect scheme of things',[30] which is treated as a matter of urgency. It assumes the coming of a rational and harmonious community, in which men's wills coincide – 'some ultimate, logical, exclusively valid social order', 'some preordained and final denouement of the historical drama', 'a uniform spiritual pattern', 'some uniformly rational behaviour in an integrated society', 'with contradictions resolved, anti-social impulses checked, and man's desire for happiness satisfied'.[31] Such a condition of social harmony is one in which the antinomies between freedom and absolute purpose, liberty and virtue, individualism and ideological absolutism, finally disappear. This supposed totalitarian image of harmony closely resembles that ascribed to modern Nazism and Communism by Norman Cohn, at the conclusion of his account of medieval millenarianism. The essence of militant, revolutionary chiliasm is, Cohn argues, 'the tense expectation of a final, decisive struggle in which a world tyranny will be overthrown by a "chosen people" and through which the world will be renewed and history brought to its consummation'. The coming society is conceived as 'a state of total community, a society wholly unanimous in its beliefs and wholly free from inner conflicts'.[32]

Such a vision of life appears fraught with danger to Talmon, as to Cohn, because men are thought of not as they are but as they were meant to be, and would be, given proper conditions. It involves a radical devaluation of the existing order, 'an acute awareness of a structural and incurable crisis in existing society'.[33] It declares war on the corrupt present, and envisages its total destruction. It conceives of a fight to the finish, and is therefore marked by 'the exclusion of shades, of diluted colours and mixed quantities from between the positive and the negative, the white and the black, the "is" and "is not"'.[34] By semantic deception it travesties liberty, which is 'realised only in the pursuit and attainment of an absolute collective purpose',[35] and extends the scope of politics to everything, thus destroying the private and independent spheres which are the necessary bulwarks of the individual against political leaders.

From this standpoint, modern totalitarianism becomes the bitter fruit of the over-reaching idealism of many political theorists. Subject to the intellectual delusion that man could be altogether liberated from dependence they, or their disciples, refused to admit their mistake and come to terms with the weaknesses of the flesh. Faced with the recalcitrance and blind obstinacy of ordinary men, they sought to coerce and beat them into a more desirable shape. Thus, according to this interpretation, terror is the logical outcome of utopianism. The excessively optimistic social theorist advocates a form of life which is literally unrealisable, because it involves the final end to something – conflict, division, alienation, pain, frustration or hierarchy – which his critic holds to be endemically or inescapably human.

Talmon regards liberalism as far saner, because it is far closer to actual human nature. It sees and accepts life as it truly is, as 'a perpetual and never resolved crisis...'[36] In Talmon's view, and this is the essential underpinning of his own positive doctrine: 'Nature and history show civilisation as the evolution of a multiplicity of historically and pragmatically formed clusters of social existence and social endeavour, and not as the achievement of abstract Man on a single level of existence.'[37] Liberalism, uncontaminated by the doctrinaire spirit, eschews ideas of 'total renovation'. Politics is regarded as an empirical matter of trial and error. Privacy is protected by limiting its sphere, and maintaining a multiplicity of social groups which are permitted to compete with each other. Liberty is regarded as spontaneity, the absence of coercion. 'Freedom has no meaning without the right to oppose and the possibility to differ.'[38]

Many other contemporary writers have contrasted the theses of totalitarianism sharply with those of liberalism, and have often cast Marx in the role of totalitarian, the precursor of Stalin – and, almost without exception, have presented Mill as the pristine liberal. Talmon himself refers to Marxism as the most vital among the various versions of the totalitarian democratic ideology, and presents a few quotations from Mill (naturally from *On Liberty*) to illustrate 'the difference between the liberal and absolutist approach'.[39] The conflict between Marxism and liberalism has been put equally sharply by Clinton Rossiter in *Marxism: The View from America*. The monism, collectivism and economism of Marx are contrasted with the pluralism, individualism and free choice of American liberal democratic theory. The author appears to be saddened by the 'confusion' of Marx and Engels over education, for it makes it 'hardly possible to set up a meaningful confrontation in this vital field'.[40] The search for meaningful confrontations has often led to their discovery where they do not exist, and this is not surprising, especially in the case of Marx and Mill, because of the central positions which they occupy in our present ideological wars. This raises an important general point. Intellectual history which is conducted as part of a continuing battle against Stalinism or totalitarianism very easily develops into a (perhaps exalted) species of propaganda, in which past thinkers are pressed ruthlessly into our procrustean categories. Ahistorical stereotypes, arbitrary and artificial lineages, emasculated histories of ideas, have grown out of the dichotomies which proliferated under the pressures of Nazism and the Cold War – liberal and totalitarian democracy, negative and positive liberty, the open and the closed society, social engineering and utopianism. The distinctions themselves are not in question. They are often useful and valuable, and, in this case, they do draw attention to some of the significant differences between Marx and Mill. But in the heat of battle the Great Simplifiers become undiscriminating defenders of the liberal citadel against aliens and enemies. Especially in accounts of the enemy forces, we are likely to find major differences overlooked, selected aspects of an individual's thought thrown into unreasonable prominence, ambiguities ignored and the historical context forgotten. It should hardly need saying that Marx's writings cannot be judged reasonably by the actions and policies of his professed disciples, that the sins of the fanatical children cannot fairly be visited upon the putative fathers, generations earlier. The liberal Mill and the anti-liberal and post-liberal – but not totalitarian – Marx are reasonable shorthands, but careful selection also makes it possible to radicalise and illiberalise Mill, and to soften Marx, so that Mill becomes the dogmatist, even totalitarian, and Marx blurs into the forerunner of the placid Bernstein, or becomes an anguished, moralistic humanist, devoid of scientific pretension, or the father of Western sociology. The existence of such diverse interpretations, each of which can be supported from the texts, at least suggests the complexity of the subjects.

1 The background

Those who experienced the rapid transformation of nineteenth-century Western European society traced it primarily to the 'dual revolution' – the political events in France between 1789 and 1815, and industrial revolution, which was most marked and far-reaching in England. The French Revolution served as a model of violent and creative change, and an indication that men could substantially alter their institutions if they wished. It was presented by many writers – not all of them revolutionaries – as a liberation of the human spirit, the self-assertion of rational men against the absurd and restrictive clutter of feudal laws and authorities.[1] Writing in 1798, amidst profound intellectual, political and technological change and uncertainty, Malthus commented on the new and extraordinary lights being cast on political subjects, and stressed above all 'that tremendous phenomenon in the political horizon, the French revolution, which, like a blazing comet, seems destined either to inspire with fresh life and vigour, or to scorch up and destroy the shrinking inhabitants of the earth'.[2] But to conservative thinkers the Revolution seemed, undeniably, a pointless and bloody carnage, and it inspired dire prophecy and encouraged repression when existing orders were threatened even marginally. The roots of universal decomposition, of the rise of anarchy and the destruction of society, were discerned in the most cautious liberalising proposals. Edmund Burke, the out-spoken and eloquent critic of the Revolution, was aware that in condemning the Revolution he was condemning the new Europe of which it was at once a symbol and a source. His attack reads as an obituary on feudal Europe and the age of chivalry by one who treasured them. 'But the age of chivalry is gone. That of the sophists, economists and calculators has succeeded, and the glory of Europe is extinguished for ever.'[3] His assault on the revolutionaries and on their predecessors and their allies, who had subverted established opinion, and especially the prejudice which linked men closely to their existing environment, and bound them together, made sense in terms of a highly romanticised account of past and present. This account stressed the probity, skill and authority of traditional rulers, the ignorance of the masses, and the harmonious and satisfying relations between them. While accepting that change, conflict and ambition were inescapable, and valuable to society, in certain ordered forms, Burke assumed the existence of close connection, attachment and obligation between the different orders of society, none of which was justified in breaking out of its accustomed place and carving a new position for itself. In conservative theory, the view that the community was divided into opposed classes was repudiated as false descriptively and untrue to human nature, and therefore destructive. Burke saw himself as a defender of the old, involved and valuable fabric of society, whose distinctions were legitimised by tradition and by natural and divine law, against impudent and irresponsible rationalists. They simplified, stripping man bare of his sustaining relationships, and reducing him to a naked and solitary abstraction. Unaware of man's intricate nature and the complexity of societies, they imagined that they could reconstruct at will. The corrosive mentality, the uprooting metaphysics of the Enlightenment broke up stable and happy societies, which dissolved into a chaos of 'elementary principles'. The 'disbanded people' were deprived of the decent draperies', 'the coat of prejudice', the habits of subordination and the traditional signposts which had hitherto given meaning and order to their lives. All that remained was 'the dust and powder of individuality'. With the cracking of the chain of traditional connection, affection withered and society fell apart. Torn out of his natural environment, the common man was left alone, miserable and insecure, and the ensuing social chaos could only be checked and controlled by brute force. In common with many other conservative thinkers, Burke was alarmed and angered by insurgent violence and novel eruptions. He denied the existence of real evils demanding radical response, and scorned the capacity of revolutionaries to reconstruct society around some new source of affection and allegiance.

Burke was concerned primarily with the threat to social order – to hierarchy, status and prejudice – posed by political reformers, armed with critical and abstract standards of judgment. He remained strangely unaware of the pace and cost of economic change, preferring romantic and sentimental accounts of the common condition. But the feudal nostalgia which was to become widespread during the early nineteenth century was provoked by forces more blatantly destructive than reason – industrialism and laissez-faire. Speaking broadly, the issue was whether society itself should become a market-place, subject only to economic laws and criteria and driven forward by an endless thirst for gain.[4] Dissatisfied groups, especially entrepreneurs and manufacturers, battled against the frustrations and confinements of traditional economic life.

The struggle against ecclesiastic authority was supplanted by a struggle against the paternalistic state and the non-economic images and standards linked with it. The rich, supportive network of social relationships associated with traditional life, and the laws, conventions and habits which helped protect it, were denounced as impediments to the free, productive individual. The new individual of liberal theory was the master, not merely of nature but of his own economic and social destiny, and he was deemed capable of looking after himself in equal competition with others, who were conceived as rivals rather than fellows. 'Rights of man' doctrines – political analogues of the capitalist economic system – propagated a view of the isolated and competitive individual, to whom society and other men were alike means towards private ends. However, it became more and more obvious during the nineteenth century that the free status and equality of men were matters of theory rather than reality, as inequality and power of an extremely damaging kind emerged. Outraged by what seemed to them large-scale social devastation, forward-looking socialists along with conservatives complained of the costs of progress, and contrasted present decomposition with warm human communities, which they sometimes located in the actual past. They were appalled by many aspects of the fragmented, differentiated, contractual and individualistic society which was emerging. Their golden age, past or future, had many features of what Tönnies[5] understood by *Gemeinschaft* – 'a community of fate' or true solidarity, intimate, instinctive and uncalculating – while their own society seemed increasingly to resemble a *Gesellschaft*, an association for the rational pursuit of self-interest, without close moral ties, unifying traditions or concern for others. It was the market-place writ large – divided, abstracted, cold, and pervaded by a selfish and calculating utilitarian morality. Engels, who at times romanticised pre-industrial England, complained of the brutal indifference, the unfeeling isolation and the narrow self-seeking of industrial capitalist society, which was revealed above all in the great towns, where man's spiritual matched his physical plight. 'The dissolution of mankind into monads, of which each one has a separate principle, the world of atoms, is here carried to its utmost extreme.'[6] Additions to vocabulary expressed critical perceptions of the changing society, and themselves embodied or implied distinctive social theories and views. They reflected, without necessarily defining, the profound changes of societies – their great and obvious contrast, their rapid over-turnings and reversals of status and fortune, their crimes and conflicts and uncertainties. The new evaluative words, loaded against the emerging world, bore witness to a deep concern with social decomposition, which was traced commonly to 'liberalism' and 'industrialism' – both recent coinages. To critics of the developing industrial order words such as 'anarchy', 'egoism', 'atomism' and 'individualism'[7] seemed to catch its essence – the division and opposition between man and society, the apparent disappearance of a sense of social duty and attachment, and the lack of guiding rules and comforting relationships. But the savage rhetoric and the laments of communitarians of left and right were in vain. Marx, who himself sometimes contrasted the warmth and security of feudalism with the inhumanity of capitalism, had little patience with backward-looking socialism or 'feudal idyllics' and, for example, dismissed Disraeli and the 'feudal socialists' for their 'total incapacity to comprehend the march of modern history',[8] and their preference for an old, pre-capitalist form of exploitation. He refused to shed romanticism's bitter tear. For, although the problem of community was a real one, it could not be settled within the recommended conservative forms, which oppressed man while satisfying some of his affective needs, and which could not be recreated after their time, anyhow. Hence, while there were common terms and even some common elements in conservative and radical denunciations of the nineteenth-century capitalist world, there were substantial differences over the sources of social disintegration, the value-laden descriptions of the old and the new worlds, and the conceptions of history within which the changes were perceived. Most social critics preferred community and closeness to division and anomie, but some looked back to an harmonious, patriarchal, and unequal system, or sought its resurrection within vastly different conditions, whilst others looked forward to a co-operative, equalitarian social order, marked by widespread and diverse individual achievement, which had been never previously created by man. The latter group wanted neither the anarchy of laissez faire nor the sham solidarity and happiness of the past but, literally, a new world.

A new world of a different kind was emerging, above all, in England. It was heavily industrialised by the middle of the nineteenth century, and the capitalist rode high. Sometimes England was taken to be a model for the rest of the world, either in the weak sense that others could follow its progressive example if they chose, or in the stronger sense that they were bound to develop in a similar way. To Marx and Engels England was the paradigm 'bourgeois society', in which other nations could see 'the image of their own future' – although its experience was unique in the sense that the industrial second-comers would make their way in a different economic world, of which an already industrialised England was an integral part. According to Engels, England was the classic soil of industrial development and its concomitant social changes, particularly the rise of the proletariat. 'Only in England can the proletariat be studied in all its relations and from all sides.'[9]

Industrial development, and especially machinery, transformed the economic system and corroded established habits and institutions. Of course, machinery neither came out of the blue nor acted in a vacuum, and its rapid expansion presupposed as well as stimulated capital accumulation and investment, trade and changing social relations. Its impact on society was decisive and far-reaching.[10] During the last two decades of the eighteenth century a sharp increase in production took place, especially in the cotton industry, the first example of modern large-scale industry. By the end of the Napoleonic Wars it was England's major textile industry and the most important British manufacturing and export industry, and its period of most rapid growth was only beginning. It was concentrated increasingly in large factories, which are commonly taken to be the most distinctive feature of the age, with a city such as Manchester as the epitome of the factory town and a foretaste of the future. But it should be noted that students of industrial change in nineteenth-century Britain are apt to concentrate on what Engels called the 'universal whirl of activity', and that this natural focus on the forward-looking and the precocious rather than on the constant or slowly changing gives an exaggerated impression of the speed and spread of industrial change. Before the middle of the century factories may have become commonplace in the case of cotton, and substantial enterprises in the case of iron and coal, but in a variety of smaller industries the old production organisation and methods persisted until late in the century. Indeed, the need of factories for subsidiaries, suppliers and finishers often increased the amount and diversity of small-shop industries, old-style crafts and adaptations of the 'domestic system'. The latter in particular was a common response to increased demand. Garment-making, which grew rapidly with increased supplies of cloth and greater export opportunities, remained a put-out, domestic sweat-shop industry until the present century. And in many of these old-style enterprises, worsened through their new connection with the factory, and yet freer than the factory from legislation and inspection, there was a decline in the status and the working conditions of the labourers, both in urban areas and in such rural purgatories as the lost villages of the Black Country.[11]

The major influence in the development of the factory was steam power. It 'transformed the process of production, halved labour costs and brought spinners and weavers alike into the factory system'.[12] It vastly quickened urban concentration and transformed labour relations. The period of rapid technical change culminated in the 1840s and 1850s, which is commonly designated 'the railway age'. The substantial heavy industry – iron and steel – was able to absorb large amounts of capital, both at home and abroad. During the first half of the nineteenth century the quickly growing iron industry produced primarily for the home market, but by the 1850s it relied heavily on exports, like much of English industry. After 1870, English capital was exported in large quantities for railway building, especially in the United States, Russia and India. Any danger of stagnation was thereby reduced, though the depression of the seventies did stimulate a search for new markets and provided an economic rationale for imperialism. Overseas expansion provided outlets for investment and for English goods, and acted as a major source of stabilisation within England itself.

The precise economic, social and political effects of industrialisation – its effects on standards of living, quality of life, and the crystallisation of classes – are matters of considerable and continuing dispute. Argument has prospered partly because of the complexity of the evidence, but more so because of different emotional and moral attitudes towards industrial capitalism, which has led to different criteria for its evaluation. Events, situations and processes are perceived through layers of myth and feeling. The modern argument about the industrial revolution is related clearly to present political concerns and conflicts, as much in the case of optimists, who argue that a general – though not universal – improvement in standards of living occurred between the early 1790s and the early 1840s, as in the case of pessimists, who assert either that there was a positive decline in the living standards of significant sections of the people, or, more cautiously, and partly as a result of the optimist assault on the old pessimistic orthodoxy, that the optimistic view has not been confirmed statistically.[13]

It is undisputed that the process of industrialisation put English institutions under considerable strain. Population was increasing fast;[14] urbanisation, which was quicker than mechanisation, made misery at least more obtrusive – by 1851 roughly one-half of the English population lived in large towns;[15] conditions in the factories were often very bad and trade fluctuations frequently had disastrous social effects. In the dark picture of unregulated industrialism – which underrates the extent of regulation and reform – the emphasis is on the growth of unsanitary, filthy and crowded factory towns such as Manchester, and on the abundant examples of proletarian or mass misery, insecurity, slovenliness, prostitution, drunkenness and thieving. Misery was widespread and intense, especially in the industrial towns of the Midlands and south Lancashire, where many of the Irish migrants were concentrated, and which provided horrifying examples of degradation and suffering, as Engels showed at length. That the demoralisation of the urban poor is highlighted sometimes by its depiction against a fictitious backdrop of pre-industrial health, harmony and happiness does not detract from its reality. The poverty of the proletariat was the other side, the 'unintended consequence', of the remarkable expansion of nineteenth-century capitalism. Alexis de Tocqueville wrote of Manchester, in words that might have come from Marx or Engels: 'From this foul drain the greatest stream of human industry flows out to fertilise the whole world. From this filthy sewer pure gold flows. Here humanity attains its most complete development and its most brutish, here civilisation works its miracles and civilised man is turned almost into a savage.'[16] There were blatant contrasts – though probably less than a century earlier – between wealth, power and creativity on the one hand, and suffering, slavery and dismal toil on the other. Yet some contemporary writers, dazzled perhaps by the wonders of technological progress, rich evidence of man's resourcefulness and strength, overlooked or disregarded the plight of the labourers. Despite everything, Andrew Ure, the zealous champion of industralisation, could describe the factory system as 'the great minister of civilisation to the terraqueous globe', diffusing 'the life blood of science and religion to myriads still lying in the region and shadow of death'.[17]

The socialist critic of the industrial revolution might concede that living standards, measured simply in terms of food and housing, did not worsen for the bulk of the labourers during the first half of the nineteenth century. The ground of the radical assault then becomes, as it has always largely been, not the economist's computation of average wages and what they could buy, which are themselves extremely hard to calculate, but the insecurity and the misery attendant upon what is perceived as the devastation of a way of life. Once again, the picture of pre-industrial man standing in rags but standing on his feet, enjoying a secure status and intimate contact with other human beings, may be overdrawn, but a critique of industrialisation in terms of 'social catastrophe' and 'the disintegration of the cultural environment',[18] seems, nevertheless, very much to the point. The essence of the indictment, which is concerned with the less tangible environment of attitudes, beliefs, habits, expectations and status, is that the industrial labourer was thrown into a new, distinctive world, whose instruments or weapons, forms of work, working and living patterns and social links, were very different from those with which he or his forebears were familiar. It is not mere pedantry to ask just how many labourers went through this process themselves and, for those who did, whether it seemed to them as good at the beginning and as bad at the end as writers such as the Hammonds or Hobsbawm have suggested.[19] For if we are speaking of the different experiences of different men, for example, of the father working in the fields and the son coming to maturity in an industrial town, we cannot speak of their cultural shock or disintegration. They are not the same person. But there seems to be no question that the mass of industrial labourers were subordinated to a novel work rhythm and to the clock, and that they were kept at work by a firm disciplinary system inside and outside the work place, as well as by their own desperate need, that life in the factory and in the urban conglomerations was hazardous and unpleasant and that the transformation of men into 'hands' or 'instruments' did mark a real loss of contact with superiors. Deference, though a ready ally of exploitation, at least implies a human relationship. And along with the division between men which is summed up in the cold phrase, 'cash nexus', went a division between man and his labour, or what E. P. Thompson has called 'a violent technological differentiation between work and life'.[20]

The argument about living standards appears to be more stringent and narrow than discussion of the fate of the labourer during the period of rapid industrial change. But the validity of any particular thesis depends, naturally, on the precise claims which it makes, and on those elements which it excludes or treats as marginal. These marginal elements may seem crucial to another observer. For example, Max Hartwell has organised a good deal of evidence suggesting that the real wages of most, though certainly not all, English workers rose between the 1790s and the 1840s, and he goes on to explain this by a fall in the cost of important consumer goods - in turn explained primarily by mass production and the fall in tariffs, especially after 1840 - without any corresponding decline in money wages.[21] Hartwell's major opponent, Eric Hobsbawm, has tried to construct the debate in his own terms, by arguing, not that there was a positive decline in the living standards of significant sections of the people, but that the hypothesis of a substantial general improvement is most improbable. He wins well against this straw hypothesis. At times he suggests that there was not much change during the period under discussion, that there was 'no significant general improvement', and at others that 'on balance the condition of the common people took a turn for the worse between the 1790s and the 1840s'.[22] Hobsbawm talks more of social considerations than does Hartwell - though Hartwell also regards them as important - and Hobsbawm also focusses more on the fate of outcasts and losers - agricultural labourers, especially in the south and the east of England, handloom weavers and other workers in declining industries and occupations, the Irish, and seamstresses and others in 'sweated' industries. Hobsbawm also proposes a relative - rather than absolute - pauperisation thesis, which could mean that real wages steadily improved during periods of expansion, though Hobsbawm himself does not take this view.

The broad claim that the bulk of English labourers did not do as badly, in literal economic terms, as the early pessimists asserted - a weakened version of the optimistic case, as many of Hobsbawm's general

declarations are weakened versions of a full-blooded pessimistic case –
is quite compatible with a recognition that their conditions were bad
and that they were treated inhumanely, and that certain sections of the
labouring force and certain regions endured almost unbroken poverty
and misery, and continuous decline. The facts leave ample room for
fundamentally opposed judgments of this period of industrialisation
and of the various attempts to mitigate some of its most blatant ill-
effects. To the harsher foes of the industrialists and their friends, the
humanitarianism which was one of the products of industrialisation
will seem piddling and hypocritical, given the huge costs and sufferings
upon which they focus. To others, such reforms as the shortening of
factory hours, limits on female and child labour, controls over the
exploitation of chimney sweeps and efforts to improve town health –
even if sometimes half-hearted, ill-conceived or blighted by self-interest –
lie near the centre of the pictures of social change. Such differences
foreshadow contemporary conflicts over social evaluation: to the champion of human liberation, reforms tend to be seen as mere tokens and
deceptions, and as totally inadequate to satisfy human needs. At a
more clearly empirical level, we cannot generalise about the fate of
the English people during the first part of the nineteenth century. The
different conditions of different groups and different regions, the variable
incidence of unemployment and high employment,[23] and the diverse
political effects of similar economic conditions must be emphasised.
Moral outrage and ideological commitment have led some of the most
eloquent and perceptive critics of the industrial revolution to organise
an untidy process too much and, by exaggerating the constancy of certain pressures on the labourers, to overrate their strength, purpose and
cohesion.

The nature or form of the nineteenth-century proletariat, which was
not constant, cannot be inferred from views of its objective economic
position. It is a matter of how masses of men, living and working in
changing and often dismal circumstances, perceived themselves and their
relationship to society or the state, and how, in terms of their changing
consciousness, they organised themselves and pursued their goals. Their
social behaviour was related to their perception of things, not ours. In
contemporary scholarship, the character and degree of unity of the
nineteenth-century working classes is as essentially contested as is their
economic condition.

Contemporary observers commented incessantly on the division within
the nation, and especially on the growing political and social segregation of the labourers. In the new urban areas, two separate communities seemed to coexist uneasily, without connecting links of any kind.
Thomas Chalmers, worried at the poor prospects of evangelism in the

large towns, commented in 1821 that in those towns 'the poor and the wealthy stand more disjoined from each other. It is true, they often meet, but they meet more on an arena of contest, than on a field where the patronage and custom of one party are met by the gratitude and goodwill of the other.' There was 'a mighty unfilled space between the high and the low of every large manufacturing city'.[24] Thirty years later a census report referred to the 'labouring myriads...forming to themselves a world apart'.[25] The division within the nation often seemed wide and dangerous, though possibly it was exaggerated because of the common idealisation of pre-industrial society, with its gentle, organic concepts and metaphors. Conservatives were haunted by that spectre of modern political and social theory – the masses, the 'lawless and furious rabble', Cobbett's 'Multitude of Horrid Barbarity' – and feared drastic and destructive assaults on established institutions. Their illusions were matched by those of the more fanatical and utopian labourers. Although England remained free of serious and dramatic confrontations, fantasy and rigidity, especially on the part of authorities, provoked clashes, which usually showed that the radical forces had exaggerated their strength.

There is a natural tendency amongst Marxist historians to present the various engagements between labourers on the one hand, and employers and authorities on the other, as part of a continuous class war. Sporadic conflicts between fluid social forces become part of a battle between capital and labour, rather than a series of limited guerrilla forays on 'the system', inspired by diverse experiences and a variety of goals. Hobsbawm defines the novel, class-conflict situation, as follows: 'What was new in the labour movement of the early nineteenth century was class consciousness and class ambition... A specific class, the labouring class, workers, or proletariat, faced another, the employers or capitalists. The French Revolution gave this new class confidence, the industrial revolution impressed on it the need for permanent mobilisation.'[26] This seems to be reading too much theory into class development, which here implies not simply a particular objective economic relationship between individuals but consciousness and mobilisation as well, and Hobsbawm himself appears to weaken his bolder claims about class identity as he proceeds.[27] Often the proletariat seemed far more like a crowd than an army.

E. P. Thompson's notion of class is at once more subtle and less firm. Reacting against both the authoritarianism of certain Marxists, who know class interests better than the labourers themselves, and the dismissiveness of certain conservatives, who treat class as 'a pejorative theoretical construct, imposed upon the evidence',[28] and find it divisive and disturbing to boot, he stresses the need to watch men in their historical development, and to observe 'patterns in their relationships, their ideas, and their institutions'.[29] Class is an historical phenomenon and relationship, and not a mechanical or static structure or thing. It 'happens' when 'some men, as a result of common experiences (inherited or shared), feel and articulate the identity of their interests as between themselves, and as against other men whose interests are different from (and usually opposed to) theirs'.[30] Thompson's research, which is inspired by sympathy and respect for the labourers, and especially the most suffering and vulnerable, in their own historical situation, and which does not move towards some ordained point, Marxist or otherwise, nonetheless leads him to the conclusion that, in the years between 1780 and 1832, 'most English working people came to feel an identity of interests as between themselves, and as against their rulers and employers'.[31] Such a conclusion is compatible with recognition of the divisions within the ranks of the labourers, and the failure and eventual disappearance of particular sections of them, and it does not imply that such feelings of identity were powerful or had any lasting political significance, or that the class acted for itself. Thompson's working class certainly did not grow along a single stem, and certainly failed to live up to his image of the way 'the working class' ought to behave.

The period between Waterloo and the European eruptions of 1848 seems to support a Marxist analysis more strongly than the later part of the century – though not nearly as strongly as Marxist historians have claimed. It was a time of considerable poverty and suffering, especially in relation to that which came after, and of widespread agitation and disaffection, and occasional revolt. The group consciousness of a significant proportion of labourers, inarticulate as well as articulate, was high, particularly in the hey-day of Chartism. After the middle of the century, the situation changed and the more prosperous and 'multiple' society of Victorian England emerged.

During the earlier period, there were strong grounds for working-class resentment at economic conditions and at the political status of the various labour organisations. These organisations were restricted severely, and both the letter and the administration of the law served the masters well. At the turn of the century, the position of the labourers was extremely vulnerable. The old paternalistic legislation was gradually abolished and police measures, such as the 1799 Act against Combinations,[32] were passed during the fiercely anti-Jacobin aftermath of the French Revolution. There were few chances for labour organisations to develop as political weapons. The war years were years of particular economic difficulty, during which prices rose substantially. Violent conflict, born of desperation, often occurred, e.g. the Luddite attacks on machines and mills, seeming causes of the labourers' plight. The Luddites are presented commonly as backward-looking and hence re-actionary, and their outbreaks and assaults are seen as absurd, demented Jacqueries. And, certainly, their attacks on machines and mills seemed to rest upon an equation of symptoms with causes, as even Marx assumed, in suggesting that it took time and experience for the workers to learn to 'direct their attack, not against the material instruments of production, but against the particular social form in which these instruments are used'.[33] They have been scorned and patronised by posterity, in whose eyes they were blind and weak opponents of the irresistible flow of history and progress. For example, the Webbs pre-sented the Lancashire cotton-spinners as a group without cohesion, vision or strategy, as they frantically but sporadically rebelled against change. 'Their ephemeral combinations and frequent strikes were, as a rule, only passionate struggles to maintain a bare subsistence wage... outbursts of machine-breaking and outrages, with intervals of abject submission and reckless competition.'[34] Tidy socialists as well as stern liberals have portrayed them as wild and lunatic, as if they should have accepted their historical decline without fuss or protest.

Although the anachronistic character of much of the theory and the action of these threatened labourers must be acknowledged, it is easy and common to exaggerate the primitive element. The bulk of Luddite activity was discriminating, in that it was directed at specific targets and not at machinery as such, it was directed against powerful and significant things, and it arose out of the absence of any adequate means of constitutional expression and protest. Appeals to parliament in the early years of the century had proved, repeatedly, both expensive and pointless, and it seemed more and more that the constitutional rights of the common man were being torn away. Given a decline of the common law restrictions on economic malpractice and on innovation, and given a loss of status without constitutional recourse, it was natural that skilled workers should appeal to the values of the past, to corpora-tive law and to immemorial custom, although these were already deeply eroded, and that they should seem the enemies of innovation itself. The handloom weavers, the stockingers and the framework knitters, increasingly dispossessed by the mills after the Napoleonic Wars, were probably the most disastrously affected by industrialisation, and fought – often despairingly and irrelevantly – against its spread. But, while they saw labour-saving machinery as a challenge to employment, it was pre-eminently unscrupulous and tyrannical masters who suffered from their attacks. They won the sympathy and sometimes the support of farmers and small businessmen, whose own livelihoods were threatened by the growth of large and competitive enterprises. Cotton weavers also won the support of aristocrats against the weaver manufacturers. Hobsbawm has pointed out that this form of 'proletarian' action might be used by all sorts of people, 'from independent small producers, through the intermediate forms so typical of the domestic system of production, to more or less fully-fledged wage-workers'.[35] Luddism won considerable public sympathy, especially in the West Riding and in the Midlands.

Luddism contained divergent elements and aspirations. It was, on one side, a cry of pain and rage, and a struggle, not for a new, open and equal world, but for an idealised traditional way of life, some aspects of which were temporarily protected by the Speenhamland system. But, as Thompson asserts, it was not simply a retreat to a dead paternalistic code, or a mass of spontaneous riots directed against the new order as a whole. His account emphasises the body of forward-looking, radical theory which emerged in the course of this transitional conflict – the demands for a minimum legal wage, for prohibitions on shoddy work, for the rights of trade unions, for arbitration. In these demands to control and civilise capitalism he sees – generously – the rudiments of an alternative political economy. 'All these demands looked forwards, as much as backwards; and they contained within them a shadowy image, not so much of a paternalist, but of a democratic community, in which industrial growth should be regulated according to ethical priorities and the pursuit of profit be subordinated to human needs.'[36]

Whether we describe these efforts to subordinate industrialism and capitalism to moral standards as forward-looking or backward-looking does not matter particularly. But these terms are generally used lightly and polemically, and without sufficient attention to what they presuppose. Self-proclaimed realists commonly dismiss ethical endeavour as mere moralism or a remnant of the past, outside the normal and perhaps determined flow of social change. To many people, moralism will seem backward-looking no matter how modern its inspiration or radical its thrust. There is frequently a rift between values or general goals, such as liberty or fraternity, which are themselves neither progressive nor reactionary, and the particular social forms in which they are supposedly embodied, which may be beyond men now, or beyond recall. The important thing for the serious and constructive moral critic is to make his ethical values explicit and to indicate clearly what would constitute embodiments or realisations of them, and how they might be approximated in actual social life. Thus we might accept the genuineness of the needs and the importance of the values which found expression in Luddism, while rejecting as utopian the particular images of economic and social life advanced by Luddites. In the early nineteenth-century cravings for warmth, community, and even spontaneity, were inevitable, as were critiques of novel institutions in terms of them. But these yearnings were satisfied only partially by the self-conscious attempts to preserve local customs and provincial diversity, and by the growth of friendly and mutual aid societies as protections and social centres for the labourers, against the encroaching industrial civilisation and the savage individualism which was part of it. However, the defences were inadequate, and soon the industrial city and capitalist morality caught the old world in their grasp, transforming it physically and spiritually, and subordinating it to new standards of discipline, method and efficiency.

Engels described Luddism as the first manifestation of proletarian opposition, as a class, to the bourgeoise.[37] But the organisation and mobilisation of the working class clearly took a far more serious form with the development of the Chartist movement in the violent decade following the financial crisis of 1836 and the economic crisis of 1837. Chartism was the most successful effort to weld the various agitating and injured labouring groups into a cohesive radical movement. The People's Charter of 1838 contained a radical programme of political reform and, while it did not explicitly demand economic and social transformation, it was frequently assumed to have implications of this kind, and economic themes loomed large in Chartist agitation and propaganda. Many of its battles were fought in clear-cut class terms, and many of its supporters came to suspect and oppose the middle-class Anti-Corn Law League, which claimed to represent the general social interest. The Chartists were battling for status and security for labour, and appeals for the reconciliation of classes easily seemed mere evasion or side-tracking from this great object. But Chartism was never a united national movement with clear, agreed goals. It was a movement which fed on a variety of local grievances, and which meant different things to different supporters. It was 'a rich and many-sided popular movement, the heir of a radical political tradition but equally the child of poor harvests and the poverty, bad housing, ill health, and unemployment that attended the growth of a new industrial society'.[38] Its social composition was very mixed, and its supporters included handloom weavers and domestic outworkers, looking back to the past, agrarian primitivists, and factory hands who accepted industrialism and sought to remedy its evils. Its leaders were as diverse as its members, and included middle-class democrats, trade union organisers, Jacobins and socialists such as Ernest Jones, a sometime favourite of Marx and Engels.[39] While its characteristic activity was that of gathering signatures for immense national petitions, which were presented to the House of Commons with a notable lack of effect, it was associated with numerous strikes and industrial disputes, and drew in a variety of dissatisfied groups which were not attracted by its specifically political objectives. This large but fluctuating movement had lost its momentum by 1848, largely because of internal divisions and the incapacity of its leaders, the waning of the trade depression, and the completion of the rail network, which tended to equalise food prices – by undermining local bread-price fluctuations due to weather and the manoeuvres of local monopolists and hoarders.[40] By this time, the middle class had no ground at all to fear an English revolution, which was never remotely possible in nineteenth-century England, though reformers raised its spectre to push reluctant governments into action.

The familiar rhetoric of class war, even during the period of greatest conflict, tended to underrate the various differentiations within society, and to exaggerate the impact and the scope of the newer elements in it. John Vincent, admittedly working within very narrow confines – electoral politics btween 1826 and 1872 – has claimed, correctly, that in all types of town and city, 'the electorate was predominantly involved in pre-industrial types of activity'.[41] The fact that urbanisation preceded mechanisation had considerable political significance, in that the towns contained large numbers of small individual proprietors and producers, which helps explain both radicalism's high respect for property and the emergence of liberalism. Vincent offers, as a working hypothesis, the generalisation that 'over the country in general the economic growth with which it (the industrial revolution) was associated worked for quite a long time in favour of a wider distribution of small property and a diminution of the relative power of large property'.[42] His researches contribute to a view of society as complex, not sharply polarised, and present private property, and the hopes and illusions surrounding it, as influencing deeply the consciousness of the masses. But those researches already had a particular interest – in the factors and forces diluting class, and diverting the workers from particular, 'proletarian' loyalties and modes of behaviour – and this angle of concern, combined with the concentration upon electoral or constitutional politics, to the omission of the masses outside, makes the confrontation with the Marxists somewhat tangential.[43] Vincent's work, however, certainly tells us more about the fifties and the sixties than it does about the earlier period, for the relative prosperity after 1848 softened class antagonisms, and the change was reflected in social theory, which stressed 'an almost endless series of social gradations' rather than 'the broad contours of class division'.[44] The talk was very much of social balance, the blending of classes, and the peaceful if selfish pursuit of interests. The reversal of the earlier tendency was sharp and permanent – so much so that by the time the workers gained the franchise, the famous one-third was prepared to vote Tory.

The heterogeneity of the proletariat and the lack of a clear and historically decisive line between 'it' and the rest of society were features of the second half of the century, although it was during this period that a factory proletariat and class patterns of voting began to emerge. The 'reserve army of the unemployed', where it existed, encouraged competition between the unskilled, checked wages and made organisation difficult. Ignorance and hostile employers intensified the problem. The skilled workers, with a keen sense of status and, frequently, a strong bargaining position, normally opposed the notion of a general union. Their organisations, such as the Amalgamated Society of Engineers, preferred to advance the vested interests of their own members, which included keeping skilled labour scarce. The labouring élite did not wish to confuse itself, or be confused with, the mass of labourers. As Thomas Wright observed in 1867, there was 'a certain understood dignity and exclusiveness of caste pertaining to the artisan class which every individual of it is compelled to respect and support. A mechanic when out of work can scarcely take work as a labourer, even if it is offered him'.[45] The persistence of status and other divisions allowed particular interests to triumph regularly over the presumed general interests of the proletariat. Maurice Dobb's words express the general position well:

> Not until the last quarter of the century did the working class begin to assume the homogeneous character of a factory proletariat. Prior to this, the majority of the workers retained the marks of the earlier period of capitalism, alike in their habits and interests, the nature of the employment relation and the circumstances of their exploitation. Capacity for enduring organisation or long-sighted policies remained undeveloped; the horizon of interest was apt to be the trade and even the locality, rather than the class; and the survival of the individualist traditions of the artisan and the craftsman, with the ambition to become himself a small employer, was for long an obstacle to any firm and widespread growth of trade unionism, let alone of class consciousness. The differences within the Chartist movement had reflected very clearly the contrast between the factory workers of the northern towns, with their clogs and 'unshorn chins and fustian jackets' to whom Feargus O'Connor directed his appeals, and the artisans of London skilled trades who followed Lovett and the small master craftsmen of the Black Country.
>
> By this heterogeneity of a still primitive labour force the dominion of Capital over Labour was augmented.[46]

Yet the British working class, divided and subject to serious political restrictions for much of the century, was in a much stronger position than its continental counterparts by the end of the century. After the defeat of the European workers in 1848, working-class organisations were closely supervised and restricted, and the more radical leaders were pursued, exiled and imprisoned during the following generation. The virtual choice was compliance or conspiracy. As Marx discovered, the task of organising the International in France was an extremely difficult one. Economic and political activity was checked more closely at all levels. Bismarck and Napoleon III not only hounded their working classes – except where their organisations took a conservative, 'economist' form, as with the Lassallean movement in Germany – but they controlled business life. The bourgeoisie in these countries had far less independence than did the English. Largely as a result of this institutional inflexibility, political change on the continent tended to be much more sudden and violent than it was in Britain, where proletarian movements took a less radical and political form.

In Britain, especially during the second half of the century, pressures by the working class and its middle-class allies and champions helped bring about a series of gradual changes which regulated the laissez-faire system and spread the rights – and the complacencies – of citizenship more and more widely. Social legislation safeguarded not merely the obviously weak sections of the work force, but eventually the bodies and livelihoods of adult males, and progress was made towards a more equitable and impartial legal system. In the sphere of unionism and employer–employee relations working-class leaders were able to gain considerable improvements, especially in the 1860s and the 1870s. In the 1860s the trades unions gained national leadership and organisation, and were well if prudently led by the conservative Applegarth, who did a great deal to improve the standing of the unions in the community. Efforts were made to extend the vote to the working men, most of whom were, until the Second Reform Act, outside 'the pale of the constitution'. The value of the vote in securing industrial reform was stressed in their propaganda. 'Recollect also, that by obtaining these rights we shall be able more effectually to secure our legitimate demands as Unionists.'[47] Political pressure, combined with intelligent, moderate leadership of the unions, led to far-reaching changes. In 1867 the greater evils of the Master and Servant law were eliminated. In 1869 the relatively friendly report of the Royal Commission on Trade Unionism helped improve the public image of the unions, and in February 1871 they were given fuller legal recognition. The strength of the organisations did not, of course, remain constant, but varied, especially with changing economic circumstances. In the late seventies, for example, unionism was, owing to an economic downturn, a less dynamic force than it had been at the beginning of the decade.

Extensions of the franchise reflected growing acceptance of the status of the working class, although the implications of political representation for economic and social change were exaggerated by some of its friends, as well as its enemies. The Reform Act of 1867 gave the vote to the artisans, through the provision of household suffrage in the towns. It was passed by a conservative administration, which defined the extent of the change in terms of its own imagined electoral advantage,[48] but the reform followed a long period of co-operation between moderate working-class leaders and middle-class radicals, to whom political democracy recommended itself primarily as a means of drawing the working class into society and thus reducing the extent and the dangers of class conflict. It was necessary to be 'wise in time'. Bright, who with Mill and Gladstone was a leading theorist and guide of the middle-class Reform Union, indicated the important prudential ground for reform when he argued that 'great discontent and turbulence might arise if the working men felt that they are distrusted, that they are marked as inferiors, that they are a sort of pariahs'.[49] The vote was conceived as both an incentive to good behaviour and as a reward for good conduct – an appropriate gift to men who had demonstrated their virtue, and especially their conservatism. The middle-class radicals and some working-class leaders sought to improve the moral, intellectual, social and economic conditions of the workers, in the hope that they would gain the qualities of the ideal 'bourgeois' worker – prudence, rationality, decency and deference. They hoped for an increase in the number of 'intelligent and respectable artisans', who would be free from the more absurd proletarian prejudices. As early as 1858, an editorial in the *Manchester Guardian* held that education had 'made the lower classes more intelligent, more self-reliant, more energetic, has taught them to think more justly of their fellow countrymen, to feel ashamed of their former prejudices, and to acknowledge that it rests with them and not with any Government to ameliorate their social condition'. Even in strikes, the writer observed, 'moderation and order are generally manifested in their proceedings, and there is a better appreciation of the laws that govern the rise and fall of wages'.[50] The Radicals envisaged increasing co-operation between the two classes in what Cobden called 'the great struggle against feudalism', by which he meant the struggle against the Anglican, aristocratic, landed structure which, with rare subtlety, had drawn leading business families into its embrace. Cobden, Bright, Ashworth and Mill spoke in their different ways for a new class, unrestrained and uncontaminated by ties with the old regime. The final defeat of feudalism, superstition and corruption, was to lead to the unrivalled supremacy of the middle class, whose aspirations were only partly satisfied by the 1832 Reform Act,[51] though as a matter of fact, 'feudalism' and the assertive bourgeoisie adapted to each other, and there was no serious, systematic, clear-cut bourgeois warfare against the established order. The result was a compromise, and not a new world.

The middle-class friends of the proletariat did not conceive the gradual conversion of the disaffected and uncivilised workers into satisfied citizens as a process of genuine equalisation. To its middle-class allies, the emancipation of the proletariat meant essentially its political enfranchisement and its continued subordination to middle-class values and to middle-class leadership – though the new citizens were conceived less as pliable, manipulated stuff than as sturdy, right-minded individuals. These boundaries were accepted, though often neither consciously nor openly, by many working-class leaders in the late nineteenth century. They accepted liberal leadership and pursued piecemeal improvements within the existing system.

The history of the nineteenth-century labour movement can be written in large part in terms of the non-fulfilment of the Marxian expectation that the working class would be reduced to a mass of 'abstract undifferentiated labour power', and that radical political possibilities would thereby emerge. There was no constant, widespread and recognised opposition of interests between classes, nor were the clashes that did occur responses to common economic conditions. There was certainly no mechanical cause-and-effect relation between poverty or misery and political action, though the link was occasionally close, for example, between the worsening of the depression in the late eighties and the rise of the new unions. Whether or not clashes took place depended, not simply upon the degree of poverty, measured absolutely or relatively, or on the extent of segregation, repression and inequality in the society, but on the qualities of leaders, the traditions and coherence of local working-class organisations, and the expectations and hopes of workers themselves. Throughout the century the conflict between labour and capital ebbed and flowed, and altered in form. At all times, but especially in the second half of the century, individual mobility, the illusions and the prospects of property,[52] increments of political and legal change, and significant divisions within classes, worked against social polarisation and against the self-consciousness and mobilisation of the proletariat. The electoral system absorbed and diverted possible structural conflicts. Vincent concludes, from his study of the poll books, that the practical moral for the politician of the nineteenth century was that 'there is almost no quarter in which votes may not be sought and won, no interest so sharply hostile that it is not worth placating, that in short the electoral situation is profoundly plastic and responsive to political art'.[53] Captured so subtly, Marx's proletariat remained almost as mythical as 'the people', identified and promoted by J. S. Mill and the philosophic radicals.

There were, of course, exceptions and unresolved problems and conflicts. Isolated revolutionaries still talked of class war, and socialism emerged as a political force by the end of the century – considerably later than in France. Traditions of great battles and courageous victories grew and flourished in the folk-lore of the working class and in the imaginative reconstructions of some highly influential Labour historians, supplanting its somewhat more mundane history. At the edges of power and influence the sense of outrage, demands for a vastly different future and the denunciation of all property, persisted. There was a clear and sometimes theoretically fruitful tension between the radical promise of democratic doctrine, with its talk of equality and autonomy, and the actual social institutions that emerged in its name. But despite subterranean rumblings and the occasional assaults of radical theory, it seems fair to say that the British working class had gained respectability and had been absorbed into national society by the early part of the present century. In the home of the industrial revolution, the inchoate radical movements of the 1830s and the 1840s were succeeded by a mass-based and largely peaceful labour movement, empty of revolutionary aspirations and content with maintaining or increasing its share of rising productivity. It was utilitarian and pragmatic, almost untouched by revolutionary or Marxist social doctrines. The 'sovereignty of the people' became so much rhetoric, class conflict faded, and the search for community, which had moved so many of the early critics of industrial change, seemed irrelevant as wages rose and as social reforms mitigated the more obvious evils of the laissez-faire state.

THE BACKGROUND OF THEORY – CLASSICAL POLITICAL ECONOMY

The one body of doctrine which strongly influenced both Mill and Marx was the classical political economy of Smith, Malthus and Ricardo, which seemed to friends and enemies alike to be peculiarly appropriate to the society in which it emerged. Although the responses of Marx and Mill differed greatly, their social theories were each influenced particularly by certain key notions and concerns in the classical economics – ideas of the space available for human development, of the sources and character of social harmony, and of the nature of politics. They both saw that the existing economic system might explode because of its failure to satisfy the demands made upon it, and developed the implications of the primitive classical accounts of class relations in their own more class-conscious society.

Classical political economy, which was a major ingredient of nineteenth-century liberalism, was portrayed by its socialist critics as class-based polemics – at best a bourgeois science and at worst unashamed bourgeois apologetics or anti-proletarian pseudo-science. Eric Hobsbawm describes the classical political economists as 'very confident champions' of the middle class.[54] And it is true that the theories of Smith, Malthus and Ricardo, which were developed during times of marked economic expansion, growing private or free enterprise and considerable optimism in business and manufacturing circles, did constitute a handy philosophy for modern capitalism, despite their occasional gloom and fear, and that the values and capacities they praised – freedom, prudence and self-realisation – seemed remarkably fitting to a rising and educated middle class. The classical theory – a shifting and many-sided thing – was construed fairly as a defence of a particular system of private property against its varied opponents. Adam Smith, for example, put the defence of property at the centre of his historical account of government. 'Till there be property, there can be no government, the very end of which is to secure wealth (i.e. to make wealth secure), and to defend the rich against the poor.'[55] Nonetheless, as Marx justly indicated, the early classical economists were disinterested inquirers carrying out impartial investigations, though within bourgeois horizons, unlike the 'hired prize-fighters' and vulgar apologists who, he believed, became dominant after 1830.[56]

Adam Smith's optimism is based upon a picture of the supposed operation of the free, competitive market. His criticisms were aimed principally at the 'pernicious regulations' which interfered with the system of perfect liberty.[57] These included restrictions on occupations, land tenure, industry and foreign trade, all of which were taken to frustrate individual initiative and thus economic efficiency. While the claims of laissez-faire may have been strengthened by 'the avarice and injustice of princes and sovereign states',[58] they did not depend upon particular governmental shortcomings, which might have been removable, and Smith's general principle would continue to apply in the case of a disinterested and efficient government and bureaucracy. He opposed interventionism as such. He was as much against restraints imposed by the virtuous to ensure virtue as he was to the restraints imposed by selfish rulers for their own supposed advantage. In advancing the claims of society and challenging those of 'adventitious' institutions such as the state, he took issue not merely with mercantilists but with those modern and arrogant philosophers whom he described as 'projectors' or 'men of system'. Like Burke's arithmetical constitution-monger, or Matthew

Arnold's Jacobin, they wished to fashion societies in terms of general principles or plans. 'Projectors disturb nature in the course of her operations on human affairs, and it requires no more than to leave her alone and give her fair play in the pursuit of her ends that she may establish her own designs.'[59] The 'man of system' pursues his 'ideal plan' regardless of individual variations and processes.

> He seems to imagine that he can arrange the different members of a great society with as much ease as the hand arranges the different pieces upon a chess board, he does not consider that the pieces upon the chess board have no other principle of motion besides that which the hand impresses upon them; but that in the great chess board of human society, every single piece has a principle of motion of its own altogether different from that which the legislature might choose to impress upon it.[60]

Whatever the goal or the inspiration, Smith doubted the competence of centralised authorities, ecclesiastical or civil, just or unjust, reforming or conservative, to bring about their desired ends. The greatest possible economic and social good would be attained where individuals produced and consumed freely. The role of the state was basically that of enforcing domestic peace and commutative justice, providing for external defence, and carrying out essential public works, including education, which could not be satisfactorily or profitably carried out by private enterprise. The state is thus presented as, essentially, the guarantor of the system of natural liberty, which means that its role is that of maintaining the framework within which free, effective competition can take place. But its precise role is left somewhat flexible – public works, and especially the provision of a system of education, go beyond the maintenance of a legal framework which would enable individuals to pursue their business in peaceful and orderly ways, although education may contribute to order, and certainly would be necessary to an informed business community. Such an extension to Smith's principle, whereby the state should concern itself with all those things which are conditions of the widest possible enjoyment of natural liberty, would clearly lead to a quite different political outcome from that which he envisaged. In addition, Smith supported certain particular cases of governmental intervention without indicating any relevant general principles under which they might be subsumed.[61]

Although government is in this sense inescapable – and hence one might be inclined to regard it as part of the natural order – the general argument is anti-political. Society does not require an extensive political framework or straitjacket in order to exist and to prosper. Indeed, political interference is likely to destroy possible gains. The emphatic distinction between the state and society, between the political and the non-political, with the political being frequently downgraded, was extremely significant in eighteenth- and nineteenth-century social theory. This often exaggerated, simplified or arbitrary distinction helped men to formulate their ideas of the goods which social man should, or would in particular circumstances, realise. Proudhon, speaking for the assorted champions of society, clearly indicated the antagonism.

> We must understand that outside the sphere of parliamentarism, as sterile as it is absorbing, there is another field incomparably vaster, in which our destiny is worked out; that beyond these political phantoms, whose forms capture our imagination, there are the phenomena of social economy, which, by their harmony or discord, produce all the good and ill of society.[62]

Government becomes more than simply a badge of lost innocence, for it sustains a lack of innocence and stands in the way of community. Politics breeds force and destructive conflict, and gives rich rewards to the unproductive and the parasitic. On the other hand, man manifests his good, productive side in society, which is spontaneous, natural and co-operative. There were, of course, significant differences within the ranks of those who made use of this general distinction, and who championed society – differences over, for example, the legitimate extent and permanence of politics or force, the character of social ties and of the spontaneous or 'natural' social order, and the causal power of society in relation to the state. There was also tension within individual thinkers, for example Adam Smith, over such matters as the legitimate powers of the state. But Scottish philosophic historians of the eighteenth century and utopian socialists, anarchists and Marxists and laissez-faire liberals did, in their separate ways, accord society an almost religious veneration, and indicated the concrete senses in which man was a social creature, and thereby helped lay the foundations of sociology. And for many of them the ideal became that of a society in which politics played the minimum possible part, which could be no part at all, as the oppressive, arbitrary and wasteful state withered away, and government dissolved into administration. To those consumed by this ideal, it seemed manifest that the various things they valued would prove compatible in the future, and that any necessary procedures for making decisions would remain uncontaminated by politics and force.

Adam Smith, who accepted the permanent need for a state apparatus, occupies a central place in this continuing debate over the state and society. His economic theory, which contains so much general social analysis, provided many arguments and images for the opponents of the state. In his view, society was largely autonomous, self-regulating or self-moving, and hence he could focus his attention upon the co-operation, the agreements and the values which held it together. It is characterised by non-coercive or 'natural' co-ordination, realised through the peaceful economic pressures of the market. The problem of order is not considered against assumptions of intense social conflict or man's instinctive barbarism. The classical liberal psychology has self-interest, directed, restrained and modified by laws and institutions, at its centre, and this basic force can find adequate outlet and scope for its creativity only in a free polity. The natural effort of every individual to better his own condition, and not altruism or benevolence (which was described by Smith as the ornament rather than the pillar of political life), binds men together in communities.

> Society may subsist among different men, as among different merchants, from a sense of its utility, without any mutual love or affection; and though no man in it should owe any obligation, or be bound in gratitude to any other, it may still be upheld by a mercenary exchange of good offices according to an agreed valuation.[63]

The social order is the unintended result of self-interest, and not the product of reason or authority or contract. The Scottish historians who influenced Smith assumed that society had a 'natural history', and emphasised the unplanned character of institutions. As Adam Ferguson wrote: 'Nations stumble upon establishments, which are indeed the result of human action, but not the execution of any human design.'[64] The spontaneous or blind growth of the complex social order is brought out clearly in Smith's account of the division of labour. The division of labour is not the result of human calculation, although the social mechanism is so ingenious that it bears the appearance of design (an 'invisible hand').[65] It results from a certain propensity in human nature – 'the propensity to truck, barter, and exchange one thing for another'.[66] Whether or not this disposition is natural or derived from something else is irrelevant to Smith's purposes. He was concerned with the way in which the trucking disposition had woven a highly disciplined, integrated and co-operative social order, which seemed to serve the individual extremely well. The productivity of labour was vastly increased by the specialisation of men in the area where their talents lay – and these particular talents, Smith was careful to point out, were perhaps more the product than the cause of specialisation. The quality of life is the product of 'the assistance and co-operation of many thousands', which acts as a social cement.[67] Co-operation arises naturally and without concern for the interests of others. 'It is not from the benevolence of the butcher, the brewer, or the baker that we expect our dinner, but from their regard of their own interest. We address ourselves, not to their humanity but to their self-love, and never talk to them of our necessities but of their advantages.'[68] In a well-governed society this system of reciprocal services or division of labour will produce a universal opulence spreading to the lowest ranks of the people – 'a general plenty diffuses itself through all the different ranks of society'.[69]

Smith's assumption that the competitive market system was natural faces several difficulties. Nature is a jack of all trades in social theory, and generally raises more problems than it resolves. What are the criteria for distinguishing natural from unnatural behaviour and institutions? The concept 'natural' is normally introduced to suggest that certain institutions are unnecessary or unreasonable or illegitimate, rather than that they are not original to man, though denunciations of the 'unnatural' may be dressed up in an historical garb. In Smith's case we are considering a civilised society which presupposes a particular legal or institutional framework, and the status of that framework, vis-à-vis nature, must itself be considered. At what point and why does the structure of laws become unnatural? The guarantor system itself excludes, or interferes with, certain kinds or forms of economic activity, and these exclusions and interventions must be justified in terms of criteria which, in principle, could extend much further than Smith allowed, in his own concrete prescriptions. In addition, there are questions of an empirical, or at least quasi-empirical character, particularly concerning the likely effects of the spontaneous operation of natural forces. How sensible was Smith's preference in relation to the ends he valued – economic efficiency, freedom and social stability? It may have been a far more reasonable choice in the 1770s than it had become by the mid-nineteenth century, because of the intervening economic and social changes. Smith's claim, reduced to bare essentials, was that the competitive market was the best mechanism for allocating resources and distributing the product. He assumed that a hidden law of co-ordination and integration was operative in a free economy.[70] But the law operated only in the ideal case, which presupposed the rational economic man, growing markets and effective competition. His abstracted model of the existing society, despite the descriptive analysis which underlay it, contained valuations and prescriptions which related less to actual tendencies within society than to ideal notions from the natural law and the utilitarian traditions. Smith was well aware that people often misunderstood their interests and that his economic model was not – nor was it meant to be – an adequate description of economic practice. Obstacles to the free market or the 'natural' or spontaneous operation of economic forces included interfering governments and sectional economic interests. Smith was especially conscious of the danger of monopoly, which grew from an undesirable kind of self-interest – from 'profit hunger', which conflicted with the general interest. Economic liberty was threatened, not by the prudent business man – sober, industrious and frugal – but by the insatiable capitalist of the kind later portrayed by Marx. Smith stressed the advantages of the masters over the men in the struggle for resources.

> The masters, being fewer in number, can combine much more easily; and the law, besides, authorises or at least does not prohibit their combinations, while it prohibits those of the workmen. We have no acts of parliament against combining to lower the price of work; but many against combining to raise it ... In the long-run the workman may be as necessary to his master as his master is to him, but the necessity is not so immediate.
>
> We rarely hear, it has been said, of the combinations of masters, though frequently of those of workmen...Masters are always and everywhere in a sort of tacit, but constant and uniform combination, not to raise the wages of labour above their actual rate.[71]

Smith frequently condemned merchants for vulgarity, partiality, avarice and deceitfulness, and indicated the ease with which they could keep the price of goods well above the natural price, and so defeat the public interest.

Monopoly thus represented a deviation from the pure system, in that individual producers were able to determine prices – of raw materials and finished goods – rather than adapting themselves to the market. The free, competitive system required that price changes were not controlled by any individual producer. Smith was certainly no supporter of large inequalities and economic concentration of the kind which emerged during the expansion of capitalism in the nineteenth century, often under the cover of laissez-faire theory, which became increasingly a hollow euphemism. But it is not simply a question of the failure of men and the shortcomings of the system at that particular time: given ignorance and scarce resources, it seems doubtful whether any society could meet the specified conditions and hence approach the system of perfect liberty. Moreover, even if that system had been approached, there was no guarantee that it would survive the social tensions to which certain aspects of the 'natural' order, especially inequality and poverty, could be expected to give rise.

Classical political economy contains a primitive sociology and, as times changed, reveals a growing awareness of the social or class problems facing men. Smith referred, not yet to classes, but to 'orders' and 'interests', and distinguished between 'the three great, original and constituent orders of every civilised society'.[72] He conceived the interests of landowners, capitalists and labourers to be reconcilable. However, the problem of social order in a world in which the alleged decrees of nature were likely to be widely resented, emerges clearly, though not explicitly, especially in his discussion of the wages of labour. All commodities have a natural price – 'the central price, to which the prices of all commodities are continually gravitating'.[73] That 'central price', or value, can be measured practically in terms of the labour embodied in it, and hence the relationship between commodities, in terms of their values, reflects the productive and class relationships between men. Men, too, have an ordinary or average price or wage, which approximates to their subsistence costs. But the actual level of wages varied significantly, over time and place, and depended upon the bargaining position of the respective parties, as Smith brought out in his chapter on 'The Wages of Labour'. The competitive situation is determined by the rate of change of stock and the number of labourers in the community. The market price may at times be 'the lowest which is consistent with common humanity',[74] or may even fall temporarily below the level necessary to ensure mere brute survival. Smith commented on the minimum level: 'A man must always live by his work, and his wages must at least be sufficient to maintain him. They must even upon most occasions be somewhat more; otherwise it would be impossible for him to bring up a family, and the race of workmen could not last beyond the first generation.'[75] The minimum level is approached in backward or stationary societies, where intense competition takes place for insufficient jobs, and especially in declining or decaying societies in which the already oversupplied labour market would be enlarged by the addition to it of 'the overflowings of all the other classes'. In the latter case, as in China, want, famine and early death are widespread, and prevail until the number of inhabitants in the country is reduced 'to what could easily be maintained by the revenue and stock which remained in it'.[76] In these circumstances the law of population is revealed in its cruellest form.

> Every species of animals naturally multiplies in proportion to the means of their subsistence and no species can ever multiply beyond it ... the demand for men, like that for any other commodity, necessarily regulates the production of men; quickens it when it goes too slowly, and stops it when it advances too fast.[77]

Smith was here stating what he believed to be a law, and was not justifying or approving of the situation which he had described. Marx was later to praise Ricardo for equally technical observatioins on wages.

Ricardo had been aware that labourers were bought as productive instruments, like machines. Marx accepted his comparison of the effect upon wages and upon the price of hats of a fall in the respective costs of production of men (e.g. cheaper food) and hats. Wages and hats would each fall to their new natural price. Marx commented that: 'Ricardo's language is as cynical as can be. To put the cost of manufacture of hats and the cost of maintenance of men on the same plane is to turn men into hats. But do not make an outcry at the cynicism of it. The cynicism is in the facts and not in the words which express the facts.'[78] For Smith as well the cynicism was in the facts, which he was seeking to state as accurately as possible. However, he did at times criticise the existing system because of its effects upon the workers. In particular, he felt that the increasingly specialised division of labour was leading to their intellectual and moral deterioration, and destroying the martial virtues. Confinement to narrow tasks and the lack of education led to the 'drowsy stupidity' of the mass of the people. He noted the apparent injustice of the system. 'So it may very justly be said that the people who clothe the whole world are in rags themselves.'[79]

In some communities the relationship between population and resources was a happy one, keeping wages well above a mere subsistence level, and perhaps contributing to a higher standard of what constituted subsistence. Smith thought conditions in England reasonably good, but the main example of a prosperous and advancing community was America. In this thriving and fast-growing society wages were high, and because of abundant employment opportunities large families were a source of prosperity rather than of poverty. This progressive state was 'the cheerful and the hearty state to all the different orders of society'.[80] America featured prominently in the writings of the classical economists and in liberal and socialist theories as a richly endowed, almost limitless society, free, at least for a long time, of the bitter, unremitting pressure of men upon resources which characterised many of the older European countries. Malthus charged Paine with ignoring England's differences from America in his vision of a property-owning democracy and a decline in the role of the civil power. While there were relatively few propertyless people in America, he commented, 'the redundant population of an old state furnishes materials of unhappiness unknown to such a state as that of America'.[81] And Jefferson, using Malthus, made a similar point when he contrasted 'the man of the old world...crowded within limits either small or over-charged, and steeped in the vices which that situation generates' with the man of the new world, who moved easily and unconfined.[82] However, as both de Tocqueville and Mill were to stress, material abundance and opportunity remained quite compatible with an oppressive philistinism.

While economists and politicians could stress America's peculiar good fortune, which postponed the evil day, the emphasis was on its peculiarity. The problems of Europe were far more pressing, and there is a vein of pessimism if not despair in many accounts of its future. Smith was not, as is sometimes supposed, a facile optimist. He did not envisage any long-term condition of economic plenty, in which all the needs and claims of men could be satisfied, nor was he unaware that dissatisfied social groups might challenge the best of all possible worlds. For the social drama is generally played out against a background of considerable economic scarcity. Men are consigned to a certain, limited condition, and the limits are set by the wealth and the social and political organisation of each particular country. A generation later, with Malthus, the natural limits to economic and social growth and improvement were presented more starkly, though in the second edition Malthus tried, in the words of his own understatement, to 'soften some of the harshest conclusions of the first Essay'.[83] Malthus saw his researches into the population question as part of general speculation on the perfectibility of man and society. In his view, utopians such as Godwin were blind to the imperious all-pervading laws of nature, especially the law of population, which stressed the limitedness of space and resources. Malthus condemned his fellows for living in a fool's paradise of procreation and extravagence, unaware of the terrible costs of the growth of population beyond the means of subsistence. When population outstripped the food supply, the pressure tended 'to subject the lower classes of society to distress, and to prevent any great permanent amelioration in their condition'.[84] The limits to the expansion of the system had been ignored by men in the desperate and selfish pursuit of their own advantage. However, Nature could do something to restore the balance between men and resources – a balance which was attained in different societies at different points, depending partly on their particular standards and expectations. Nature employed certain positive checks, which increased the death rate. 'Misery', through famine, high infant mortality, the diseases associated with urban overcrowding and lack of sanitation, and so on, killed off surplus population, and was peculiarly strong in the most despotic and worst-governed states. But more to the moral point were preventive checks, involving the planned limitation of the birth rate. In Malthus's scheme, the ideal preventive checks were the avoidance of 'early and improvident marriages' and the voluntary and rational setting of limits to the size of families. Malthus strongly rejected one possible preventive check – 'vice' or the 'improper arts', which included contraception – on the assumption that chastity was the proper moral response to poverty, being dictated by nature and sanctioned by revealed religion.[85]

Malthus was concerned deeply about a real problem and real suffering, but because of his particular single-cause explanation of misery and poverty, and his related prescriptions to end or sharply reduce it, critics declared that the ideological function of his theory – and perhaps his own dishonesty or superficiality – was manifest. For Malthus located the real source of the plight of the labourers neither in the private property system nor in governmental mismanagement, but primarily in the common man's lack of forethought and self-discipline. He spelled out the message explicitly:

> That the principal and most permanent cause of poverty has little or no direct relation to forms of government, or the unequal division of property; and that, as the rich do not in reality possess the power of finding employment for the poor, the poor cannot, in the nature of things, possess the right to demand them, are important truths flowing from the principle of population, which, when properly explained, would by no means be above the most ordinary comprehensions.[86]

Governments might contribute to social evils, and might not contribute much to social prosperity, but institutions were light in comparison with the true causes of distress. Malthus stressed again and again that it was vital to spread the knowledge that 'the principal cause of want and unhappiness is only indirectly connected with government and totally beyond its power directly to remove'.[87] Reacting sharply to the disorders and turbulence of his own time, he attacked false teachers and instant reformers not merely for ignorance, but for undermining liberty, because the agitation inspired by their shallow doctrines encouraged anarchy and excessive, illiberal responses on the part of those in authority. Radical, unrealistic aspiration bred tyranny by tainting reform and frightening the erstwhile friends of liberty into abandoning it. 'The most successful supporters of tyranny are without doubt those general declaimers who attribute the distresses of the poor, and almost all the evils to which society is subject, to human institutions and the iniquity of government.'[88] The spread of his facts would, he hoped, increase social stability by encouraging working-class patience and moderation. For those conversant with the facts, revolutionary action and civil commotion could have no possible point – as Francis Place and other lower class Malthusians tried to convince the more aggressive political radicals, including the Chartists.

Malthus thought the Malthusian problem soluble, although distress could not be alleviated at once. The title of the second edition of the *Essay* refers to 'the future removal or mitigation of the evils' occasioned by the principle of population, and he concluded the work with the claim that, though the virtue and happiness of mankind could not be expected to keep pace with the brilliant career of physical discovery, the 'partial good which seems to be attainable is worthy of all our exertions, is sufficient to direct our efforts and animate our prospects'.[89] Men and not the objective environment were to blame for their plight, and education and prohibitive measures, primarily in relation to the working class, could vastly improve the general position by reducing the number on the raft to what it could safely hold. If men could only adapt their appetites to the situation of scarcity, the gloomy analysis could be followed by cautious hope.

Education was called upon to inculcate the lessons of nature. It was to encourage men to sacrifice temporary to permanent gratifications, to readily accept 'moral restraint' based upon individual prudence. The virtues stressed by Malthus were knowledge, foresight, sobriety, industry, respectability, pride, independence and cleanliness – virtues which, given his view of the facts, seemed unlikely to challenge social order. Education was especially valuable where it enabled a man to acquire 'that decent kind of pride and those juster habits of thinking which will prevent him from burdening society with a family of children that he cannot support'.[90] It would strengthen tendencies to demand a higher standard of living, which would naturally limit both marriages and the size of families. Malthus believed that man's prudential habits would grow immensely if he became less content with a condition of wretchedness, and that such a process would be encouraged principally by 'liberty, security of property, the diffusion of knowledge, and a taste for the conveniences and comforts of life'.[91] Education, equal laws and political participation would improve men and draw them into common moral action with their fellows, and would make them fearful of any personal degradation, including loss of material advantages. In this way the master-spring of industry, 'the desire of bettering our condition, and the fear of making it worse',[92] could become a far more powerful force for good than it already was.

Malthus stated quite explicitly that these qualities – prudence, elevation of sentiment, self-improvement – were characteristic of the middle class, and that the social problem was, from one angle, that of subordinating the labourers to middle-class standards, where it was not possible to raise them into it. He wrote that it is probable that 'our best-grounded expectations of an increase in the happiness of the mass of human society are founded on the prospect of an increase in the relative proportions of the middle parts'.[93] With a lowering of population pressure, more labour-saving devices, and a consequent increase in the relative numbers of the middle class, it was possible that 'each labourer might indulge a more rational hope of rising by diligence and exertion into a better station; the rewards of industry and virtue would be increased in number; the lottery of human society would appear to consist of fewer blanks and more prizes; and the sum of social happiness would be evidently augmented'.[94] It was not possible to change the social structure utterly, and there would always be a class of labourers and a class of proprietors, but Malthus did hope that 'the condition of each, and the proportion which they bear to each other, may be so altered as greatly to improve the harmony and beauty of the whole'.[95]

Malthus thus sought a resolution of the population problem primarily in moral and cognitive change within individuals. Their socialisation amounted to their acceptance of bourgeois values and bourgeois virtues. The framework within which this goal was to be consummated was an unequal society which offered self-interested individuals the prospect of rising or falling, and which rested upon the laws of property and marriage. Prudent men, knowing the limits of possible change and cherishing their own prospects and advantages, would come to abhor the absurd doctrines of those who thought that political manipulation and institutional change could make a new world.

Ricardo, who wrote during a time of economic growth accompanied by war, uncertainty, conflict and social discontent, concentrated not upon production, but on the more problematical and urgent theory of distribution. He wrote to Malthus in 1820 that political economy should be called 'an inquiry into the laws which determine the division of the produce of industry among the classses which concur in its formation'.[96] The division of interests is a basic assumption of his major work, *On the Principles of Political Economy and Taxation*, which was published in 1817. There he expressed his concern with the way in which the produce of the earth was divided among the three classes of the community – 'the proprietor of the land, the owner of the stock or capital necessary for its cultivation, and the labourers by whose industry it is cultivated'.[97] He offered little hope to the workers, arguing that the combination of the laws of population and diminishing returns in agriculture determined wages at subsistence according to the price of corn, and hence limited progress because profits tended to decline as rents rose.[98] The general tendency of increases in both the level of wages and the number of workmen was a declining marginal return on capital, leading to a gradual drying up of investment. In a pamphlet published in 1815 he concluded that economic progress, which involved increasing population and capital accumulation, 'would leave the wage earners with a static subsistence wage, the capitalists with decreasing profits on stock, and the landlords with increasing rents'.[99] While the substitution of machinery for human labour was 'often very injurious to the class of labourers',[100] and while it was a distinctly harmful influence insofar as it diverted labour from the production of consumer goods, and drew on the wage fund rather than savings, it did not explain the labourer's general plight. The appropriate counters to the natural tendency of profits to fall, with corresponding injurious effects upon the labourers, were a free, self-regulating market economy and free trade, and the Malthusian means of encouraging expectations of higher living standards (changing the habits and customs of the people) and ensuring public disapproval of improvident marriages.

The apparent confidence of the classical political economy evaporated in Ricardo's cool and sharp analysis. He had pointed to a clear division of interests between the landlords, seeking to maintain a destructive protectionism, and the other sections of society. His account of the landowners' interests, and his assertion of the need to import cheap food to England, amounted to a declaration of war on the established authorities, and pointed to a serious class conflict at the heart of the new system. In addition, Ricardo's theory implied that capitalism was subject to a process of internal degeneration. Its problems were not to be dismissed easily as the results of external causes, such as Nature. In its ordinary process of development it seemed to be undermining the motive for accumulation, which was essential to its continuing expansion. As Meek puts it: 'Not even the best of all possible economic systems, it was maintained, could overcome the obstacle of diminishing returns in agriculture.'[101] Even if the stationary state was far distant, and was characterised as not a state of stagnation, doubts were cast upon the easy confidence of the capitalist. It was not surprising that the Political Economy Club should, in the thirties, devote much of its effort to demolishing such pessimistic doctrines as Malthus's principle of population, the inverse ratio of wages and profits, the stationary state, the real conflict of interest between landlords and others, and the concern with distribution, as well as more distinctively socialist beliefs such as the interpretation of value as embodied labour. Mountifort Longfield, in a series of lectures in 1833, emphasised the need to develop and spread a political economy which in no way threatened the existing order, by encouraging the working men to follow their 'real interests'. In his words, 'it only remains to be considered, in what manner a true sense of their real interests may be most effectually brought home to them...It depends in some degree upon every person present, whether the labourer is taught that his interest will be best promoted by prudence and industry, or by a violent demolition of the capital destined to his support.'[102]

For Smith, Malthus and Ricardo, man was necessarily confined in room, and it was a major concern, above all for Malthus, to ensure that the population was kept at or below the level which the society could adequately support. Each recognised the possibility of serious social conflict when downward pressures were strongest. They could explain why things were as they were, and especially why distribution was as it was, and they could recommend prudence, but they realised, in general, that a statement of the truths of political economy to men suffering from its supposedly impersonal compulsions, would not always be sufficient to restrain them. While emphasising the natural limits to social mobility and to the satisfaction of economic claims, and in many cases to the satisfaction of basic needs, they saw that men collided over precisely these issues. Their own accounts of inequality – though not always existing inequalities, which they often condemned – and scarcity as necessary features of the economic system were not accepted by many underprivileged groups, which were quite capable, as the younger Mill was to complain, of committing fallacies of political economy in the hope of improving their economic position. Smith, too, had complained of the inability of the labourer to comprehend the social interest or its connection with his own interest. Hence the problem becomes, essentially, one of education and communication – the diffusion of useful knowledge – although the classical political economists recognised existing irrationality, and feared attempts, based on false economics, to triumph over the laws of nature and ignore the limits of the system of natural liberty, when that existed. In such circumstances, property rights would not remain secure. Theirs was no complacent philosophy of individualism and social harmony. These sober and worried political economists were not seekers after perfection, but sought the greatest possible achievements within the real world. Although they could conceive of no better economic system, they were not blindly optimistic about the economic prospects of laissez-faire: where they revealed considerable faith, and even here it was sometimes hedged, was in the expectation that men could be persuaded to accept the so-called natural limits to the improvement of their economic lot. The laws of nature of the classical economists were soon to be dismissed as part of an interested defence of an unjust order, which because of the conflict and suffering to which it gave rise, could and should be destroyed.

Socialist condemnations of the market economy and its supporting theories generally focussed on its destructiveness, its inefficiency and its artificiality. The disagreements were not simply empirical, for the socialists articulated a very different social ideal from the laissez-faire economists. They sought reintegration after the stresses and divisions of individualism and industrialism. In their assaults on the notions that poverty was a necessary and indispensable feature of society, and that substantial inequalities were natural and useful, they interpreted certain

classical doctrines in new and more radical ways, and denied the natural-
ness of the economic order which the classical writers had described
and justified. More profoundly, they condemned the classical writers for
abstracting economic life from its human context, and giving it a false
autonomy. In stricter economic terms, subversive and moralistic lines of
argument were developed from the classical theory of costs, which
attached major significance to labour. The labour theory of value, when
applied to the distribution of the social product, could have far-reaching
implications, particularly if it was assumed that the labourer was the
sole or even the main creator of value. If value was embodied labour,
profit readily came to be seen as a kind of surplus value. William
Thompson was expressing a common radical view when he said that the
producer was the creator of value. The existing and unjust distributive
system was normally explained in terms of interlopers, parasites and
exploiters depriving the useful and productive classes of their due
rewards. No law could legitimise a situation in which 'he who produces
everything receives almost nothing while those persons who produce
nothing revel in superfluity'.[103] One underlying assumption was that
existing distinctions were arbitrary, and hence social critics could
blame the rich and the powerful, not nature or the undisciplined poor,
for the evils they perceived. 'From the present constitution of society,
the millions are a doomed class,' wrote J. F. Bray in 1839, 'from the
position in which they stand with regard to capital and the capitalist,
their condition is unimprovable and their wrongs irremediable.'[104] The
Ricardian socialist Thomas Hodgskin wrote:

> It is the overwhelming nature of the demands of capital, sanctioned
> by the laws of society, sanctioned by the customs of men, en-
> forced by the legislature, and warmly defended by political econo-
> mists, which keep, which ever have kept, and which ever will
> keep, as long as they are allowed and acquiesced in, the labourer
> in poverty and misery.[105]

Hodgskin, whose ideal was less socialist than radical individualist,[106]
anticipated Marx in many respects, developing theories of surplus value
and the class nature of law, amongst others. But perhaps the most interesting aspect of his writings lies in his emphasis on the difference
between social regulations or positive laws and natural laws, and in his
argument that the property system and the resultant poverty were
themselves products of human interference with a beneficent natural
order. Freed from restrictive law, he felt that human ingenuity was
such that the productive power of society could far surpass the limited
achievements permitted man in the classical political economy. He
therefore felt that Ricardo had not only dignified passing, artificial and

unjust social conditions with the title 'natural', but that he had seriously underestimated the productive potential of a properly organised society. Agreeing that harmonious and uninterrupted progress would not occur under capitalism, he complained of Ricardo's pessimistic doctrines, which seemed 'to set bounds to our hopes for the future progress of mankind in a more definite manner even than the opinions of Mr Malthus'.[107]

Marx, like some of his socialist predecessors, stressed the conservative, deflating function of much of the classical political economy, and its ahistorical presentation of a particular mode of production as 'eternal' or 'natural'. He directed his most savage polemic at Malthus, claiming that his *Essay on Population* owed its popularity solely to party interest.

> The French Revolution had found passionate defenders in the United Kingdom; the 'principle of population', slowly worked out in the eighteenth century, and then in the midst of a great social crisis, proclaimed with drums and trumpets as the infallible anti-dote to the teachings of Condorcet, etc., was greeted with jubilance by the English oligarchy as the great destroyer of all hankerings after human development.[108]

Marx, too, presented the future society as not only a genuine community but as a consciously controlled and extremely efficient economic system, in which man was fully in command of his own life and destiny, and was able to enjoy far more space for human development than had ever been suspected in the gloomy science of classical economics.

PART 2 MARX

2 Man and community

The proclaimed starting point of the whole Marxian theory is real, corporeal man – no abstraction, or figment of the speculative imagination – as he goes about the business of producing and consuming, in the course of which he transforms the physical universe, society and himself. Seeking to satisfy his changing needs, man changes nature through tool-making and purposive activity, and through that activity he transforms himself, and transforms himself in certain particular directions. Hence life and society are essentially historical, and human nature changes, and will change drastically in that paradise of human achievement which Marx confidently anticipated. Thus Marx repudiated static conceptions of human nature, which confined human capacities arbitrarily, and underlay the ordinary conservative defences of established institutions and existing distributions of power and resources. Burke's theories, for example, though appropriate in their time, diminished man by denying his potentialities and the possibility of a radically new social order in the future. Historical deficiencies were made part of man's nature, and hence the masses were assigned permanently to a particular, limited station. The contingent and the necessary were confused, and such historical forms as private property and inequality were presented as innate or pristine, and surrounded with rich layers of myth and legitimation. The conservative was correct in claiming that 'you can't change human nature', in the sense of suddenly creating a new man according to reason or plan, and he was also correct in observing the deep links between men's appetites and desires and existing institutions, such as private property. Men's appetites and the most powerful existing institutions mutually reinforced each other. But while Marx acknowledged the present limitations of men, and the potency of appetites which he found dehumanising, he was more struck by the continuity of historical change, with which man's nature changed, as did his achievements and social institutions. History was the record of man's as yet unfinished self-creation. His diverse creative powers, his distinctive capacities and abilities, emerged historically, and were demonstrated and unfolded in the process of technological and social change, though they

55

were exercised still within a restrictive and damaging framework. *Homo faber* suffered in his work, finding his powers frustrated and crushed therein. Men were estranged in a physical and social world which they had helped create, and could not either see it as their own product, or seize it for themselves. That world, and their perceptions of it, were alike twisted and one-sided.

Marx's account of historical change and of the different forms of human society, culminating in the powerful, sweeping and bitter anthropological critique of capitalism, must be read against a particular view of human needs and powers. In much of Marx's writings, such a view is presented indirectly or obliquely, in the various accounts of dehumanisation. For any account of dehumanisation presupposes a notion of what is human or truly human and, indeed, gives broad guidance as to the content of that notion. If we know that a man is being impeded in the expression of his powers and the satisfaction of his needs, we gain at least a rough image of the unimpeded and fulfilled man. The vision of man on which Marx's hostile analysis of capitalism rested, and which he presented sometimes indirectly, sometimes directly, is of a free, creative, self-determining and social being. Moved by this vision he condemned the social principles of Christianity which, he said, 'preach cowardice, self-contempt, abasement, submission, dejection, in a word all the qualities of the canaille, and the proletariat, not wishing to be treated as canaille, needs its courage, its self-feeling, its pride and its sense of independence more than its bread'.[1] Illusions – and, of course, the social realities which sustained them, and which were defined more precisely by Marx as his work progressed – had to be destroyed if men were to stand on their own feet, to fulfil their human nature or to realise their capacities, which meant expressing powers and satisfying needs which were, by and large, frustrated, hidden or non-existent in pre-communist societies. All this was necessary for man to become the highest being for man, to 'revolve around himself as his own true sun'.[2] The abolition of religion is proclaimed in the following terms: 'The criticism of religion ends with the doctrine that man is the supreme being for man. It ends, therefore, with the categorical imperative to overthrow all those conditions in which man is an abused, enslaved, contemptible creature.'[3] Marx's strong concern for human autonomy or freedom, and for man's ultimate self-realisation in co-operation with others, underlay his mature as well as his early writings. He envisaged, as the outcome of history, man unconstrained by his social environment, active, versatile, revealing a variety of creative powers, enriched, a whole man. To this vision, man's existing state was counterposed. For he was, under capitalism, not self-determining but the victim of circumstances, not creative, versatile and whole, but chained to specialised and soul-destroying tasks, and not genuinely co-operative but isolated and egoistical.

Marx did not conceive this view of man as an independent, ahistorical moral standard or goal, nor as a picture of natural man. He had no conception of an historical man separated from some natural or abstract self, nor a romantic view of civilisation corrupting an original virtue, tumbling a complete man out of paradise. Capitalism, the productive system which he condemned so profoundly, had created possibilities for human development which had not existed before, and in this sense human emancipation presupposed man's whole previous development. The creative tension within the existing society was not between historically constant powers or potentialities and capitalism, but between human possibilities which had emerged only in capitalism, and its distinctive relationships and institutions, which prevented the realisation of these possibilities.

History is thus two-sided. On the one side, change is constant and cannot be held back, new qualities and situations emerge, human freedom is made possible and, even within oppressive and inhumane class societies, man's supreme productive capacity, and sporadic examples of versatility, co-operativeness and fraternity could be observed. In addition to technology – the awe-inspiring manifestation of human ingenuity and power – there were particular achievements, foreshadowing or heralding the future. On the other side, men were constrained and deformed by the conditions and the relationships in which they worked and lived. They had not yet made history freely and consciously, expressing their full powers in it. The process whereby man begets or completes himself through activity is in many respects – and for some far more than for others – an exceedingly painful one.

THE SELF-CREATION OF MAN

History is no metaphysical subject of which men are the bearers. History is human history. It is the process of man's active self-creation, in interaction with a changing natural environment and other men. The act and the process of production lie at the centre of Marx's account of history. Man's concrete productive activity is the birthplace of history, and world history is essentially the history of production. Labour is essential to man and characteristic of all forms of society. The labour-process is 'the everlasting Nature-imposed condition of human existence, and therefore is independent of every social phase of that existence, or rather, is common to every such phase'.[4] Naturally the conditions of labour varied enormously, and could not be deduced from the process of production.

As the taste of porridge does not tell you who grew the oats, no more does this simple process tell you of itself what are the social conditions under which it is taking place, whether under the slave-owner's brutal lash, or the anxious eye of the capitalist, whether Cincinnatus carried it on in tilling his modest farm or a savage in killing wild animals with stones.[5]

In labouring in various and frequently damaging conditions, man reveals a technological inventiveness, a 'universal' productive capacity, which distinguishes him from animals. 'The use and fabrication of instruments of labour, although existing in the germ among certain species of animals, is specifically characteristic of the human labour-process, and Franklin therefore defines man as a tool-making animal.'[6] Marx held, precisely, that man creates himself through labour and distinguishes himself by labour – that he must be characterised as a labouring rather than a rational or any other kind of animal. But the animal is contained within its sphere, limited by a biological and instinctual structure which admits of little development or variation. In contrast, human labour is characterised by its freedom, for it is planned, conscious and purposive, regardless of whether man understands his place in the world or his relationship to the objects which he makes. Speaking of exclusively human labour, Marx wrote that

> what distinguishes the worst architect from the best of the bees is this, that the architect raises his structure in imagination before he erects it in reality. At the end of every labour-process, we get the result that already existed in the imagination of the labourer at its commencement. He not only effects a change of form in the material on which he works, but he also realises a purpose of his own that gives the law to his modus operandi, and to which he must subordinate his will.[7]

Nature, which exists independently of human activity upon it, is the field of man's labour, the *Gegenstand* of production. It furnishes the natural conditions of his labour – it is 'the inorganic nature which he finds and makes his own, the objective body of his subjectivity'.[8] Man does not react passively to nature but acts on it and changes it, thereby putting a human stamp upon it and drawing it into human history. It is transformed gradually from raw nature to humanised nature, which is increasingly man's own work. The distinction between the natural and the human disappears as the physical world embodies and reveals the creativity of man, who 'contemplates himself in a world he has created'.[9] In the 1844 *Manuscripts*, Marx refers to society as 'the consummated oneness in substance of man and nature – the true resurrection of nature – the naturalism of man and the humanism of nature both brought to fulfilment'.[10]

This natural–human world, which is more and more the product of past human labour, reveals and embodies man's powers. But this picture of the world as man's work is quite compatible with the claim, made insistently by Marx, that in his work the labourer has generally suffered intensely from the partiality, the enslavement and the exploitative character of production and consumption. Labour is distinctively human but has been enforced and endured in truly inhuman ways. Existing conditions have contradicted man's humanity. Things have remained objects of possession, and have not been absorbed through the whole range of man's senses and imagination. The world has not yet been grasped as human, by humans.

Marx attacked Hegel and the Young Hegelians for failing to appreciate the significance of labour, both causally in history, and as man's defining characteristic. He praised the classical economists and the Scottish sociological historians of the eighteenth century for their recognition that civil society, the sphere of man's productive activity, was central to the explanation of human life and thought. But if Hegel had to be condemned for his idealism, the classical economists were to be attacked for accepting the permanence of a particular, alienated mode of labour and life. An Hegelian historical sense and a notion of genuinely human labour were poised against the classical economy, while the economist's materialism helped reveal the separation of Hegel's philosophy from the world, and to identify the dynamic elements within history.

Marx's view of history as human history, rooted in human labour – a history of 'real individuals, their actions, and their material conditions of life'[11] – emerged in opposition to the idealism and elitism of the Young Hegelians. Marx thought that Hegel himself had misunderstood the nature of real man, 'man living in a real, objective world and determined by that world'.[12] His philosophical writings, which falsely opposed abstract thought to sensible reality and reversed the subject and the predicate of history, constituted 'an abstract, logical and speculative expression of the historical process'.[13] The rich substance of history evaporated, and man became the vehicle of a spectral, supra-human process. History became a mere history of 'pseudo-ideas, a history about spirits and spectres, while the real empirical history that forms the basis of this ghostly history is only utilised to provide bodies for these spectres'.[14] In its Hegelian form, this mysterious process, which overturned reality, nonetheless had a rational core, and a thrust driving it beyond the system which contained it. But the Young Hegelians merely added to the mystification without Hegel's ingenuity or genius.

Man was separated from his conditions of life and a number of false antitheses were made – between spirit and matter, God and the world, and the philosophic elite and the masses. As in religion, man was divided into two – spirit and matter – which both tore him apart and inverted the actual relationship of his inseparable constitutents. The Young Hegelian accounts of 'consciousness', 'thought as such' and so on, tended to give the impression that theory was self-sufficient, self-developing and all-powerful. The true dynamic of change was ignored for the sterile whirlings and circlings of thought, which moved eternally within itself. Things were left precisely as they were. Reclassification merely posed as genuine change. Even Hegel's profound *Phenomenology* was conservative and positivistic, as it left the material, objective bases of estrangement unchanged. 'Thus the whole destructive work results in the most conservative philosophy because it thinks it has overcome the objective world, the sensuously real world, by merely transforming it into a "thing of thought", a mere determination of self-consciousness, and can therefore dissolve the opponent, which has become ethereal, in the "ether of pure thought".'[15] Hence, despite the radicalism of some of Hegel's particular political views, he had helped legitimate the *status quo* and man's persisting estrangement – though admittedly at an abstract theoretical level – and had left 'change' without any actual force. That which is taken up in another concept does not, for that reason, cease to exist.

Detaching consciousness from life, and placing consciousness at the centre of their theories, the Young Hegelians ignored the material requisites of freedom and talked airily of philosophic liberation, which left man's real chains intact. From a perspective according to which human history was inseparable from the history of industry and exchange, and consciousness itself was a secondary phenomenon, the sources of man's frustration and misery were material, and had to be removed by material means. From Marx's standpoint, once he broke with the Young Hegelian emphasis on rational criticism, purely theoretical disputation was a waste of time, a repetition of Bauer's 'theological error' – considering religion in the abstract, independently of its secular roots.[16] This was simply the substitution of changed interpretations of the world for a changed world, the confusion of the symptoms of the disease with its source. All mystifications and mythologies, including religion, would disappear only with the destruction of their social roots, which was a practical and not a conceptual task – though as a matter of fact Marx declared intellectual war on those who reduced man's real, palpable yokes and struggles to problems of thought. *The Holy Family* begins strongly: 'Real Humanism has no more dangerous enemy in Germany than spiritualism or speculative idealism which substitutes "self-consciousness" or the "spirit" for the real individual man.'[17] But while it was necessary to challenge illusions by argument, the dynamic of change was not criticism but revolution, and it was this which, in the end, would sweep away 'false consciousness' and 'idealistic humbug', end the domination of alien forces over men, and free the 'massy communist workers' from their material bondage. Only in action, and not in the enlightened and critical contemplation of the world, could men seize the world as their own and understand their place in it. Only in Praxis could they see it as it truly was.

Marx's historical theory asserts the primary significance, within an organic system, of certain activities and forces – narrowly, technological, more broadly, economic – and the dynamic impact which they have on existing social forms, which are gradually and inevitably subverted. Despite the mystifying character of his philosophy, Hegel had grasped 'the self-creation of man as a process' and had conceived 'objective man (true, because real man) as the result of his own labour'.[18] In common with many other thinkers of his time, Marx's emphasis is on process, movement, development. In *Capital* he stressed the way in which productive developments altered men and their communities, as well as nature. 'By thus acting on the external world and changing it, he at the same time changes his own nature. He develops his slumbering powers and compels them to act in obedience to his sway'.[19] In a typical statement in the *Grundrisse,* it is pointed out that the act of reproduction changes not only the objective conditions, for example, transforming village into town, but 'the producers change with it, by the emergence of new qualities, by transforming and developing themselves in production, forming new powers and new conceptions, new modes of intercourse and new speech'.[20] Thus human nature is transformed through man's incessant productive activity, the impetus to which is provided by human needs, which themselves change and diversify.[21] Men, seeking to satisfy their physical and other needs, continuously create new and more diverse needs, whose satisfaction requires greater productivity – which, in turn, creates further needs. Primitive needs were few and simple: 'But then needs were only slight in the beginning, and only developed with the productive forces.'[22] Production arises to satisfy existing needs, and constantly creates new ones, and provides new means of satisfying old ones.

Certain of man's needs pertain to him as a biological creature, although a human manner of satisfying them is different from the animal's satisfaction of its natural needs. Perennial and elementary needs are in fact satisfied in a variety of historically and culturally qualified ways. 'Hunger is hunger; but the hunger that is satisfied by cooked meat eaten with knife and fork differs from hunger that devours raw meat with the help of hands, nails and teeth.'[23] Other needs are distinctively human, belonging to man as man and not as a natural creature. Man becomes himself when he satisfies all his species or human needs, the wealth of needs and creative dispositions which will emerge in socialism.

> In fact, however, when the narrow bourgeois form has been peeled away, what is wealth, if not the universality of needs, capacities, enjoyments, productive powers, etc., of individuals, produced in universal exchange? What, if not the full development of human control over the forces of nature – those of his own nature as well as those of so-called 'nature'? What, if not the absolute elaboration of his creative dispositions, without any preconditions other than antecedent historical evolution which makes the totality of this evolution – i.e., the evolution of all human powers as such, unmeasured by any previously established yardstick – an end in itself? What is this, if not a situation where man does not reproduce himself in any determined form, but produces his totality.[24]

It is clear that this account of human needs provided Marx, not merely with a major source of historical change, but with a standard by which to evaluate the various social orders. Affirming all men's needs and appetites, he nonetheless found some of them narrow, partial, abstracted and deformed. Such human activities as eating, drinking and sex, may be pursued as mere biological needs, crudely and desperately, and hence will not be satisfied in any distinctively human way. Man's needs and functions, when abstracted or incomplete, become animal, and indeed, were manipulated and narrowed to the advantage of particular individuals. The extension of products and needs, he wrote in 1844,

> falls into contriving and ever-calculating subservience to inhuman, refined, unnatural and imaginary appetites. Private property does not know how to change crude need into human need...no eunuch flatters his despot more basely or uses more despicable means to stimulate his dulled capacity for pleasure in order to sneak a favour for himself than does the industrial eunuch – the producer – in order to sneak for himself a few pennies...He puts himself at the service of the other's most depraved fancies, plays the pimp between him and his need, excites in him morbid appetites, lies in wait for each of his weaknesses...every real and possible need is a weakness which will lead the fly to the gluepot.[25]

Man's needs and desires have been limited and perverted within societies, and especially within capitalism. At this point Marx hints at a theory of false, unreal and artificially created needs, the domination of which amounts to a renunciation of life and humanity. From one angle, communism is that condition marked by a wealth of human needs, human sensibility and human senses, enabling man to freely and fully appropriate the world and its rich possibilities. This means, in essence, the emergence and satisfaction of a radically new structure of true human needs.

Marx's Hegelian claim, against Proudhon, that 'all history is nothing but a continuous transformation of human nature',[26] is by no means self-explanatory, and requires some analysis at once. The main distinction to be considered is that between those human drives and needs which are unvarying, and common to all men – though they may be expressed and satisfied in such vastly differing ways as to seem quite different things – and those which are historically contingent, varying with different social conditions. In addition, the revolutionary character of Marx's theory of human nature must be stressed – certain needs, drives and powers are to become common to all men in particular, specified circumstances, while being not yet constituent parts of man. Such distinctions are necessary before we can state adequately Marx's views on the transience or otherwise of existing institutions, with which inhuman, depraved and unnatural appetites and needs are closely connected, and must be if radical change is to seem at all feasible. If the destructive needs and appetites are anterior to the damned institutions, the grounds of optimism become more questionable. A new world must be characterised, not by institutional change alone, but by the transformation or humanisation of those appetites and drives which divide and limit men, and which, presumably, are to be explained historically.

The general character of Marx's view emerges clearly in his criticism of other conceptions of man. He opposed most vigorously any assumption that human nature was a static abstraction. The tendency to present an abstract essence as man seemed to him to be deep-rooted in German philosophy, and he singled out for attack Feuerbach's *Wesen* and Stirner's *Einziger*. In *The German Ideology*, Feuerbach, Stirner and others of his countrymen are castigated for the double error of treating man and the world as being eternally the same, and of not recognising that both are the result of continuous technological change. Feuerbach assumed that there was an absolute human nature or essence. He 'says "Man" instead of "real historical man". "Man" is really "the German" '.[27] Max Stirner ignored man's definite historical needs, so that ' "Man" appeared instead of actual individuals, and the striving for a fantastic idea, for freedom as such, for the "freedom of Man", appeared instead of the satisfaction of actual human needs'.[28] Naturally, such errors had conservative political effects, because of the concentration upon the human condition and human nature rather than upon the class condition, class nature and class warfare analysed by proletarian theory. Hence Marx attacked the German True Socialists for not being concerned with the interests of the proletariat, but with 'the interests of Human Nature, of Man in general, who belongs to no class, has no reality, who exists only in the misty realm of philosophical fantasy'.[29] Moral exhortations to the suffering proletarian, to love his bourgeois brother, were stupid and dangerous – stupid because they ignored the overwhelming fact of class, and dangerous because they undermined the perception necessary for radical political action.

Marx also objected to Jeremy Bentham's utilitarianism, which misrepresented human nature by ignoring history.

> To know what is useful for a dog, one must study dog-nature. This nature itself is not to be deduced from the principle of utility. Applying this to man, he that would criticise all human acts, movements, relations, etc., by the principle of utility, must first deal with human nature in general, and then with human nature as modified in each historical epoch. Bentham makes short work of it. With the dryest naïveté he takes the modern shopkeeper, especially the English shopkeeper, as the normal man. Whatever is useful to this queer normal man, and to his world, is absolutely useful.[30]

Particular institutional prescriptions rested upon such ahistorical views of man. In criticising Carlyle – as well as in criticising Bentham – Marx stressed the tendency of philosophers to claim permanence or universal validity for a particular and passing state of affairs. In Carlyle's view, the entire historic process

> is not determined by the evolution of the living masses themselves, who naturally depend on definite but historically produced and changing conditions, it is determined by an eternal law of nature, immutable for all times...Historically created class differences are made into natural differences which people must recognise and revere as part of the eternal law of nature by bowing before wise and noble ones in nature: the cult of genius.[31]

Malthus is similarly condemned for taking features of his own age – in this case the situation expressed in the general law of population – as characteristic of all ages. According to Marx, 'every special historic mode of production has its own special laws of population, historically valid within its limits alone. An abstract law of population exists

for plants and animals only, and only in so far as man has not interfered with them.'[32] Indeed, that biological world might be interpreted
in terms of man's world, and it sometimes seemed to Marx that Darwin
had projected bourgeois economic relationships into natural history,
though he also enthusiastically accepted Darwin's book because it provided 'a natural-scientific basis for the class struggle in history.'[33]

The readiness to design permanent sets of institutions, suitable for all
times and places, was particularly marked in eighteenth-century philosophy,[34] and the sketched ideals were naturally, in many cases, conso-
nant with the interests of powerful classes. Unaware of the sources
and the status of their ideas, class spokesmen insisted that their own
institutions, values and ideals were natural or legitimate and perhaps
universally appropriate as well, and failed to recognise the transience
and the limitations of their particular social orders. Each new class was
compelled to 'give its ideas the form of universality, and represent them
as the only rational, universally valid ones...it appears as the whole
mass of society confronting the ruling class'.[35] For example, the rising
capitalists believed themselves to be struggling for universal ends and not
merely for particular class interests. And Marx admitted that, in a sense,
progressive classes could claim properly to be representing the common
interest of society, in that they played a necessary part in the general
social progress. The capitalists, for example, undermined conservative
feudal institutions and created the technological basis for the future
communist society. In relation to the emancipation of the proletariat,
Marx wrote in one of his early essays:

> No class in civil society can play this role without arousing a
> moment of enthusiasm in itself and in the masses, a moment in
> which it fraternises and merges with society in general, becomes
> confused with it and is perceived and acknowledged as its general
> representatives, a moment in which its claims and rights are truly
> the claims and rights of society itself, a moment in which it is
> truly the social head and the social heart.[36]

But while such universal pretensions were not simply fraudulent and
confused, it was – in capitalist society – wrong of classes other than
the proletariat to assume the identity of their interests with human
interests in general. The bourgeoisie could not properly appropriate
for itself the abstract language of freedom, and condemn the communists
for attacking freedom itself, rather than the 'bourgeois freedom' which
was their real target. The bourgeoisie had 'selfish misconceptions' of
itself, and consecrated its own interests, presenting them as 'eternal
laws of nature and reason'.

For Marx, explicitly at least, human nature was no abstraction inherent in each separate individual, no essence independent of particular forms of society and common to them all. He found 'Man as such' a figment of the imagination, or a disguised image of contemporary class man. Historical men – German petty philistines, English shopkeepers, the strong and the advantaged – were made the paradigms of human nature. Marx rejected such frozen and limited conceptions of man, and the derivation of supposedly natural or necessary social structures from these conceptions, as ahistorical and metaphysical. And yet, while one might break the link between particular views of man and the institutional prescriptions which seemingly flow from them, and acccept the, by now, commonplace charge that men do universalise the behaviour and institutions of their own societies, Marx's own account of human nature leaves some crucial questions unanswered. Did Marx, despite these criticisms of the philosophers, and despite certain explicit statements to the contrary, himself believe in some general human nature, some common capacities or qualities shared, or to be shared, by all men? How did he answer the question which he asked in the *Rheinische Zeitung* in 1842? 'Is there not a universal human nature just as there is a universal nature of plants and heavenly bodies?'[37] What was the 'human nature in general' to which he referred in his criticism of Bentham? What changes historically and what – if anything – is constant? What are the essential powers revealed by man in history, and does their existence imply a human essence? How does one identify the effects on human nature of successive productive systems or historical epochs? The broad account of historical change offered by Marx and Engels provides the beginnings of an answer to these questions.

THE RISE OF THE SORDID PASSIONS

Human progress, and especially rapid technological advance, are won at the cost of great conflict and suffering. Marx and Engels tended to portray the relationship between progress on the one hand, and regression and suffering on the other, as neat, almost mechanical. The supposed relationship is one of inverse ratio. Engels wrote, for example, that monogamy, along with slavery and private wealth, inaugurated 'that epoch, lasting until today, in which every advance is likewise a relative regression, in which the well-being and development of the one group are attained by the misery and repression of the other...everything engendered by civilisation is double-sided, double-tongued, self-contradictory and antagonistic'.[38] The assumption of polarities, antitheses, necessary contrasts and even direct inverse ratios was deep-rooted in German philosophical circles in the forties, and fitted well with early observation of the dramatic contrasts of capitalism. This aspect of dialectical thinking, in relation to capitalism, pointed to a fundamental contradiction between manifest wealth and productivity, and the poverty of the masses. Marx dwelt on the beauty, the palaces, the marvels, the leisure and the intelligence available to the rich, while the lot of the workers was deformity, hovels, privation, barbarous toil and cretinism. The destructive element in progress was most clearly evident in the emergence and consolidation of bourgeois society, which is presented as the most brutal and inhuman of the progressive forms of social life. Human contact, warmth and integration were at a minimum, and the 'sordid' appetites so frequently condemned by Marx and Engels were predominant. Primitive communism, or gentile society, the classical *polis*, oriental society, and the feudal societies from which Western capitalism grew were far richer in terms of associative life, albeit at a crude level, and despite their shortcomings in other respects.

The fullest account of the dissolution of primitive society offered by Marx or Engels is contained in *The Origin of the Family*, by Engels. In that work, Engels gave a broad view of a cohesive primitive society and an account of the emergence and power of the sordid appetites, and indicated strongly the shortcomings of capitalism in terms of social virtues. Making use of anthropological studies,[39] the work suggested that primitive societies were free of classes and therefore of class struggles, that they were free, in fact, of the interrelated evils of subsequent societies – an unnatural and damaging division of labour, private property, classes and class conflict, exploitation, egoism and the state. The constitution of the primitive societies was, according to Engels, remarkably simple. 'Everything runs smoothly without soldiers, gendarmes, or police; without nobles, kings, governors, prefects or judges; without prisons; without trials. All quarrels or disputes are settled by the whole body of those concerned – the gens or the tribe or the individual gentes among themselves...All are free and equal – including the women.'[40] The men were dignified, straightforward and strong. Engels did not deny their cruelty, their religious illusions and their technological backwardness, but he remained impressed by the absence of exploitation, oppression, inequality and class division, and by their paternal authority patterns, communal ownership of the main productive instruments, production for direct needs, and physiologically based division of labour. This is obviously a highly idealised account of the primitive gens, whose lack of viability Engels recognised and sought to explain.

Marx also commented, in general terms, on the inadequacy of primitive communism. Although society was free of alienation, as wealth was seen to lie in natural objects, not commodities, human objectification did not exist either, and as a consequence men could not realise total, diverse capacities. Hence primitive communism 'cannot serve in any way as a model for fully developed communism that presupposes alienation as well as its abolition'.⁴¹ Whatever the precise sources of its degeneration, it had to give way to a succession of more developed social forms if human potentialities were ever to be fulfilled.

Engels – unlike Rousseau who, in portraying the origins of inequality, presented, as he put it, 'mere conditional and hypothetical reasonings' – sought to provide a generalised factual account of the appearance of class division and inequality in the pre-existing society. In addition, he accepted the necessity of civilisation, and its contribution to human development, whereas Rousseau remained far more pessimistic and doubtful. However, both he and Rousseau explained social degeneration in roughly the same way, and each failed to provide a satisfactory and consistent account of the relationship between the different destructive forces – property, the division of labour, masters and slaves, new wants, the decline of community feeling, and the rise of self-interest – and there is, in fact, a good deal of conjecture in Engels's allegedly historical story.

Engels traced the collapse of the gens to the development of the division of labour with the domestication of animals and the breeding of herds. This produced new social relationships within the gens by giving a source of wealth and power to the males, which undermined mother-right and led ultimately to the antagonism of the sexes and the class oppression of females which, in Engels's view, persisted to his own day. Man's economic predominance led to the monogamous family based upon male lineage and the right of inheritance from the father. The monogamous family was 'the first form of the family based not on natural but on economic conditions, namely, on the victory of private property over original, naturally developed, common ownership'.⁴² Pastoralism gave slaves a new utility and introduced surplus value, thus establishing the first great form of servitude. The property system and class exploitation began. Between the different communities and spheres of production a system of exchange developed, leading to a new division of labour and the transformation of products into commodities.

This decisive revolution was pictured as a decline, though one which could not have been avoided.

> The power of these primordial communities had to be broken, and it was broken. But it was broken by influences which from the

outset appear to us as a degradation, a fall from the simple moral grandeur of the ancient gentile society. The lowest interests – base greed, brutal sensuality, sordid avarice, selfish plunder of common possessions – usher in the new civilised society, class society; the most outrageous means – theft, rape, deceit and treachery – undermine and topple the old, classless, gentile society.[43]

Thus new instincts and passions, especially the great driving force of greed, emerge within society. As Engels commented in relation to Hegel's theory of history, 'it is precisely the wicked passions of man – greed and lust for power – which, since the emergence of class antagonisms, serve as levers of historical development – a fact of which the history of feudalism and of the bourgeoisie, for example, constitutes a single continual proof'.[44]

While Engels failed to analyse sufficiently the origins of what he called 'the wicked passions of man' – in fact, they come very much out of the blue – it is clear that they are not natural to man, but emerge in the process of historical change. These appetites or passions, which Marx, unlike Engels, treated as human but partial or one-sided, and the institutions which create or stimulate them – especially the division of labour and private property – reinforce each other and destroy man's happy and primitive condition. New economic factors – money, creditors, exchange, commodities, private ownership and the accumulation and concentration of wealth – proved incompatible with the simple structure of the early communities. The money system, for example, 'penetrated like a corroding acid into the traditional life of the rural communities founded on natural economy'.[45] The profound change involved in the emergence of that necessary guardian of order, the state, and the beginning of politics, had to occur because of the preceding economic transformation – in the general theoretical terms of historical materialism, political structures must eventually come into conformity with economic conditions. In this case, the conflict between rival economic groups required a special public authority in order to control the (otherwise) irreconcilable antagonisms which had emerged within society. The state proved necessary, Engels argued, because of the emergence of classes, though he does not indicate whether or not the emergence of classes – or whatever it was that produced classes – was itself necessary.[46]

This story of decline is to some extent repeated in Marx's account of the emergence of capitalism, although capitalism developed within societies which were already characterised by class division and exploitation. Yet these societies provided more security and associative life

than did capitalism, though they also enslaved man more. The corporations, especially the guilds, the social ranks or estates and the related
privileges, bound men closely together. Within the guilds, formed
initially by the workers for self-protection, the masters influenced the
whole lives of the journeymen, who were held together by a bond of
opposition to other journeymen. The craft-guilds were tight, warm
associations, which often acted as substitutes for the older associations –
family and village – that their members had foregone. The medieval
towns were 'true associations called forth by the direct need, the care
of providing for the protection of property, and of multiplying the
means of production and defence of the separate members'.[47] The
'privileged exclusivities' – trades, guilds and corporations – were 'dis-
jointing' elements in civil society as a whole, but were cohesive elements
in the lives of their individual members. Political life was embodied in
the various distinct societies within feudalism. In the words of the
young Marx, the political spirit was 'dissolved, fragmented and lost
in the various cul-de-sacs of feudal society'.[48] Lacking attachment to
the (emerging) nation or state, men were linked by motley feudal ties
to a determinate, limited social environment – family, guild, estate,
locality. But, as in the case of Engels's version of primitive society,
powerful acquisitive urges and subversive economic practices were
destroying these direct and close, though servile, relationships.

The energetic and grasping bourgeoisie had destroyed, or was destroying, the backward societies of both feudal Europe and the Orient.
Striving to make the whole world capitalist, or subservient to capital,
the dynamic, history-making Westerners drew the static East into
history, transforming its communications, its systems of land tenure,
its weak and youthful industries, the needs and wants of its people.
The East, according to Marx's Western-oriented theories, lacked any
internal dynamic force. The passive, stagnating, unchanging social in-
frastructure was disguised only thinly by the rapid movement on the
political surface. To develop – and develop it must, if the proletariat
were ever to win – outside intervention was crucial. Marx recognised
the historical role of the bourgeoisie, in terms of his broad analysis of
social development, though he also – without wishing to change the
character of that intervention one whit – fiercely attacked its moral
qualities, and especially denounced the hypocrisy of Western 'civilisation mongers'. 'Has the bourgeoisie ever done more? Has it ever
effected a progress without dragging individuals and peoples through
blood and dirt, through misery and degradation?'[49] In India, unrestrained by the conventions of the home society, its representatives
tore up established institutions and murdered and pillaged at will. 'The
profound hypocrisy and inherent barbarism of bourgeois civilisation lies

unveiled before our eyes, turning from its home, where it assumes respectable forms, to the colonies, where it goes naked.'[50] But Marx's indignation was not intended to produce a change of heart. He did not tell the bourgeoisie to stop, for greed and the vile interests were contributing profoundly to ultimate historical progress.

Marx recognised the costs of innovation, especially in terms of the elements of community present in these cramping anachronistic forms. They had social strengths, and perhaps even durability.[51] However, the primitive condition was not happy and virtuous, and Marx revealed no sympathy for such backward-looking forces as the sepoys in the Indian Mutiny. The society they valued was extremely rigid, destructive and violent. Marx reminded those who were inclined to romanticise the village communities of India that these communities had always been the solid foundation of Oriental despotism,

> that they restrained the human mind within the smallest possible compass, making it the unresisting tool of superstition, enslaving it beneath traditional rules, depriving it of all grandeur and historical energies...We must not forget that this dignified, stagnatory, and vegetative life, that this passive sort of existence evoked on the other part, in contradistinction, wild, aimless, unbounded forces of destruction, and rendered murder itself a religious rite in Hindustan. We must not forget that these little communities were contaminated by distinctions of caste and by slavery, that they subjugated man to external circumstances instead of elevating man to be the sovereign of circumstances, that they transformed a self-developing social state into never-changing natural destiny, and thus brought about a brutalising worship of nature, exhibiting its degradation in the fact that man, the sovereign of nature, fell down on his knees in adoration of Hanuman, the monkey, and Sabbala, the cow.[52]

The tribal system, oriental despotism and the classical polis were all relatively simple and socially limiting forms, which were characterised by a close unity of the individual and society. As Marx wrote in the unfinished Introduction to *A Contribution to the Critique of Political Economy*:

> The further back we trace the course of history, the more does the individual, and accordingly also the producing individual, appear to be dependent and to belong to a larger whole. At first, the individual in a still quite natural manner is part of the family and of the tribe which evolves from the family, later he is part of a community, of one of the different forms of the community which arise from the conflict and the merging of tribes. It is not until the

eighteenth century that in bourgeois society the various forms of the social texture confront the individual as merely means towards his private ends, as external necessity. But the epoch which produces this standpoint, namely that of the solitary individual, is precisely the epoch of the (as yet) most highly developed social (according to this standpoint, general) relations.[53]

As Avineri[54] brings out clearly, Marx conceived these communities to be naive, undifferentiated and unsophisticated, and consequently incapable of satisfying and fulfilling the needs, capacities and powers of the free, socialised individual. But their inadequacies in terms of the presumed needs of non-existent, fully human beings cannot provide a source of historical movement in the present: if they break down it cannot be because of their incompatibility with a future good, but because of their incapacity to accommodate and satisfy the mundane pressures, demands and forces which grew up within them. In the case of feudalism, it was not the unrealised humanity of any class, but the unrelenting quest of the bourgeoisie for gold which drove it forward, and let no barrier stand in its way. The expropriation of the immediate producers was effected 'with merciless vandalism and under the stimulus of passions the most infamous, the most sordid, the pettiest, the most meanly odious'.[55] The brutal story of the breakdown of the primitive gens is even more savagely re-enacted. 'If money, according to Augier, "comes into the world with a congenital blood-stain on its cheek", capital comes dripping from head to foot, from every pore, with blood and dirt.'[56] This was the period in which the fall of man, and his utmost degradation, was consummated. Marx put it lyrically in *The Poverty of Philosophy*:

> Finally, there came a time when everything that men had considered as inalienable became an object of exchange, of traffic, and could be alienated. This is the time when the very things which till then had been communicated, but never exchanged; given, but never sold; acquired, but never bought – virtue, love, conviction, knowledge, conscience, etc. – when everything, in short, passed into commerce. It is the time of general corruption, of universal venality, or to speak in terms of political economy, the the time when everything, moral or physical, having become a marketable value, is brought to the market to be assessed at its truest value.[57]

MAN AND COMMUNITY UNDER CAPITALISM

Marx analysed man's dehumanisation and loss most directly in his theory of alienation, which is an anthropological critique of industrial capitalism, largely in terms of the condition of the labourer and his relationship to the world. Marx's writings on alienation articulate a conception of human nature through a critical analysis of particular, concrete social conditions, which divide men within and from each other, and which enslave them to alien and destructive forces. In mastering nature man has imprisoned himself, and become dependent or servile. In these circumstances, he lacks the power to realise himself in the rich sense conceived and valued by Marx. Sometimes dismissed as metaphysical nonsense and the outpourings of juvenile romanticism, this early theory, or important elements of it, have been supported powerfully by critics of contemporary, industrialised, bureaucratic states, 'communist' or otherwise, in which it is felt that man's freedom, individuality and communality are being denied or frustrated. As a theory it has been developed profoundly, and as a polemical notion it has been used sharply and deftly, but more commonly it has become an inflated blanket term under which the evils of modern civilisation are gathered indiscriminately.[58] Marx's view of alienation was complex and specific, and must be clearly distinguished from popular uses of the term to mean mere human frustration, or the meaninglessness of life, or man's situation when he is treated as a means rather than an end, or as the slave rather than the lord of creation. There are overlaps and links, but Marx's notion cannot be reduced to such humanistic or existential catch-cries.

Marx believed that man's plight was at its most excruciating in bourgeois society. Alienation reached a peculiar intensity and depth in the condition of the wage-labourer under capitalism, though it also characterised – to a lesser degree, and in different ways – other classes and pre-capitalist societies. The alienation of the proletarian was not, then, to be counterposed to the non-alienation of the capitalist, or of feudal society, but to the unalienated world of communism, which had now come within historical reach.

> In the present epoch, the domination of material conditions over individuals, and the suppression of individuality by chance, has assumed its sharpest and most universal form, thereby setting existing individuals a very definite task. It has set them the task of replacing the domination of circumstances and of chance over individuals by the domination of individuals over chance and circumstances.[59]

In order to emancipate themselves, men needed to read the hieroglyphics of their alienated societies, to resolve superstition into history, to see that the social world is an (alienated) human world. They had to see both the alienated nature of the world and the fact that their manacles were man-made: part of man's alienation was his inability to recognise it as such, and to perceive his own role and responsibility.

Although the gist of Marx's critique is clear, the various aspects or forms of alienated labour are not clearly defined and separate, but overlap with each other, and interconnect causally, and both critics and disciples differ strongly over just how much of his early assumptions and approaches Marx was to accept after 1844 or 1846 or 1847, or whenever a crucial disjuncture was supposed to occur. While it is not possible for me to enter into the intricacies, the far reaches, and the contemporary political significance of these disputes, I must at least declare my attitude to them. In general, I find the distinction between ideology or moralism or vision on the one hand, and science or naturalism on the other, a real one, but one which is exaggerated or over-sharpened by some zealous social scientists, as well as by some of the advocates of an epistemological or theoretical break in Marx's writings in the mid or late forties. In the study of society, scientific pretensions are usually marred – or, alternatively, the study is broadened or human-ised – by moral preferences and goals, which may rarely be stated openly, and which influence analysis in various ways. In particular, I find the 'change' from youthful to mature Marxism neither as conscious nor as considerable as writers such as Hook and Feuer suggest,[60] though one is left with the problems of specifying the dimensions along which change or continuity are to be traced, and of avoiding such vague but tempting responses as, for example, that 'moral vision in-forms the later writings', or that there is 'some unity' in his writings.

In the preface to the 1844 *Manuscripts*, Marx writes that his results have been won 'by means of a wholly empirical analysis based on a conscientious critical study of political economy' (p. 18). Yet, despite its obvious bearing on most of his work, we can hardly take this as a statement of a concern and a method that was clear at the outset, and which was simply elaborated during the following half century, so that Marx's life work becomes the completion of a task undertaken in the early forties. Marx changed his views in some respects, shifted his area of concern, altered his emphasis and modified his language – for example, the notion of human essence disappears during the forties. What does remain constant – though the elaborations vary – is the vision of the complete or authentic human being, frustrated and fragmented in a world that man himself has created. Within the difficult and often opaque writings of the early forties, social analysis in materialistic and class terms is clearly present, and notions of community and communism, productive labour and human autonomy, underlie and sustain the apparently technical analysis of *Capital* and the other largely economic studies. In *Capital* the term estrangement appears several times, and what it signifies is crucial to Marx's analysis of capitalism at that time – that man's own power has passed to capital, which has become the ruling power in society. I am not claiming that this is an adequate general characterisation of *Capital*, nor that *Capital* is some kind of mythology or philosophy decked out in the apparently firm terminology of economics, nor again that the early writings are as important as *Capital*. Clearly, *Capital* is more significant in Marx's Marxism than is his juvenile love poetry. In any defence of the continuity thesis – that a particular conception of man and of human labour not only persists throughout Marx's writings, but remains crucial to his social analysis – the *Grundrisse* of 1857–8 plays an important, linking part, as it carries over much of the moralistic phraseology and conceptualisation of the early writings.[61] The change in Marx is from a relatively fuzzy view of bourgeois society, dominated by philosophical conceptions, to a clearer, tougher and more fact-based perception of that society, though that sharper, more empirically solid analysis is riddled still with old notions of man's characteristic attributes and powers, of his universal, freely creative nature.

The fact of political economy from which the Marxian analysis began was man's alienation. Alienation arises in man's labour itself, which denies his universal or species-being (*Gattungswesen*), in his relationship to the diverse objects and things which he produces, and in the relations between man and man. As alienation arises first in man's labouring activity, in the process of labour, it seems appropriate to begin the account there.

Marx counterposes a view of free, creative labour to labour under capitalism, which appears consequently as dehumanising and divisive. In developing the notion of species-being or species-character, he was advancing a moral and critical notion of distinctively or truly human life, activity and community. The notion is the result of conceptual analysis, embodying an ideal, and is not a piece of empirical psychology or sociology. The core of the notion, which has clear affinities with the familiar German ideal of the romantic aesthete, is the view of man as a free or self-determining and productive being, self-conscious, controlling his own productive activity and thus his own evolution. He is distinguished from the animals, which produce only under the dominion of physical need, by free, self-conscious activity, which constitutes his species-character, and by his power to appropriate the whole world for his own use. Man 'produces even when he is free from physical need and only truly produces in freedom therefrom'.[62] The distinctively human mode of production is not carried out to satisfy biological needs, as it is under capitalism, but when man, free from external compulsion, fashions things in accordance with the laws of beauty. In capitalist society, man's labour is forced, uncreative and detested. It is pictured as a process of self-estrangement, self-alienation or loss of self. Marx found detailed confirmation of his view in contemporary studies of working conditions, especially the writings of such early critics of industrialism as Schulz, Sismondi, Pecqueur, Loudon and Buret. Their views are incorporated in Marx's more abstract account of external labour in the manuscript entitled *Estranged Labour*. The well-known passage runs:

> What then, constitutes the alienation of labour? First the fact that labour is external to the worker, i.e. it does not belong to his essential being; that in his work, therefore, he does not affirm himself but denies himself, does not feel content but unhappy, does not develop freely his physical and mental energy but mortifies his body and ruins his mind. The worker therefore only feels himself outside his work, and in his work feels outside himself. He is at home when he is not working, and when he is working he is not at home. His labour is therefore not voluntary, but coerced; it is forced labour. It is therefore not the satisfaction of a need; it is merely a means to satisfy needs external to it. Its alien character emerges clearly in the fact that as soon as no physical or other compulsion exists, labour is shunned like the plague. External labour, labour in which man alienates himself, is a labour of self-sacrifice, of mortification. Lastly, the external character of labour for the worker appears in the fact that it is not his own, but someone else's, that it does not belong to him, that in it he belongs, not to himself, but to another. Just as in religion the spontaneous activity of the human imagination, of the human brain and the human heart, operates independently of the individual – that is, operates on him as an alien, divine or diabolical activity – in the same way the worker's activity is not his spontaneous activity. It belongs to another; it is the loss of his self.
>
> As a result, therefore, man (the worker) no longer feels himself to be freely active in any but his animal functions – eating, drinking, procreating, or at most in his dwelling and in dressing-up, etc.; and in his human functions he no longer feels himself to be anything but an animal. What is animal becomes human and what is human becomes animal.
>
> Certainly, eating, drinking, procreating, etc., are also genuinely human functions. But in the abstraction which separates them from the sphere of all other human activity and turns them into sole and ultimate ends, they are animal.[63]

Labour – man's distinctive, creative activity – hence becomes a means to an outside end, the satisfaction of merely animal or biological needs; the labourer is forced to work under appalling conditions, which destroy his mind and body; and he ruins himself in labour for someone else, an outside person.

In the first place, labour is undertaken, not for its own sake, but as a means to the maintenance of life. It becomes enslavement to crude needs and selfish wants, which themselves are manipulated continuously by other persons. The worker sells his life-activity to another person 'in order to secure the necessary means of subsistence. Thus his life-activity is for him only a means to enable him to exist. He works in order to live. He does not even reckon labour as part of his life, it is rather a sacrifice of his life.' Consequently, he draws a sharp line between life and labour, which seems in no way a manifestation of his life. 'On the contrary, life begins for him where this activity ceases, at table, in the public house, in bed. The twelve hours' labour, on the other hand, has no meaning for him as weaving, spinning, drilling, etc., but as earnings, which bring him to the table, to the public house, into bed. If the silk worm were to spin in order to continue its existence as a caterpillar, it would be a complete wage-worker.'[64] And, as if this were not bad enough, the life left over cannot become, in existing conditions, a sphere of genuine human enjoyment and fulfilment. The work-place invades free time, leaving the worker, in his leisure, a person without the energy, vision or interest to build a rich domestic and private life.

The division of labour is the most direct and profound source of man's alienation from the process of labour and of his dehumanisation. It provoked some of Marx's fiercest prose and some of his most visionary passages. Increasingly damaging under capitalism, it stunted men's lives and made them mere fragments, confining them to repetitive tasks leaving no scope for the imagination. Man thus became a small part of his whole self – as Schiller earlier put the common view, he became 'nothing more than the imprint of his occupation or of his specialised knowledge'.[65] The division of labour manifested itself in a series of historical separations – between mental and physical labour, between town and country, between rulers and ruled, between operative and overlooker, between workmen in their myriad narrow specialisations. In all cases, apart from the original division between man and woman, it confined men and created conflict.

The antagonism between town and country can only exist within the framework of private property. It is the most crass expression of the subjection of the individual under the division of labour, under a definite activity forced upon him – a subjection which makes one man into a restricted town-animal, the other into a restricted country-animal, and daily creates anew the conflict between their interests.[66]

The division of labour does not arise from natural differences, but creates the special, limited abilities which the economic system requires. It creates certain kinds or fragments of men rather than others – capitalists, lawyers, teachers, soldiers and, more importantly, workers, in their various occupations. It forces the worker to become dependent 'upon a particular very one-sided machine-like labour'.[67] It increases the productive power of labour but 'impoverishes the worker and reduces him to a machine'.[68] Marx continually spoke of labour under capitalism as being abstract, i.e. one-sided or incomplete, separated from the whole spectrum of human activities and abilities. Consequently the human beings subject to it, and formed by it, were crippled and deformed, in relation to what they might be. Marx meant this quite literally. The means of production became means of not only dominating and exploiting the producers, but of creating them, mentally and physically:

> they mutilate the labourer into a fragment of a man, degrade him to the level of an appendage of a machine, destroy every remnant of charm in his work and turn it into a hated toil; they estrange from him the intellectual potentialities of the labour-process in the same proportion as science is incorporated in it as an independent power; they distort the conditions under which he works, subject him during the labour-process to a despotism the more hateful for its meanness; they transform his life-time into his working-time.[69]

Manufacture revolutionised labour and converted the labourer 'into a crippled monstrosity, by forcing his detail dexterity at the expense of a world of productive capabilities and instincts; just as in the states of La Plata they butcher a whole beast for the sake of his hide or his tallow'.[70] Modern machine industry destroyed detailed handicraft specialisation, sweeping away by technical means

> the manufacturing division of labour, under which each man is bound hand and foot for life to a single detail-operation. At the same time, the capitalistic form of that industry reproduces this same division of labour in a still more monstrous shape; in the factory proper, by converting the workman into a living appendage of the machine.[71]

The labourer – ignorant, deformed, unhealthy, stultified – adapted himself, body and mind, to the machine that ruled him.

The division of labour was significant as an original cause of alienation, and a primary source both of man's alienation in the labour-process and in making his own deed or activity an alien power opposed to him. In the words of *The German Ideology*:

> each man has a particular exclusive sphere of activity, which is forced upon him and from which he cannot escape ... This fixation of social activity, this consolidation of what we ourselves produce into an objective power above us, growing out of our control, thwarting our expectations, bringing to naught our calculations, is one of the chief factors in historical development up till now.[72]

The division of labour is thus a primary determinant of men's actual natures and capabilities: it shaped them in specific and limiting ways, by dividing intellectual and material activity, enjoyment and labour, production and consumption, and by imposing destructive forms of each. The subordination to minute tasks, preventing the many-sided play of muscles and the development of diverse gifts, reached its greatest intensity in the case of the industrial labourer, who was branded as not merely the property but the product of capital. The serf and the handicraftsman owned the instruments of their labour, and engaged in a whole round of tasks necessary to self-subsistence. The guild-workers needed to be proficient in their whole craft. Their interest and their proficiency made it possible for them to rise to 'a narrow-artistic sense', although they generally had a 'slavish, contented relationship' to their work.[73] They were much more subjected to it, and absorbed in it, than the industrial labourer, whose work was a matter of indifference to him. Hence their relationship to their work was a closer and more genuine one – self-earned private property was grounded on 'the fusing-together of the isolated, independent labouring-individual with the conditions of his labour'.[74]

Private property is treated as the direct product of estranged labour, and both the alienation of the product and man's alienation in his own activity – and hence his alienation from his species-being – are explained largely by the division of labour. But those things which were not causes of alienation originally may nonetheless contribute powerfully to it in their own right, and Marx not only treats private property as a source of alienation, but treats it and the division of labour as identical expressions: 'in the one the same thing is affirmed with reference to activity as is affirmed in the other with reference to the product of the activity'.[75] In any case, the coerced, frustrated, confined and unhappy labourer is ruled over by the things, the private property, that he produces, and plays no part in determining the process of his labour or the fate of its results.

He is alienated further from his activity because his labour is the product of another. He works under the yoke of the capitalist and for his private gain – an aspect of alienation which was transformed easily into a theory of exploitation, and the view that private property was the root of evil, so that it had to be overcome if human emancipation was to be achieved.

The three destructive aspects of the process of labour under industrial capitalism were to be abolished or profoundly modified in communist (truly human) society, which is characterised by the disappearance of private property and the capitalist (the other person), the abolition or transformation of the division of labour, and a plenitude of resources to satisfy human needs in all their variety, and to end the coercion arising from scarcity and the fear of starvation. It must be noted that Marx did not attack labour as such, nor – with the exception of one or two utopian passages – did he anticipate the elimination of labour and necessity altogether.[76] He attacks the specifically capitalistic form of labour, and while accepting that labour has always seemed repulsive – a sphere of slavery and misery – in its historical forms, he condemns Adam Smith for offering 'a purely negative definition' of labour as sacrifice. Smith was, Marx said, 'thinking only of the slaves of capital. For example, even the semi-artistic worker of the Middle Ages cannot be included in his definition'.[77] In the future man would realise his species-being, in the sense of creating spontaneously and co-operatively, after Schiller's model of the artist as the free labourer. And certainly such labour was neither light nor painless. Really free labour, such as musical composition, is at the same time, Marx acknowledged, 'damned serious and demands the greatest effort'.[78] Alienation is to be ended, not by ending labour, but by making it human.

The worker is constantly active, making things. In an alienated state, he transfers his essence and reality to the things which he creates, so that these come to constitute an alien, objective world opposed to him. At this point it is necessary to distiguish objectification, which, as the creation of external objects in which man expresses himself, is characteristically human, and alienation from the object, which arises when the object is separated from and dominant over man. Man as man objectifies, whereas alienation is objectification in a specific productive order.[79] It grows from a particular concrete relationship between man and his objects. In that relationship, the labourer, subject to external compulsion, fails to realise himself in the object, and hence his activity is described as loss and servitude to the object or thing. Alienated man is subjugated to outside forces and powers, which press down upon him in various ways, and from which he is increasingly cut off. Marx argued strongly, against Stirner, that 'within the framework of definite modes of production, which, of course, are not dependent on the will, alien practical forces, which are independent not only of isolated individuals but even of all of them together, always come to stand above people'.[80] Industry, religion and property are described as 'alienated life elements'.[81] Men make masters and prisons for themselves. Ideologies, such as the classical political economy, commodities, machines, money, gods, classes and social institutions become fetishes, with apparently real lives of their own, while men become impotent and dependent creatures, means rather than ends, 'the playthings of alien powers'.[82] In the words of *The German Ideology*, 'the productive forces appear as a world for themselves, quite independent of and divorced from the individuals, alongside the individuals', because the individuals, whose forces they actually are, exist 'split up and in opposition to one another'.[83] Things, products, inhuman powers, rule over the person, and a more and more weighty world bears down upon him. 'With the increasing value of the world of things proceeds in direct proportion the devaluation of the world of man.'[84] Under the domination of the bourgeoisie, with the immense expansion of man's productive power, men are more than ever subjected to 'the violence of things'.[85]

Man's alienation from the results of his own activity is revealed pre-eminently in religion, commodities and money, and the state. Marx, like Feuerbach, presented an anthropological account of religion. He saw it as an expression of social realities, an epiphenomenon, a functional part of a particular historical world – a divided and twisted world, in which men are frustrated, lost and unhappy. Religious belief becomes intelligible given the inadequacies of man's social environment. It is the spiritual aroma of an alienated class society. Marx's most famous statement on religion reads as follows:

> The basis of irreligious criticism is: Man makes religion, religion does not make man. In other words, religion is the self-consciousness and self-feeling of man who has either not yet found himself or has already lost himself again. But man is no abstract being squatting outside the world. Man is the world of man, the state, society. This state, this society, produce religion, a reversed world-consciousness, because they are a reversed world. . .Religious distress is at the same time the expression of real distress and the protest against real distress. Religion is the sigh of the oppressed creature, the heart of a heartless world, just as it is the spirit of a spiritless situation. It is the opium of the people.[86]

Man is driven by suffering to these consoling delusions, and subordinates himself to religious figments, creatures of his own imagination.

Money – the substance of exchange relationships and the measure of commodities – is an essential source and part of human estrangement. In his discussion of the Jewish question, in which he brought out strongly the dual meaning of *das Judentum* (Judaism and commerce), Marx's attack on the money system – and on the modern Jew as the symbol of the money and market society – is at its most savage.

> Money is the jealous God of Israel, beside which no other God may exist. Money abases all the gods of mankind and changes them into commodities. Money is the universal and self-sufficient value of all things. It has, therefore, deprived the whole world, both the human world and nature, of their own proper value. Money is the alienated essence of man's work and existence, this essence dominates him and he worships it. The god of the Jews has been secularised and has become the god of this world. The bill of exchange is the real God of the Jew.[87]

Marx described the development of exchange values and money relationships as the same thing as 'general venality and corruption'.[88] Money becomes an 'alien mediation', standing between men, their products, activities and relationships, and subordinating the most heterogeneous things to a common, crude measure of value. It is a most destructive intermediary, separating men's powers off from themselves, and transforming everything into articles of commerce. The universal equivalent undermined human individuality, morality, virtue and reputation, by ignoring specific needs and qualities. Man's being and his powers were determined by his wealth. Marx complained that anything – work, duty, love – could be bought with money, which is 'the object of eminent possession' and 'the almighty being'.[89] It has become 'the pimp between man's need and the object, between his life and his means of life'.[90] It reverses all values, as a favourite quotation from *Timon of Athens* indicated: 'Thus much of this [gold] will make black white, foul fair, wrong right, base noble, old young, coward valiant.'[91] It degrades man by achieving for him what he cannot gain through exercising his own powers himself.

> The less you are, the more you have: the less you express your own life, the greater is your alienated life – the greater is the store of your estranged being. Everything which the political economist takes from you in life and in humanity, he replaces for you in money and in wealth: and all the things which you cannot do, your money can do. It can eat and drink, go to the dance hall and the theatre; it can travel, it can appropriate art, learning, the treasures of the past, political power – all this it can appropriate for you – it can buy all this for you: it is the true endowment.[92]

Money and religion, both products of alienated man, tyrannise over men, and live lives of their own, so that, for example, trade in money becomes an independent transaction, and money seems itself to create more money. The process produces and brings out men's shortcomings.

Objectification is the practice of alienation. Just as man, so long as he is engrossed in religion, can only objectify his essence by an alien and fantastic being; so under the sway of egoistic need, he can only affirm himself and produce objects in practice by subordinating his products and his own activity to the domination of an alien entity, and by attributing to them the significance of an alien entity, namely money.[93]

Speaking historically, the growth of exchange value and of the power of money are interconnected, and the whole exchange relationship 'establishes itself as a force externally opposed to the producers, and independent of them'.[94]

Under capitalism, and especially in the money-form, social relations between men assume, in their eyes, the fantastic form of a relation between things. Marx spoke of commodities as fetishes, 'independent beings endowed with life' – a transformation which embodied and exposed the character of capitalist labour. The commodity was no trivial thing, but in reality 'a very queer thing', abounding in 'metaphysical subtleties' and 'theological niceties'. For example, the table as commodity becomes a mysterious, transcendent object. 'It not only stands with its feet on the ground, but, in relation to all other commodities, it stands on its head, and evolves out of its wooden brain grotesque ideas, far more wonderful than "table-turning" ever was.'[95] Marx found it revealing to draw an analogy between commodity fetishism and the mist-enveloped regions of the religious world. 'In that world the productions of the human brain appear as independent beings endowed with life, and entering into relation both with one another and the human race. So it is in the world of commodities with the products of men's hands.'[96] Marx described the 'personification of things and conversion of production relations into entities' as 'the religion of everyday life'.[97] In this 'enchanted, perverted, topsy-turvy world', manufactured objects seemed to be themselves living, endowed with powers and moving men at whim, absorbing their qualities and forcing them to adapt. In the market, where commodities exchanged, anti-human forces – the products of alienated labour – ruled. The exchange relationship – buying and selling – had been split into two separate parts, indifferent to each other, and less and less subject to human control and manipulation. Men were enriched suddenly, and just as suddenly broken and cast aside. Capitalism could not even maintain an inhuman regularity. The uncontrolled system bred economic crisis, with harmony being gained only by 'allowing the most extreme disharmonies to run their course'.[98] And even its extreme irregularities were presented under the form of external law, so that apparently men were faced with a blind and imperious necessity.

Clearly this aspect of alienation – man subordinated to his own forces, which are misconceived by him – remains crucial in the work of the mature Marx. Much of volume I and parts of volume II of *Capital*, which lays bare the anatomy of civil society, is concerned with precisely this. Broadly speaking, the analysis is as follows. Man is separated from the objective conditions of production as alien property – historically, the immediate producers are expropriated, the means of production literally torn away from them – which is counterposed to him as capital. The labourer produces wealth in the form of capital which becomes 'an alien power that dominates him',[99] 'an alienated independent social power which stands opposed to society as an object'.[100] Man is confronted by machinery and capital as independent ruling forces which, although categories of production and not units or substances, apparently acquire a personality of their own – or, what Marx treats as the same thing, are 'the property of a personality other than the workers'. Capitalist property, like landed property, represents the master's power and appears as his property, though the master, too, is enslaved. The division of labour is the main cause of this reversal of the proper relationship between men and things, but it is strengthened both by the private property system and by the sheer mass of capital and machinery confronting the worker. He faces a dense, weighty, complex world, which is impervious to his individual plans, and in which human relationships are hidden, appearing instead as relationships between things. Human relations were more transparent in simpler, earlier societies based upon personal dependence than in societies founded on apparent independence.[101]

The claim that the relations between men and things is upside down brings out a crucial feature of the Marxist anthropology, and underlies its vision of the future. The point is made repeatedly that, in bourgeois society, accumulated, past, materialised labour – or capital – dominates over, and pumps dry, direct, living labour. Petrified human activity employs and consumes the labourer instead of being employed and consumed by him. The means of production consume 'the ferment necessary to their own life-process'. Marx treats 'this complete inversion of the relation between dead and living labour, between value and the force that creates value', as peculiar to and characteristic of capitalist production.[102] It is here that man is most sharply and decisively separated from the objective world, the inorganic conditions of labour.[103] The message is clear enough. Whereas living labour was then a means to increase accumulated labour, in the future the dead would serve the living, and the present dominate the past. Capitalism was clearly incompatible with human freedom and the ending of alienation, and Marx could dismiss with derision the bourgeois claim that individuality and freedom were consummated in capitalist society.[104] Continuous technological advance, in a form which crushed rather than freed man, was of the essence of capitalism.

The state is a further external and hostile force, to which man submits involuntarily. Its laws are not absorbed or internalised, and man accepts their validity 'not because they are the laws of his own will and nature, but because they are dominant and any infraction of them will be avenged'.[105] Men regard the 'social power' as 'an alien force existing outside them, of the origin and goals of which they are ignorant, which they thus cannot control, which on the contrary passes through a peculiar series of phases and stages independent of the will and the action of man, nay even being the prime governor of these'.[106] Men fail to participate meaningfully in political life, and fail to see political institutions as their own.

Man is thus alienated, in the sense that he is dominated by his own creations, of whose true nature he is unaware. Gods, money, commodities and political institutions share the characteristic that they were created by man, but that they escaped his control, and he made himself their subject, bowing to and worshipping them. They were not merely external to him but – and this is a stronger and more questionable claim – they are presented as hostile, threatening and devouring forces. Men fawn before their own products, and become the victims, the passive recipients, of history. Because man imputes his qualities to objects, and thus misreads history and capitalist society, seeing it all as mysterious and external, he allows dead things to exercise real power over him. His inescapable blindness helps fasten his chains, and keeps him ignorant of the interests that prosper while he loses. Only when he gets behind the secret of his own social products, recognises his own powers as such, and absorbs them back into himself, will he become emancipated.

Man, chained in labour and subject to his own creations, is alienated from his species-life and thus from others, who are similarly alienated from human life. Man's species-life includes his character as a social being, his recognition of himself as a member of the human species, in community with other men, aware of his human essence or essential human nature, which is manifested in his generic social existence. He is only a true or authentic man when he does recognise the community of men. In this context alienation means that he treats his generic social existence as a mere means to the satisfaction of private and partial interests. His social relationships are, consequently, narrow and impoverished.

Political society is, naturally, characterised by alienation, which flows through to it from the sphere of labour and production. Under capitalism social relationships are external and contractual, and are embodied or crystallised in particular political institutions – representative government and the rights of man. Bourgeois society is distinguished by the apotheosis of the isolated individual, a creature of fantasy. The dissolution of feudalism has freed the egoistic man and introduced new political forms. The modern bourgeoisie required a strong, centralised state which would destroy rival authorities, privilege and discrimination, and establish an individualistic society based on formal political equality or right. 'The representative system is a very specific product of modern bourgeois society which is as inseparable from the latter as is the isolated individual of modern times.'[107] The modern state brought about political but not human emancipation, which means that it established general liberties which on the face of it destroyed certain traditional grounds of distinction between men, while remaining compatible with – and attached to – alienation, private property and class. It introduced formal equality or the rights of man, which were the rights of the egoistic and anti-social individual, pursuing his private interests. But man entered no true, satisfying community simply because political and economic independence were assured. In *The Holy Family* Marx spelled out what the demolition of the 'privileged exclusivities' of feudalism actually amounted to:

> The modern 'public system', the developed modern state, is not based, as Criticism thinks, on a society of privileges, but on a society in which privileges are abolished and dissolved; on developed civil society based on the vital elements which were still politically fettered in the privilege system and have been set free. Here no 'privileged exclusivity' stands opposed to any other exclusivity or to the public system. Free industry and free trade abolish privileged exclusivities. In its place they set man free from privilege – which isolates from the social whole but at the same time joins in a narrower exclusivity – man, no longer bound to man even by the semblance of common ties. Thus they produce the universal struggle of man against man, individual against individual. In the same way civil society as a whole is this war among themselves of all those individuals no longer isolated from the others by anything else but their individuality, and the universal uncurbed movement of the elementary forces of life freed from the fetters of privilege.[108]

The mask is cast off and community standards weaken, as property is freed to follow its own volitions and establish its own rules, virtually unrestricted by the tinctures of morality. Modern capitalistic property is 'pure private property, which has cast off all semblance of a communal institution and has shut out the State from any influence on the development of property'.[109] The individual is 'freed' from patriarchal and natural relationships,[110] such as guild and family, and now appears as an isolated monad, an economic man and a political citizen. Civil society loses the political character which it had possessed under feudalism, and dissolves into a loose gathering of egoistic individuals. Liberalism is the triumph of the private man over the communal being or 'moral person'.

In his discussion of *The Jewish Question* Marx indicated the significance, in terms of individual and group life, of the rise of bourgeois society. Man is portrayed as a divided creature, unable to reconcile his universal and rational essence with his selfish and empirical nature. He has his feet in the mundane world of civil society, while his head is in the clouds, where an imaginary universality prevails. The conflict, within the individual and within society, is presented variously as between the particular and the general interest, the bourgeois and the citizen, civil society and the state, individual life and species-life, and the private person and the public person. In the developing liberal societies of his own day Marx believed that the egoistic and private life of civil society was dominant. The separate 'political' sphere which had emerged recently was subordinated to financial power and property rights, and consequently equality before the state was empty. Men regarded themselves as pure individuals and treated others as instruments. Man 'treats other men as means, degrades himself to the role of a mere means, and becomes the plaything of alien powers'.[111] Self-estrangement and estrangement from others are inseparable. In Marx's words in the *Manuscripts*, 'one man is estranged from the other, as each of them is from man's essential nature'.[112] Each man contains the larger historical divisions within himself – he is divided within, or is in contradiction with, himself. Inside him, the atomic, egoistic man of civil society wars with the universal political citizen.

The relations between men become relations between class-members and property-holders, who perceive society from their own partial, narrowing standpoints, and cannot, given their limiting social existences, do otherwise. The politically free individual, e.g. the inhabitant of New England, takes Mammon as his idol, and in his view 'the world is no more than a Stock Exchange'.[113] Again: 'Trade has seized up all his thoughts, and he has no other recreation than to exchange objects.'[114] Society becomes fiercely competitive. The spirit of civil society is that of 'the sphere of egoism and of *bellum omnium contra omnes*'.[115] Political institutions express the differentiation of men and their separation from the community. Marx describes political democracy as Christian, in the sense that it considered man as 'a sovereign being, a supreme being', while as a matter of fact its 'sovereign being' was man already lost, split, corrupted and alienated. Society was perceived as something external to the individual, and an encroaching force against which defensive barriers had to be erected. Assuming an antithesis between society and the individual, which seemed plausible in terms of man's actual, alienated relationships under capitalism, democratic theory reduced the realm of citizenship – the political community – to a mere means of preserving the rights of man, and reduced men themselves to self-sufficient entities. The rights of man are founded, then, upon the separation of man from man – they are the rights of the circumscribed, self-interested individual, withdrawn into himself, and protecting himself against others. 'Security is the supreme social concept of civil society; the concept of the police. The whole society exists only in order to guarantee for each of its members the preservation of his person, his rights and his property.'[116] These misconceptions of man and society, which reflected a deficient world, were embedded in language and aided by it. As Marx was to argue later, it was easy for the ideological spokesmen of the bourgeoisie, given appropriate (and new) language, to identify bourgeois interests with the general social interest.

> For the bourgeois it is so much the easier to prove on the basis of his language, the identity of commercial and individual, or even universal, human relations, since this language itself is a product of the bourgeoisie and therefore in actuality as in language the relations of buying and selling have been made the basis of all others.[117]

The market-place provided an image of human relationships. Hence Adam Smith considered society under the form of exchange and commerce. 'According to Adam Smith, society is a commercial enterprise. Every one of its members is a salesman. It is evident how political economy establishes an alienated form of social intercourse as the true and original form, and that which corresponds to human nature.'[118] Political economy, itself an expression of alienated life, formulated 'objective' laws which assumed the continuance of alienated conditions, and themselves defined and regulated man's activity.

Marx rejected liberalism and the rights of man because of the underlying views of man as a sovereign being – when he was not in fact sovereign but subject to overwhelming outside forces – and of society and other men as means towards private ends. He attacked both the counterposition of the free man to society, and sociological individual-ism – the isolated individual as the starting-point of analysis, as in con-tract theory or the classical political economy, in which the competitive individualist was simply projected backwards into history. Man was idealised in his partiality and incompleteness as in the classical political economy, with its 'egoistic man', falsely conceived to be 'the true and authentic man'. The citizen, the full member of the political commun-ity, was subordinated to the 'egoistic man': 'it is man as a bourgeois and not man as a citizen who is considered the true and authentic man'.[119] Political economy was concerned only with man as wealth-seeker and labouring instrument and, by incorporating private property into the essence of man, succeeded only in formulating the laws of alienated labour. Political economy was concerned solely with men in-side the labour-relationship. The inability to see man in his wholeness, in all his aspects, is revealed in the conflicts between the various sys-tems of thought – religion, economics, law, ethics, and so on – which took fragments of man as the essential man, and treated him as if he were subject to their laws alone. Hence there were conflicts, e.g. between the claims of morality and those of political economy, which were further evidences of the alienated world in which men lived.[120]

Men assert their individuality against others and against society. Their apparent independence is actually indifference – 'independence, that is, to collide with one another freely and to barter within the limits of this freedom'.[121] Others are perceived narrowly, abstractly and par-tially. The self-enclosed isolates were incapable of recognising the need or the potentiality of their fellows, though they could see their useful-ness to their own distorted ends. In the relations between man and woman, which Marx believed to be the most natural of all relation-ships, and which revealed the extent to which man's natural behav-iour had become human, their separation was revealed clearly, as men failed to recognise the species relation itself, and regarded women merely as objects of lust. They disregarded the reality, variety and distinctive-ness of others, who were conceived as atoms, stereotypes, competitors, instruments and enemies. Marx was to claim in 1847, as critical social analysis, that social relations were 'not relations between individual and individual, but between worker and capitalist, between farmer and landlord, etc.'[122] Even feudal relationships, which seemed personal, were frozen in economic and social categories, and men only related to each other 'in determined roles, as a feudal lord and his vassal, a landlord and his serf, etc., or as a member of a caste, etc., or of an estate, etc.'[123] The relations between individuals became class and property relations, devoid of any free and mutual consideration. The man was lost in the role and the category, and the capitalist as much as the proletarian lacked an individual personality. He was subsumed in his class and under material powers – a perception which underlay *Capital*. 'The persons exist for one another merely as representatives of, and, therefore, as owners of, commodities. In the course of our investigation we shall find, in general, that the characters who appear on the economic stage are but the personifications of the economic relations that exist between them.'[124]

In these circumstances – abstracted, cut into pieces and isolated from his fellows – man suffered immensely. Family and other social ties were torn apart as men, women and children were turned into articles of commerce and instruments of labour. The proletarian in particular was separated from the fellowship of true social life. 'This social life, from which his own labour excludes him, is life itself, physical and cultural life, human morality, human activity, human enjoyment, real human existence.'[125] This isolation is pervasive, unbearable and horrible, for true fellowship is much wider and more encompassing than political fellowship, just as man is far more than a citizen. In reviewing Peuchet's book on suicide, Marx indicated more feelingly the shortcomings, in relation to communal life, of the societies of his own day. 'What sort of society is it, in truth, where one finds several millions in deepest loneliness, where one can be overcome by an irresistible longing to kill oneself without anyone discovering it. This society is not a society; it is, as Rousseau says, a desert populated by wild animals.'[126]

Yet these divided, anarchic and individualistic societies hung together. Somehow the 'crazy fabric' held. Marx's explanation, following Hegel and the classical political economists, was that economic interdependence, based on the division of labour, was the main source of social union. He began at the beginning, with man's natural needs. Men produced goods for exchange on a market, and thus depended upon each other, co-operating for specific economic purposes in civil society.

> It is natural necessity, essential human properties, however alienated they may seem to be, and interest that hold the members of civil society together: civil not political life is their real tie. . .only political superstition imagines that social life must be held together by the state whereas in reality the state is held together by civil life.[127]

But its stability was illusory. Men were both united and divided by exchange relationships within the private property system – united as producers and consumers, making and devouring products within the exchange process, and divided as competitive and self-seeking class individuals, advancing to the disadvantage of others. Money was the bond of all bonds and the solvent of all ties. 'It is the true agent of divorce as well as the true binding agent – the universal galvano-chemical power of Society.'[128]

Thus society or civil society is the foundation of the state. Men are linked not by law or by love, but by the community of material need which Hegel took to be synonymous with civil society – the area of human labour and the satisfaction of human needs – which binds men together by forcing them to take account of the interests of others.[129] Hence capitalist society is analogous to a commercial enterprise rather than to a genuine community, or a political order maintained by law, convention and coercion. Yet, men, twisted and broken as they are, dimly perceive the state as their own work, and cling to it as an illusory community, a partial expression of the real and satisfying community which they unconsciously crave.[130] They desire and need a real community of men, in which they can realise their humanity. For this, the sham and shallow 'heavenly' universality of the state, which cannot take up and genuinely resolve the conflicts and the clashing egoisms of civil society, is no substitute. Political links are superficial, while the deeper bonds of self-interest are transitory.

INTIMATIONS OF THE FUTURE

The shortcomings of alienated, class man, in terms of Marx's vision of the creative, versatile, autonomous and communal man, are obvious. Marx's assault on capitalism is set against an image of a world in which man is completely developed, in which his human relations and standing depend upon his own abilities and powers, and not upon some external measure or force, and it can only be comprehended in relation to that image.

But how is the enormous gulf between present and future, between existence and essence, to be bridged? How is man to gain his human nature? What combination of economic change and political action can create the conditions for human transformation, by destroying the tyrannous institutions and the powerful, one-sided appetites which have made him a slave in his own world? What view of man's nature and historical change underlies the far-reaching hope for the future? Or, putting the question pejoratively, what were the grounds of Marx's faith? In essence, the following three chapters pursue these questions, but certain general points can be raised at this stage.

To begin with, Marx's view of societies as constantly changing, through a process of internal dissolution, is compatible with a radically optimistic view of man's prospects, though it does not necessarily lead to such a view. Similarly, the general assertion that human nature changes is compatible with any number of accounts of its content and its process of development. However, a record of substantial and constant social change certainly suggests that the various forms of human society are contingent,[131] and uproots the static conservative doctrine that we all move – and must move – eternally in the same ruts. But even were it true that societies alter incessantly, and that men develop new qualities and capacities along with the development of society, the Marxist vision would not yet have gained sufficient underpinning. Precisely what powers develop in the course of social evolution? How does one show that history is progressive and meaningful in terms of the capacities which are valued? Why should societies develop in one way rather than another – and, indeed, why should they develop rather than regress? And how is it shown that a genuinely new society is both feasible and on the way?

In the early writings Marx adopted what was then a philosophical commonplace – the notion that, as Lorenz von Stein put it in 1844, the destiny of man is 'his completion, or the realization of all those abilities which are in him'.[132] For Marx, history, including that which was still to come, was an unfolding of tendencies already present. Rational process or destiny was an essential feature of the world he studied. And that process was not one in which an unknown potentiality is realised; Marx found the germs of a particular future within history and within the present. That future – communism – presupposed both the achievements and the sufferings of capitalism, both the wealth and the poverty of previous development. Emerging within the capitalist order were institutional foundations, models, glimpses and intimations of the future. Marx showed how capitalism had made conditions vastly different from what they were before, in terms of intensified alienation and brutalisation of the many, and a remarkable technological and institutional creativeness. It had not only built the economic and technological prerequisites of a free society – large enterprises, and joint stock companies and workers' co-operatives, which were embryonic socialist forms within the old society – but had forged a political force to bring the existing order down. It had simplified class antagonisms and stripped the workers bare, facing them directly with a brutal reality, removing the veils so that their connections and their isolation were not disguised by personal dependence or by communal or affectionate ties. In the horror lay the seeds of emancipation. Capitalism had brought certain historical contradictions to their height, so that the conditions for, as well as the necessity of, their final resolution, existed. In this sense, capitalism had subverted its own bases, and could grow no further, collapsing over the contradictions between the means and the relations of production, between private appropriation and social production. Things had come to the point whereby men could move forward, societies grow and the historical movement be completed, only with the destruction of capitalism.

In terms of the discussion of human nature, it needs to be pointed out that capitalism did not simply enslave, destroy and deprive man, while establishing conditions for his ultimate emancipation. Men were already revealing powers and feelings of a kind which Marx valued and praised. Human labour was embodied in objects which stood as a permanent witness to man's power, however restrictive and harmful the circumstances in which they were made. Industrial development under capitalism was the supreme demonstration hitherto of the ability of man to manipulate his physical environment. In the 1844 *Manuscripts* Marx wrote that 'the history of industry and the established objective existence of industry are the open book of man's essential powers'.[133] What Marx appears to mean by this is that man has shown, historically, that he has certain powers, which are characteristically human. These are his powers as tool-maker, craftsman, industrial inventor and so on. While these powers, which had developed throughout history – in which man develops his slumbering powers – had reached, by Marx's time, a remarkable degree of sophistication, genuine creativity was limited to a very few, and labour remained, for most men, gruelling and monotonous. History was certainly not characterised by a free, steady and progressive unfolding of human capacity. Not everybody revealed the distinctively human qualities: men's powers were not 'actualised' or 'realised' positively. Similarly, the conception of man as rational is not a conception of all men at all times as rational. It assumes a capacity for reason, which is perhaps embodied above all in the great systems of ideas, which bear lasting testimony to human rationality though not to the rationality of every man.

Hence Marx did not claim that man was as a matter of fact a free, creative, versatile and social labourer, but that he had it in him to become so in specified conditions, and that there was sufficient historical evidence of human abilities, and of the development of the human senses, and enough productive power, industrial training and particular achievements under capitalism to treat these human powers as potentialities in the process of realisation, and capable of full development in a new social order, rather than as parts of an empty utopian moral ideal. Under the restrictive conditions of capitalism he found examples of human versatility but, more significantly, far-reaching changes in the process of modern industry itself, which were subverting specialisation. Modern industry, though not capitalism, required variation of labour, fluency of function and universal mobility of labour. Through its catastrophes, it made it necessary to recognise, as a fundamental law of production,

> variation of work, consequently fitness of the labourer for varied work, consequently the greatest possible development of his varied aptitudes. It becomes a question of life and death for society to adapt the mode of production to the normal functioning of this law. Modern industry, indeed, compels society, under penalty of death, to replace the detail-worker of today, crippled by life-long repetition of one and the same trivial operation, and thus reduced to the mere fragment of a man, by the fully developed individual, fit for a variety of labours, ready to face any change of production, and to whom the different social functions he performs, are but so many modes of giving free scope to his own natural and acquired powers.[134]

Even the weak education clauses of the Factory Act revealed the possibility of combining manual labour with education and gymnastics, while the limited time spent on formal education enabled some factory children, despite their toil, to come to it with unusual freshness and energy. Marx held that Robert Owen had shown how the factory system had produced 'the germ of the education of the future, an education that will, in the case of every child over a certain age, combine productive labour with instruction and gymnastics, not only as one of the methods of adding to the efficiency of production, but as the only method of producing fully developed human beings'.[135] Men and children – though not, as yet, women – were being formed already for diverse, many-sided activity.

Marx and Engels emphasised the dehumanisation of the contemporary proletariat. They recognised that most men did not reveal their species powers, but were crude, limited, ignorant, with senses distorted and potentialities seemingly withered, hardly different from the brutes themselves. They admitted, analysed and scarified the assassination of the people under capitalism, and blamed powerful institutions and interests for their fate. They saw man's shortcomings, and the divisions between men, as historical and social creations, and not as natural or fixed features of the world. Neither greed nor love of domination were inescapably human, and would wither away with the transformation of the system which constrained and malformed men. In their view, things were put the wrong way round, as explanations of existing institutions began too late, or stopped too early; for example the division of labour created differences between men but was in turn legitimised by them. Guided by a particular analysis of history and view of human nature, they denied the longevity of man's contemporary limitations, and remained hopeful about his power to humanise circumstances. Marx indicated that communists shared radical and optimistic assumptions with the French materialism of the Enlightenment.

> There is no need of any great penetration to see from the teaching of materialism on the original goodness and equal intellectual endowment of men, the omnipotence of experience, habit and education, and the influence of environment on man, the great significance of industry, the justification of enjoyment, etc., how necessarily materialism is connected with communism and socialism.[136]

In Marx's case, however, history was seen to be a process in which man's powers were gradually drawn out and developed, so that ultimately, after many ups and downs, he becomes fully human in Marx's sense of the term. Communism seemed feasible given assumptions about man's technological skill and achievement, his versatility, and his collective and large-scale industrial enterprises. Existing social life, despite its shortcomings and contradictions – which were dynamic in their effects – revealed man's capacities, though generally in a twisted form and in restrictive circumstances. Marx did not rest his case on the number of complete or developed men that there already were, though he did provide examples of particular men or groups of men who were, in existing conditions, inventive geniuses, versatile individuals, and genuine brothers. There emerge, amidst accounts of the most painful and injurious industrial toil, sudden flashes of enthusiasm and hope. Where French socialist workers meet together, for example, 'the brotherhood of man is no empty phrase but a reality, and the nobility of man shines forth upon us from their toil-worn bodies'.[137]

Marx did not present flat or static moral criticism of capitalism. He believed himself to be describing, not one goal or possibility amongst others, but 'the actual emergence, the actual future realisation for man of his nature and his nature as actual'.[138] History was not merely the exotic revelation of man's essential powers, nor merely a sphere of misery and enslavement. Already within capitalist society the future could be glimpsed, as men revealed, sometimes directly – as half-liberated or semi-realised men – and sometimes in an alienated or corrupted way, those powers and aspirations which would be, under communism, elaborated, fulfilled and widely spread. The sacrifice of human nature could be ended, Marx argued, when the 'definite presuppositions and conditions' which inhibited man in making history, and brought him misery, were themselves ended. Mankind could not be freed within those presuppositions and conditions.

The vision is, of course, that of Marx. We may find his instances of man's approximation to his species-being, and the rest of his supporting argument, too sparse to warrant his hopes. We may find those weighty influences and powers that hover so relentlessly over capitalist man too tenacious for the liberating forces to remove, and, especially if not friends of the dialectic, we may remain unconvinced by the idea that man is at his most alienated and brutalised immediately prior to the final stages of his emancipation. That historical divide seems to be crossed too often merely by a process – often very alluring – of dialectical thinking. But, for Marx, the tenacity of the powerful controlling and perverting institutions of capitalism was illusory, and things were already and rapidly building up towards their destruction. And then the future would be remarkably open and productive. If slaves could create so much, what might free men not do? Marx's optimistic and generous view of human nature could not be substantiated by previous history, though Marx himself thought that his analysis and his expectation were rooted in historical actuality, unlike utopian appeals to the distant and vacuous goddesses of Justice, Freedom, Equality and Fraternity. But whether Marxism itself is empty, assertive, ethical idealism, a desperate and fruitless Promethean assertion of man against demeaning and crippling circumstances, or whether it describes man's destiny, can only be shown, within its own terms, by political action and the actual process of self-emancipation. It was not something to be read fatalistically from the historical record, nor was it to be awaited passively, though it did presuppose certain economic conditions and processes, which were outlined most fully in *Capital*.

3 The disintegration of capitalism

Marx regarded capitalism as a concrete economic system, occupying a particular point in time.[1] But the method of analysis which he employed in *Capital* begins with an abstract or simplified account of capitalism – in order to reveal the inner mechanisms of capitalist production without being distracted by the complex play of surface phenomena – and only concludes with the location of the concrete forms growing out of the movements of capitalist production as a whole. In volume III, the various forms of capital approach the form which they assume 'on the surface of society, in the action of different capitals upon one another, in competition, and in the ordinary consciousness of the agents of production themselves'.[2] By means of this approach, Marx hoped to bring out the essential features of capitalistic economic relations, and to expose the concrete human relationships which were disguised by economic formulae and the flux of appearance. Capitalism as such was no artificial construct, though certain of the features which Marx thought crucial to it had not yet emerged fully or clearly. His approach was necessarily and fundamentally historical, treating the object in its development, and revealing the tendencies and potentialities – the future – which lay within it. Beginning from the contemporary economic facts described in the classical political economy, the theory at once lagged behind events and sought to reveal and help shape the destiny of the system.

Scientific analysis of the capitalist mode of production demonstrated that it was 'a mode of production of a special kind, with special historical features'.[3] It shared key institutional characteristics with preceding class societies – private ownership of productive resources, commodity production, surplus value, class conflict and the social and political as well as the economic predominance of one class. Each of these took on a new and distinctive form in capitalism. To Marx, the particular character of commodity production and surplus value, both of which existed earlier, were definitive of capitalism. In their new forms they were its 'specific traits'. The commodity aspect of things had become their dominant characteristic, basically in the emergence of the 'free' labourer as the seller of a commodity – his labour power. He owned

97

nothing but his labour power – a condition which presupposed the expropriation of direct producers from the land – and he could dispose of it as he wished, though his actual alternatives might be very slight. The second distinctive feature of capitalism was 'the production of surplus-value as the direct aim and determining motive of production'.[4]

Marx and Engels were interested largely in those features of capitalism which were subverting it. Their accounts of its rise, zenith and decline showed that there were revolutionary forces at its very heart, driving it irresistibly towards destruction. Theory and practice alike went beyond the existing order – dialectical thought grasped the negative or contradictory elements within reality and became itself active, defining and promoting practical-critical or revolutionary activity. The Marxist critique of capitalism thus offers an analysis of its general tendencies which purports to be both scientific and creative. It is not moralistic, in the sense of condemning an evil society in terms of abstract ethical values – justice, equality and the like – and attempting to persuade rational men to create a humane social order out of the blue, as it were. The communists stressed the impotence of ethical attacks on the capitalist system, and of exhortations to men to behave more morally. 'The communists do not preach morality at all, such as Stirner preaches so extensively.'[5] They do not advise people to love each other or to cease being egoists, for 'they are very well aware that egoism, just as much as self-sacrifice, is in definite circumstances a necessary form of the self-assertion of individuals'.[6] Communist theory was based explicitly, not on moral indignation at the inhumanity of capitalism, but on 'the inevitable collapse of the capitalist mode of production which is daily taking place before our eyes to an ever greater degree'.[7] Yet, while Marx condemned sentimental assaults on capitalism for its brutality, and commonly phrased his own account in the cold, dead language of economics, he made it quite clear that the objective tendencies of social development led towards a future which was desirable in terms of his own conception of human nature. He did not legitimise social trends *per se*. Fact and value – his own facts and his own values – are fused in his grand vision of the development and transformation of capitalism.

The character of capitalist development had been indicated, rather fuzzily, in the classical political economy, of which Marx's economic theory was a continuing critique. Marx believed that the classical system had disclosed many important economic relations but had not provided an adequate theoretical framework for their comprehension. The political economists did not see how far their laws and categories arose from the 'very nature of private property' and were 'but the expression of a necessary course of development'.[8] Their analysis assumed a bourgeois framework, presupposing private property and alienation, and employing abstracted economic categories. While producing genuine social theories, and not merely tools of technical economic analysis, they did not define adequately the social reality which lay behind their economic concepts. The class struggle was revealed rather than recognised in their writings – a fact which could be explained by their times and their class situations. Moreover, they tended to treat their own distinctions, and the capitalist system or market economy itself, as natural and essential rather than historical, bound to disappear with the consummation of that class war of which they had caught occasional glimpses.

Marx asserted the historicity of the society which was frozen in the classical political economy, and exposed the social relations which were obscured in its fetishistic categories. Professing to have put himself wholly at the standpoint of the political economist,[9] he developed an internal critique of its economic categories, which was also, inevitably, a critical exposure of the bourgeois economy itself. Bringing out the contradictions which co-existed within the existing study, he pushed beyond competition and mutual exploitation to a very different image of the future.

> We have proceeded from the premises of political economy. We have accepted its language and its law. We presupposed private property, the separation of labour, capital and land, and of wages, profit and capital, and rent of land – likewise division of labour, competition, the concept of exchange-value, etc. On the basis of political economy itself, in its own words, we have shown that the worker sinks to the level of a commodity and becomes indeed the most wretched of commodities, that the wretchedness of the worker is in inverse proportion to the power and magnitude of his production; that the necessary result of competition is the accumulation of capital in a few hands, and thus the restoration of monopoly in a more terrible form; and finally the distinction between capitalist and land-rentier, like that between the tiller of the soil and the factory-worker, disappears and that the whole of society must fall apart into two classes – the property-owners and the propertiless workers.[10]

While Smith and Ricardo denied the importance of deliberate design in human affairs, and stressed the unintended results of actions, they anticipated – on the whole – continuing economic efficiency and harmony. Marx also treated the lack of conscious social regulation of production as a central feature of bourgeois society, but in his case the invisible hand or the Cunning of Reason had an end-product of chaos and fundamental change. Of course, Marx stressed the amazing and revolutionary technological progress of capitalist societies, and their tendency to drive relentlessly onwards and outwards, until the whole world was gathered in one net, and subordinated to a common standard. There was a profound energy and restlessness in the continuous search for new markets and materials. The political successes of the French bourgeoisie, for example, brought economic vitality and rapid advance, 'a storm and stress of commercial enterprise, a passion for enrichment, the frenzy of the new bourgeois life whose first self-enjoyment is pert, light-hearted and intoxicating'.[11] But his study of the society within which economic development was set, and of the economic barriers met by capitalism at various points during its development, led him to the belief that this in-built and unceasing technological change would ultimately prove self-defeating, and that eventually capitalism would be destroyed by forces which it had itself created.

Marx's pursuit of his major task – laying bare the economic law of movement of bourgeois society – does raise a serious interpretative problem, concerning his whole approach to economic phenomena. This problem must be considered prior to any examination of his detailed economic-cum-sociological doctrines. Marx claimed that his economic analysis and predictions were descriptive or empirical in character. The view of Marx as scientist assumes the derivation of his economic theories more or less directly from economic facts. For example, Schumpeter, who draws such a picture of Marx, admits that he employed certain formal analogies with Hegelianism, but asserts that nowhere did he 'betray positive science to metaphysics'.[12] Yet the original source of many of the neat, symmetrical conceptions of Marxian economics – inverse ratios, the proletariat as the absolute negation of capitalism, absolute impoverishment counterposed to absolute wealth, the polarisation of classes – appears to be philosophical rather than empirical, though the two are generally mixed in social inquiry, and it is quite wrong to suggest that, because of this, conclusions are thereby invalidated. Marx's economics cannot be understood independently of Hegelian dialectics, stripped of its mystical form so that the rational kernel remains.[13] More than most economists – or, at least, more obviously than most – Marx's views on economic and social developments seem at many points to flow from assumptions about the nature of the universe which are external to the study, narrowly conceived, and indeed the vast economic study was preceded by a philosophical preface. The schema with which he approached the detailed study of economic phenomena has been neatly labelled the 'Hegelian choreography'[14] – a set of clear, definite, logical relations which are seen as inherent in the historical process itself. To oversimplify, what was needed from Marx was the addition of specific and concrete historical actors to the abstract framework of negations and contradictions. The vital, world-transforming role of the class with radical chains, the dissolution of society, was conjured up out of Hegelian metaphysics, and the movement of capitalist society was seen from a distance as a clear embodiment of dialectics. There are a number of specific economic hypotheses in the 1844 *Manuscripts*, but the point is that Marx's approach at this time was directed by anterior philosophical considerations, which continued to battle with an increasingly rich and solid grasp of social reality, including an unsystematised body of observations which pointed to a very different future for capitalism than that which he anticipated in the middle and late forties. The conflict between the image of simplifying social processes and clear-cut social outcomes, to which Hegel was the primary contributor, and the more complex views which arose out of close study of various capitalist and semi-capitalist societies, was never finally resolved by Marx himself.[15]

The problem is thus a larger one than that of the relationship between simplified economic models – proper and unavoidable creations of the economist – and the complex social reality whose essence the models are intended to grasp. If, for certain purposes, we do stress the methodological value of Marx's simplifying procedure, it must be remembered that Marx was not merely employing methodolgical devices – though he did do this – but was expounding a total and overriding vision of the historical process, which has been criticised by some writers as 'a quasi-apocalyptic phantasy'.[16] But if we did take Marxism at its own 'scientific' face value, and elicited its particular scientific method, we would discover, at one level, fundamental principles or laws, to which are then appended, as occasion arises, auxiliary hypotheses whose function is to explain, or explain away, apparent deviations from the alleged general tendency. In Marx's case we find throughout his work – from the 1844 *Manuscripts* to volume III of *Capital* – a simple two-class model of society which is held to apply to the late stage of capitalism, as a result of certain presumed economic tendencies. It did not represent an actuality in the present, in relation to which Marx was usually perceptive and subtle, elaborating often on the untidiness and the variety of class groupings. But it was more than an abstraction assumed for the purposes of analysis, and rather more than a model of capitalism as it would develop if left undisturbed, as the comments on Marx's philosophical heritage suggest. On the view that Marx simply presented a model of capitalism as it would develop if left undisturbed – elaborated, amongst others, by A. D. Lindsay[17] – Marxism becomes an *if, then type* social theory, whose laws are only true *ceteris paribus*, i.e. if present conditions hold, then a fundamental clash between capital and labour will ensue. Given Lindsay's view of the logical status of Marxism, it becomes impossible to refute or confirm Marx's predictions by an appeal to 'unanalysed historical facts'.[18]

While it is true that critics are sometimes clumsy or unfair in opposing 'historical facts' to Marx's predictions, and that the variations of his position (e.g. on wages or on revolution) in different historical circumstances are sometimes forgotten, it does seem to me that Marxism is susceptible to this kind of test, i.e. against historical evidence – regardless of the source of his views. We may wish to explain the differences between his predictions and some of the major tendencies in advanced capitalist societies in terms of forces counteracting 'pure capitalism', e.g. Factory Acts and other laws transforming the laissez-faire system internally, or the growing power of trades unions – though there are disagreements as to whether such developments deviate from, or are part of, his central theory of capitalism.[19] It is certainly reasonable in some cases to appeal to 'short-run tendencies' and 'temporary variations'. But such appeals often turn out to be evasions – evasions of the fact that Marx presented a number of apparently empirical hypotheses concerning the present and the future of capitalism, and that some though not all of them have turned out to be incorrect. Marx sometimes suggested that the condition of the proletariat would deteriorate or at best remain constant, while the wealth of others grew, and he believed that this would have drastic political consequences. This claim is concrete and significant, and can properly be examined against the history of the countries with which he was primarily concerned – which history must, of course, itself be interpreted – and against his own divergent claims. The essential point is that Marx believed that the tendencies which he had observed in capitalist societies, and above all in England, would hold and even, he argues at times, 'work out with iron necessity towards inevitable results'.[20] Capitalist production, he wrote, 'begets, with the inexorability of a law of Nature, its own negation'.[21] Not that history or the dialectic or capitalism or the forces of production wage any battles of their own. But men, subjected to certain pressures within a concrete social system, are expected and encouraged to respond in certain ways, to overcome the profound and dynamic historical conflict between capital and labour, and thus to overcome class conflict altogether.

Marx presented a dichotomous image of capitalism in terms of a primitive philosophic vision, which was to emerge in its sharp simplicity as capitalism approached its end. He also simplified as a methodological procedure, believing abstraction to be inescapable, and likening himself to the physicist studying physical phenomena where they occur 'in their most typical form and most free from disturbing influence'[22] –

though without claiming that his laws and necessities were of the same order as those of physics. England is presented as the classic case, in which the laws of capitalist production, with their supposed social consequences, were most clearly working out. But even England did not embody all the characteristics of bourgeois society, which became something of an ideal type. As Engels put it: 'Generally speaking, for the economical development of the bourgeoisie, England is here taken as the typical country; for its political development, France.'[23] However, what was combined in theory was not combined in fact, and the imposing theoretical edifice, with its generalised picture of bourgeois society, soon fell apart.

Marx insisted that he was offering no master-key for all history, no 'historic–philosophic theory of the general path every people is fated to tread'.[24] The use of such abstractions as 'production in general' did not imply that one could speak of economic and social development in general, and much of Marx's writing is devoted to ingenious analysis of the impurity of concrete historical forms, and to the explanation – if not the accommodation – of the peculiarities and variations of particular societies. He recognised that the lines between epochs were not hard and fast, that the old lived on and penetrated the new, and that the transition from our epoch to another could take place in a variety of ways. He was particularly conscious of the peculiarities of German development, and wrote in relation to it: 'Alongside of modern evils, a whole series of inherited evils oppress us, arising from the passive survival of antiquated modes of production, with their inevitable train of social and political anachronisms. We suffer not only from the living, but from the dead. Le mort saisit le vif.'[25] But, while recognising, in principle at least, that each society had to be examined empirically, and while often exploring anachronisms and divergences flexibly, he believed that capitalist processes were steadily removing unevennesses, within particular societies and throughout the world, that as a matter of historical fact social conflict was being simplified and intensified, and that social reality would ultimately conform to his simple image. The Hegelian myth, with its sharp and clear antitheses and its heady final resolution of conflicts and contradictions, still hovered over Marx's reading of history, and he never completely freed himself from it.

THE LABOUR THEORY OF VALUE AND THE THEORY OF WAGES

Marx's critical analysis of capitalism must be approached from one of the basic doctrines of the classical economists, which was also the centrepiece of his own theoretical system – the labour theory of value.

This theory which, in technical economic terms, represented an attempt to discover why commodities exchanged at particular prices (and, as such, is highly questionable), derives most of its weight from its ethical and sociological content. It is no merely descriptive theory (if such things exist), but a critical and transforming doctrine which, along with its offspring – the theory of surplus value – explains how man, the producer of his own world through labour, comes to be alienated and exploited.

Marx sought the common substance, the 'unifying quantitative principle', which would explain the rate of exchange of commodities. He saw the act of exchange as unconnected with the use-value of things, which was not a function of human labour, and involved qualitative differences, whereas exchange was concerned merely with quantities. Commodities shared the characteristic of being simply definite masses of 'congealed labour-time'. The firm measure of their value was the labour power embodied in their production, which included that directly involved and an allowance for products already consumed during the productive process. This determined their primary or natural price or exchange value, which could diverge from the actual market price. As stated by Ricardo, interpreted by Marx, the view was that labour was 'the foundation of the exchangeable value of all things, excepting those which cannot be increased by human industry'.[26] Ideal cases of simple communities were used to illustrate the doctrine. Ricardo used as an example the exchange between a hunter's and a fisherman's daily catch and Adam Smith held that the measure applied in the 'early and rude state of society', but that in 'improved and civilised society' a more complex calculation was necessary.[27] Neither Smith nor Ricardo nor Marx believed that in their own societies labour time could serve, alone and unanalysed, as the determinant of price. Differences of energy, training, skill and technical development had to be taken into account. Marx therefore described abstract uniform labour or socially necessary labour time as the true source of value – though more time might be spent on producing a particular commodity than was socially necessary. Socially necessary labour time is defined as 'that required to produce an article under the normal conditions of production, and with the average degree of skill and intensity prevalent at the time'.[28] It was a function of competition to determine this time by distinguishing between useful and useless labour. 'Is your hour's labour worth mine? That is a question which is decided by competition.'[29] Again, more explicitly: 'What determines value is not the time taken to produce a thing, but the minimum time it could possibly be produced in, and this minimum is ascertained by competition.'[30] Thus labour must be of average efficiency or normal goodness, working with the usual degree of intensity.

The problem of unequal skill – the differences in labour power of skilled and unskilled labourers – was met at the theoretical level by simplifying the analysis and reducing all labour to units of 'unskilled average labour' and, as far as the realities of capitalist society were concerned, by the claim that differences of skill were becoming less and less important as labourers were equally subordinated to the machine.

> If the mere quantity of labour functions as a measure of value regardless of quality, it presupposes that simple labour has become the pivot of industry. It presupposes that labour has been equalised by the subordination of man to the machine or by the extreme division of labour; that men are effaced by their labour; that the pendulum of the clock has become as accurate a measure of the relative activity of two workers as it is of the speed of two locomotives. . .Time is everything, man is nothing; he is at most, time's carcase. Quality no longer matters. Quantity alone decides everything. . .this equalising of labour is. . .purely and simply a fact of modern industry.[31]

Hence it was assumed that, as a matter of fact, price or exchange value tended to approximate more directly to labour time.

The labour theory of value linked up directly with Marx's views of class conflict and the future of capitalism when it was applied to the commodity of labour, or labour power. It helped form his view of the condition and the destiny of the labouring class. Labour power is a commodity, an object for sale, subject like any other to the law of value. In the transaction with the capitalist, the labourer alienates his own essential power, his 'general activity and reality', and in effect loses his own essence, which becomes the property of another, in order to survive. Labour is 'bought as an instrument of production, as a machine would be bought'.[32] The labourer appears as a productive force of capital, 'as bare material labour-power, as a commodity'.[33] As a commodity, his value is determined, not by the worth of the products he makes, but by the amount of socially necessary labour time required to maintain him. Wages, or the price of labour power, amount to what is necessary for the life, reproduction and perhaps reasonable efficiency of the productive instrument, i.e. the labourer, and this was an appropriate fact of political economy at that time. The tendency of wages to lie at or about subsistence level had been emphasised by the classical economists, but they had generally been content to announce the irreversibility of nature's decision, and had not, on the whole, explored the possible effects of poverty on the behaviour of the labouring class.

Marx was strongly impressed by the subsistence wage theory, though he did not share the classical view of the causes of low wages. In the

1844 Manuscripts he had noted Smith's discovery that the ordinary wage was 'the lowest compatible with common humanity (that is a cattle-like existence)'. [34] The workers were regarded and treated as productive instruments which, in the interests of profit-making, were to be serviced at the minimum possible cost. The average price of labour is the minimum wage, 'that quantum of the means of subsistence, which is absolutely requisite to keep the labourer in bare existence as a labourer'.[35] Marx did suggest that the value of labour power was fixed by historical and social elements, as well as by the physical element – what was required for mere brute survival – and that custom and culturally conditioned expectations could raise it above the physiological minimum.[36] But he believed that, commonly, the labourers had no choice but to eat the cheapest and poorest foods, e.g. potatoes, a situation which he naturally felt would be transformed under socialism, when social utility would determine the distribution of time and resources, and much of the consumable part of surplus value would be spent on social consumption. Economic analysis and moral revulsion mingle, even in the more 'scientific' works, and Marx and Engels bring out – directly, or indirectly, through treating human beings within the concepts of the existing political economy – the costs, in terms of dehumanisation and physical mutilation and suffering, of reducing human beings to commodities or productive instruments.

Various writers have pointed out that labour power, which Marx wanted to treat as an ordinary commodity, lacks 'the equilibrating mechanism of supply and demand'[37] which operates in the case of other commodities. Producers of labour power do not compete in the manner of producers of ordinary commodities.[38] In the absence of that form of competition which, through resource re-allocation, generally approximates price to value, it might seem that there is no good reason why wages should fail to rise along with capital accumulation, and perhaps even to its full extent. The labour theory of value, in its application to wages, merely asserts their tendency to lie at about subsistence level under capitalism: it does not answer the crucial questions which arise at this point. Why is it that the workers are in no position to peacefully improve their lot, especially in the case of a general increase of productivity? Why must they continue to suffer under capitalism? What is the source of the despotism of capital? What are the boundaries or limits of the capitalist system? Why is it that the capitalist can compel the working class 'to do more work than the narrow round of its own life-wants prescribes'?[39]

In pursuing Marx's answers to these questions we are driven to consider the sociology of capitalism, the distribution of power within that system. The plight of the proletariat, the class which owns only its labour power, arises from its relationship with the small class of owners of the means of production. Low wages are partly explained by the pressures on the capitalist to exploit and to accumulate, which was his characteristic and, indeed, defining activity. The other part of the explanation, which is more directly relevant at this point, concerns his ability to do so because of the nature of the labour force. Marx, who normally argued that a permanent and general rise in wages was unlikely, held that this was so not because of an abstract commitment to the labour theory of value, but because of the assumption that there would ordinarily be a buyer's market for labour, i.e. the bargaining situation would favour the capitalists because of the supply of labour available. Marx assumed that capitalism had a general tendency to produce a surplus labour force, or what he called a reserve army of the unemployed. This was the special law of population of the capitalist method of production. The process which Marx described was a favourite one, whereby a system generated the conditions of its own continued existence, and ultimately the conditions of its supersession. In his words:

> It is capitalistic accumulation itself that constantly produces, and produces in the direct ratio of its own energy and extent, a relatively redundant population of labourers...this surplus population becomes...the lever of capitalistic accumulation, nay, a condition of existence of the capitalist mode of production. It forms a disposable industrial reserve army, that belongs to capital quite as absolutely as if the latter had bred it at its own cost. Independently of the limits of the actual increase of population, it creates, for the changing needs of the self-expansion of capital, a mass of human material always ready for exploitation.[40]

Within a mature capitalist system the major source of the industrial reserve army was the constant, feverish revolutionising of the means of production, which led, in Marx's view, to a relative decrease in employment opportunities. In technical economic terms the relative magnitude of variable capital (the wages bill) progressively declines in relation to constant capital (machines and other capital equipment – the means of production).[41] This is the normal process of capitalist accumulation and production. In the early days, owing primarily to the lack of a capital market, the transformation was slow: in mature capitalism the rate of conversion of profits to capital equipment, dictated by competition, is extremely quick and far-reaching. Machines increasingly devour men, who are used up, destroyed and cast aside in the process of production. The process of accumulation is characterised by the growing inability of the system to provide employment for new workers and its tendency, as the classical euphemism put it, to 'set free' labourers who had hitherto been employed. Thus technological change, which quickens the 'concentration' and 'centralisation' of capitals, is presented as labour-saving in character. In addition to asserting an increase in the number of semi-employed and unemployed workers, the size of which varied with the trade cycle, Marx claimed that skilled men were gradually being supplanted by unskilled and cheaper labourers, especially women and children, and that a significant casual labouring section and a submerged mass of paupers were emerging. This transformation of the labouring force was technically feasible as well as more profitable for the capitalist. Naturally such a situation, with a plenitude of potential strike-breakers, would increase the bargaining strength of the employers, and was defended in precisely these terms. Andrew Ure, the 'Pindar' of the factory system, praised the new machinery because it led to 'the equalization of labour', by dispensing with the special aptitudes of the 'self-willed and intractable' skilled workman.[42]

Marx suggested, reasonably, that in some cases machinery was introduced with the deliberate intention of establishing control over a rebellious or prosperous labour force. The farmers who were faced with a rise in agrarian wages during the 1850s did not wait until an increased birth rate, offshoot of prosperity, had provided them with bargaining strength again. They introduced more machinery and thus rendered many workers once more superfluous.[43] In *The Poverty of Philosophy* the point is generalised.

> In England, strikers have regularly given rise to the invention and application of new machines. Machines were, it may be said, the weapon employed by the capitalists to quell the revolt of specialised labour. The self-acting mule, the greatest invention of modern industry, put out of action the spinners who were in revolt. If combinations and strikers had no other effect than that of making the efforts of mechanical genius react against them, they would still exercise an immense influence on the development of industry.[44]

Hence machinery helped create that surplus of labourers whose existence Marx took to be a vital need of capitalism. He claimed that relative surplus population was 'the pivot upon which the law of supply and demand of labour works. It confines the field of action of this law within the limits absolutely convenient to the activity of exploitation and to the domination of capital.'[45]

Marx was endeavouring to describe and explain a general tendency of capitalism. He recognised that there were boom periods and that there were privileged sections of workers at all times but, while admitting these exceptions to his analysis, he did not alter his long-term predictions as a consequence. When labourers were relatively scarce, either in particular industries or in the economy as a whole, as in some periods of rapid economic growth, the market wage could exceed the subsistence wage. For Ricardo, the subsistence wage theory was protected by the argument that boom conditions produce counteracting forces, as high wages made it economically possible for the labourers to maintain large families. Hence within a generation (or even a few years) of the time of prosperity, the supply of cheap redundant labour reappears, and wage levels are once more depressed. In this way the Malthusian population theory acted as a crucial support for the classical doctrine of wages. Such a theoretical solution of the problem was quite unacceptable to Marx, though he did compliment Malthus for recognising that overpopulation was necessary to modern industry.[46] In Marx's own view, shortage of labour and a rising real income for the proletariat leads to a fall in profits, a lag in accumulation, and eventually a cutback in investment, and hence once more to substantial unemployment. Alternatively, high capital expenditure would eventually cause overproduction because of the inability of the masses to purchase more than their subsistence requirements. In either case, at a certain point profits are sharply reduced and the eventual effect of this is widespread unemployment. 'The capitalist mode of production meets with barriers at a certain scale of production...It comes to a standstill at a point determined by the profit, not by the satisfaction of social needs.'[47]

Marx's normal account of capitalism assumes widespread poverty on the part of the working class, though with varying income levels between different sections of the class. He rejected prevailing theories of underconsumption as tautologous and as suffering from more substantial weaknesses, but stressed the significance of mass poverty and the contradiction between production and consumption, and rejected the notion that capitalism could save itself by creating a rich domestic working-class market. In volume III of *Capital* he sought to explain the disproportion between production and consumption by the lack of effective demand on the part of the workers, which was partly determined by the laws of wages and partly by the fact that they were only employed when it was profitable for the capitalist class. 'The ultimate reason for all real crises always remains the poverty and restricted consumption of the masses as opposed to the drive of capitalist production to develop the productive forces as though only the absolute consuming power of society constituted their limit.'[48] Hence low mass consumption was one part of the total situation, the other side of which was the overproduction of capital.

The explanation of proletarian poverty, and thus the general explanation of crisis, is in terms of the unemployment which is inseparable from technological advance in both agrarian and industrial spheres. Given a chronic supply of unemployed labour – and here we remain within the terms of the Marxist system – it is clear that the employer is in a position to keep wages low. The pressure of the market, without legal compulsion, could, as Marx and Engels often complained, demoralise and divide the working class, making it difficult to organise a coherent and homogeneous proletarian political movement. They showed how competition forced those already working to overwork, and cited the high mortality rate, to which overwork contributed, amongst young workers. In the 1844 *Manuscripts* Marx had pointed out how, even in an economically advancing society, intense competition lowered the price of labour, and how, with the increase of workers, competition became 'all the more intense, unnatural and violent'. The workers caught the capitalist mania to enrich themselves. 'The more they wish to earn, the more they must sacrifice their time and carry out slave-labour, in the service of avarice completely losing all their freedom, thereby they shorten their lives'.[49] Driven by want, the workers compete with each other on the same bad terms, hindering class unification and forcing wages to contract even further. In normal times some workers do well, e.g. the fine spinners or craftsmen in exclusive unions, the more fortunate of the ordinary workers gain the minimum wage, and some earn less, living utterly brutish lives or dying. With such a favourable bargaining position the capitalists could call the tune, and it naturally became one of Marx's main purposes to organise the labour movement, nationally and internationally, so that its initiatives would not be destroyed by the workless.[50]

THE CAPITALIST

The unceasing progress of technology which, within capitalism, is the main source of proletarian misery, results from the activities of the capitalist. It is his unremitting pursuit of his own interest that has such dramatic historical effect. Marx portrayed him as a man dominated by the desire for profit, or the surplus value from which profit arises, which is the goal of capitalist production.[51] He isolated this desire as that which is typically capitalist: 'it is only in so far as the appropriation of ever more and more wealth in the abstract becomes the sole motive of his operations, that he functions as a capitalist, that is, as capital personified and endowed with consciousness and a will.'[52] He has historical value only as an agent or embodiment or personification of capital. Thus a specific aim, motive or function is chosen and isolated, and its consequences outlined and predicted, while other motives are excluded, at least for the time being. If a reasonable prediction is to be made in the real world, the other determinants of human behaviour would obviously have to be introduced at a later stage. The method of abstraction was defended also by J. S. Mill, who claimed that the 'geometrical approach', presupposing an arbitrary definition of man, yielded 'abstract truth' if successful, and that 'when completed by adding or subtracting the effect of the non-calculated circumstances, they are true in the concrete, and may be applied to practice'.[53]

Marx certainly wanted concrete and not abstract truth. He was not playing the methodological games of some modern economists, but was trying to disclose the dynamic elements underlying radical social change. It makes sense to ask whether his abstraction can bear the historical weight that he puts upon it. Even if one were to admit the historical validity of his 'bill of indictment' of the bourgeoisie, especially the English bourgeoisie, it would still be reasonable to ask whether capitalist qualities and drives were as deep-rooted and significant as he suggested, or whether pity or fear or anxiety or fellow-feeling might not restrain or complicate the quest for wealth. Is it conceivable that 'the capitalist' – or some capitalists – should pursue art or domestic happiness or the welfare of the poor or moderation in business as serious goals? To answer this question, and to determine its importance, we need to consider both the motivations or functions ascribed to the capitalist and their supposed sources, especially when they seem to derive largely from the confining and oppressive economic environment which they inhabit. If these are not as Marx described them, greed, egoism and avarice might continue without driving the system to destruction, and Marx's analysis would become the grounds of an empty prophecy.

Marx believed that the capitalist of history was subject to an overpowering lust for profit, and that divided and deviant individuals were generally insignificant. He regarded the non-class attributes or interests or loyalties of individuals as irrelevant to the historical process, and claimed that deviation from a class position has 'as little effect upon the class struggle as the secession of a few nobles to the *tiers état* had upon the French Revolution'[54] – a poor example in view of the actual significance of their secession. His typical capitalist is portrayed in strong, crude colours, which was necessary if his more ambitious predictions were to seem credible. He stressed the compulsive character of the capitalist's desires. The capitalist aims at the 'restless neverending process of profit-making', he has a 'boundless greed after riches' and engages in a 'passionate chase after exchange-value'.[55] The rhetoric tumbles boldly. 'Accumulate, accumulate! That is Moses and the prophets!'[56] For their insatiable greed Marx condemned the British capitalists as 'curs' and 'swine'.[57] Attempts to remove such furious appetites by moral persuasion would clearly be absurd.

Marx assumed the capitalist to be both greedy and driven on by the pressures of the competitive system. While the origins of greed are not explained satisfactorily, it is usually depicted as a product of society, and especially of the highly competitive capitalist system. Thus the power of appropriating exchange values awakens the greed for money, which is consequently no natural or innate human appetite.[58] The capitalist becomes, in fact, the victim or plaything of the economic and social order, whose demands he cannot resist. Capital governs the capitalist himself. Hence Marx wrote that the passion for wealth is, in the capitalist,

> the effect of the social mechanism, of which he is but one of the wheels...competition makes the immanent laws of capitalist production to be felt by each individual capitalist, as external coercive laws. It compels him to keep constantly extending his capital, in order to preserve it, but extend it he cannot, except by means of progressive accumulation.[59]

Marx did not analyse capitalism in terms of individual choices and attitudes, nor was his critique focussed on the moral shortcomings of the capitalists. To treat the capitalist as idiosyncratic or immoral was incompatible with his view of economic evolution as a process of natural history. From no standpoint was it less reasonable to 'make the individual responsible for relations whose creature he socially remains, however much he may subjectively raise himself above them'.[60] Marx sought to explain the system within which the capitalist psychology developed, and which made capitalist modes of behaviour appropriate and inescapable. The capitalist entered definite and unavoidable relations independent of his will and he did what it was his task or function to do. The conflict between the capitalist as purchaser and the labourer as seller of labour power is a conflict between equal rights. 'There is here, therefore, an antinomy, right against right, both equally bearing the seal of the law of exchanges.'[61] Each acts as the agent of a mode of production. Capitalists must buy and sell commodities at their values, which naturally clashes with the interests of sellers of the commodity of labour. Class conflict is inherent in their historical roles.

While the capitalist is greedy for money, he is no miser, accumulating to hoard. Presented in the truly moral science of political economy as the ascetic but extortionate miser, the 'working, sober, economical, prosaic industrialist',[62] the frugal and thrifty upholder of the Puritan ethic, certain desires nonetheless push him beyond the mere pursuit of accumulation. As time passes, avarice and the desire to get rich – the ruling passions during the early period of capitalist production – are complicated by the appeals of an extravagant life. The capitalist is increasingly tantalised by the thought of good living, so that there develops in his breast 'a Faustian conflict between the passion for accumulation, and the desire for enjoyment'.[63] In addition, the thirst for accumulation is fed by love of the power which money confers – an aspect of the desire to get rich which had been perceived clearly by Luther, for which he was complimented by Marx.[64]

The pressure on the capitalist to accumulate or perish was intensified, in Marx's view, by the falling rate of profit, which referred to an inherent, general tendency of capitalism, though one which might be counteracted in the short run.[65] The notion of the falling profit rate follows from the theories that the ratio of constant to variable capital regularly increases (with mechanisation) and that surplus value or profit is extracted from variable capital only, though alternatively the rate could fall because of a decline in the rate of surplus value, resulting from shortening of the working day or wage increases. The progressive decline in the 'relative magnitude' of variable capital not only increases the general level of unemployment, but it drives the capitalists into ever fiercer competition with each other, in the course of which old and inefficient enterprises are destroyed. It intensifies competition – both 'avarice and war amongst the avaricious'.[66] Planning and regulation, though attempted at times, and though sometimes successful, are incompatible with the competitive system. Capital and labour flow into the most advantageous areas, but their presence and competition quickly reduce its special profitability, and bring about an approximation to average profits in the various spheres of production. While it is possible for a particular capitalist to make a quick killing, any advantage he steals over his fellows is short-lived, as others follow suit and profits fall back again. Marx wrote that 'competition seeks to rob capital of the golden fruits of their power by bringing the price of the commodities back to the cost of production'.[67] He once suggested that falling profits may blunt the stimulus to gain, but he normally assumed that the capitalist, recognising that there were profits available for some, would leave his neighbour to bear the losses, and would assume that his world would not collapse until after he had gone. Preoccupied with his own gain, he would make as much as he could from the failing system. Driven on by 'sordid avarice' and desperate competition, each capitalist would continue to follow the law 'which gives capital no rest, continually whispers in its ear: Go on! Go on!'[68] In this frantic and ultimately unsuccessful effort to maintain profits the capitalists undermine the foundations of their power, and lay the grounds for radical social change.

While Marx stressed the potentially revolutionary effects of the bitter internal war between the capitalists, the falling profit rate was compatible with other, less far-reaching outcomes, if it was linked with a rise in the mass of profits. In fact, while there was a tremendous decrease in the price of finished articles during the late eighteenth and early nineteenth centuries – often without a comparative decrease in the costs of production[69] – total profits rose substantially, as Marx himself noted. If these tendencies continued, if the rate and mass of the surplus grew, the capitalists might still compete fiercely with each other, but their relations with the proletariat could become much more flexible, as the worker's impoverishment became unnecessary to the capitalist's survival, and the class structure of capitalism could reveal significant variations as a substantial middle class emerged, living off the surplus which arose out of labour's rapidly increasing productivity. These possibilities were observed by Marx in his later writings, though they were not incorporated into his theory of revolutionary political action.

THE SUFFERINGS OF LABOUR AND THE BREAKDOWN OF THE SYSTEM

Marx accepted and legitimised capitalism within his theory of history. He approved of Ricardo's clear-eyed cynicism, 'his having an eye solely for the development of the productive forces, whatever the cost in human-beings and capital values – it is precisely that which is important about him. Development of the productive forces of social labour is the historical task and justification of capital. This is just the way in which it unconsciously creates the material requirements of a higher mode of production.'[70] Capitalism's restless striving after a general form of wealth explains why it is productive: 'it is an essential relationship for the development of the productive forces of society. It only ceases to be so when the development of these productive forces themselves meets a barrier in capital itself.'[71] But its immense contribution to the productiveness of labour at the same time plants the seeds of its self-destruction. In a word, its economic success necessarily worsened the plight of labour and created a force whose future lay in a new world. High productivity and wealth, and the sufferings of the proletariat, were different sides of the same coin, twin poles of a contradictory world. Given such a vision, a pauperisation or immiseration (*Verelendung*) hypothesis seemed compelling, though as a matter of historical fact it did not apply, in the form commonly ascribed to Marx, to the advanced capitalist states. But, as there is a good deal of disagreement over what Marx both said and meant, and as his views were not consistent, a fuller characterisation of his claims is necessary.

Marx clearly indicated the various ways in which the employers were forced to worsen the situation of the proletariat. They sought the maximum possible labour from the labourer at the minimum possible cost. They sought to lengthen the working day as far as was physically possible, which would increase 'absolute surplus value', and rapidly introduced new and better machinery, which increased 'relative surplus value' by reducing the amount of time needed to cover the labourer's own costs. It was, he said, a basic tendency of capitalism to increase relative surplus value. With either an absolute or a relative increase, the rate of exploitation grows. And the actual sufferings of the workers mount as capital consummates its ends. In Marx's words, 'in its blind, unrestrainable passion, its were-wolf hunger for surplus labour, capital oversteps not only the moral, but even the merely physical maximum bounds of the working-day. It usurps the time for growth, development, and healthy maintenance of the body.'[72] What does this mean precisely in relation to the changing and variable conditions of the workers under capitalism? Are the various declarations about the wretchedness of proletarian life largely rhetoric, or are they – and are they intended to be – accurate historical or predictive statements? In considering the doctrine of increasing misery it should be observed that it has four possible meanings – which are not mutually exclusive – depending on whether the increase of misery is taken to be absolute or relative, and whether it refers to material standards or to psychological and other considerations. At some times Marx claimed that there was an absolute material deterioration, at others that there was no improvement in proletarian conditions, and at others again that there was a relative deterioration – in relation to social wealth in general, or to the wealth of particular groups. The plausibility of the hypothesis obviously depends upon the version which is adopted, and the concrete historical circumstances to which it supposedly applies. Any version – an absolute decrease of real wages, a relative decrease of real wages, an absolute or a relative increase of mental anguish, insecurity and so on – might apply to particular groups at particular times, but difficulties gather as soon as one version is seen to describe a general tendency of capitalism. The greatest difficulties face the narrow and extreme account of increasing misery as an absolute worsening of the worker's concrete, material position – a view which seems implicit in the general law of capitalist accumulation, and which is put forward directly by Marx on several occasions. In the 1844 *Manuscripts*, when the proletariat equalled 'absolute impoverishment', and in 'The Communist Manifesto', he predicted a fall in wages,[73] as well as a growth of insecurity and 'mental degradation', and a loss of craftsmanship and a growing hatred of work. In 1864, addressing the International, he opened his speech by denying that misery had decreased during the previous sixteen years: 'It is a great fact that the misery of the working masses has not diminished from 1848 to 1864, and yet this period is unrivalled for the development of its industry and the growth of its commerce.'[74] Whilst it is difficult to handle the large claim that the misery of the working masses did not diminish during this period, it can be conceded that in particular periods and amongst particular sections of the work force, real wages declined – for a time – and misery grew, and that overall the workers may have participated inadequately, and may have gained relatively less than the already advantaged, from the rapidly increasing national wealth. In his later writings, Marx seems increasingly to have recognised that wages would not necessarily fall, and could increase, though not quickly or substantially, under capitalism. His criticism focussed on the non-economic senses in which he believed the position of the proletariat to be worsening – the brutalisation and crippling of workers, insecurity, the obliteration of individuality and of intimate and independent groups, and the subordination of the whole of society to capitalist processes. In these and other respects conditions could worsen whatever the wage might be. On the narrower matter of wage levels, Marx tended to argue more that the proletariat was not maintaining its proportionate share of productivity, and that its position was deteriorating socially. The theory of the widening social gap holds that, although the average wage of the worker may increase, it decreases relatively to capitalist wealth, thus widening the gulf between the classes. In 'Wage Labour and Capital', written in 1874, he wrote: 'The material position of the workers had improved but at the cost of his social position. The social gulf that divides him from the capitalist has widened.'[75] Hence, while the theories of an absolute and a relative decline in proletarian economic levels were advanced at the same time, there is a growing tendency for Marx's general statements about capitalism to stress the latter line, while noting particular cases of absolute decline. Naturally the shift of focus, which brought the doctrine closer to reality, raised serious problems for a radical theory of social change, and Marx nowhere seriously tried to make the theory of the widening gulf, in conditions of rising general prosperity, the grounds of such a radical theory – apart from suggesting that these circumstances would bring more discomfort and discontent to the workers. The vital issue is the effect of new conditions for 'the lordship of capital over labour' on the incentives and drives of the workers to act in order to change the system drastically. Where they worked shorter hours for more pay – even though more under the domination of the machine – or where a rising surplus permitted a steady improvement of average living conditions, the social outcome would probably be very different from a situation in which masses of them were kept at a bare subsistence level, or where their conditions deteriorated. As Marx commented late in life: 'The rising surplus makes it possible for the capitalist class to exchange its tyranny for a benevolent despotism.'[76] And benevolent despotism, as many social theorists – including Mill – have pointed out, tends to be a poor stimulator of radical energy.

The belief that wages would tend towards a low and perhaps decreasing subsistence level was certainly not confirmed by the history of nineteenth-century England, which furnishes a clear example of long-term improvement of working-class wages and living conditions – whatever criticisms we may make of the extent or non-extent of income redistribution. Some defenders of Marx look after his interests by focussing on the more congenial and plausible aspects of his theory, and pretending that he never had a doctrine of pauperisation.[77] Others ascribe such a doctrine to him, and defend it by all manner of transparent devices, including statistical manipulation (to prove that real wages have not risen), assertions of the growing spiritual oppression or persisting exploitation of the class, and references to particular sections of the proletariat, where the long-run tendencies are manifesting themselves and salvation is yet to be found.[78] While some of these notions may form part of a plausible contemporary critique of capitalist society, they emerge, by and large, to protect a dogma, and are scaffolding on a collapsed foundation, lacking that compelling and imaginative fusion of technical economic analysis with revolutionary social theory which we find in Marx himself.

Whatever Marx's specific theses about wages, he regarded bourgeois society as a sorcerer which could no longer control the powers of the nether world which its spells had called forth. Its lack of control over the economy as a whole was most strikingly revealed during crises, which are presented as integral features of capitalist economies and evidence of their internal contradictions and irrationality. They had a positive regulatory function – that of getting rid of wasteful and uneconomic enterprises, of destroying redundant or unproductive capital, and thus of temporarily bringing the system back to equilibrium. Marx insisted that crises were features of the system when it was functioning normally, in conformity with its own principles. He strongly rejected the liberal view that crises were abnormalities, the results of mistakes or external interferences which prevented capitalism from working naturally. These fundamental disagreements over the nature of capitalist crises were, of course, part of wider disagreements over the viability and the future of capitalism itself.

In Marx's eyes, the decennial cycle of English industry, with average activity production followed by crisis and stagnation[79] reflected a large and growing disproportion between supply and demand which, though increased by money exchange, was in large part the consequence of the size of industrial enterprises. 'Large-scale industry, forced by the very instruments at its disposal to produce on an ever-increasing scale, can no longer wait for demand.'[80] The advanced productive forces of capitalism assume an almost autonomous character, driving the capitalists to overproduction and contributing to the anarchy and inefficiency of the system. Crises brought about a momentary and forcible solution of existing contradictions, thereby increasing the immediate stability of the system, but they weakened it profoundly in the long run. Marx wrote that 'these fluctuations...bring with them the most fearful devastations and, like earthquakes, cause bourgeois society to tremble to its foundations. In the course of this industrial anarchy, in this cyclical movement, competition compensates, so to speak, for one excess by means of another.'[81] These 'epidemics of overproduction' put bourgeois society on trial, each time more threateningly. Even in the lesser crises, 'whole hecatombs of workers' perish and the miseries of unemployment spread. Capitalism reveals itself as a system based upon unconcern with human need except when it is profitable, and produces too little and too unpredictably to satisfy decently and humanely the wants of the great mass. 'Not too much human wealth is produced. But at times too much wealth is produced in its capitalistic, self-contradictory forms.'[82] When the contradiction between the expansion of capital and the absolute development of the productive forces, and between human need and wasted wealth, becomes manifest in crises, the condition of the proletariat worsens and constitutes a standing indictment of the whole capitalist system.

> The modern labourer...sinks deeper and deeper below the conditions of existence of his own class. He becomes a pauper, and pauperism develops more rapidly than population and wealth. And here it becomes evident, that the bourgeoisie is unfit any longer to be the ruling class in society as an overriding law. It is unfit to rule because it is incompetent to assure an existence to its slave within his slavery, because it cannot help letting him sink into such a state, that it has to feed him, instead of being fed by him. Society can no longer live under this bourgeoisie, in other words, its existence is no longer compatible with society.[83]

Marx believed that his economic analysis showed that the end of capitalism was near. A constantly decreasing group of capitalists wrestled with each other and, as smaller enterprises were destroyed, competition disappeared, and huge centralised enterprises, perhaps dominated by 'one single capitalist' or 'one single corporation', emerged. At the same time, the growing body of workers, checked in their demands by the reserve army of the unemployed, which was necessarily created by the process of capitalist production itself, were impoverished, injured and united by the process of industrialisation. The extension of factory legislation hastened industrial change and thus hastened the crystallisation of conflict. 'It destroys both the ancient and the transitional forms, behind which the dominion of capital is still in part concealed, and replaces them by the direct and open sway of capital; but thereby it also generalises the direct opposition to this sway.' Technical advance increases the anarchy and catastrophes of capitalist production. The destruction of small industry destroys the last resources of the redundant population, and the last safety-valve of the whole social mechanism. 'By maturing the material conditions, and the combination on a social scale of the processes of production, it matures the contradictions and antagonisms of the capitalist form of production, and thereby provides, along with the elements for the formation of a new society, the forces for exploding the old one.'[84] Capital treated the workers simply as personified labour time, obliterating the distinctions between them and destroying their ties with society and nation, thereby destroying their illusions about capitalism as well. They were stripped naked, with no stake – physical, emotional or moral – in the social order, in which they barely existed. In addition, capitalist development forced educated members of the bourgeoisie into the proletariat, and thus contributed to the enlightenment of the oppressed class. The conflict images accumulate – 'more powerful labour armies' develop, with 'more gigantic instruments of war', and society becomes an 'industrial battlefield'.[85] Such, in Marx's common view, was the general tendency of capitalism. In his vigorous prose:

> One capitalist always kills many...Along with the constantly diminishing number of the magnates of capital, who usurp and monopolise all advantages of this process of transformation, grows the mass of misery, oppression, slavery, degradation, exploitation; but with this too grows the revolt of the working-class, a class always increasing in numbers, and disciplined, united, organised by the very mechanism of the process of capitalist production itself...Centralisation of the means of production and socialisation of labour at last reach a point where they become incompatible with their capitalist integument. This integument is burst asunder. The knell of capitalist private property sounds. The expropriators are expropriated.[86]

There are two crucial problems facing Marx's account of capitalist contradictions. One concerns whether or not the alleged contradictions are in fact irresolvable, and what it is that makes them sharp and decisive. For although Marx claimed that within capitalism the contradictions between distribution and production relations on the one hand, and productive forces on the other, were deep-rooted and irremediable, he does not establish the inability of the ruling elements to maintain the central institutions of the system in some form or other. He does not establish that they lack the economic resources or the knowledge or the will to offer some combination of economic goods, political concessions and ideological blandishments to potentially subversive forces, thereby blunting the edge of the contradictions, which presuppose that the elements of social life are at once more clearly defined and more limited in their possible developments than they in fact are. The failure to show in any convincing way that the basic contradictions are irresolvable within a capitalist or quasi-capitalist system is linked closely with a failure to show directly enough the means by which the allegedly irresolvable contradictions will necessarily destroy the system (and, presumably, a system might contain irresolvable contradictions for a very long time, without the emergence of a new historical form). For the destruction of capitalism must be the work of human agency – the proletariat – and thus it is assumed that the endemic contradictions discerned by the theorist will contribute strongly to the consciousness and the activity which will overcome them. It is here that Marx's view of class – closely related to but not utterly dependent upon economic conditions, including contradictions – is vital.

THE LIFE PROCESS OF CLASSES

Marx's economic analysis is not narrowly technical, but is set within, and helps sustain, a prophetic social theory, which invests it with concrete and far-reaching political implications. Economic analysis flows into the sociology of class and socialism. The key to social transformation lies in the necessarily antagonistic relations between classes, in which the conflict between forces and relations of production loses its abstract character and is given flesh. 'The very moment civilisation begins, production begins to be founded on the antagonism of orders, estates, classes and finally on the antagonism of accumulated labour and actual labour. No antagonism, no progress. This is the law that civilisation has followed up to our days. Till now the productive forces have been developed by virtue of this system of class antagonisms.'[87] The clash between classes is not random or accidental, but arises naturally and inescapably within the process of social evolution, wherever there exists private ownership of productive resources – classes are antagonistic entities between which long-term peace is not possible.[88] Their situations are distinct and incompatible. This assumption was integral to Marx's social analysis and was vital to his general prediction of the future of capitalism, though in fact he exaggerated the importance of classes in previous societies and in his own time, and exaggerated the rift between them.

It is possible to classify men in terms of a great variety of characteristics, and this very fact renders suspect any single basis of distinction which is also taken to represent the decisive general distinction between men. We create classifications for all kinds of purposes, without necessarily believing that any particular characteristic is primary, in the sense of being the ultimate or crucial or basic ground of human behaviour. We classify people as shareholders, farmers, professional men, manual workers, and so on, and as rich or poor, advantaged or disadvantaged; we distinguish people on regional or ethnic or cultural grounds, without claiming, at the outset, that these are more than statistical aggregates, more than individuals sharing some common, objective feature. But, of course, Marx was not offering a sterile piece of classification. He treated classes as real and active, though not fixed, entities, rather than as mere abstractions or hypothetical constructs conjured up by social scientists. Classes are the actual, immediate agents of historical change and the conscious determinants of the historical outcome. They set the general character of men's lives. Class relationships are narrow, limited and alienated, as class becomes an external and dominant force, blind to individuality. It 'achieves an independent existence over against the individuals, so that the latter find their conditions of existence predetermined, and hence have their position in life and their personal development assigned to them by their class, become subsumed under it'.[89] And this, Marx thought, was both a denial of man's humanity and a vital fact about the world – though his theory of class has been condemned as itself immoral, a spur to group hatred and revolution in a world which, presumably, neither needs nor can afford such destructive fantasies.

Classes are more than aggregates of individuals passively sharing some characteristic or attribute. They have specific traditions and ideologies, their members share vital loyalties and interests, and they have particular patterns of growth. Men do not select their view of the world from amongst equally competing alternatives, but are conditioned by their economic and social position to accept certain views of the world as natural. Their images of life, the very structure of their thought, are determined by forces outside their control. Class relations – and particularly relations between owners and non-owners (producers) – provide the essential clue to the understanding of society:

> it is always the direct relationship of the owners of the conditions of production to the direct producers – a relation always naturally

corresponding to a definite stage in the development of the methods of labour and thereby its social productivity – which reveals the innermost secret, the hidden basis of the entire social structure, and with it the political form of the relation of sovereignty and dependence, in short, the corresponding specific form of the state.[90]

It must be decided whether or not there were and are social realities corresponding to the classes defined by Marx, and whether or not such groups as did exist conceived their class interests in his sense, and behaved in accordance with those interests. Definitions of class do not automatically resolve questions about the nature of class interests and the appropriate behaviour of classes. For example, the proletariat, as defined objectively by Marx, has certainly shown a preference for economic progress over freedom, and has been far more strongly influenced by nationalist than by internationalist feelings. Major empirical questions must, then, be raised. Was there a united bourgeois class, pursuing its interests in the senses defined by Marx? Was the proletariat simply an idea, an abstraction, a mythical or *a priori* concept, endowed by Marx with a far greater historical significance than it had, or has ever had? Is it the product of faith and hope rather than of close social analysis? Did Marx falsely generalise from one historical setting to others? Was he an arrogant intellectual imposing a destructive vision upon diverse historical events? Moreover, how far did he himself recognise the shortcomings of his pure or simple notion of class? To consider these questions, we must first examine Marx's definition of class, which will enable us to determine how striking and dramatic his claims in fact were.

Though class was Marx's fundamental sociological concept, he did not spend much time on definition or on drawing his various observations together. After all, the political significance of class was not dependent upon careful analysis. Marx wanted to understand and assist the process of structural change in society. He was excited by the grand scheme of history, in which he saw class conflict, arising out of the incompatibility of objective class interests, as the dynamic force. His own explicit attempt to clarify his general notion – at the close of the third volume of *Capital* – remained unfinished. However, he did at least face certain problems, and rejected identity of source of income as a principle of classification, as it provided only segments of classes – occupational groups – resulting from the division of labour. It would, for example, make physicians and officials into separate classes. 'The same would be true of the infinite fragmentation of interest and rank into which the division of social labour splits labourers as well as capitalists and landlords – the latter, e.g. into owners of vineyards, farmowners, owners of forests, mine owners and owners of fisheries.'[91] It is worth noting, though, that these segments of classes may prove historically significant, especially as sources of division within the wider classes – a fact to which Marx frequently drew attention. Again, while there is great economic inequality between different classes, income and wealth are unsatisfactory definitional criteria. 'The size of one's purse is a purely quantitative difference, by which any two individuals of the same class may be brought into conflict.'[92] To Marx, a class was a group of men related in the same way to the system of production, in that they were either owners or non-owners of the means of production. The question of property is the life-question of any class, and of any definition of class. Classes are defined primarily through ownership of the means of production – itself a complex notion – which is naturally connected closely with the distribution of the rewards of labour. Slaves own nothing, even their labour; serfs own part of their labour and normally have freehold rights as well; proletarians possess labour or labour power; and the capitalists own the various materials, including labour power, from which they extract profit. Ownership and non-ownership provide a simple principle of stratification, but one which would involve the existence of only two classes. That is, in fact, Marx's pure model, to be approached in the immediate pre-revolutionary period. However, he was quite conscious of the complexity of class groupings at most times in most societies, and this created a need for other criteria than ownership/non-ownership to define and enumerate them. The additional grounds of distinction appear to be their sphere of production and source of income (in contradiction with the claim at the end of volume III of *Capital*) and, more loosely, their historical role -- whether or not they operate identifiably as separate groups.[93] Marx did not, in practice, apply clear-cut objective criteria to define social groups, but identified them by rule of thumb, narrowing and widening the boundaries of class in different contexts, and using terms such as 'fractions' and 'strata', and group labellings, such as lumpenproletariat (implying a mass of unco-ordinated individuals) and petit-bourgeoisie, which pushed aside the problem of whether or not they constituted classes in his own more formal sense.

The proletariat is the prime example or 'ideal type' of a class. Marx's account of it, and of other classes determinedly pursuing their objective class interests, was something more than a simple description of existing realities. He was anticipating a process of class development, under the pressure of specific economic forces. He described the transformation of the proletariat into a homogeneous force, consciously pursuing its real interests, in Hegelian terms, as the transformation of a class in itself into a class for itself, or alternatively, of latent into manifest interests. The vision becomes flesh in the form of a radical, class-conscious and homogeneous proletariat, though that achievement itself assumes both the development and the dissolution of other classes. Certain conditions are necessary for such a growth of class consciousness to occur. In seeking to explain why the French peasantry failed to become cohesive, why it remained inert, sharing a fate rather than a destiny, Marx indicated some of these:

> the great mass of the French nation is formed by simple addition of homologous magnitudes, much as potatoes in a sack form a sack of potatoes. In so far as millions of families live under economic conditions of existence that separate their mode of life, their interests and their culture from those of the other classes, and put them in hostile opposition to the latter, they form a class. In so far as there is merely a local interconnection among these small-holding peasants, and the identity of their interests begets no community, no national bond and no political organisation among them, they do not form a class. They are consequently incapable of enforcing their class interests in their own name.[94]

The peasants remained scattered, lacking community sense, and any political action undertaken by them was bound to be fragmentary, isolated or random.

The proletarians, unlike the French peasants, were not a mere agglomeration of separate individuals, but experienced conditions of life which were forging them into an internally cohesive and historically effective class. Economic and technical factors – concentrated and large-scale factory production, improved communications, growing misery or a widening gap with employers and owners, and the reduction of differentiation within the class – lead to political organisation and a common consciousness.

> Economic conditions had first transformed the mass of the people of the country into workers. The combination of capital had created for this class a common situation, common interests. This mass is thus already a class as against capital, but not yet for itself. In the struggle of which we have only noted a few phases, this mass becomes united, and constitutes itself as a class for itself. The interests it defends become class interests. But the struggle of class against class is a political struggle.[95]

The proletarians have little real choice in the matter, and individual variations are insignificant.

The question is not what this or that proletarian, or even the whole of the proletariat at the moment considers as its aim. The question is what the proletariat is, and what, consequent on that being, it will be compelled to do. Its aim and historical action is irrevocably and obviously demonstrated in its own life situation as well as in the whole organisation of bourgeois society today.[96]

Revolutionary class consciousness is ultimately forced upon the workers. The proletariat thus has a definite pattern of growth – from infancy to maturity, from differentiation to unity, from ignorance to knowledge, from an incoherent mass to a self-conscious class. In its early stages it sees the world very much as the capitalist does. It believes the claims and promises which he makes, and supports his attacks on the feudal order. Its illusions are not only natural, but contribute to progress. At this time, aggressive and radical proletarian demands must be classified as objectively counter-revolutionary, as they come before their time, before the proletariat as such constitutes a revolutionary force. However, capitalist ideology increasingly fails to satisfy the proletariat, as its sufferings and uncertainties grow under the system, and its developing aspirations are thwarted. It increasingly recognises the true nature of the class rules and standards whose universal validity is constantly asserted. More and more members of the class express or accept socialist critiques of the system. Marx insisted that several of the early nineteenth-century socialists – Sismondi, Saint-Simon, Fourier and Owen, for example – had played a significant part in revealing to the workers as much of the truth about capitalism as could be revealed at the time. But, like the self-confident French bourgeoisie of the late eighteenth century, the proletariat outgrew its old ideological dress, which then only constrained it. Utopian socialism becomes counter-revolutionary, holding men in thrall to the existing bourgeois society by encouraging the false belief that capitalism was capable of gradual, piecemeal and planned modification. Its fantastic pictures of a future society diverted the attention of the workers from the tasks at hand. As Marx wrote to Sorge in 1877: 'It is natural that utopianism, which before the era of materialistically critical socialism concealed the latter within itself as embryo, can now, coming belatedly, only be stale, silly and reactionary from the roots up.'[97] With the maturing of capitalism Marxism comes into its own as the doctrine of the self-conscious working class, and competing theories become dangerous heresies, which may have helped educate the proletariat, but now extend the life of the old order.

On the other side, a homogeneous ruling class is postulated. Marx often spoke of the bourgeoisie as if it was an entity. He made the

general point clearly in his discussion of the ruling ideas of the age in
The German Ideology:

> The ideas of the ruling class are in every epoch the ruling ideas,
> i.e. the class which is the ruling material force of society, is at the
> same time its ruling intellectual force. The class which has the
> means of material production at its disposal, has control at the
> same time over the means of mental production, so that thereby,
> generally speaking, the ideas of those who lack the means of mental
> production are subject to it...Insofar...as they rule as a class
> and determine the extent and compass of an epoch, it is self-evident
> that they do this in its whole range, hence among other things
> rule also as thinkers, as producers of ideas, and regulate the pro-
> duction and distribution of the ideas of their age: thus their ideas
> are the ruling ideas of the epoch.[98]

This state of intellectual domination by a united ruling class is not
commonly presented by Marx as being the normal state of affairs, as
rival classes have their own competing ideologies, and are rarely in a
condition of complete subordination. But I am concerned here with
the notion of a cohesive ruling class. Does this notion exaggerate the
unity and the common interests of the ruling groups? Are the concepts
of class and social polarisation too crude to grasp and explain the complex phenomena of political life, and even of political conflict?

Marx faced precisely this problem in his detailed historical studies.
In the first place, there is the image of two great historical contestants,
increasingly homogeneous internally and increasingly polarised from
each other, which emerges from his more polemical and prophetic
accounts of bourgeois society. This picture of conflict points to both the
essence of the existing clash – the role of certain participants is dismissed as marginal – and to the tendencies of social development.
Polarisation is obscured and incomplete in the present, but already its
future reality could be discerned clearly. The image, vital to militant
ideologies, is one of hard, sharp lines or cleavages, of oppressed against
oppressors, poor against rich, non-owners against owners, powerless
against powerful, liberators against gaolers. The ideology requires,
at its centre, the picture of a single foe, and can ill afford the equivocations, ambiguities and subtleties of the scholar, which may easily
weaken the determination and the self-consciousness of the suppressed
forces. The simple and stirring image of conflict need not be literally
true when stated: it adds to the class momentum and ultimately becomes
true in a literal sense. Yet the prophetic vision of a single vast division
within society, which many particular clashes both intimated and aided,
did tend to disintegrate under the impact of close historical research.

In part that research was intended to explain the absence of simple, devastating conflict, and here Marx pointed to the number of intermediate or transitional classes which were alive and active in his own time, and to the divisions, conflicts and vacillations within the ranks of the bourgeoisie and the proletariat themselves. The intermediate and vestigial classes obliterate the lines of clear conflict, entering into muddling coalitions and alliances with sections of the proletariat, and leading them along false trails. Marx noted much of this, and provided a great deal of subtle and complex analysis of class and society to explain many of the situations which confronted him, but his prophetic impulses remained powerful, and he continued to insist that multiple divisions, diversity and muddle were temporary features of social life, and that simple and fundamental conflict would come as capitalist contradictions approached their height.

THE INTERMEDIATE CLASSES

In 'The Communist Manifesto' Marx and Engels, after describing history as the history of class struggles, continued:

> In the earlier epochs of history, we find almost everywhere a complicated arrangement of society into various orders, a manifold gradation of social rank. In ancient Rome we have patricians, knights, plebeians, slaves; in the Middle Ages, feudal lords, vassals, guildmaster, journeymen, apprentices, serfs; in almost all of these classes again, subordinate gradations.[99]

In nineteenth-century England class relations were also complex, though English society was the most highly and classically developed in economic structure. 'Nevertheless, even here the stratification of classes does not appear in its pure form. Middle and intermediate strata even here obliterate lines of demarcation everywhere.'[100] The three main classes, in England at least, were those derived from the classical political economy, with its three factors of production – profit, rent, and wages. The corresponding classes, defined in terms of relationship to the means of production, were the bourgeoisie, the landlords, and the wage-labourers. Attempts to maintain the conditions of an ancient ascendancy, on the part of landowners, and older antagonisms, especially between peasants and landlords, persisted, overlapping and intermingling with the essential capitalist antagonism. In addition to these four classes, those most frequently discussed were the petit-bourgeoisie and the lumpenproletariat. Marx also referred to 'ideological classes', such as government officials, priests, lawyers and soldiers – groups not directly involved in the productive process, although they generally worked on behalf of the ruling class. Despite occasional conflicts of interest with the capitalists, they were dependent on them, and could normally be classified as part of the same class. The ideological class seems to comprise part of the surplus class identified by Marx in his latest writings. That class, made possible by the surplus capital available for consumption, included the whole range of those whom Marx deemed parasitic – accountants, lawyers, bookkeepers, educators and other ideologists, and managers, as well as criminals, vagabonds and servants. The surplus to be consumed made it possible for the bourgeoisie to imitate 'the feudal system of retainers'.[101] It is clear, however, that part of this group comprises functionaries in the new large-scale economic organisations, the salaried personnel of the new capitalism – commanders such as managers, foremen and supervisors, and bookkeepers, such as accountants and clerks. Problems are posed both for the prediction that classes will disappear in the future – will such categories of worker also disappear? – and for the theory of mounting class conflict itself. For, as Marx was aware, the multiplication of such personnel, living predominantly on revenue, thickened the middle of society, and increased the social security and power of 'the upper ten thousand'. An admittedly untidy mass of service workers and unproductive consumers emerged as capitalism matured, creating problems for the theory of social change which Marx never had an opportunity to adequately consider.

Capitalist societies are characterised by complex class differentiation, the character of which constantly alters. Marx distinguished eight classes in Germany in 1848, and if we use Engels's account of rural differentiation, it is possible to distinguish nine classes.[102] The activities of these diverse classes naturally confused the pure class struggle, especially in France, where Marx frequently invoked the peasantry, the petit-bourgeoisie, and the lumpenproletariat in his explanations of the tardiness of history. The inertia, egoism and attachment to traditions of the peasantry – 'the class that represents barbarism within civilisation'[103] – is often condemned in his writings. That class, harbouring conservative small-property illusions, was behind Louis Bonaparte's accession to power, which detached the state from its old class roots and softened the edge of class collisions. The 'property fanaticism' of the peasantry, and its frequent refusal to ally itself with the proletariat on proletarian, i.e. revolutionary, terms, has remained one of the key problems of communist parties in underdeveloped countries. The peasants live for themselves, without collective consciousness, and generally without any vision of change beyond that of increasing their own individual property.[104]

The shopkeepers, small traders, cafe proprietors, handicraftsmen, independent artisans, small farmers, and so on, who make up the petit-

bourgeoisie,[105] are portrayed as the protagonists of a mode of production
– a capitalism of small enterprises – which had no future. Consequently
their aspirations and their programmes were fantasies, which led them
into one of the cul-de-sacs of history. Nonetheless, they frequently
subverted decisive class action on the part of the proletariat, by
muddling proletarian leaders, and by running to the class enemy. They
believed themselves to be elevated above class antagonisms, and this
illusion itself helped blunt conflict. As a transitional class of democrats,
it was peculiarly vulnerable to parliamentary cretinism, which 'holds
those infected by it fast in an imaginary world and robs them of all
sense, all memory, all understanding of the rude external world'.[106]
Weak, unadventurous, selfish and sentimental, blind champions of law
and order, swayed by contradictory impulses and allegiances, these
mean-thinking mediocrities lacked heroic qualities, and could never be
the stuff of tragic works of art.[107] Marx's contempt for them matches
that of the great French novelists of the mid-nineteenth century. Moreover, when the little man did decide, his decision was almost invariably
for reaction and not for revolution. Trotsky used the theory of the
conservative petit-bourgeoisie to good effect in explaining Hitler's
seizure of power in the 1930s. He, the *wildgewordene Kleinburger* writ
large, answered their hysterical craving for status and property.[108] The
category of the petit-bourgeoisie served Marx and his followers as a
convenient and abusive residual category, the use of which enabled
crucial problems of social analysis and revolutionary strategy to be
far too easily brushed aside.

The most bitterly assailed minor class or stratum was the lumpenproletariat, which is portrayed as a demoralised mass, a collection of all
the decayed and the degenerate, without cohesion or consciousness. It
becomes, at times, a moral rather than a descriptive category. Marx
listed its human types savagely.

> Alongside decayed roués, with dubious means of subsistence and
> of dubious origin, alongside ruined and adventurous off-shoots of
> the bourgeoisie, were vagabonds, discharged soldiers, mountebanks,
> lazzaroni, pickpockets, tricksters, gamblers, maquereaux, brothel
> keepers, porters, literati, organgrinders, rag-pickers, knife-grinders,
> tinkers, beggars – in short, the whole indefinite, disintegrated
> mass, thrown hither and thither, which the French term *la
> bohème.*[109]

Occasionally this brazen crew played an important historical role because
it constituted an alternative labour force and 'a bribed tool of reactionary intrigue',[110] and could therefore threaten the proletariat and undermine its revolutionary zeal, as it did in France in the confusing times

between 1848 and 1851. In 1848 particularly its members betrayed the proletariat by acting as strikebreakers.

Marx believed, however, that the role of the intermediate classes was transitory, though they might disturb revolutionary developments for the time being. The surplus class was, he felt, effectively part of the capitalist class – though its mass, its diversity and its strategic position made it a very serious obstacle to the polarisation process within society at large – and the landowners were being gradually absorbed into it, by marriage, investment and the capitalisation of agriculture. Large landed property was becoming bourgeois. On the other side, and here the key case is France, the peasants and the petit-bourgeoisie are presented as increasingly battling against 'capital's secondary modes of exploitation' – the petit-bourgeoisie against the wholesaler and the peasants against usury.[111] According to the theory, the mid-nineteenth-century French peasantry had real interests in common with those of the urban proletariat, and in opposition to those of the bourgeoisie, though it was rarely clear to peasants that this was in fact the case. The petit-bourgeoisie was moved occasionally by radical slogans and by revolutionary enthusiasm, as Marx felt it was when the Montagne and the socialists united to form the social-democratic party early in 1849. But, as a class, it remained a doubtful ally and Marx looked forward more confidently to its disintegration under the impact of capitalism, when its erstwhile members would have become proletarian. The revolutionary or 'Anarchist' side in 1849 was held by Marx to be no less a coalition of different interests than the Party of Order. 'From the smallest reform of the old social disorder to the overthrow of the old social order, from bourgeois liberalism to revolutionary terrorism – as far apart as this lie the extremes that form the starting-point of the party of "Anarchy".[112] But the writing was on the wall, as the pressure of events was dissolving the transitional and intermediate classes, and would lead eventually to the emergence of a popular revolutionary force, none of whose members would have real or even imagined stakes in the old order.

CAPITALISTS AND PROLETARIANS

Marx sometimes condemned a crucial class for failing to act according to its objective class interests, a situation which, depending on the circumstances, he related to the underdevelopment of capitalism – which would also account for the resilience of intermediate classes – or to a specific disturbing influence, such as an outside occurrence or the actions of a particular individual or group interrupting what was assumed to be the 'normal' course of events. The broad lines of future development may be predictable or inescapable, given the particular assumptions made about economic trends and limits and about class psychology, but for Marx there was no all-embracing determinism such that all class action is equally inevitable, or inevitable at a particular time. As he informed Dr Kugelmann, the world historical struggle was not taken up only on condition of infallibly favourable chances. Accidents were significant, though they tended to balance out. 'But acceleration and delay are very dependent upon such "accidents", which include the "accident" of the character of those who at first stand at the head of the movement.'[113] It is obviously extremely difficult to state the relations between objective and subjective elements, or between the determined and the free parts of history, in general terms which are illuminating – normally such attempts produce either spongy platitudes, or mechanical and unreal dogmas. It is possible, however, to dismiss at once the extreme positions – that men can make history out of the whole cloth, and that men need to do nothing but wait. For Marx, constructive historical action presupposed both a certain background, a certain level of development of productive forces, and a certain adventurousness or readiness to take a chance. There is plenty of scope for tactical choices – and conflicts – and for political decisions, in terms of one's views of the present state of the system, which may in part be derived from the fate of particular class activity. Policy and behaviour may be condemned as reactionary or foolhardy, unnecessarily prolonging the life of the old order. At this stage conflicts frequently arise between those who assume the spontaneous, unformed development of a popular and successful radical movement, and the champions of revolutionary action, who may, like Lenin, take an elitist position, contemptuous of existing mass aspirations and sceptical that they would ever, unaided, challenge the old order. The issue cannot, of course, be settled in the abstract: the appeal to wait on history or the call to organisation and the revolutionary will each, in particular circumstances, be wise or absurd.

Marx's discussion of the heterogeneity of the two key classes, and their failure to act out their historical roles, is largely confined to France and England. Occasionally the bourgeoisie was forced into unity in the course of a struggle with another class. Critical situations could draw its various factions together. The June insurrection in Paris in 1848 and its 'bloody suppression', 'united, in England as on the Continent, all fractions of the ruling classes, landlords and capitalists, stock-exchange wolves and shop-keepers, Protectionists and Free-traders, government and opposition, priests and free-thinkers, young whores and old nuns, under the common cry for the salvation of Property, Religion, the Family and Society.'[114] But the persisting common interest of the bourgeois – in profit maximisation, through exploiting the proletariat by keeping wages down and increasing relative or absolute surplus value – was a common interest of a peculiar kind, as it forced them into internecine conflict. They split into factions, on hostile terms as competitors. The system could not satisfy them all. In Marx's words: 'if all the members of the modern bourgeoisie have the same interests inasmuch as they form a class as against another class, they have opposite, antagonistic interests inasmuch as they stand face to face with one another. This opposition of interests results from the economic conditions of their bourgeois life.'[115] He regarded the provisional government which was established after the February barricades as a compromise government, which was necessary because the class interests of the victorious forces were mutually antagonistic. He identified the component parts of the French bourgeoisie as the 'finance aristocracy' (bankers, stock-exchange and railway kings), the industrial bourgeoisie,[116] the landed proprietors,[117] the savants or 'so-called men of talent', and the Bonapartists, who barely qualified. 'They were not a serious faction of the bourgeois class, but a collection of old, superstitious invalids and of young, unbelieving soldiers of fortune.'[118] Such divisions could be of considerable historical importance. The break-up of the Party of Order into the Orleanist and Legitimist factions, behind which lay respectively capital and landed property, enabled Louis Bonaparte to seize power as the embodiment of peasant aspirations.

It was not simply material interests that set the factions apart from each other, although this was the crucial source of division. What divided the factions was:

> their material conditions of existence, two different kinds of property, it was the old contrast between town and country, the rivalry between capital and landed property. That at the same time old memories, personal enmities, fears and hopes, prejudices and illusions, sympathies and antipathies, convictions, articles of faith and principles bound them to one or the other royal house, who is there that denies this?[119]

Marx did not argue that it was the persistence of cohesive forces of this latter kind – prejudices, illusions, convictions, principles – that explained the tame submission of the bourgeoisie to Louis Napoleon. It is not that the class, for some reason or other, failed to act according to its objective interests: Marx is here rather equivocal as to what these objective interests were. At one point he suggested that the parliamentary republic was the political order representing a compromise (the only possible compromise) between the bourgeois factions. Here the different bourgeois species disappeared and the bourgeois genus was

revealed: the parliamentary republic represented an interest common
to the bourgeoisie as a whole, overriding, at least in theory, those more
specific interests which tended to fragment the class. In fact, the class
revealed great and disastrous heterogeneity, which lost it political power
and enabled a 'grotesque mediocrity' to rule and perfect the state power
as an 'appalling parasitic body'. Marx berated the ordinary bourgeois
for being 'always inclined to sacrifice the general interest of his class
for this or that private motive'. He noted that a number of representatives had deserted the party 'out of lassitude, out of family regard for
the state salaries so near and dear to them, out of speculation on minis-
terial posts becoming vacant (Odilon Barrot), out of sheer egoism'.[120]
These bourgeois are not simply personifications of economic categories –
or, at least, the economic categories have become very complex. He
accused the bourgeoisie as a whole of having sacrificed its general class
or political interests to 'the narrowest and most sordid private interests'.[121] The extra-parliamentary bourgeoisie in its turn 'declared unequivocally that it longed to get rid of its own political rule in order to
get rid of the troubles and dangers of ruling'.[122] And so parliament,
'left in the lurch by its own class',[123] succumbed to the executive power.

At some points during the analysis Marx suggested that the interests
of the bourgeoisie lay in giving the class struggle more 'elbow-room',
in maintaining rather than destroying parliamentary power, which was
their own power, and therefore in keeping the executive in a position
of dependence. Its failure to pursue its interest in this way prevented
the pure political expression of bourgeois class rule from emerging, and
thus prevented the antagonism of other classes from appearing in a
pure form. Yet he also suggested that the political nullity of the bourgeois class was the condition of continued exploitation and of the
peaceful enjoyment of its pleasures. Political power, its public or class
interest, troubled it – 'it was a disturbance of private business'.[124] Its
material interests demanded strong government which it itself was
incapable of providing. 'Industry and trade, hence the business affairs
of the middle class, are to prosper in hot house fashion under the
strong government.'[125] The bourgeoisie, terrified of the proletariat and
of the dangers of universal suffrage, mouthed constitutional phrases,
and acquiesced in the destruction of the constitution. Even the revolutionary bourgeoisie desired to 'prolong the constituent period with its
conditions, its illusions, its language and its personages and to prevent
the mature bourgeois republic from emerging in its complete and peculiar form'.[126] Engels offers a similar account of the frightened bourgeoisie
in his discussion of the Prussian representatives of that class in 1874 –
they could have done great things, given determination, but they ceded
rule to powerful allies and protectors, who would maintain economic

security and keep the proletariat in place. A special, Bonapartist, ruling caste emerges, resulting – in Engels's view – from the 'equilibrium between the bourgeoisie and the proletariat',[127] and the fears and uncertainties of the bourgeoisie. The value of a political authority which was apparently above classes and class conflict was indicated clearly by Marx in relation to the mid-nineteenth-century French bourgeoisie who, had they made their political rule complete, would have had to 'confront the subjugated classes and contend against them without mediation, without the concealment afforded by the crown'.[128]

Marx thus offered a rough explanation of the untidiness of the class struggle in France, and provided a much closer analysis of the fissures within the bourgeoisie than he did anywhere else.[129] The underlying explanation, in terms of the immaturity of capitalism, was coupled with a curious anger at the failure of the class to act as the bourgeoisie is supposed to act, and must act if the class struggle is to emerge in its classical form. It was failing in its historical duty. As a result of the muddling prejudices, beliefs, illusions and fantasies, the rich mystification and the fears and doubts, class conflict did not emerge clearly and directly, and the bourgeoisie did not contribute to the hypothetical historical process as strongly as they might, had they been mere personifications of economic categories.

It is not surprising that there is also some ambivalence in Marx's various accounts and analyses of the proletariat, whose vocation it was to overthrow the capitalist mode of production. Clearly it is misleading to speak of the proletariat as if it were an entity, endowed with a universal revolutionary mission. The role of the proletariat is a role which some men – proletarians or socialist intellectuals – ascribe to masses of others, who are divided and influenced in various ways, and whose situations are rarely, if ever, identical in all major respects. Some are revolutionary and visionary, whilst others are conservative, fiercely holding on to what they have. In explaining the failures of the proletariat, whether they are failures of excessive adventurism or undue caution, Marx pointed frequently to the objective economic conditions. The popular leaders in the French Revolution, for example, were dreamers whose ideals were unrealisable on the existing economic base.

> The Revolution was a 'failure' only for the mass which did not find in the political 'idea' the idea of its real 'interest', whose real life-principle did not therefore coincide with the life-principle of the Revolution; the mass whose real conditions for emancipation were substantially different from the conditions within which the bourgeoisie could emancipate itself and society.[130]

Robespierre and Saint-Just looked backwards to what was irretrievably lost and not forward to the emerging future. They failed to understand that man 'cannot be the man of the ancient republic any more than his economic and industrial relations are those of the ancient times'.[131] Given a particular view of the normal process of development, certain aspirations and programmes are at once consigned to the byways and dead ends of history.

Proletarian defeat and proletarian conservatism are explained occasionally by the absence of necessary economic conditions – a serious proletarian programme is impossible when capitalism is hardly developed and the proletariat virtually non-existent. Defeat may prove highly instructive, as Marx believed the defeat of the Paris proletariat in 1848–1849 had been. It had lost thereby many illusions – what succumbed to defeat were 'the pre-revolutionary traditional appendages, results of social relationships which had not yet come to the point of sharp antagonisms – persons, illusions, conceptions, projects from which the revolutionary party before the February Revolution was not free, from which it could be freed, not by the victory of February, but only by a series of defeats'.[132] Lack of revolutionary effort, as much as its defeat, is explained by the relative underdevelopment of economic phenomena. Engels wrote that when the class was not ripe for emancipation, 'it will in its majority regard the existing order of society as the only one possible and, politically, will form the tail of the capitalist class, its extreme Left wing'.[133] The proletariat will not and cannot destroy capitalism before it is ready for destruction – an assertion which is rescued from circularity because the circumstances in which capitalism is ready for destruction are indicated, albeit roughly.

The obvious and important problem here is that of deciding when the proletariat is ripe for emancipation, when it can reasonably make a fundamental assault on the system. Such knowledge, which is vital to correct proletarian action, is not derived simply from theoretical analysis, but from practice – including unsuccessful practice – as well. A too optimistic assessment of chances will lead to adventurism, defeat and perhaps excessive cost to the growing proletarian movement, whilst undue caution produces opportunism. It was this latter danger which especially concerned Marx as a tactician and political organiser. It often seemed to him that the workers were spineless, ignorant of relevant facts and blind to the possibilities of their situation, and that their ignorance and blindness were culpable and were not simply a reflection of economic underdevelopment. He believed that some proletarians in his own time mistook their interests and failed to seize their opportunities, often remaining too close to the bourgeois radicals. For example, he condemned the Paris proletariat for accepting the leadership of the democratic petit-bourgeoisie in 1850, and accepting the enervating and 'classless' slogan of fraternity, although their secondary position was understandable in terms of the industrial and commercial prosperity of the period.

> By letting themselves be led by the democrats in face of such an event and forgetting the revolutionary interests of their class for momentary ease and comfort, they renounced the honour of being a conquering power, surrendered to their fate, proved that the defeat of June 1848 had put them out of the fight for years and that the historical process would for the present again have to go over their heads.[134]

This line of thought constantly appears in his discussions of the English working class. Good working conditions were, he felt, undermining potential revolutionary energy. The workers were suffering from the delusion that piecemeal progress could satisfy their long-term interests, and they were encouraged in their uncritical reformism by temporary prosperity and by some trade union leaders. In 1879 Marx presented a judgment which he had made many times during the life of the International. 'The English working class had been gradually becoming more and more deeply demoralised by the period of corruption since 1848 and had at last got to the point when it was nothing more than the tail of the Great Liberal Party, i.e. of its oppressors, the capitalists. Its direction had passed completely into the hands of the venal trade union leaders and professional agitators.'[135] It was a constant danger, in capitalist society, that the proletariat might be content with 'forging for itself the golden chains by which the bourgeoisie drags it in its train'.[136] Yet faith in the masses could be maintained by denunciation – often facile and unfair – of particular working-class leaders. Ultimately corrupting influences would be swept away. The result has been a persisting ambiguity in Marxist explanations of proletarian conservatism – bad leaders and/or an enfeebled proletariat, which had sold out on a massive scale, and which may, indeed, need a substitute, pure party or group, standing in for the actual, historical class with its undeveloped impulses. Explanations for the common conservatism of the class have varied, like those of Marx himself, between deterministic analysis of social trends, which explains class inaction in terms of its immaturity, which is understandable in terms of the economic conditions, and bitter, angry assaults on proletarian betrayal and egoism, or that of the leaders. The difference is, however, partly one of emphasis, in that economic underdevelopment can be used to explain tactical faults and moral shortcomings, though Marxists, like other revolutionaries, have not been content to put all the weight on men's circumstances. Sometimes the fault has seemed to lie less in men's stars than in men themselves.

Marx's attacks on opportunism sometimes emphasised the division between the labour aristocracy and the mass of the working class. He also stressed other sources of division, which made it extremely difficult to organise a united labour movement. In England, as Engels had noted already in 1844, the key division was that between the English and the Irish. Emigration from Ireland provided a demoralised mass of labourers whose subsistence level was extremely low, and who were therefore able to undercut the English. To economic was added nationalistic hostility.

> Every industrial and commercial centre in England now possesses a working class divided into two hostile camps, English proletarians and Irish proletarians. The ordinary English worker hates the Irish worker as a competitor who lowers his standard of life. In relation to the Irish worker he feels himself a member of the ruling nation and so turns himself into a tool of the aristocrats and capitalists of his country against Ireland, thus strengthening their domination over himself. He cherishes religious, social and national prejudices against the Irish worker. His attitude towards him is much the same as that of the 'poor white' to the 'niggers' in the former slave states of the U.S.A. The Irishman pays him back with interest in his own money. He sees in the English worker at once the accomplice and the stupid tool of the English rule in Ireland. This antagonism is artificially kept alive and intensified by the press, the pulpit, the comic papers, in short by all the means at the disposal of the ruling classes. This antagonism is the secret of the impotence of the English working class, despite its organisation. It is the secret by which the capitalist class maintains its power. And that class is fully aware of it.[137]

The Irish thus constituted a distinctive sub-proletariat – concentrated, demoralised and more vulnerable than their English fellows – which worked against the emergence of a homogeneous and class-wide socialist movement, and provided capitalism with a mass of material eminently fitted for exploitation.

Marx offered several explanations of the rift between the labour movement and socialism, which was revealed in the failure of homogeneous labour movements to develop sufficiently radical perspectives, and in serious divisions within the class itself. Some explanations focussed on economic realities – the failure of contradictions to mature, the absence of devastating crises, and the widening of the boundaries of the capitalist system through imperialism, and, especially in the case of England, industrial and trade monopolies in other parts of the world. Explanations in terms of competition between sectors of the proletariat, opportunism and laziness, and the influence of treacherous and conservative leaders were related closely to these economic phenomena, without being fully explained or determined by them. Within the working class economic progress fostered divisions between the 'labour aristocracy' and the mass of workers, who were often bemused and manipulated by the contented. The subdivisions of the class contributed to the maintenance of order. Racial and national antagonisms persisted, and emigration detached from Europe many of its radical sons. An ideology of social harmony and gradual progress spread, as key sections of the proletariat came to believe that desired social changes could be brought about by peaceful constitutional means.

4 Politics and social change

In 1845 Marx drew up a draft plan for a work on the modern state, which was to contain a consideration of some of the key issues of contemporary political theory. The proposed plan included sections on 'the origin of the modern State or the French Revolution', 'the self-conceit of the political sphere', 'state and civil society', the representative state, the rights of man, individual freedom and public authority, the federal system, parties, the division of power and 'suffrage, the fight for the abolition of the State and of bourgeois society'.[1] Things were left there. Neither Marx nor Engels offered a direct and detailed analysis of the role and character of the political institutions of capitalist society, and the degree to which those institutions might be capable of radical implementation and transformation. It is difficult to reduce their scattered and diverse observations to any consistent general theory, partly because different problems and different enemies were confronted at different times, and partly because the views of the two authors diverged in some crucial respects. But there is a distinctive Marxist theory of the state and of politics, and it is one which involves a rejection, or at least a radical redefinition, of the terms of the normal liberal discussion.

In some respects Marx was the most anti-political of social theorists. He rejected the explanation of events in political – or, more generally, ideological – terms and, frequently, doubted that existing political institutions could function as instruments of radical change, or as components of a new social order. The exercise of political skills plays a small part in his account of history. In his history, there are no creative political artists, moulding the clay of contingency and circumstance, and themselves determining events. Explanations of events in political terms, like political institutions themselves, fitted his own society. But they and the issues of traditional political philosophy – the rights of man and the limits of the state, freedom and order, law, sovereignty – would disappear, along with the world whose conflicts, egoism and inadequacy they reflected, and helped sustain.

POLITICS AND THE ILLUSION OF THE EPOCH

Marx's theory of ideology challenges sharply some of the main claims and assumptions of liberal politics, and it is therefore necessary to examine historical materialism again from this particular angle. His theory of ideology is neither simple nor internally consistent. It is unsystematised and contains numerous contradictions and ambiguities. The views of history against which he directed his main criticisms contemptuously dismissed economic factors, if they noticed them at all. 'The exponents of this conception of history have consequently only been able to see in history the political actions of princes and states, religion and all sorts of theoretical struggles, and in particular in each historical epoch have had to share the illusion of that epoch.'[2] Against such superficialities Marx stressed the distinction between material and ideological forces and processes, and the links between them which explained the emergence, the spread and the decline of particular ideas. In its more aggressive version, historical materialism portrays ideas, laws and political struggles as parts of a façade beneath which immense, powerful forces were at work – forces which Marx sometimes described in builder's metaphor as the substructure from which the derived superstructure grows. In *The German Ideology* the material substructure is equated with bourgeois or civil society, whose anatomy was to be sought in political economy. The Scottish and French historians of the preceding century are praised for giving a materialist basis to history, for writing 'histories of civil society, of commerce and industry'.[3] Writers such as Fergusson and Millar had argued strongly for the view that the most powerful influence on thinking was the manner in which men made their living. Marx followed them in claiming that the forms of consciousness had their roots in the area of human labour and the satisfaction of needs. Many general statements make essentially this point, e.g. the statements that production and commerce are the basis of social institutions and beliefs, or that the mode of production determines the general character of social, political and economic life.

On the face of it, the theory is clearly reductionist. According to it, certain superficial or derivative social phenomena are explained in terms of others. Ideas are described variously as 'reflexes', 'echoes', 'copies' or 'sublimates' of something else. Marx, like Freud or Pareto, believed that he had unmasked the roots of beliefs, exposed the unconscious grounds of thought. His general view is straightforward enough. It obviously conflicts fundamentally with the typical liberal conception of the nature and the importance of ideas. If social existence determines consciousness and determines it in such a way that the individual ordinarily cannot correctly perceive his world, then the belief that men correct error through discussion and experience, through some kind of autonomous rational process, cannot survive. Marx certainly claimed as much as this.

But he did not commit himself to the extreme or hard technological version of historical materialism, according to which the forces of production determine everything else. Those who ascribe such a view to him can refer to a handful of crude or simplistic general statements, especially the well-known passage in *The Poverty of Philosophy* which reads: 'Social relations are closely bound up with productive forces. In acquiring new productive forces, men change their mode of production, in changing their way of earning their living, they change all their social relations. The hand mill gives you society with the feudal lord; the steam-mill society with the industrial capitalist.'[4] The theory imputed to Marx would hold, not merely that tools and techniques are the key causal factors in social change, but that they produce a particular form of the division of labour and particular social relations, which in turn produce a particular ideological superstructure. The secondary elements correspond to the productive forces and are dependent upon them. The relationship is presented as functional in a technical sense – variables are correlated in such a way that changes in one can be systematically related to changes in the other, with the productive forces being, in this case, the independent variable.[5] Yet Marx clearly recognised what are often presented as serious objections to his view of social causation – that technology must itself be caused, that much more than the productive forces determines social change, and that political and socio-economic relations are necessary for the very existence of technological activity. His economic phenomena are not simple in character, and the relations between economic and ideological phenomena are described both variously and imprecisely, though it is made quite clear that the relationship is a dialectical and a dynamic one. Occasionally he spoke of economic conditions 'determining' ideology, and of ideology 'reflecting' economic conditions – claims which are not identical – but at other times the connection appears to be a much looser one, e.g. his reference to the fact that 'Greek art and Greek epic poetry are tied to specific forms of economic development',[6] or his use of such linking terms as 'bound up with'. The elastic nature of the concept of economic conditions emerges clearly, especially in discussions of science and art – the spheres most difficult to subordinate to any vulgar materialism. In *The German Ideology* Marx and Engels wrote: 'Even this "pure" natural science is provided with an aim, as with its material, only through trade and industry, through the sensuous activity of men.'[7] Of Raphael, they stated:

> Raphael as much as any other artist was determined by the technical advances in art made before him, by the organisation of society and the division of labour in his locality, and, finally, by the division of labour in all the countries with which his locality

has intercourse. Whether an individual like Raphael succeeds in developing his talent depends wholly on demand, which in turn depends on the division of labour and the conditions of human culture resulting from it.[8]

Hence all ideas can be explained within the theory by widening the causal factors to include available techniques, problems to be solved and so on. Everything is thereby conditioned, if not determined, by some material factor or other, as the notion of material or economic conditions becomes wide and fluctuating.

At the other end of what must be seen as an interactive process, ideology is conceded some independence and some causal significance, as it is explicitly by Engels in a letter to Conrad Schmidt in 1890, in which he tried to provide a sophisticated and plausible general statement of the relations between ideology and economic conditions.[9] His statement suggests, not merely that there is no simple, direct cause and effect relationship between economic conditions and ideology, but that the ideological sphere itself may be differentiated and heterogeneous. It, as much as capitalist society, is subject to uneven development, with different parts more or less remotely attached to the economic structure, more or less significant in maintaining or undermining existing orders, more or less penetrated by class interests. The thrust, as in so much of classical Marxism, is towards serious empirical investigation rather than towards the multiplication of supposedly adequate general statements. The revised general statements offered by Engels are banal and uninformative, less bold and interesting than the highly distinctive – and more questionable – claims of early historical materialism. Engels stressed interdependence but claimed that economics retains the last word – whatever that means. We are left with evasive, almost vacuous formulations, crediting ideas with relative independence and economics with ultimate power, though in fairness one must add that by their works, rather than their definitions, should they be judged.

The questions of monocausality and interdependence have caused Marxists a good deal of trouble. This is not surprising, given that the classical theory asserts a close relationship between two kinds of phenomena, but is unclear both as to their composition and the (varied) connections between them. The notion of the economic conditions is, to begin with, a spongy one and, as soon as interaction is admitted, those conditions are partly made up of those things (ideas) which they are supposedly determining. Once there is a 'complex totality', the parts of which interact dialectically, it becomes extremely difficult to fix limits to the role of ideology, which is interwoven with economic and social phenomena as a whole. These problems arise directly out of Marx's own approaches and analyses which, as any number of modern Marxists properly insist, were utterly opposed to any sharp, mechanical, abstract separation of two elements of social life. Marx treated man, the labourer, as a conscious animal, in whose life intellectual and material production interacted, and interpreted the relations between material and ideological factors concretely and dynamically. But while a continuing process of mutual interaction – as in all organic bodies – is compatible with some notion of 'basic' or 'determining' causes, it naturally becomes difficult to separate out their weight and their precise effects in each particular situation.[10]

A more specific problem, central to Marxian political strategy, concerns the relations between class, and especially proletarian, consciousness and the objective structure, which conscious men help create. Marx and Engels generally related moral, political, legal, philosophic, religious and economic ideas to classes and class interests, rather than to the economic substructure indiscriminately. These ideas serve normally as unconscious rationalisations or defences of class interests. Marx stressed the need to distinguish 'the phrases and fancies of parties from their real organism and their real interests, their conception of themselves from their reality'.[11] There is thus a difference between beliefs on the one hand, and realities and interests on the other. Ideology distorts reality and normally involves self-deception as well, for the ideologist is as a rule unaware that he believes in illusions. In *The German Ideology* Marx and Engels refer to the fact that 'in all ideology men and their circumstances appear upside down as in a camera obscura'.[12] The emphasis in Marxist social theory is on illusions, the world of appearances, the inability of men to see the world as it truly is. It holds that the material or economic roots of social conflict must be separated from the 'ideological forms in which men become conscious of this conflict and fight it out'. It is thus possible to dismiss 'all struggles within the State, the struggle between democracy, aristocracy, and monarchy, the struggle for the franchise, etc., etc.' as 'merely the illusory forms in which the real struggles of the different classes are fought out among one another'.[13] Later 'political' and 'religious' motives are described as forms of true motives.[14] The motives which people impute to themselves, the ends they consciously seek, are dismissed as misleading and superficial. Men are bemused. Scratch away the coating of principles, the universalist delusions, and the naked class interests which underlie them will be clearly revealed.

The problem here, which has been raised earlier, and will be taken up again later, concerns the appropriateness of proletarian false consciousness at any particular time, and the circumstances in which, and the means whereby, a true proletarian consciousness can emerge. Marx writes that consciousness must be explained by the contradictions of material life,[15] but does not say very much about how precisely a revolutionary consciousness grows from, or is provoked by, economic contradictions. As his political writings show, he does not regard consciousness as simply reflective and dependent, and the actual diversity of ideology, in terms of progressiveness, proximity to economic conditions and interests, and form and degree of restraint by economic conditions, presumably gives consciousness some scope and some independence in particular circumstances. With a relatively undeveloped economic and class structure, the veil of false consciousness cannot be removed, partly because the realities (the contradictions) of capitalism are still not clear-cut. It is not that men are simply confused in a situation which already exists: capitalist reality itself is not fully developed. But the proletariat's consciousness is also a constitutive part of capitalist reality, and its increasing focus upon the true character of the objective structure is crucial if that structure is to be transformed. Consciousness does not fit reality by passively reflecting it – whatever that would be like. Within the terms of Marxism, the degree to which, and the points at which, thought can critically grasp reality cannot be settled in abstract doctrines or in detailed formulae, but must be resolved in political practice itself.

Marx had, nonetheless, to confront those who thought that consciousness, mind, morality or intelligence were free, and could conjure up new worlds out of nothing. He played down the power of the human will in his attacks on utopian socialism and anarchism, which are presented as sharing a romantic voluntarist assumption that men could choose, at any time, and regardless of the 'objective situation', whatever social arrangements they desire. It is the characteristic delusion of political thought that it fails to recognise the element of constraint or determination imposed on man by the economic system, social relations, ideologies and other parts of class society, and that, as a consequence, it imputes an unreal freedom to him. 'The principle of politics is the will. The more partial, and the more perfected, political thought becomes, the more it believes in the omnipotence of the will, the less able is it to see the natural and mental limitations on the will, the less capable is it of discovering the source of social evils.'[16] Man, in an abstract and unreal form, was credited with imaginary powers and choices – by liberals, anarchists, utopian socialists and Hegelians, in their various ways. Marx rejected Hegel's view of punishment as the right of the criminal on the ground that Hegel, 'instead of looking upon the criminal as mere object, the slave of justice, elevates him to the position of a free and self-determined being'. He added a crucial question: 'Is it not a delusion to substitute for the individual with his real motives, with multifarious social circumstances pressing upon him, the abstraction of "free will" – one among the many qualities of man for man himself?'[17] Such assumptions might prove politically useful, however, as in the case of authorities who criticised and punished defective – and supposedly responsible – individuals, focussing attention upon them rather than on the system or structure whose servants they were.[18] Marxian theory challenged the dominant structures, and notions of individual guilt and individual responsibility were foreign to Marx's basic doctrines.

The fundamental thrust of the argument is that man – the criminal, the proletarian, the dominant capitalist even – is the slave of circumstance, an object and not a subject, a being who is not individually responsible for his actions. It is, of course, true that man is always in a determinate social situation, and always in relationships independent of his will, when he acts, whether or not he is free, and whether or not he is morally responsible. Marx claimed – and this is an old but true claim – that man enters a world which is already formed and structured, and that this world at once forms and limits him, destroying certain potentialities and depriving him even of powers and freedoms which are his theoretically. He claimed that human autonomy and moral responsibility had – and could have – no concrete reality in the present society, which leads on to crucial questions concerning the exact conditions and forces which restrict man, whether and how far they are removable, what would be required for man to be autonomous, and what he would then be like.

It was clear to Marx and Engels that men could not become autonomous and human within capitalist society, and that its political mechanisms, including representative institutions, were conceived by the dominant groups as means of maintaining the existing order, and not as vehicles for its transformation. Marx and Engels tended to dismiss democratic constitutions and parliaments as 'political shams' and 'mock democratism', propping up the real despotism of capital. They remained ambivalent about the likelihood of fundamental, gradual social change through existing institutions, and were uncertain how far reforms could go in peacefully subverting the system. The socialist movement naturally regarded the capitalist state with a good deal of suspicion and hostility.

THE CAPITALIST STATE

Marx and Engels did not see the state in identical ways. Avineri points the contrast sharply, claiming that Marx conceived the modern state as 'a perpetual tension between the idea of universality, ideally a bulwark against the particularist interests of civil society, and these antagonistic interests themselves', whereas for Engels, allegedly, it was 'nothing more than an external organization for coercion mechanistically directed by the dominant economic powers'.[19] Avineri's comments properly warn against the assumption that there was one simple Marxist view of the state, and focus on the contradiction upon which Marx believed the state to be based. But Avineri sharpens the contrast too much. At many points throughout his study he counterposes a philosophically profound Hegelian Marx to a more vulgar and shallow Engels, working from a quite different tradition, so that it becomes a manifest intention to free Marx from the incubus of Engels (and several other incubi besides). However, Marx was the heir of non-Hegelian traditions as well, and made plenty of random observations which do not derive from any of the traditions which he acknowledged. In relation to the state, at many points he treats it 'mechanically' as a machine of repression and as a key instrument in the class struggle. It may reflect 'a perpetual tension' between the idea of universality and the egoism and partialities of civil society, but this neither defines nor limits its function. In addition, although Engels did present the state as essentially a repressive institution serving class ends, he indicated frequently – as did Marx – that the state develops special interests, that bureaucratisation occurs and that the political force develops a momentum of its own. In his introduction to the 1891 edition of *The Civil War in France* Engels wrote: 'Society has created its own organs to look after its common interests, originally through simple division of labour. But these organs, at whose head was the state power, had in the course of time, in pursuance of their own special interests, transformed themselves from the servants of society into the masters of society.'[20] In *The Origin of the Family* he argued that the state, which had become necessary because tribal institutions were incapable of harmonising conflicting class interests, became increasingly a special organism, standing above society.

> But in order that these antagonisms, classes with conflicting economic interests, might not consume themselves and society in sterile struggle, a power seemingly standing above society became necessary for the purpose of moderating the conflict, of keeping it within the bounds of 'order', and this power, arisen out of society, but placing itself above it, and increasingly alienating itself from it, is the state.[21]

The state is here presented as a mechanism which emerged to protect the common interests of society, primarily through moderating class conflict, and as one which develops its own peculiar interests, which are not always simply those of the ruling class. Nonetheless, even here the common, vulgar Marxist notion of the state – that treated by Avineri as the conception of Engels – finds an entrance, in that the maintenance of the social and economic order is obviously of greatest moment to the wealthy and the powerful, who have most to lose from conflict.

Situations in which the state is 'classless', or not subject to the domination of the appropriate class, are seen by Engels as atypical. The exceptional periods were those in which, because of the roughly equal strength of the warring classes, the state assumed a position of comparative independence. The examples cited include the absolute monarchies of the seventeenth and eighteenth centuries, which allegedly held the balance between nobility and burghers, and the new German Empire under Bismarck, in which 'capitalists and workers are balanced against each other and equally cheated for the benefit of the impoverished Prussian cabbage junkers'.[22] The key instance of this atypical independence of the state was under Louis Napoleon's Second Empire, which Marx analysed in detail. The nationalistic regime, representing the latent interests of the peasantry, and characterised by the enormous development of the state as a parasitic apparatus, rested on a stalemate between bourgeoisie and proletariat. 'In reality, it was the only form of government possible at a time when the bourgeoisie had already lost, and the working class had not yet acquired, the faculty of ruling the nation.'[23] Divisions between the bourgeoisie and the political rulers easily develop. Engels wrote to Marx in 1866 that it was becoming clearer to him that

> the bourgeoisie had not the stuff in it for ruling directly itself, and that therefore where there is no oligarchy, as there is here in England, to take over, for good pay, the management of state and society in the interests of the bourgeoisie, a Bonapartist semi-dictatorship is the normal form. It upholds the big material interests of the bourgeoisie even against the will of the bourgeoisie; but allows the bourgeoisie no share in the power of government.[24]

In a number of significant cases, including some of the most highly developed capitalist societies, there is no clear-cut class rule – the lack of a dominant class is reflected in state power, which may even serve the interests of some class other than the key contenders. In addition to these situations of class balance, Marx and Engels noted a general tendency towards bureaucratisation, towards differentiated and specialised groups of officials, recruited from all classes, which became increasingly unresponsive to popular control.[25] These cases of blurred class rule and of non-class despotism, and the recognition of bureaucratic tendencies, make it clear that classical Marxist discussion of the state is more complex and varied than many of its critics assume.

However, the state is held to be, in 'all typical periods', the property or instrument of the dominant class. 'The cohesive force of civilised society is the state, which in all typical periods is exclusively the state of the ruling class, and in all cases remains essentially a machine for keeping down the oppressed, exploited class.'[26] The general historical function of the state is to safeguard the mode of production and maintain order through its characteristic coercive weapons. In the case of the modern representative or parliamentary state the bourgeoisie had gained exclusive political sway. 'The executive of the modern State is but a committee for managing the common affairs of the whole bourgeoisie.'[27] It is used by that class in an effort to maintain the existing economic system and social structure, which is, from its viewpoint, the best of all possible worlds. With the development of capitalism, its class character became clearer and clearer. 'At the same time at which the progress of modern industry developed, widened, intensified the class antagonism between capital and labour, the state powers assumed more and more the character of the national power of capital over labour, of a public force organised for social enslavement, of an engine of class despotism.'[28] Whatever the particular form of political system in capitalist societies, power usually remains, according to the theory, in the hands of the capitalists, who use the law, the various socialising institutions and the means of propaganda, to protect themselves. A body of pervasive and stabilising beliefs emerges, to mask and defend the real domination of a class. These attractive abridgements of a class way of life, which are in effect so many subtle barricades against any erosion of its power, are not invented for the purpose, nor are they simple and direct responses to class needs. But however diverse its origins, social morality is interpreted as particular class rules and norms, which their protagonists falsely identify with reason and the general interest. Marx and Engels did not deny that all societies required order and a body of rules,[29] but they were primarily concerned with the content of the rules (and norms and beliefs) of particular societies. They were interested in the specific social and moral ties, the specific patterns of authority and so on within societies, and with their relationship to class interests, and were little concerned with the functional prerequisites of societies as such. They argued, not that classes, economic activities and technology existed in a vacuum, or could exist prior to or independently of moral and legal codes, but that particular moral and legal codes were interpreted best in terms of the interests of social groups.

Marx and Engels believed that their general account of the state received abundant confirmation from the structure of laws under capitalism. Laws are taken to express or reflect economic relations. A given civil law is 'but the expression of a certain development of property'.[30]

'Legislation, whether political or civil, never does more than proclaim, express in words, the will of economic relations.'[31] The ruling individuals in societies characterised by the division of labour and private property

> besides having to constitute their power in the form of the State, have to give their will, which is determined by these definite conditions, a universal expression as the will of the State, as law – an expression whose content is always determined by the relations of this class, as the civil and criminal law demonstrates in the clearest possible way.[32]

Legal inequality matches and confirms social and economic inequality. As *The Holy Family* has it, 'the credo of most states starts by making the high and low, the rich and the poor, unequal before the law'.[33]

Marx and Engels each provide numerous examples of the class character of law. According to Engels, in 1844 society was in 'the juvenile state of capitalist exploitation',[34] in which class manipulation of the legal system was supposedly clear-cut. He cited several instances of anti-proletarian bills in the legislature – some of which did not, in fact, pass into law – and complained particularly of the New Poor Law of 1834. This measure, which established peculiarly unpleasant and barbarous workhouses for the poor, was a clear revelation of the bourgeois conception of its duties toward the proletariat – 'that the non-possessing class exists solely for the purpose of being exploited, and of starving when the property holders can no longer make use of it'.[35]

The domination of capital was revealed, not merely in the content of laws – the crimes and the penalties – but in their enforcement, and their accessibility to a small section of the people only. Police and justices of the peace were partisan, assuming the guilt of the proletarian, and treating him rudely and brutally, while the occasional middle-class defendant was given privileged treatment. Marx, in his historical account of the struggle for a normal working day in England, provided numerous examples of the political power of the bourgeoisie, such as the Labour Statutes which compulsorily lengthened the working day and the defeat of many measures for the improvement of working conditions. When Factory Acts were introduced, Marx pointed to the fact that many of the reforms were nominal, remaining a dead letter, that the law-makers purposely left escape-routes in the law, which were easily discerned by the 'lynx eye of capital', that in critical cases the capitalists carried out a 'pro-slavery rebellion in miniature', and that the intention of the Acts was frustrated in those courts in which 'the masters sat in judgement on themselves'.[36] He also indicated the advantages of revolutionary change over the pragmatic, gradualist and untidy progress of reform in England. The French revolutionary method 'once for all commands the same limits to the working-day in all shops and factories without distinction, whilst English legislation reluctantly yields to the pressure of circumstances, now on this point, now on that, and is getting lost in a hopelessly bewildering tangle of contradictory enactments'.[37] English law was muddled, irrational and complex, and the task of interpreting it was a highly skilled one, which was well beyond the means and the abilities of labourers. To understand the nature of class rule it is necessary to consider, not merely the structure of formal law, but the possibilities which it offers for interpretation and evasion, and the manner in which it is enforced, and by whom.

In addition to the partiality and oppressiveness of the law, the labourer suffered, because of his lack of power, in one vital area. This was the area of free contract between capitalist and labourer. The law defined the rules of free competition, and declared that the contracting parties were legally free and equal, but the force of economic sanctions – given the profound inequality of the contending parties – ensured that one side would generally come out on top. The labour contract is presented as a key demonstration of the nature and the weight of economic power. 'The magnitude of wages is determined at the beginning by free agreement between the free worker and the free capitalist. Later it turns out that the worker is compelled to allow the capitalist to determine it, just as the capitalist is compelled to fix it as low as possible. Freedom of the contracting parties is supplanted by competition.'[38] Engels put the argument clearly:

> The labour contract is supposed to be voluntarily entered into by both parties. But it is taken to be voluntarily entered into as soon as the law has put both parties on an equal footing on paper. The power given to one party by its different class position, the pressure it exercises on the other – the real economic position of both – all this is no concern of the law. And both parties, again, are supposed to have equal rights for the duration of the labour contract, unless one or other of the parties expressly waive them. That the concrete economic situation compels the worker to forego even the slightest semblance of equal rights – this is something the law cannot help.[39]

Marx, writing of the sphere of the production of commodities, wherein the purchase and sale of labour power were effected, described it as 'a very Eden of the innate rights of man. There alone rule Freedom, Equality, Property and Bentham. Freedom because both buyer and seller of a commodity, say of labour-power, are constrained only by their own free will. They contract as free agents, and the agreement they come to, is but the form in which they give legal expression to their common will.' In these free transactions, the appearance of the *dramatis personae* changes. 'He, who before was the money-owner, now strides in front as capitalist; the possessor of labour-power follows as his labourer. The one with an air of importance, smirking, intent on business; the other, timid and holding back, like one who is bringing his own hide to market and has nothing to expect but – a hiding.'[40]

The general critical point underlying these claims is that an account of decisions or choices in terms of political processes and formal rights alone is superficial, because it treats men as abstract legal beings rather than as concrete social creatures. The possessor of formal rights is prevented from making free choices of the kind envisaged in traditional liberal theory by the actual conditions of life, and especially by the differentiation of power along class lines. The choosing proletarian was subject to the formidable extra-parliamentary power of the bourgeoisie, which meant primarily the economic whip. The Marxist analysis of the labour contract seems to have been reasonable in relation to mid-nineteenth-century England. It recognised that the power of the individual to determine his own life was challenged, not merely by political or legal tyranny, but by economic sanctions (aided by law). T. H. Green emphasised this point in his lecture on *Liberal Legislation and Freedom of Contract* in 1880. He said, in relation to Irish tenants and their landlords, that it was nonsense to talk of freedom of contract because of the extreme inequality of the parties. The economic strength of the landlords gave them immense coercive power. If the peasant could be confronted with the choice of accepting his master's terms or being evicted, which carried the penalty of starvation, his freedom of choice was very restricted. Marx also commented on the relations between the Irish tenant and the English lord, which *The Times* had spoken of as relations between two traders. Marx rejoined: 'As well you might call the relationship between the robber who presents his pistol, and the traveller who presents his purse, a relation between two traders.'[41] The claim that men are unfree when they are so imposed upon by others and by circumstances does face a technical difficulty, in that there is a sense in which free choice does exist in such conditions – one could choose starvation or prison or execution in preference to surrendering. The opponent of a totalitarian system, for example, may have a choice between silence and imprisonment or death. But when we speak of freedom or free choice or rights we normally have in mind at least a particular kind of institutional context and a range of choices not all of which are hazardous or destructive, though we may have in mind new men and new societies. It is, of course, an extremely complex task to define the necessary conditions for free choices, in that – even within a very limited context – they may demand knowledge of a wide range of alternatives, as well as access to at least some of them. Even to become aware of certain alternatives requires a special kind of education or a wealthy home or some other resources that are not generally available. In practical terms the advocate of 'free choices' will seek to maximise the condition under which (all) people can visualise and realise alternatives, though there will always be a ceiling, perhaps changing, to his demands.

Marx argued in many places that men are not, and cannot be, free and self-determining in capitalist society, because of the variety of pressures and restraints upon them. The law, economic pressures, and ideology are the most obvious and specific determinants of the situation within which they made their choices. They are limited in that some alternatives are directly excluded by the powerful, and others could not be envisaged because of the way in which opinion is formed and controlled in capitalist societies. Given these limitations, how could relations between the socialist movement and capitalist democracy be conceived?

DEMOCRACY, CHANGE AND THE POLITICS OF THE PROLETARIAT

The existence of democratic institutions within capitalist states posed problems for classical Marxism. The situation encouraged hopes of easy – or, at least, peaceful – proletarian success. In Britain the franchise was extended to many members of the working class in 1867 and to country areas in 1884. A form of universal suffrage existed in France at different times during the century. In Germany it was introduced into the North German federal parliament by Bismarck in 1867, though it was not extended to Prussia until the twentieth century. The extension of the franchise was associated with a democratic theory which stressed the power and prospects of the newly enfranchised groups. That theory interpreted the democratic political order as one based upon the consent of the governed. It spoke, in somewhat idealistic terms, of communities of participating individuals, of the equality of political rights and powers, of rational and individual choices of political policies, or, at least, of political leaders. Institutionally the keys were majority rule and civil liberties, which were together taken to be capable of producing something approximating to the will of the people. Both proponents and enemies of democracy took its claims seriously, believing that the majority could utilise universal suffrage to rule in fact. To democratic socialists, universal suffrage provided the means for successfully opposing the numerical strength of the proletariat to the social power of capital. To conservative foes of democracy, this amounted to the potential domination of the most numerous, ignorant and poorest class, who were likely to use their new-found power to destroy the market economy and private property.

Yet from the very beginning the real significance or extent of the process of democratisation was questioned. The effectiveness of formal democratic rights was doubted, partly because of the nature of the consent or choice exercised by the democratic citizen. Critics, including Marx, stressed the influences or pressures upon political choice, the total environment within which it operates, and its effects. They believed themselves to be tearing away the mask, penetrating beneath what Burnham later called 'the abstract, empty, sentimental rhetoric of democratic idealism',[12] to reveal the facts of capitalist society, or the oligarchic power which characterises all societies. Marx doubted the effectiveness of democratic institutions in capitalist societies, believing that those who owned the instruments of production retained a decisive say in political life, and that they would continue to use political power to maintain the existing institutions against any peaceful proletarian threat. Political democracy, one of the great achievements of the bourgeois revolution, became a means of preserving bourgeois power, while the theory of representative government concealed the actuality of class rule. But Marx did more than expose the fraudulence and the contradictions of seemingly democratic devices and developments: he thought that they might, in one form or another, serve the real interests of the proletariat.

He stressed the steady internal subversion of its own foundations by capitalism, not simply in the economic and industrial sphere, but in the area of legislation as well. Welfare legislation had been passed in capitalist states, and in some societies the political power of the working class had grown. In 1892 Engels, now immensely optimistic about the prospects of social democratic movements, affirmed the gradual civilising of capitalism, and the growing freedom granted to working-class organisations, especially the trades unions:

> The Revolution of 1848, not less than many of its predecessors, has had strange bedfellows and successors. The very people who have put it down have become, as Karl Marx used to say, its testamentary executors. Louis Napoleon had to create an independent and united Italy, Bismarck had to revolutionise Germany and to restore Hungarian independence, and the English manufacturers had to enact the People's Charter.[43]

The admission of achievements within capitalism, in the fields of welfare and political representation, raised crucial questions which faced, and divided, revisionists and revolutionary Marxists towards the end of the nineteenth century. How could welfare legislation be accounted for, and what were its limits under capitalism? Could capitalism be transformed through a gradual and peaceful accumulation of reforms, and could a peaceful and fundamental redistribution of political power take place? And, if such changes did occur, would they lead to a new socialist world?

Marx argued that basic changes were occurring in the economic structure of capitalism, and that the result would be eventual changes in political conditions, whatever the will of political leaders. The source of innovation lay outside political institutions – hence Marx denied that parliament was the decisive force in the politico-legal regulation of English capitalism. It simply responded to forces over which it had no control.

> In England combination is authorised by an Act of Parliament, and it is the economic system which has forced Parliament to grant this legal authorisation. . .The more modern industry and competition develop, the more elements there are which call forth and strengthen combination, and as soon as combination becomes an economic fact, daily gaining in solidity, it is bound before long to become a legal fact.[44]

In discussing the regulations for the working day which were laid down in the Factory Acts, he wrote:

> It has been seen that these minutiae, which, with military uniformity, regulate by stroke of the clock the times, limits, pauses of the work, were not at all the products of Parliamentary fancy. They developed gradually out of circumstances as natural laws of the modern mode of production. Their formulation, official recognition, and proclamation by the State, were the result of a long struggle of classes.[45]

That class struggle resulted in the defeat of bourgeois political economy, which assumed the blind rule of supply and demand, by proletarian political economy, which preached planned social production.[46]

While Marx here plays down the role of parliament as a creative institution, he admitted its capacity to recognise changing economic facts – it responded to outside pressures and transformed the law, to the immense benefit of the working class. It is possible, of course, to characterise and explain bourgeois reforms in a variety of ways. The legal regulation of capitalism was explained by Marx as a necessary social response to the monstrous exactions of capital, and as a result of persistent civil war and a recognition of increasing proletarian power, and hence as a product of prudence or 'frightened avarice' rather than of humanitarianism or reforming zeal. It was the product of enlightened conservatism, stabilising the capitalist system by mitigating its greatest evils. But, whatever the motives of individuals, the reality of social change is admitted, and the historical tendency towards socialism asserted. Even if parliament is cleverly denigrated – as merely ratifying, or expressing in legal terms, an already existing situation or a shift of strength, so that the precedence of economic over legal and political facts can still be asserted – its reaction to outside circumstances might nonetheless be highly significant. It may respond at the last possible minute, but its responses could continually take the initiative away from radical movements, if not improve or civilise the system. In this respect, the role ascribed by Marx to the factory inspectors – the agents of parliament – is interesting. The inspectors, some of whom were denounced by the factory owners as revolutionists, constantly pointed to the evils of the industrial system, and fought those factory owners who sought to avoid the new legislation. They are portrayed by Marx as both important agents of change and disinterested humanitarians. Given such competent and concerned reformers – whose bourgeois social background fits badly with Marx's general claims about class – and a parliament which responds eventually to industrial change, and depending upon one's view of the flexibility and the economic prospects of capitalism, it might be plausibly argued that the proletariat, with or without the franchise, could exercise its power in such a way as to gradually transform the capitalist system in its own interest. But Marx, more than Engels, remained uncertain about the effectiveness of peaceful proletarian political action in winning socialism. In the end the capitalists – myopic and fighting for survival – would have to dig in their heels or disappear.

The interpreters of Marx have disagreed strongly over his conception of the nature and possible scope of proletarian action within capitalism. Marx certainly talked of the forcible overthrow of the bourgeoisie, of the imminence of revolution, and of force as the midwife – rather than the propagator – of the new order. He also spoke rather loosely about the smashing of the old state machinery and the bursting asunder of the old world. It is, of course, possible that the large threats and promises, the rhetorical language, conceals as much as it reveals, and that it contains no specific commitment to revolution, conceived as a violent seizure of power. Indeed, revolution need not imply streets deep in blood, and there is certainly a tradition according to which it means only fundamental and relatively quick change in some area or other. Marx saw the collapse of capitalism as the result of a long development of its own inner mechanisms, and thought that the worker–capitalist struggle might be less terrible and bloody than the feudal conflict which gave rise to capitalism. But we are not justified in imputing to him a firm general view for or against a violent proletarian seizure of power, though he did reject that violence which reflected premature proletarian action, without the requisite structural supports. His attitude to violence was dependent upon the actual conditions obtaining in particular societies, which included the readiness of dominant groups to accept peaceful proletarian advance, and he was not at all inconsistent or immoral for insisting that strategies must relate to the specific conditions in which men found themselves.

Hence it is not surprising that, in discussing political rights, Marx (and Engels) could offer no simple recommendation, no general line on whether or not universal suffrage provided an adequate means of achieving proletarian ends, or some of them. Avineri makes the matter simpler than it is by focussing upon the philosophical meaning of universal suffrage – what its 'effective existence' implies, what it would lead to 'by itself', what its achievement of its ends or its 'necessary consequences' amounts to. According to his interpretation, universal suffrage abolishes the state by abolishing the contradiction upon which the state is founded. Ensuring that the political structure utilises all its potentialities, the effective existence of universal suffrage 'implies the dialectical overcoming and disappearance of the state as a distinct organism'.[47] Avineri distinguishes sharply between universal suffrage and parliamentarism, which is 'the limited parliamentary rule of the mid-nineteenth century, socially and functionally almost a total antithesis of the universality implied in universal suffrage'.[48] And he stresses how bourgeois legislators, aware of the revolutionary possibilities of universal suffrage, tried to prevent it achieving its ends.[49] My objections are to both Marx and Avineri. To Marx, insofar as he sees revolution occurring through universal suffrage simply because universal suffrage is the resolution of the conflict between the state and civil society:[50] because something resolves a conflict or a contradiction, it has not yet gained any historical force. It remains a myth, and we deal still in categories, not facts. Avineri suggests, against Marx, that the historical and the philosophical may not be as permanently united as Marx imagined,[51] and I employ that distinction in questioning Avineri's account of universal suffrage: his philosophical analysis brings out the meaning or the essence of the idea of universal suffrage, but does not allow sufficiently for the perverted, limited and partial forms which it takes in fact. History, for Marx, was more than a process of entities fulfilling their internal logic. He was seeking a definite goal for mankind, and while his philosophical assumptions helped him define social phenomena, and encouraged optimism, he had to examine concrete institutions, real concentrations of power, and to overcome obstacles which prevented his 'ideas' tidily working themselves out. Universal suffrage, in its empirical sense, was a right squeezed out of rulers, and a right which they tried systematically to limit. For it to achieve its ends or effectively exist, their power had to be overcome by a strong, self-conscious and radical proletariat. Thus the social context gives a concrete meaning to universal suffrage, which becomes a tool of fundamental change only in certain circumstances. In other cases its implications may be squashed and a violent seizure of power imposed upon the proletariat. Philosophic analysis of the idea of universal suffrage cannot settle questions about the nature of the proletarian accession to power in actual capitalist states.

Although universal suffrage, broadly and philosophically conceived, brought about the *Aufhebung* of the state, its actual historical effect was dependent upon particular political cultures and social arrangements, which strongly influenced proletarian consciousness and the nature of capitalist and governmental responses to proletarian activity. In France under the Second Empire experience with the universal franchise was hardly promising. In Germany Lassalle's short alliance with Bismarck – exchanging labour support for an extension of the franchise – seemed to Marx to be unprincipled and dangerous, compromising the labour movement, making the suffrage a vehicle of conservatism,[52] flirting with nationalism, and possibly laying a foundation for Bonapartism. Marx complained that Lassalle overlooked the lessons of the Second Empire with regard to universal suffrage. The question was one to be viewed historically, not in the abstract. Popper claims that Marx's 'ambiguity' on the matter of violent revolution and peaceful democratic change was a product of his historicist approach, and gives the impression that Marx formulated his predictions and recommendations as he did in order to prevent their falsification.[53] This view is incorrect, for what made Marx uncertain were the changes and the variations in historical circumstances and opportunities. His 'ambiguity' was the product of the varied experience of universal franchise and of the economic and political changes which occurred during the century. In the later writings, while democratic clichés are still challenged, there is a growing acceptance of the possibility of peaceful and far-reaching changes in some bourgeois-democratic societies, whereas the writings up to 1848, strongly influenced by the example of 1789, suggest that it would probably be necessary to overthrow existing social conditions forcibly.

Marx and Engels argued that working-class agitation for full political freedom, including the vote, was crucial to its development. Frequently the stress was less on the social reforms which the struggle might produce than on the role of conflict in educating and organising the class.

And they recognised the advantages, in terms of class organisation and solidarity, of a relatively free environment. The workers would be awakened, they would be brought to demand their due, by political activity. They would cease to be pawns in the hands of the capitalists. In 1870 Marx advised the French workers to 'calmly and resolutely improve the opportunities of Republican liberty, for the work of their own class organisation'.[54] Twenty years earlier he had commented, again in relation to France, on the achievements and the shortcomings of universal suffrage. The limitations of the appeal to universal suffrage were revealed when, in mid-1850, the petit-bourgeois democrats united with the bourgeois liberals to crush the proletariat. 'Universal suffrage had fulfilled its mission. The majority of the people had passed through the school of development, which is all that universal suffrage can serve for in a revolutionary period. It had to be set aside by a revolution or by the reaction.'[55] Trades unions were also schools of development, ramparts for the workers in their struggles with the employers. Marx and Engels expected an increase in class consciousness from guerilla warfare against the system, which would eventually be transcended by a political movement against the system as such. The democratic republic, with its rights, is recognised as an advance on more dictatorial and restrictive states. It provided 'islands of proletarian democracy within bourgeois democracy', as Trotsky was later to say, in bitter opposition to Comintern policy.[56] Naturally political agitation and organisation were conceived as means of bringing out and strengthening the class struggle. As Marx said of France in 1848, if universal suffrage was not the miracle-working magic wand for which republican worthies had taken it, it did unchain the class struggle, and gave it greater clarity.[57] It encouraged the emergence of the proletariat as a separate and independent force.

Proletarian assertiveness within the bourgeois state is presented as a process of self-emancipation – a process which is not opposed to, or incompatible with, the need to organise and the notion of a vanguard party, which best interprets the hidden sense of the existing class struggle. Marx and Engels did not deny that the workers could and must profit from education and leadership, though naturally the degree of emphasis placed upon one or other part of the process – leaders or class – could diverge sufficiently to produce substantially different theories of proletarian development, Lenin or Luxemburg. Marx and Engels, asserting that the emancipation of the working class must be conquered by the working classes themselves, declared their inability to co-operate with 'people who openly state the workers are too uneducated to emancipate themselves and must be freed from above by philanthropic big bourgeois and petty bourgeois'.[58] The workers had to be prevented from remaining playthings in the hands of the ruling classes, as their pretended saviours and superior spokesmen – even if inspired by some form of socialism – would leave them. The danger seemed particularly strong in Germany, where authority and its regulations were virtually unquestioned. In 1868 Marx rejected the arguments for a proposed centralist organisation of German trades unions on these grounds. Germany was the last place for such a scheme. 'Here where the worker's life is regulated from childhood on by the bureaucracy and he himself believes in the authorities, in the bodies appointed over him, he must be taught before all else to walk by himself.'[59] But the stress on the 'historical initiative' of the workers – whose development included, amongst other things, the influence of Marxist theory – leaves open the questions of just how far they might be allowed to go, and how far they might choose to go, within the bourgeois state. Their initiative might be arrested by authorities, with the possible effect of provoking violent revolution, or their resolution might be softened and weakened by a mixture of rewards, threats and subtle influences.

If the various democratic rights, and particularly universal suffrage, were to become vehicles of peaceful revolution, two empirical conditions would have to be met – the ruling classes must remove themselves, and allow the battle for democracy to succeed, and the working class must pursue whatever it is that constitutes the revolutionary achievement. As already mentioned, Marx believed that the possibility of peaceful transformation depended upon the institutions, traditions and customs of the country in question. Favourable conditions included a proletarian majority and the lack of a strong bureaucracy. Much impressed by the development of democracy and the internal, dialectical transformation of capitalism, Marx did not insist that violence was an indispensable source of radical social change. Engels, like Marx, stressed the legislative results of proletarian pressure, as in the case, touched upon already, of the Ten Hours Bill in England. 'This law has been won by English factory workers by years of endurance, by the most persistent, stubborn struggle with the factory owners, by freedom of the press, the right of association and assembly, as well as by adroit utilisation of the splits in the ruling class itself.'[60] Marx interpreted the Chartist demand for universal suffrage as

> the equivalent for political power for the working class of England, where the proletariat form the large majority of the population...
> The carrying of universal suffrage in England would, therefore, be a far more socialistic measure than anything which has been honoured with the name on the Continent. Its inevitable result here, is the political supremacy of the working class.[61]

Addressing the First International in 1872, his consideration of the question was more general, and showed his lack of a doctrinaire stance. The commonly quoted passage reads, 'we do not deny that there are countries such as America, England, and I would add Holland if I knew your institutions better, where the working people may achieve their goal by peaceful means'. The passage continues – though this is quoted less commonly: 'If that is true, we must also recognise that in most of the continental countries it is force that will have to be the lever of our revolutions; it is force that we will some day have to resort to in order to establish a reign of labour.'[62] The possibility of peaceful change is suggested again in 1880, in a letter to Hyndman. Marx wrote: 'If you say that you do not share the views of my party for England I can only reply that that party considers an English revolution not necessary, but – according to the historical precedents – possible. If the unavoidable evolution turns into a revolution, it would not only be the fault of the ruling classes, but also of the working classes.'[63]

Engels considered the possibility of the peaceful, democratic achievement of socialism more fully than did Marx, especially in his writings during the relatively placid years following Marx's death. He became a strong believer in gradualism, though not for its own sake. His main subject was Germany, on which he had already commented in 1868: 'The splits within the ruling classes are more favourable to the workers than they ever were in England, because universal suffrage compels the ruling classes to court the favour of the workers.'[64] Confronted with the remarkable growth of the German Social-Democratic Party during the last three decades of the nineteenth century, he argued that the German workers, now at the centre of the international working-class movement, had shown their fellows how to use universal suffrage, which had often been dismissed as a snare. They had transformed the franchise 'from a means of deception, which it was before, into an instrument of emancipation'.[65] Revolution, as the violent seizure of power, had become, in Engels's view, to a large extent obsolete, as developments in weapons, the professionalisation of armies and the change in the lay-out of the cities, made it extremely costly to the workers and, more importantly, because proletarian ends were now being secured by other means. Slow propaganda work and parliamentary activity had become the immediate tasks of the party, whose accession to political power had become inevitable. The growth of the German social-democracy 'proceeds as spontaneously, as steadily, as irresistibly, and at the same time as tranquilly as a natural process'.[66]

The growing assertiveness and power of the proletariat confronted the bourgeoisie and its allies with a great dilemma. Marx and Engels never forgot the counter-revolutionary propensities of the bourgeoisie which, in their view, had no genuine belief in liberal-democratic institutions, despite its liberal-democratic rhetoric. To secure power it had needed proletarian support, and this had both pushed it further than it wanted to go and had dragged the restless masses into the political arena. It now turned its back on its heroic past, and tried to undo the existing structure of right and liberties because they could not be confined within set limits, but had revolutionary potentialities. Its position came to seem extremely vulnerable, especially in France. Marx pointed to the comprehensive contradiction of Marrast's constitution, which consisted in the fact that it put the oppressed classes in possession of political power through universal suffrage. 'It forces the political rule of the bourgeoisie into democratic conditions, which at every moment help the hostile classes to victory and jeopardise the very foundations of bourgeois society.'[67] Marx wrote of the mid-nineteenth-century France: 'The bourgeoisie had a true insight into the fact that all the weapons which it had forged against feudalism turned their points against itself; that all the means of education which it had produced rebelled against its own civilisation, that all the gods which it had created had fallen away from it.'[68] It carried the assault on the now inconvenient civil liberties even to its own press, which was not sufficiently servile. Its savagery was most pronounced when the working class asserted itself forcefully.[69] Marx also argued, in relation to France, that the bourgeoisie had to strengthen the executive vis-à-vis the legislature if it was to survive – a charge which communists commonly make against capitalist states in general. Marx assumed that civil liberties – two-edged weapons – were never safe under capitalism, and were most in danger when the proletariat was beginning seriously to challenge the system. The capitalists were expected to fight savagely against a peaceful process of democratisation and social reform, using constitutional manipulation and other forms of political manoeuvring, and perhaps violence, in a desperate effort to maintain their power and privileges. For gradual changes could threaten their interests just as much as could more rapid ones, and in these circumstances their adherence to the rules of the game could not be confidently anticipated. Even in England, where civil liberties seemed to be fairly secure, Marx sensed the possibility of Bonapartism, under that most successful of British politicians – Palmerston. In 1857 he argued that, in the event of Palmerston's success in the forthcoming elections, his dictatorship would be openly proclaimed.

A *coup d'état* might then, in due course of time, follow Palmerston's appeal from the Parliament to the people, as it followed Bonaparte's appeal from the Assemblée Nationale to the nation. That some people (the parliamentary majority) might then learn to their damage that Palmerston is the old colleague of the Castlereagh–Sidmouth Cabinet, who gagged the press, suppressed public meetings, suspended the Habeas Corpus Act, made it legal for the Cabinet to imprison and expulse at pleasure, and lastly butchered the people of Manchester for protesting against the Corn Laws.[70]

Engels, after claiming, incorrectly, that Marx's studies had led to the conclusion that 'at least in Europe, England is the only country where the inevitable social revolution might be effected entirely by peaceful and legal means', continued that he 'certainly never forgot to add that he hardly expected the English ruling classes to submit, without a "pro-slavery rebellion", to this peaceful and legal revolution'.[71] While some societies, at some times, seemed to offer prospects of peaceful and far-reaching change, such change was likely to be blocked by force at a certain stage – by the bureaucracy in Germany and France, and by the bourgeoisie in England and the United States.

Engels himself taunted the German bourgeoisie with the legal progress of the working class, and suggested that the rulers might have to break this 'fatal legality' and breach the constitution, returning to absolutism. Then there would be no binding rules at all. 'If, therefore, you break the constitution of the Reich, the Social-Democracy is free, and can do as it pleases with regard to you.'[72] In 1891, in his *Critique of a Draft for the Erfurt Program*, he complained of the failure of the draft to take account of the undemocratic character of the German state. He wrote:

> We deceive ourselves and the Party in asserting that 'present-day society is growing into socialism' if we do not ask whether it is not consequently necessary for this society to grow out of its old political constitution – to burst, like a crab, forcibly from this old shell. Must not present-day society in Germany break the chains of its half-absolutist, unspeakably entangled, political order?[73]

But at the same time he suggested that, where the people's representatives had all power, as in England, France and the United States, it was conceivable that the old society would grow peacefully into the new.

The assumption of a steady and substantial alteration of the capitalist system through peaceful and constitutional reform did not entail the further view that there were no limits to such reform, and that socialism could be achieved without violence. How far the proletariat could realise socialism – if it wished to do so – by peaceful means is left open, for it depended upon particular circumstances which had diverse tactical implications. Marx and Engels argued that the chances for a non-violent proletarian attainment of power were considerable in England and the United States, to which Engels added France and Marx, possibly Holland. But experience showed that ruling groups were rarely prepared to simply get out of the way of the progressive or democratic forces, and hence it was remembered always that the threatened bourgeoisie may employ violence, and whatever other means were available, against a 'lawful' proletarian power.

But would the proletariat demand socialism, or something else with which the bourgeoisie might reasonably co-exist? For the peaceful route had one great danger, which could well increase with its achievements. Marx and Engels both feared that improving economic conditions and democratic political institutions might corrupt the working class, in the sense that it would be sucked into capitalist society, accepting the wage system and class division, and believing in social harmony and gradual progress. For on the one hand the proletariat is called upon to utilise the political institutions of the capitalist state, to gain the vote and to use it and other legal rights to struggle for economic reforms, thereby coming to maturity, and on the other it is expected to advance from the improvement of economic conditions and the expansion of political rights to the liberation of man, which involves the elimination of wage labour and classes. The problem was that of ensuring that the means (the political struggle) did not alter or put off the end (the socialist society) or, as it emerged in the common socialist distinction, that pursuit of the minimum programme, designed to protect proletarian interests within the present system, e.g. by shortening the working day, did not shift attention away from the maximum programme. There was obviously a serious danger that the proletarian party would become contaminated through operating peacefully within a society whose disintegration it both envisaged and sought. Negotiations, continuous peaceful dealings and agitation, and material rewards are enemies of the righteousness, the sense of mission and the feelings of separate identity which, in the bulk of Marxist theory, are the conditions of a radical proletarian assault on the system. To speak abstractly, each step forward, each economic or political gain, may well make the successive steps seem less pressing, insofar as they are conceived as steps towards a new society rather than as demands for more goods and resources. Programmes for short-term gain could continually undermine the prospects of both capitalist collapse and of the realisation of communism. In the circular letter attacking an article by Höchberg, Bernstein and Schramm on the proper role of the German Social-Democratic Party, Marx and Engels stated that their opponents wanted the party to work amongst the bourgeoisie, devoting itself 'to those petit-bourgeois patchwork reforms which, by providing the old order of society with new props, may perhaps transform the ultimate catastrophe into a gradual, piece-meal and as far as possible peaceful process of dissolution'.[74] Indeed, it might be doubted whether it would be a process of genuine dissolution at all. The issue – the extent and nature of the change demanded by the proletariat – naturally became central in the party which arose out of the fusion of the Lassallist wing, stressing political representation and activity within the middle-class state, and the classically Marxist Eisenacher wing. Marx's attack on the Lassallean–Bismarckian compromise paralleled his attack on Proudhon, who was condemned for his willingness to preserve such basic institutions of bourgeois society as marriage and private property, and hence for seeking merely partial changes, the removal of outstanding grievances, which would ensure the continuing stability of the system. Proudhon's proposed changes were 'by no means the abolition of bourgeois relations of production, an abolition that can be effected only by a revolution, but administrative reforms, based on the continued existence of these relations'.[75] This was a crucial argument used by Marx against many of his socialist contemporaries and predecessors – that they wanted changes within the framework of bourgeois society, that such categories as 'capital' and 'private property' were still accepted and that hence contradictions remained unreconciled within their systems. 'The philanthropists, then, want to retain the categories which express bourgeois relations, without the antagonism which constitutes them and is inseparable from them.'[76] They did not want to abolish the antagonism between capital and wage labour, but to soften it, to have both harmony and classes. In many cases the class struggle was pushed aside, and a vacuous, enervating love of humanity was put in its place.[77] Constitutional successes dissipated revolutionary energy. Marx condemned 'parliamentary idiocy', with its tendency to 'draw the teeth of socialism'. Parliamentary cretins laboured under the illusion that their resolutions could change the face of Europe. They, in common with those who came to be known as revisionists and with the anarchists, offered superficial analyses of capitalism and failed to strike it at the decisive point.[78] These connected criticisms – of goals amounting to reformed capitalism, sitting still on the old contradictions, of a lack of attachment to the class struggle and shallowness in identifying the vital points of change, and a corresponding tendency to illusions about the power of parliaments and legislators – indicate clearly Marx's perception of the dangers of parliamentary and peaceful politics.

The people, confused and comforted by these various myths, were inclined to relax, anticipating legal but not revolutionary triumphs. Engels, as already mentioned, referred to the pressure which a voting proletariat might exert upon a divided ruling class, but he was also concerned about something which has divided the socialist movement ever since – that parliamentary socialists might seek support by offering the public roughly what it wants, and thereby sacrifice the moral dynamism and revolutionary fervour of the movement. As he asked Bebel:

> is the struggle to be conducted as a class struggle of the proletariat against the bourgeoisie, or is it to be permitted that in good opportunist (or as it is called in the socialist translation: Possibilist) style the class character of the movement, together with the programme is everywhere to be dropped where more votes, more adherents, can be won by this means?[79]

Operating within the system could thus have a drastic effect, undermining the integrity of socialist parties, and leading the trades unions to pursue, as ultimate aims, wage increases and the reduction of working hours. By the late nineteenth century the labour movement in Western Europe seemed to be in a serious dilemma, threatened by reformism on one side and sectarianism on the other. The dangers were well put by Rosa Luxemburg. 'One is the loss of its mass character, the other the abandonment of its goal. One is the danger of sinking back into the condition of a sect, the other the danger of becoming a movement of bourgeois reform.'[80] The preachers of social integration were thus destroying the cutting edge, the clear and separate identity and radical character of the proletarian movement. The gravediggers of capitalism were becoming its contented slaves, living in a reformed society, an ersatz community which was stable, but which lacked the economic progressiveness, the new and more human social bonds, and the individual freedom and creativity which characterised communism, as Marx and Engels conceived it.

5 *Communism*

Capitalism was to be transformed, not by theoretical assaults or by piecemeal tinkering, but under the impact of mass, proletarian revolutionary action. The exact manner of its collapse, and the role of violence, are not indicated in clear or general terms, but remain to be determined in the particular case. But if the form of revolution is uncertain, its content is indicated clearly enough. It is a political act, or series of acts, which destroys the existing ruling power, frees hitherto oppressed classes, and dissolves existing social relationships – although the final turbulence, or period of rapid, clear change, presupposes certain determinate conditions and a long and complex process of development. It confirms and puts the seal on a steady accumulation of changes. The presumed advantages of a period of rapid and striking change over gradual incremental change was that it cleared away the debris more decisively, as it involved a new start, a sharp break with the past, in certain crucial respects, and consequently freed consciousness more cleanly and quickly from the myths, allurements, illusions and values of the past. This was especially important in the final, proletarian revolution which, striking the old society at its vital points, would lead – though not immediately – to a far more radical negation of previous social conditions than had followed any previous revolution. It would lead, ultimately, to general human emancipation and not simply to another class society. The various evils of capitalist society – the division of labour, class, private property, the state, alienation – were linked closely, both conceptually and empirically, and would not have to be destroyed separately, one by one, through a series of disparate radical reforms. Limited change, and the total process of change, would make inroads on each of them. Many new features would come spontaneously into being as the original and historical causes or roots of their corrupt predecessors withered away. Marx's idealism was in some respects as great as that of the most radical French revolutionaries, with their new calendar for their new world, but it was not recognised as such by him. He felt that he was appealing to facts, and that this was science, although events did lead to the kind of future that humane men desired.

Marx and Engels were sparing in their references to the final stages of what Marx called 'the process of human emancipation and discovery'.[1] There are a few general statements, rather mystical in character, and we can make various inferences from the fact that communism represents both the negation and the fulfilment of capitalism, but there is no tough, rigorous analysis of the possible problems of the future. There are off-the-cuff comments and rhetorical flourishes. Marx was, in fact, careful to avoid anything approaching a detailed account of communism, believing that such attempts were mere utopian fantasies, which could become reactionary attempts to impose programmes on the future. Scientific socialists do not speculate on the precise character of economic distribution or the design of buildings in the future. What is to be done depends upon the specific conditions at the time – and then it will be known, immediately, what has to be done. In his words:

> no equation can be solved unless the elements of its solution are involved in its terms. . .had any eighteenth-century Frenchman the faintest idea beforehand, *a priori*, of the manner in which the demands of the French bourgeoisie would be forced through? The doctrinaire and necessarily fantastic anticipation of the programme of action for a revolution of the future only diverts one from the struggle of the present.[2]

Marx and Engels became almost exclusively preoccupied, from 1848 onwards, with the analysis of existing societies, and especially with the changes which they were undergoing. It seemed to them more important for communists to reveal the means by which the new society was to come into being, and to act appropriately, than to ask concrete questions about the communist future. Moreover, such questions were, in terms of Marx's philosophy, unanswerable in principle, for according to it thinking individuals can have no clear idea of realities which do not yet exist, particularly when those future realities presuppose the dialectical transcendence of the existing order, and the appearance of men with different values and goals – a different consciousness – from the men of Marx's own time.

MATERIAL AND INSTITUTIONAL FOUNDATIONS

The future society, which differs in basic respects from the old, grows from it as it breaks away. The proletariat has no ideals to realise, but to 'set free the elements of the new society with which the old collapsing bourgeois society is pregnant'.[3] At times the proletarian take-over seems astonishingly easy: the revolutionaries seem less the harsh and angry gravediggers of capitalism than the placid beneficiaries of its productive labours. Again and again Marx honoured capital's contribution to man's future. Natural science had invaded and transformed human life through the medium of industry ,'and has prepared human emancipation, however directly and much it had to consummate dehumanisation'.[4] The two-sidedness of capitalist industrialisation – the tremendous technical achievements and possibilities, and widespread human suffering and degradation – and its implications for man's future is spelled out more fully in a passage from *Capital:*

> machinery, considered alone, shortens the hours of labour, but when in the service of capital, lengthens them; ...in itself it lightens labour, but when employed by capital, heightens the intensity of labour; ...in itself it is a victory of man over the forces of nature, but in the hands of capital, makes man the slave of those forces; ...in itself it increases the wealth of the producers, but in the hands of capital makes them paupers.[5]

Capitalism was a contradictory and transitory form, which laid foundations for communism, but had proved increasingly unable to spread the benefits which technological development had made possible. Concerned only with producing profit, unconcerned with ministering to wants, capital ensured that 'a rift must continually ensue between the limited dimensions of consumption under capitalism and a production which forever tends to exceed this immanent barrier'.[6] But at least material abundance, which was a premise of communism, was now within reach, and under wise social management would rapidly become a reality.

Capitalism presented socialism with more than technological mastery, more than powerful instruments of production which needed only to be freed from limiting social relationships. Marx and Engels stressed the existence of transitional, linking institutions which arose out of the internal socialisation of the capitalist system, though it is not clear precisely how these institutions are to be conceived. The general claim, which is made especially in the third volume of *Capital*, is that as capitalism develops, there is a growth in collective ownership, which – naturally – falls short of ownership by the associated producers. Joint stock companies, big monopolistic concerns, the credit system and large co-operative enterprises are presented as steps towards communism, as signs and concrete foundations of the impending new order. The stock company is a social enterprise, involving 'the abolition of capital as private property within the framework of capitalist production itself', though it remains 'ensnared in the trammels of capitalism'.[7] In the co-operatives the antithesis between capital and labour is overcome partially.

The cooperative factories of the labourers themselves represent within the old form the first sprouts of the new although they naturally reproduce, and must reproduce, everywhere in their actual organisation all the shortcomings of the prevailing system. . . The capitalist stock companies, as much as the cooperative factories, should be considered as transitional forms from the capitalist mode of production to the associated one, with the only distinction that the antagonism is resolved negatively in the one and positively in the other.[8]

The banking and credit system 'does away with the private character of capital and thus contains in itself, but only in itself, the abolition of capital itself'.[9] Finally, large-scale expropriation – still within capitalism – centralises industry, thereby making it more manageable by the proletariat.

The relationship of these various developments to the old and the new orders is not absolutely clear and, of course, we are not justified in assuming that they bear the same relationship. All bear witness to the social character of production or of capital, and presumably highlight the contradiction between this fact and individual appropriation. Centralisation, in the form of joint stock companies, credit facilities and expropriation of smaller owners, reveals the degree of maturity attained by capitalism, and provides institutions and arrangements ripe for takeover by the associated workers. Assuming the substantial transformation of capitalist private property, already resting on socialised production, into socialised property, Marx believed that the transition to communism would be less protracted, violent and difficult than that from feudalism to capitalism. These changes provide the form, though obviously not the content, of genuinely social devices and institutions, but so great is the difference still that they must be characterised as ultimate developments within capitalism rather than as embryos of the new order. They may also serve as 'powerful levers' during the transition between modes of production.[10] But the most constructive and novel creations within capitalism are the co-operative factories, great social experiments which reveal something of the shape and the possibilities of the future. They have shown that large-scale, scientific production may occur 'without the existence of a class of masters employing a class of hands; that to bear fruit, the means of labour need not be monopolised as a means of dominion over, and of extortion against, the labouring man himself; and that, like slave labour, like serf labour, hired labour is but a transitory and inferior form, destined to disappear before associated labour plying its toil with a willing hand, a ready mind, and a joyous heart'.[11] The co-operatives seem to be, unambiguously, 'elements of the new society', though they require expansion and development, whereas the other main institutional forms emerging in late capitalism are valued for their universal characteristic – breaking down distinctions and divisions – and for their fruitfulness as levers of change when in the hands of the workers.

THE PERIOD OF TRANSITION

The emergence of elements of the new society within the old provides some reason for confidence in a steady march forward, but does not indicate the political character of the transition – what men do, and how the process of transition affects them. For the constructive elements born out of capitalism – machines and institutions – cannot achieve anything alone. As consciousness lags behind reality, it must be 'old' men, men in the grip of old concepts, values and desires – at least in the early stages – who make the new society, and they will be opposed by other men who unashamedly prefer the old order.

Marx and Engels did offer some detailed discussion of the crucial transition period – between capitalist and communist society – which they came to call the dictatorship of the proletariat, though the term itself only appears a handful of times in their writings. In 1852 Marx wrote to Weydemeyer that the class struggle necessarily leads to the dictatorship of the proletariat, which itself only constitutes the transition to the abolition of all classes and to a classless society.[12] In his *Critique of the Gotha Programme* he stated that: 'Between capitalist and communist society lies the period of the revolutionary transformation of the one into the other. There corresponds to this also a political transition period in which the state can be nothing but the revolutionary dictatorship of the proletariat.'[13] The nature of the transitional period is determined by the problems which it has to face, and in particular by the existing level of the proletariat and the strength of its enemies. If the proletariat was assumed to be ignorant and demoralised, as it was by such proponents of minority revolution as Blanqui and Weitling, an extremely rigorous dictatorship of the most advanced and class-conscious revolutionaries probably seems necessary, whereas those who assume the maturity of the class, perhaps trained through democratic struggle, will generally advocate a much more liberal political or quasi-political form. Naturally this proved a major issue of conflict between the Bolsheviks and such leading Western Marxists as Kautsky and Rosa Luxemburg. Kautsky strongly attacked the élitist conceptions of Blanqui and Weitling – whose scheme he likened to that of the dictatorial Jesuit Messiahs in Paraguay – and he attacked even more strongly the Bolshevik view of the transitional period, for establishing and justifying a repressive minority dictatorship which seemed to have little to do with the classical Marxist doctrine.[14]

Marx himself doubted that state apparatus could be dismantled easily and rapidly. Even in *The Civil War in France*, in which he was extremely generous to the Communards, he showed that he was aware of the great problems which any proletarian order would face at its inception, even if it was more than 'the rising of a city under exceptional conditions'.[15]

> The working class did not expect miracles from the Commune. They have no ready-made utopias to introduce *par décret du peuple*. They know that in order to work out their own emancipation, and along with it that higher form to which present society is irresistibly tending by its own economical agencies, they will have to pass through long struggles, through a series of historic processes, transforming circumstances and men.[16]

Why are there long and difficult struggles before the victorious proletariat can leap into the realm of freedom where man's dignity and his potentialities are realised fully?

Difficulties arise in the first place because of the normal condition of the working class when revolutionary change is attempted. In most of his writings Marx speaks of the proletariat as broken, crushed and mutilated by capitalism. It is increasingly alienated, dehumanised, oppressed or emiserated, especially as a result of the division of labour. In the later writings, although the terms of discussion are more strictly economic, the moral fervour survives, and at most times a sense of the terrible degradation of the bulk of the workers emerges clearly. On the whole the picture is not one of the enslavement of a noble and idealistic class: the slaves degenerate and catch, in addition to their own characteristic vices, those of their masters. There are occasional moods of contrast, when particular sections of the proletariat, especially in France, are credited with vision, nobility and self-sacrifice. Marx was impressed deeply by the moral qualities of the Communards. He has, indeed, been praised by one recent commentator, Eugene Kamenka, for his desire to believe that the proletariat, in its misery, 'yearned for initiative, enterprise and freedom, that it rejected servility, careerism and the concern with security as Marx himself had rejected them'.[17] However, Kamenka attacks Marx for his loss of faith in the better instincts and hopes of the workers, which led him to stress the impersonal laws of history lying behind proletarian political activity, and to downgrade the passion for liberty as an existing social force. Marx's supposed reliance on 'history', which contrasts unfavourably with his own early conceptions and with those of the anarcho-syndicalists, prevented Marxism from mounting a moral assault on capitalism when the Western workers displayed a preference 'for rewards and security over freedom and struggle'.[18] This criticism, which makes sense in terms of a particular view of moral or genuine human action, must be confronted with analysis of the actual forces moving men in capitalist society. To appeal to freedom and enterprise as historic traditions operating in any society is certainly not servile, but it may be silly. The anarchist appeal to men to throw off their chains in a radical, libertarian and conscious gesture may be more exciting and stirring than Marx's common depictions of a degraded and unidealistic class acting out of sheer economic necessity, or of complacent opportunists peacefully working within the capitalist system. We may well prefer Sorel's producer ethic, according to which liberty is valued far more than material welfare, to his tamer ethic of the consumer, concerned with securing ends and gaining things. But for one who seeks, above all, revolutionary social change, the focus must be on the possible foundations for political action in the societies with which he is concerned. To Marx, the thin declamations and posturings of some anarchists must have seemed like spitting into the wind. What was the likelihood of a proletarian uprising for freedom? Marx stressed the need for the workers to act independently – and hence accepted, with caveats, the democratic struggle – but he usually presented the class which was pitted against the old world as one which was not only oppressed in that world, but was contaminated deeply by it. He opposed the holiness of the word 'proletariat', and did not ascribe its historical role to the class because he considered proletarians to be gods. Some, but only some, were capable of recognising the degradation and inhumanity of their society, and of fighting consciously for a future marked by individual creativity and genuine community, and others would learn in the struggle and developments of the transitional period. Of course, Marx may have been no wiser than his anarchist foes, for his 'history' and his 'prophecy' may have been as unrealistic as their generous psychological theory and facile images of change.

Given Marx's picture of the proletariat, one is bound, at the very least, to question its capacity to bring about its own emancipation, to carry out a grand act of 'reappropriation'. Is it in any position to leap out of the realm of necessity? Marx's first and indirect answer to this question is presented in his discussion of 'raw communism' in the 1844 *Manuscripts* – a devastating account of early communist theory and, according to some commentators, a parallel account of immature communist man, which reads in places as if it was written by the most violent and disgusted enemy of communism.[19] I think that we are quite unjustified in assuming a complete equivalence or identity between the early theoretical depictions of communist society and how Marx conceived it at this time,[20] and certainly Marx's later accounts of early communism, with its rich material base and the educative contributions of class political action and mature communist theory, suggest that the man of the transition will not be as desperate and shallow as he is portrayed here. But as his vision and his values will remain seriously deficient during the early phases of emancipation – Marx assumes this in all his discussions of this phase – it is worth briefly considering Marx's account of the related deficiencies of early proletarian theory and early proletarian revolutionary aspiration.

In raw, primitive communist theory, the labourer remains consumed with acquisitive feelings in the immediate post-revolutionary period. He remains alienated. Society remains property-ridden. Communism in this form means 'universal private property', with the community as the common capitalist, the extension of the category of labour to all men, and universal prostitution. It is a time of levelling down, not of elevation, and is one form in which 'the vileness of private property[21] comes to the surface. 'General envy constituting itself as a power is the disguise in which avarice re-establishes itself and satisfies itself, only in another way ... The crude communism is only the consummation of this envy and of this levelling down proceeding from this preconceived minimum. It has a definite, limited standard.'[22] As a result, there is no 'real appropriation', no true emergence of man. It is, indeed, a revelation of the backwardness of those who rise up – it reveals 'the unnatural simplicity of the poor and undemanding man who has not only failed to go beyond private property, but has not yet even attained to it'.[23] The curse of selfishness, and limited notions of possession, persist. Man demands to possess things in an egoistic manner, to have them, and perceives both things and others in this way. His perceptive and artistic faculties have not yet developed. He remains stupid and one-sided, like the dealer in minerals who can see only the mercantile value of the mineral, and remains dead to its unique value and its beauty. There is no sense of the individuality of women, who are regarded and treated brutishly – 'in the approach to woman as the spoil and handmaid of communal lust is expressed the infinite degradation in which man exists for himself'.[24] While much of Marx's discussion is rather opaque, it emerges clearly that, in this picture of communism, man is not the free and immediate creator of a satisfying and fully human world, but is brutalised and warped by the previous society, and stands, a debased creature, on the threshold of history.

This account of a conception of the immediate post-revolutionary period which is appropriate in an early stage of historical development, bears parallels with his own view of the problems and shortcomings of the intermediate period in his *Critique of the Gotha Programme*. There, deeply conscious of the continuities between capitalism and its successor, and the limitations which this implied, Marx maintained that communism would not burst on the world in one glorious moment. There would be no sudden conversion of the proletariat, no immediate and fundamental institutional change. The birth of the new order would prove difficult and painful. 'What we have to deal with here is a communist society, not as it has developed on its own foundations, but, on the contrary, just as it emerges from capitalist society: which is thus in every respect economically, morally and intellectually, still stamped with the birth marks of the old society from whose womb it emerges.'[25] Unequal individual endowments still produce unequal rewards. There will be economic differentiation, though it is not clear how much. 'But these defects are inevitable in the first phase of communist society as it is when it has just emerged after prolonged birth-pangs from capitalist society. Right can never be higher than the economic structure of society and its cultural development conditioned thereby.'[26] The traditions and values of the old order weigh heavily before and after the revolutionary period, in the first case hindering the development of radical forces, and in the second threatening to disrupt the hard-won victory. Certain aspects of capitalist organisation and morality persist. They will not disappear at once, but will die gradually as material and institutional changes interact with and support changes in human nature.

It is not of vital importance to this study to decide whether Marx's account of 'raw communism' represented his own early view of man's condition when he began seriously to emancipate himself, though it is important if this was Marx's own view in 1844, and if it is similar in content to the brief version in the *Critique*. It seems quite clear, however, that the *Critique* differs more than merely in the restraint of its language,[27] in that it assumes different material conditions of existence, a higher economic structure and level of cultural development, than were or could have been assumed by Marx in 1844. That this led to a more concrete and direct account of the condition of human emancipation goes without saying. But what is vital is that in both 'raw communism' and 'the first phase of communist society', as presented by Marx, and regardless of whether the birth marks of the old society are identical in the two cases, Marx continued to recognise the disfigurement of socialism, the immense difficulties which it would face, because of the conditions out of which it would emerge. But he could hardly leave things there. He distinguished his own theory from that of the utopians on the ground of its recognition of, and contribution to, forces capable of transforming the evil, self-contradictory world of capitalism into a harmonious future society. And, given his realistic view of the problems of the intermediate stage – and, even then, it may not be realistic enough – the means of transformation would need to be extremely powerful. He often offered neatly rounded myths and largely verbal formulations which fob off rather than confront difficulties, but he also provided a serious account of the mechanisms and the content of future social change.

Marx's most important general claim in this respect was that institutional changes and changes to human nature coincide. Man transforms himself in the revolutionary process, which is itself the product of his activity. As the third of the pithy *Theses on Feuerbach* puts it: 'The coincidence of the changing of circumstances and of human activity or self-changing can be conceived and rationally understood only as revolutionary practice.'[28] Man is product and producer of the world, and the process is always an interactive one, in which objective circumstances set limits to what he can do. He asserts himself as producer, as subjective agent, more directly and fully in this revolutionary period than at any other time: it is his closest approximation, hitherto, to autonomous activity. Marx's predictions assume continuous change, to which subjective human agency – which is at the same time being expanded, developed and altered – contributes. Because of the continuous transformation of the world, and of men's standpoints in relation to it, Marx avoided efforts to pin down the future concretely and in detail.

The most encouraging changes are those to human nature. Co-operative and spontaneous activity transforms man and, in particular, the proletarian revolution becomes a great, purging experience, in which meanness and the acquisitive instincts lose something of their potency, and the workers catch an elevating glimpse of the future. The revolution not only destroys the old order – it develops, according to *The German Ideology*, 'the universal character and the energy of the proletariat, without which the revolution cannot be accomplished; and in which further the proletariat rids itself of everything that still clings to it from its previous position in society.'[29] And again:

> Both for the production on a mass scale of this communist consciousness, and for the success of the cause itself, the alteration of men on a mass scale is necessary, an alteration which can only take place in a practical movement, a revolution; this revolution is necessary, therefore, not because the ruling class cannot be overthrown in any other way, but also because the class overthrowing it can only in a revolution succeed in ridding itself of all the muck of ages and become fitted to found society anew.[30]

These comments suggest that the process of revolutionary change – here, presumably, involving violence, though much else besides – itself helps men develop the qualities necessary for the new world. The revolution becomes the supreme act of human mastery, the change of self which coincides with the change of circumstances. The logic of Marx's position, to which I shall return later in considering critically his theory of communism, is that no experience of historical revolutions could be simply counterposed to his version as disproof. At this point, I simply wish to stress the difference in tone from both the 1844 *Manuscripts*, which came earlier, and *The Critique of the Gotha Programme*, which came later. In neither of these works did Marx concede that in revolution the 'muck of ages' might be washed away – though he did not say otherwise, and it is possible that in the latter work he assumed *some* improvement in the quality of the proletariat during the revolutionary period. It seems that his degree of optimism fluctuated and that his readiness to encourage optimism varied, as it naturally would given his role in a movement whose parts were at different stages of development and facing their own concrete historical problems and opportunities, and also that in *The German Ideology* his vision was less constrained than at most other times.

Even allowing for some moral growth on the part of the proletariat during the democratic struggle and the revolution, a period of proletarian dictatorship will prove necessary. Building on the achievements of capitalism and presumably led or inspired by the most advanced and resolute members of the working class, it will complete the task of laying the foundations for communism. The task will not be simple, nor will these times smell of the oil of roses.

Marx did not examine very closely the political or institutional structure of the proletarian dictatorship, which is presented in general terms as a democratic system, a government by the whole people. His one concrete account of the intermediate period is provided in *The Civil War in France*, an angry pamphlet written on the occasion of an unexpected and heroic event – the establishment of the Paris Commune in 1871. Marx was inspired by the fervour and the high hopes of the Communards, storming heaven. In April 1872 he wrote: 'What elasticity, what historical initiative, what a capacity for sacrifice in these Parisians! ...History has no example of a like greatness.'[31] And yet his view of the historical commune can by no means be taken as an unequivocal avowal of it. He was strongly against the proposed insurrection before it occurred, believing that the condition of the French proletariat, demoralised and divided through its experience under Bonaparte, made it a most unlikely agent of constructive revolutionary change, even if other historical conditions were favourable, which they were not. He deeply distrusted the Jacobin and petty bourgeois elements, irresponsible and half-hearted revolutionaries, which he saw – before and after – as the moving spirits in the uprising. As Avineri points out, in the course of a perceptive analysis of the various pressures and considerations which Marx had to take into account when discussing the Commune, the fact that it became a symbol of proletarian solidarity forced him to mute his criticisms, and, more significantly, his adherence to the Commune was less to its achievements than to its promise. He saw a difference between the actual Commune and its principles, how it appeared when its potentialities were projected into the future.[32]

Marx took the Commune to contain the rudiments of a completely new historical creation, towards which it aspired. Hence it was quite unlike the medieval commune, for it had assumed the revolutionary task of breaking the modern state power and attempting a socialist revolution. Engels referred to the Commune as 'no longer a state in the proper sense of the word'[33] – an estimate which may have been encouraged by the assault of the Communards on what was an extremely formidable bureaucratic system. The Commune seemed at the time to be in many respects a fair model of the proletarian dictatorship, despite the special difficulties which it faced. Engels, though not Marx, later wrote: 'Look at the Paris Commune. That was the Dictatorship of the Proletariat.'[34]

Marx thought that the political achievements and aspirations of the Commune were its most significant characteristic. In particular, the efforts to establish popular control over bureaucracy and executive marked a growth of social as against political power. Marx outlined the governmental structure – and the actual political achievement – of the Commune as follows:

> The Commune was formed of the municipal councillors, chosen by universal suffrage in the various wards of the town, responsible and revocable at short terms. The majority of its members were naturally working men, or acknowledged representatives of the working class. The Commune was to be a working, not a parliamentary, body, executive and legislative at the same time. Instead of continuing to be the agent of the Central Government, the police was at once stripped of its political attributes, and turned into the responsible and at all times revocable agent of the Commune. So were the officials of all other branches of the Administration. From the members of the Commune downwards, the public service had to be done at workmen's wages. The vested interests and the representation allowances of the high dignitaries of State

disappeared along with the high dignitaries themselves. Public functions ceased to be the private property of the tools of the Central Government. Not only municipal administration, but the whole initiative hitherto exercised by the State was laid into the hands of the Commune.[35]

In this way, the separate and increasingly independent organs of the state were drawn back into the body of society – a foretaste of the process in which all alienated social powers would be seen as man's own and subordinated to him. Accountability to the people and the removal of the pecuniary temptations of office were to destroy the corruption which had spread throughout the Assembly, the judiciary, the police force and the standing army – indeed, throughout the whole body of state functionaries, down to the lowest level. The standing army was to be replaced by a national militia. The power of the Church – the spiritual force of repression – was to be broken by separating it from the state and from state aid, and making it dependent on voluntary contributions. This would have freed the educational system, and given the peasant 'enlightenment by the schoolmaster in the place of stultification by the priest'.[36] In these ways the Communal Constitution would have 'restored to the social body all the forces hitherto absorbed by the State parasite, feeding upon, and clogging the free movement of, society.'[37]

Marx was quite convinced that this would not amount to the abolition of all the functions hitherto exercised by the state. 'While the merely repressive organs of the old governmental power were to be amputated, its legitimate functions were to be wrested from an authority usurping pre-eminence over society itself, and restored to the responsible agents of society.'[38] Authority and officials remained necessary. The task was to ensure that vested interests did not develop, to keep the authorities in check, and one of the means to this end was the shortening of terms in office and the establishment of independent local bodies, on the basis of which a pyramidal political structure was to be built.[39] In these circumstances, with local self-governing bodies managing what they could, the role of the central authority would naturally diminish. There were, even then, intimations of the moral order of the future. The crime rate had fallen sharply and the public burning of the guillotine – the symbol of repression – was a highly popular act.

The working class revealed supreme initiative in its organisation of economic life, where it sought to destroy the conditions of class rule by transforming the means of production into 'mere instruments of free and associated labour'. Production was taken over by co-operative societies, working under a common plan. It was primarily because of this that Marx could praise the Communards, not merely for heroism and self-sacrifice, but for creating an expansive political form. The Commune was the glorious harbinger of a new society, and its main achievement was summed up as follows: 'It was essentially a working-class government, the product of the struggle of the producing against the appropriating class, the political form at last discovered under which to work out the economic emancipation of labour...With labour emancipated, every man becomes a working man, and productive labour ceases to be a class attribute.'[40]

Two years later Marx played down the image of the Commune as a free and inspired political form, saying that the communal councils were only temporary organs of the revolution, and implying that the Commune could not be taken straightforwardly as a model for the proletarian dictatorship. 'The workers must...aim at the most decided centralisation of power in the hands of the State authority. They should not allow themselves to be confused by democratic talk of freedom of the communities, of self government, etc.'[41] That this marks a sudden shift from his 1871 position must be doubted. In 1871, even when he was carefully bringing out the positive side of the Commune, he stressed the extent of the problems faced and the need for a national political apparatus, and complained of the innocence-cum-frivolity of the Communards in their perilous situation. After all, Blanqui was a far stronger intellectual influence on the Communards than was Marx, and amongst those members of the International who participated, more were Proudhonist than Marxist. Marx claimed that they tried to go too far, when they could have reached a reasonable and fruitable compromise with Versailles. The Communards were neither firm enough nor practical enough.

The general comments of Marx and Engels on the proletarian dictatorship stress that it is a political form resting on mass support, which nonetheless requires a centralised, autocratic structure of power. For it is a dictatorship, whose existence and political character are unavoidable because of the enemies it confronts as well as the indecisiveness and divisions in the ranks of its supporters, who remain in many respects the product of the capitalist past. As Marx informed a questioner in 1881: 'One thing you can at any rate be sure of: a socialist government does not come into power in a country unless conditions are so developed that it can immediately take the necessary measures for intimidating the mass of the bourgeoisie sufficiently to gain time – the first desideratum – for permanent action.'[42] Shortly after Marx's death, Engels also pointed to the enemies which the new regime would have to face, necessitating the adaptation of the state to new functions. 'But to destroy that [the state] at such a moment, would be to destroy the only organism by means of which the victorious working class can exert its newly-conquered power, keep down its capitalist enemies and carry out that economic revolution of society without which the whole victory must end in a defeat and in a massacre of the working class like that after the Paris Commune.'[43] The White Terrors of 1848 and 1871 were strongly etched in their minds, leading to a fear of premature proletarian attempts to seize power, and to the demand that, when in power, the proletariat must use political coercion to continue the struggle against its remaining opponents. Once the proletariat had taken power, it could not relax, for it had to destroy capitalism and all the roots of ancient political institutions before the state could be finally transcended. The changes which the proletarian dictatorship is called upon to effect include the transformation of the economic and political foundations of capitalism – its economic institutions, its personnel and its values. During this period certain classes, whose ultimate objectives differ from those of the proletariat, will have to be checked and uplifted, for example, such erstwhile revolutionary allies as the peasantry, still cherishing small property illusions.[44]

But precisely what methods will be employed by the dominant power during the transitional period? It is clear that social education and communal experience have a significant part to play, but so too may coercion and violence. It is true that Marx was extremely hostile to any such notion as a Jacobin dictatorship, which he saw as a minority regime based upon rampant political power and an inflation of the political will, and thus based essentially on terror. Marx's proletarian dictatorship is one based upon the prior existence of economic and other conditions which ensure the existence of a conscious, united proletarian majority – though not immediately at the collapse of capitalism. If the economical agencies tending towards a higher form of society had developed to their utmost possible extent within capitalism, then revolution would approximate to a natural transfer of power, and would be nothing like a *putsch* or a *coup d'état*. If, on the other hand, the proletariat or its alleged spokesmen seized power prematurely, they might well use terror to compensate for economic undevelopment and the strength and variety of their enemies, and would eventually go under in a melée of chaos and violence. Had the Communards behaved ferociously, this would simply have brought out, more strongly than did their eventual defeat, that they had asserted themselves without the required supporting conditions. But the rejection of Jacobin dictatorship – which some see as a premonition of Bolshevism – and the assumption that the more violence, the less are conditions ripe for change, does not suggest that a successful proletariat will not have to employ violence. Economic developments do not gently push aside and supplant its enemies. Revolutionary violence may shorten the birth-pangs of the new order, by pursuing its resolute foes. Circumstances will be difficult, and blind faith in spontaneity or libertarian social devices could lead to the defeat of even a numerically predominant proletariat. The precise amount of 'legitimate' coercion and violence required to establish and maintain the new order will obviously depend upon the stage at which the revolution occurs, and the mechanisms, and forms through which it has taken place – though leaders, who do not know everything in advance, may use more or less violence than is needed. Thus the method of expropriating the expropriators may be peaceful. In his reformist days Engels wrote that whether or not the big landowners and manufacturers were to be compensated depended on the circumstances. 'We by no means consider compensation as impermissible in any event; Marx told me (and how many times!) that in his opinion we could get off cheapest if we could buy out the whole lot of them.'[45] Avineri, in conformity with his general presentation of a 'soft' Marx, holds that private property was not to be seized, by political fiat, but would co-exist with more progressive economic and political arrangements, until it proved unviable and had to transform itself.[46] It seems doubtful whether Marx's 'raw communists', as portrayed by Avineri, would happily wait such a result, nor indeed, that Marx's capitalists, as portrayed in *Capital*, would be ready for anything but last-ditch resistance to the enemies of bourgeois property. My point is not that Marx was committed to violence, but that Avineri exaggerates his commitment to peaceful transformation. Marx was committed to the realisation of a new society by whatever policies and tactics proved necessary to and compatible with that goal: hence violence might be necessary but terror could neither contribute to nor was it compatible with the achievement of communism. For Marx and Engels the policies of the future could not be defined in advance. In this area, at least, they were pragmatic and flexible, which is not to say that they set no limits to possible action, or that they had no firm ideas as to what would be required.

The replacement of capitalism does not lead immediately to economic equality or to a distributive system based upon needs. In his attack on the Gotha Programme Marx admitted that rewards would have to be determined by contributions – 'it tacitly recognizes unequal individual endowment and thus productive capacity as natural privileges'.[47] Wage labour persists, but the system differs from capitalism in being a genuine meritocracy. The criteria for evaluating contributions are not discussed, however. Thus the parasites have disappeared, as have certain unjustifiable discrepancies, but the new economic order – adjusted to men's individual needs and qualities – has not yet come into being. Everyone has become a worker: men have not yet become fully human.

Marx anticipated a substantial shift in public expenditure during the intermediate period. From the product of labour certain deductions must be made for social purposes, 'to satisfy the general social needs', as is the case in all societies.[48] On one hand, the amount necessary for the general costs of administration not belonging to production will substantially diminish, and will diminish further as the new society develops. In his account of the Commune Marx had described proletarian government as cheap government, because of the disappearance of the great mass of state functionaries, the replacement of the standing army by a national militia, and the equalisation of salaries. On the other hand, the central directing body will be responsible for the common satisfaction of social needs, such as health, education and relief of those who cannot work. Expenditure on social services will be greater than it was under capitalism, and will increase further with the development of the new society.

COMMUNISM

Communism is a return to lost innocence and a completion of reality. But it is a return which arises out of and presupposes capitalism and the whole of previous development, and hence, although it will be structurally similar to the primitive communist societies, man will be immensely more powerful, self-conscious and developed. According to Marx's grand historical myth, men are to witness the final disappearance of the connected evils of class societies. True communism is described, in the metaphysical language of the 1844 *Manuscripts*, as 'the genuine resolution of the strife between existence and essence, between objectification and self-confirmation, between freedom and necessity, between the individual and the species. Communism is the riddle of history solved, and it knows itself to be this solution.'[49] This truly human world is characterised by a deep and productive solidarity between men, now undivided and unrestricted by any of the traditional sources of conflict. The elimination of the causes of self-estrangement involves a radical transformation of man's relations with nature and the world of production, with his fellows and with his own, labouring activity, in which his plight was expressed most deeply. Outside forces will no longer constrain him, as he masters chance and circumstances: he will be free, undeluded, creative and co-operative.

Marx attached supreme importance to human self-determination, to which the capitalist labour process was a major obstacle. Under capitalism men failed to manifest their essential powers, to develop their faculties, but remained partial creatures, confined to specific and limited tasks. In *The German Ideology* he spoke of the necessity of abolishing labour, by which he meant the abolition of that destructive specialisation which separated and opposed life and labour, with life beginning where labouring ended. The division of labour offered man no choice, it left him no opportunity to develop his latent capacities, but forced a particular, exclusive sphere of activity upon him.

> He is a hunter, a fisherman, a shepherd or a critical critic, and must remain so if he does not want to lose his means of livelihood; while in Communist society, where nobody has one exclusive sphere of activity but each can become accomplished in any branch he wishes, society regulates the general production and thus makes it possible for me to do one thing today and another tomorrow, hunt in the morning, fish in the afternoon, rear cattle in the evening, criticise after dinner, just as I have a mind, without ever becoming hunter, fisherman, shepherd or critic.[50]

It is tempting to draw a sharp decisive line between the appealing rural vision of the early writings and the more realistic assessment of the possibilities of industrialism, especially in relation to the division of labour, which was presented in the probing and predominantly economic analysis of capitalism of the later works. But, while the later writings reveal more recognition of the limitations imposed by industrialism – reflecting his greater knowledge of concrete economic phenomena and the growth of large-scale industrial enterprises during the century – Marx's hatred of the division of labour remained too deep-rooted for him to simply surrender to any apparent demands of the system. His whole vision of man conflicted absolutely with existing specialisation. The rich human being, the emancipated and creative man of the early writings, is one who has had all the human senses and attributes freed. The world of sense is restored to man, and his needs are enriched and emancipated from alienated and distorted forms. Wealth is found in the development of human capacities rather than in the things or objects possessed. Man becomes versatile, multi-specialised and independent, not the mere instrument of outside persons and institutions, of which the most repressive and frustrating is the division of labour. Activity, not dictated by needs external to itself, for example the need to survive, will be spontaneous, creative and many-sided. The stupidity and partiality imposed by the system of private property, and in particular the desire for exclusive possession, will end as new desires and needs emerge. The autonomous man resembles the artist of romantic literature, for whom the distinction between work and play, or at least the distinction between work-time and free-time, has disappeared. He is close to his creation, confirms his individuality in it and expresses and sees his genuine self in all that he does.

Marx's later comments on the division of labour show that this vision of man persisted, and that his efforts to see that vision embodied in productive and social arrangements continued, even though the degree of possible emancipation came to seem more limited. In a well-known passage in the *Critique of the Gotha Programme* he put the transformation of the division of labour at the very centre of scientific socialism.

> In a higher phase of communist society, after the enslaving subordination of the individual to the division of labour, and also therewith the antithesis between mental and physical labour, has vanished; after labour has become not only a means of life but life's prime want; after the productive forces have also increased with the all-round development of the individual, and all the springs of co-operative wealth flow more abundantly – only then can the narrow horizon of bourgeois right be crossed in its entirety and society inscribe on its banners: From each according to his needs![51]

In the first volume of *Capital* he frequently condemns individual enslavement to specialisation, and visualises the end of such enslavement. He discovered, even under the restrictive conditions of capitalism, examples of human versatility, foreshadowing things to come. Technical and agricultural schools and craft training already helped develop the various capacities of the individual and undermined the old division of labour. In the third volume of *Capital* the major problem – that of combining a productive and sophisticated economy with individual freedom and development – is directly acknowledged and faced. There Marx argued that the shortening of the working day was the crucial means of emancipation, for freedom begins where necessary labour ceases. It lies outside the sphere of natural material production.

> Freedom in this field can only consist in socialized man, the associated producers, rationally regulating their interchange with Nature, and achieving this with the least expenditure of energy and under conditions most favourable to, and worthy of, their human nature. But it nonetheless still remains a realm of necessity. Beyond it begins that development of human energy which is an end in itself, the true realm of freedom, which, however, can blossom forth only with this realm of necessity as its basis. The shortening of the working-day is its basic prerequisite.[52]

The assumptions underlying this significant statement need to be brought out. The first assumption is that a substantial general reduction in labour time is now possible. 'Disregarding the class contradiction, the whole nation would now need only one-third of its time for direct

production, whereas earlier it had needed two-thirds. With equal distribution, everyone would now have two-thirds of his time for unproductive labour and for leisure. But in capitalist production, everything
appears and is contradictory.'[53] Capitalism had developed the means
whereby a larger product could be produced with less direct labour,
through the invention of powerful mechanical agents, which restricted
human labour to 'watching and supervising the production process'.[54]
Of course, capitalism was not itself capable of realising the possibilities
which it had introduced, partly because it was an exploitative system,
resting on surplus labour, and partly because it was wasteful and inefficient, squandering labour power outrageously.[55] In socialist society the
working day could be shortened through the fullest possible application
of science to production, along with the abolition of profiteering, superfluous employments and sheer waste, and the transformation of the
labourer himself. However, actual labour time would not be cut back
to the absolute minimum, which would be less than necessary labour-
time under capitalism because of increased productiveness. Necessary
labour time would be greater than capitalism's hypothetical minimum
because the notion of the 'means of subsistence' would expand, with
the labourer – as a rich human being with diverse and complex needs
– claiming and receiving a far higher standard of living, while a part
of surplus labour – that providing a fund for reserve and accumulation
– would then be counted as necessary labour.[56]

The second underlying assumption is that leisure time can be time
for free development, free development of the kind which had been
integrated into the labour process in the pastoral utopia of *The German
Ideology*, and that free time and work would mutually reinforce each
other, thereby reducing the antagonism between work and life. 'Free
time – which includes leisure time as well as time for higher activities –
naturally transforms anyone who enjoys it into a different person, and
it is this different person who then enters the direct process of production.'[57] Hannah Arendt's criticism of Marx's view that free time can lead
to the emancipation of labour founders because it abstracts from the
relationship between, and the general context of, working and free
time, ignoring both the interaction between them, and the broader social
relationships within which they are set, as Marx conceived them.
Miss Arendt accuses Marx of sharing

> the illusion of a mechanistic philosophy which assumes that labour
> power, like any other energy, can never be lost, so that if it is not
> spent and exhausted in the drudgery of life it will automatically
> nourish other, 'higher', activities...A hundred years after Marx
> we know the fallacy of this reasoning; the spare time of the animal

laborans is never spent in anything but consumption, and the more time left to him, the greedier and more craving his appetites.[58]

Marx conceived free and labouring activity as feeding each other, and favoured an educational system which would contribute to this end. In many connections he stressed the vital linkage of production and education, of work and education, of practical and theoretical education. One of the ten revolutionary measures for the proletariat includes the combination of education with industrial production,[59] whilst in the *Critique of the Gotha Programme* an early combination of productive labour with education is described as 'one of the most potent means for the transformation of present-day society'.[60] Marx had no conception of the drudge freely and productively engaging in 'higher' activities when he escapes the factory: his conception was one of the removal of drudgery through shorter working hours and better conditions, where science had removed the backbreaking labour which was sheer sacrifice and misery, and where the total social environment gave men ample opportunity for participation and self-development. Hence Marx, like most other socialist critics of industrial capitalism, wanted to alter society as a whole, and not merely what happens within the factory walls. He, like them, assumed that the worker's perception of his work could be changed substantially through increased participation, involvement and equality in the larger society. Marx and Engels naturally called for an overall transformation of social institutions and social relations, which would make each feel a full member of the community, neither subjugated nor exploited.

While it is true that, for Marx, labour remained the main constituent of the human personality, and that much of the language of *Capital* is identical with that of the *Manuscripts*,[61] it is important to note that in his later writings Marx did see the framework of industry and labour as more restrictive than he had earlier. Engels tended to assert the restrictiveness of technology and productive arrangements more firmly than did Marx, especially in a short piece which he wrote in 1872, insisting on the need for detailed organisation and hence authority in modern industrial enterprises. He was taking issue with certain anarchistic views of authority, which he found historically retrogressive, and this helps explain his uncompromising tone.

The automatic machinery of a big factory is much more despotic than the small capitalists who employ workers have been. At least with regard to the hours of work one may write upon the portals of these factories: *Lasciate ogni autonomia, voi che entrate!* (Leave, ye that enter in, all autonomy behind!) If man, by dint of his knowledge and inventive genius, has subdued the forces of nature, the latter avenge themselves upon him, in so far as he employs them, to a veritable despotism independent of all social organisation. Wanting to abolish authority in large-scale industry is tantamount to wanting to abolish industry itself, to destroy the power loom in order to return to the spinning wheel.[62]

To Marx, technology could not act despotically as an autonomous force, in abstraction from the total society of which it was part. But what Marx did accept was that, in advanced industrial societies, the factory and its characteristic instruments would continue to make demands on the individual which were not compatible with his own early hopes. The hellishness of industry could not be blamed solely on capitalism. Modern production methods and modern technology had their own unpleasant imperatives, which might be sharply reduced within socialism, but which were not to be dispelled with a sudden wave of the philosopher's wand.[63] It is incorrect to treat as a central and persisting part of his account of labour the views that labour and necessity might be eliminated altogether, that under communism all professions would become hobbies or play, and that he left us with 'the rather distressing alternative between productive slavery and unproductive freedom'.[64] For Marx, men could not abolish the realm of necessity without destroying society, but their labour could be reduced in absolute terms, and that which remained essential could be carried out in conditions appropriate to their humanity – with the additional benefit of increasing industrial efficiency. The rural idyll of the 1840s faded, and self-realisation became something to be found primarily in free time, though the sharp and demoralising rift between work and free time, which had so disfigured capitalism, was to be reduced substantially.

The characteristic and central institutional goal of communists is normally taken to be common ownership of the means of production. Engels gave it a central place in 1846, when he wrote that the objectives of the communists included the achievement of the ends of the proletariat through the abolition of private property and its replacement by a community of goods.[65] Yet this theme was never thoroughly developed in the works of classical Marxism. In the early writings the point is sometimes brough out in critiques of the limited perspectives of such socialists as Proudhon. Like Marx's alienated man, Proudhon stressed the possession of material things rather than the emancipation of the senses. In the words of The Holy Family: 'But as his criticism of political economy is a prisoner of the premises of political economy, he still understands the very reappropriation of the objective world as the political-economic form of possession.'[66] Proudhon, like many other reformers, was a living contradiction, unable to reconcile his petit-bourgeois and his socialist ideas. The various redistributionist ideologies were damned by their acceptance of the principle of private property. Marx's condemnation was twofold – the ideal of private property for all was impossible, and it could not make men free. It was a mirage. As Marx informed those German immigrants in America who sought land reform within capitalism, the wish that 'all people shall be property owners' can be as little realised as 'the wish to make all people emperors, kings and popes'.[67] More importantly, not only could man not be freed by the possession of property, but human emancipation was incompatible with the institution of private property. The raising of wages would not help towards human emancipation – it would be 'nothing but better payment for the slave, and would not conquer either for the worker or for labour their human status and dignity'.[68] Vulgar socialism, with its concentration on distribution, remained fettered within the old system, unable to appreciate the dependence of distribution upon the prevailing mode of production. Marxism itself permitted reward according to contribution during the transitional stage – right can never be higher than the economic structure of society – but remained deeply antagonistic to what it dismissed as a petit-bourgeois conception of justice, with its vain ideal of 'just exchange' within capitalist society.

In Marx's scheme, the total productive forces of the community pass into the hands of the associated producers, i.e. everybody. The institution of private property will disappear. 'From the standpoint of a higher economic form of society, private ownership of the globe by single individuals will appear quite as absurd as private ownership of one man by another.'[69] Private property was not merely the foundation of other capitalist institutions: it supported the vices, especially egoism, and thus blighted and twisted man's enjoyment of his world. Marx envisaged the abolition of private property in productive resources, and thus of the capacity to exploit and enslave, and the transcendence of old notions of exclusive possessiveness. True personal property, the new form of appropriation, would not involve selfish claims, exclusive plots, and forebidding titles, but the whole world and its riches would belong to all men, to use and enjoy but not to accumulate and keep.[70]

The abolition of private property will, by definition, lead to the disappearance of classes, which are defined in terms of private property. In Marx's view classes as such had to be destroyed. He felt that it was futile to seek long-term harmonious relations between entities which were by nature antagonistic, and bitterly attacked talk of the political, economic and social equalisation of classes. 'The "equalisation of classes", literally interpreted, is nothing but another way of saying the "harmony of capital and labour" preached by the bourgeois Socialists. Not the logically impossible "equalisation of classes" but the historically necessary "abolition of classes" constitutes the final aim of the International Working Men's Association.'[71] Where relations of exploitation and conflict were obscured, reformers might envisage the harmonisation of classes, as was the case with the popular American economist C. H. Carey, who interpreted rent, profit and wages not as 'conditions of struggle and antagonism', but as 'conditions of association and harmony'. 'All he proves, of course', Marx commented, 'is that he is taking the "undeveloped" conditions of the United States for "normal conditions".'[72] For Marx, the harmonisation of classes was, like the goal of private property for all, an impossible aspiration, and one quite inadequate to realise human emancipation.

The disappearance of classes (and of capitalism specifically) leads naturally to the disappearance of the state, which is the product, expression, servant and strengthener of class society. If the state is an organisation of which the main object is to secure, by force, the subjection of the working majority to the wealthy minority, it certainly makes sense to argue that it will pass away when the wealthy minority does, along with all other classes, and if the state is an organisation resting upon a certain contradiction, it also makes sense to hold that it will disappear when that contradiction dissolves. However, it may have developed, or always have had, other functions or uses which would make its continued existence more likely, and even within Marxist theory its role is not confined to that of a repressive class force, nor is it presented as simply a parasitic institution. But, leaving that question aside for the moment, the general Marxist claim is that political institutions, conceived in a narrow sense as instruments of class rule, will ultimately disappear because of a series of transformations in more basic parts of the social order. Thus 'the communist revolution, which removes the division of labour, ultimately abolishes political institutions'.[73] Engels, whose view of the state arose out of a different and less complex theoretical background than did Marx's, made the most familiar Marxist declaration on the subject. 'State interference in social relations becomes, in one domain after another, superfluous, and then withers away of itself; the government of persons is replaced by the administration of things, and by the conduct of the processes of production. The state is not "abolished". It withers away.'[74] It is not surprising that the meaning of such a large assertion was not spelled out in detail. In *The Critique of the Gotha Programme* Marx did at least ask the key question, though he did not attempt to answer it. 'The question now arises: what sort of change will the form of the state undergo in communist society? In other words, what social functions will remain then still in existence analogous to the functions now performed by the state? This question can only be considered scientifically.'[75]

Marx and Engels wished to retain the advantages of large-scale industrial society while removing as many of its defects as possible. They regarded the common focus of utopian socialists upon small communities and small-scale enterprises as essentially retrograde, despite the admirable goal of reducing the destructiveness of labour and satisfying the needs and capacities of all men. Yet they themselves did not make clear what institutional form, what political-administrative organisation, would be necessary to manage the large and complex industrial societies which they envisaged. In what sense was the political apparatus to wither away or disappear or be transcended?

St Simon, who did seriously consider the 'political' problem of large states, saw government (politics) as the maintenance of order by the use of force. It involved the domination or coercion of most men, normally by men who were themselves ignorant and selfish. On the other hand, administration, in his idealised notion, is concerned with the most efficient management of the resources of the community. It was to be conducted by impartial and disinterested experts, exercising their technical skills like doctors or scientists. Although St Simon's particular brand of élitism made him a questionable champion of a non-political world, his theory urged the replacement of government by administration, and this involved, at least, the disappearance of the coercive, brutal aspect of political power. It meant this also for Marx and Engels. They envisaged, ultimately, the disapearance of the traditional enemies of socialism – police forces, prisons, armies, courts and bureaucracies. There would be no more crime, owing to the disappearance of its historical causes. For the criminal was driven to his crimes by economic necessity, as in *Les Misérables*, or he was an heroic protester against an evil class society. Without classes, and without poverty, crime and laws against crime would wither away, and law would be replaced by self-imposed restraints.

The question of whether or not the Marxist claim is as radical as it seems now arises. The prediction that the state will wither away rests upon an extremely narrow definition of the realm of politics, so that many people, in looking at the substance of Marx's account of the future, would deny that politics had completely disappeared. Marx and Engels both distinguish between repressive class functions, which they associated with the state, and the 'legitimate functions' of social authorities, such as those which Marx thought the Communards were seeking to wrest back from the state, and those which Engels described as the indispensable and proper tasks of the early state. Insofar as these functions arise from the existence of disputes and abuses of authority,[76] they raise significant political issues at once, and even if they are limited to the 'mere superintendence of production',[77] they presuppose authority or authorities and, moreover, the superintendence of production is hardly as mere as mere can be. Marx and Engels made it clear that in the complex economic order which they envisaged, tasks of management and supervision would remain. Production, no longer determined by the mechanism of the market, would be regulated by 'the direct and conscious control of society over its working time'.[78] In the final volume of *Capital*, which contains many clues to his position on the future management of the economy, Marx emphasised the need for social regulation, for a commanding will to co-ordinate and unify the economic processes. Regulation and order were indispensable elements of any mode of production. He did not envisage spontaneous proletarian organisation of separate enterprises. The need for planning, supervision and management, and for the organised extraction of a surplus for social expenditure, remains and may even increase. In Marx's words, 'after the abolition of the capitalist mode of production, but still retaining social production, the determination of value continues to prevail in the sense that the regulation of labour-time and the distribution of social labour among the various production groups, ultimately the bookkeeping encompassing all this, becomes more essential than ever'.[79] The implications of such general comments are not spelled out, and it is not clear what they – and such apparently straightforward suggestions as that accountancy or book-keeping remain crucial – actually entail in the way of division and distribution of authority and the presence of control. But for Marx and Engels, the necessary business of the future society becomes strikingly simple and clear. The general production is regulated smoothly, without a clash of wills. Conscious collective planning of the future ends the domination of uncontrolled social forces and hence realises the liberal vision of a self-regulating economic system,[80] in that men are no longer subjected to legal compulsion or to external economic sanctions and forces. In one sense what has happened is that society has reasserted itself against the independent political forces, so that the state is transformed from an organ superimposed upon society into one completely subordinate to it.[81] To man – a social creature rather than a political animal – human unity is restored, as production is concentrated in the hands of a free and vast association of the whole people.

This account of the communist future, with its echoes of Rousseau – disagreements or cracks in society are distortions, clear imperfections – leaves many things unsaid, and says many others far too readily. At present, however, I wish only to outline as fully as possible Marx's vision and the grounds he gave for thinking it feasible. It is quite clear that he was making a very large and serious claim – even if not as large as it is sometimes believed to be – when he stated that, in the association which excludes classes and their antagonisms, 'there will be no more political power properly so-called, since political power is precisely the official expression of antagonism in civil society'.[82] He was predicting an end to significant social conflict, and to the political institutions which contradiction and conflict had produced, and which had in turn served the interests of the economically powerful. While he admitted the need for authorities to manage the economy, he believed that constituional gadgetry would be unnecessary to restrain rulers. When societies are divided into classes, constitutional guarantees of individual rights were patently inadequate: when, on the other hand, the community had become one and indivisible, with the disappearance of the old sources of conflict, there would be no need for them. Is the suggestion, then, that the distinctions which had once proved politically significant no longer have divisive results – due, perhaps, to an increase in the moral and cultural level of society – or are the distinctions themselves to disappear? Engels suggested that some inequalities would persist. 'Between one country and another, one province and another and even one locality and another there will always exist a certain inequality in the conditions of life, which it will be possible to reduce to a minimum but never entirely remove. Alpine dwellers will always have different conditions of life from those of people living on the plains.'[83] It is not clear whether Engels is sugesting the obvious point that climate – and hence productivity – varies and will vary in different parts of the world, or whether he has in mind a differential distribution of economic goods, which may arise from diversity of conditions of life. Marx certainly admitted differential rewards in the intermediate period, when men were to be rewarded according to an equal standard, labour. 'This equal right is an unequal right for unequal labour. It recognises no class differences, because everyone is only a worker like everyone else; but it tacitly recognises unequal individual endowment and thus productive capacity as natural privileges.'[84]

The claim that everyone is now a worker, that no class differences are recognised, and the more far-reaching claims that man will live in free, egalitarian communities unhampered by political institutions and by hierarchy, are not particularly interesting until the grounds of belief are offered. Marx's main grounds are two. In the first instance, productivity is assumed to be enormously increased, and productive arrangements made more simple and rational, in the new society, after the appalling wastage of resources under capitalism. Marxism condemns the anarchy of capitalism rather than its distributive injustices, but it also has a profoundly egalitarian thrust, so that a changed distribution of resources is envisaged along with much greater economic efficiency and a coresponding increase of social wealth. There is no longer a desperate pursuit of food and wealth. The diminution of the economic pressures on men and the wakening of their productive energy enables their diverse needs to be satisfied without the exploitation of any section of the community.

More important than the mere provision of ample resources for men is the change or development in human nature, that fulfilment of potentialities to which economic changes and experience of new, freer social conditions strongly contribute. The replacement of the state by *Gemeinwesen* or commune, of the contractual conflict-ridden world of capitalism by a free, harmonious and self-conscious community, obviously presupposes far-reaching changes in man himself, as old contaminations and deformities gradually disappear. His motives, goals and values profoundly alter. The penalties, goads and incentives of the past, including the prospect of personal gain at the expense of others, prove unnecessary as people choose to perform their public duties, not recognising them as impositions. This is the shift from force and violence to custom and public opinion, from hatred and compulsion to sympathy and free choice, which Lenin sketched in *The State and Revolution*. People observed the elementary conditions of social justice 'without force and without subjection'. Agreement is to be secured through public opinion, which is to act peacefully and in tune with the individual's own instincts. Because public opinion is so penetrative and its sanctions so various, the role of law can diminish and coercive laws eventually disappear. It is, presumably, freely formed and accepted by the great bulk of the people, and elevated and correct, threatening only the primitive, the violent and the wicked, where they persist.[85] Although Marx did not discuss the role of social education at this stage, it is fair to assume that he expected it to play an important part in removing the need for law. He envisaged a substantial change in human drives. The acquisitive urge and the lust for power were to disappear and in their place a new disinterestedness and community sense were to develop. Sydney Hook, during his Marxist phase, took the argument against Michels, relying on education and the change from politics to administration to show why the economic and social presuppositions of oligarchy could be expected to disappear.

> In a socialist society in which political leadership is an administrative function, and, therefore, carries with it no economic power, in which the processes of education strive to direct the psychic tendencies to self-assertion into 'moral and social equivalents' of oligarchi-

cal ambition, in which the monopoly of education for one class has been abolished, and the divisions of labour between manual and mental worker is progressively eliminated – the danger that Michels' 'law of oligarchy' will express itself in traditional form, becomes quite remote.[86]

Man's energies and goals are redirected by social education, and the changes in his economic and social environment remove misery and the objective grounds for discontent. Individuals, neither defined nor determined by groups, greet each other in a true fraternity. Their relations are clear, close, direct and free. The long pre-historical travail of man is over. He moves from necessity toward freedom, loses ideological delusions and becomes self-determining and dominant in a universe whose benefits and beauties all men now share. A condition of enduring, though not static, social solidarity now begins, in which the motor of social change and development is no longer systematic structural conflicts within society.[87]

This vision of society is deeply individualistic, far removed from Kasernenkommunismus or barracks-communism, which implied an undifferentiated mass controlled down to the very details of their lives, and which Marx took to be Bakunin's actual goal as well as the natural consequence of his wild inflation of the political will against social circumstances. Marx presents the communist society, explicitly, as one in which the various constraints on man have been eliminated, in which he has emerged as an individual, developing fully, freely and in an all-round way, which presupposes life in a genuine community. The institutions and the social groups which were signs of his imperfection have disappeared, leaving 'socialised humanity' or the 'genericosocial man', without any restraining political discipline, or any need for it. This was the gist of Marx's moral attack on capitalism – that it frustrated and crushed the individual in many ways, and it was natural that he should depict communism as a fulfilment of the individualistic goals which liberalism had proclaimed but had been unable to realise. What Marx sought was genuine democracy, genuine liberty for all, a genuine laissez-faire system which secured maximum economic efficiency, stability, justice and self-development. It was to be co-ordinated in a non-coercive manner, without constraint, contradiction or failure. That, at least, was the declared ideal. It may be argued, on empirical or quasi-empirical grounds, that the removal of all the limiting institutions of liberal capitalist society, which both constrain and define men, would lead, not to the emergence of the free and co-operative individual, but to an even more restrictive and destructive social order.

CRITICISMS

My criticisms by no means exhaust the possible criticisms of Marx and Engels on communism, but they are the ones most relevant to my theme. My concern is with three points of criticism, the first two of which touch on the third and crucial one, which is the general problem of diverse values and interests in circumstances in which there can be only single or concerted action. This is the case wherever general policies must be undertaken within an association, the most important of which is obviously the state or nation, and such general policies include even those which provide for or recognise diversity and conflict. The normal difficulties placed before the Marxist view that significant conflict would end if some particular institution or body of institutions disappeared are that, whatever structures are acknowledged to remain, or whatever structures the critic sees as necessarily remaining, will themselves secrete or produce certain special interests and divisions, and that vital sources of conflict and division exist which were never acknowledged in the classical theory. In my view, the problem is even more deep-rooted: admitting a hypothetical and almost unimaginable condition in which there is no structural differentiation whatsoever, in which there were no bureaucracies or oligarchies or special interests of the familiar kind, and assuming all men to be thoroughly altruistic, I would still hold strongly that such a condition would be characterised by different and competing values and visions of good, and that inevitably some general decisions would prove disturbing to some people, whose resultant actions might require, in the end, that they be somehow constrained. At present, given imperfect approximations to the vision of a profoundly consensual society, the utopian attention is focussed upon particular and apparently transient impediments to its fuller realisation – bourgeois conceptions and interests, mass incompetence and vulnerability, the power of particular oligarchies, the nefarious effects of traditional education, and so on – as if, were they obliterated, men would share the same constructive view of the world. I do not share this vision, and would not share it even if I could envisage the disappearance of all impediments to man's self-development and to his direct and unhampered association with his fellows.

I

A number of problems emerge in relation to the internal adequacy and completeness of the Marxist theory. Many of Marx's comments on the self-transformation of the proletariat and the achievement of communism appear to have some explanatory or empirical content, but prove on analysis to be empty or circular. Radical claims are sometimes secured by the movement of definitions and Hegelian concepts. Teleologies are common; for example private property provides the foundation for the transition to communism, because it cannot be abolished until it has been fully developed, but this tells us nothing about the prospects of change in the real world, though it appears to intimate a fundamental transformation. Again, the assertion that absolute poverty is a necessary condition for the absolute realisation of wealth tells us nothing about the behaviour and the aspirations of the absolutely poor. Or, to take Marx's far-reaching claim at the conclusion of *The Poverty of Philosophy*: 'The condition for the emancipation of the working class is the abolition of every class, just as the condition for the liberation of the third estate, of the bourgeois order, was the abolition of all estates and orders.'[88] Now it is clear that the working class will be emancipated or abolished if every class is abolished, because it is itself one of them – and subject to the exploitation which, by definition, exists in class society. In this respect, the comparison with the liberation of the bourgeoisie is significant because of the difference in the terms employed. The bourgeoisie abolished all estates or orders but established a regime of classes: is it not possible that the abolition of classes will lead to the establishment of some other kind of social division or stratification? The question is not only why should the proletariat be the last class, but why class division should be the last form of social division.

A more important issue arises in relation to the historical story of the origins of classes. This is of vital importance to a theory which envisages the disappearance of the old relations of domination and subordination. Remaining at present within the confines of Marxist theory, communism can only seem a possible form of society if it is explained how the basic or original causes of class division are to be eliminated – or, alternatively, if some new factor or factors are introduced which will prevent the forces which devastated the ancient gens from having similar or identical effects in the future. Why are the original sources of conflict not reproduceable? What accounts for the entrance and the exit of evil and contradiction in history? Marx sometimes gave the impression that the elimination of property would be enough to abolish classes. In *The Holy Family* this is clearly suggested in a passage which also seems to be circular.

> The proletariat executes the sentence that private property pronounced on itself by begetting the proletariat, just as it carries out the sentence that wage-labour pronounced on itself by bringing forth wealth for others and misery for itself. When the proletariat is victorious, it by no means becomes the absolute side of society,

for it is victorious only by abolishing itself and its opposite. Then
the proletariat disappears as well as the opposite which determines
it, private property.[89]

If this is a hypothesis linking the disappearance of classes with the
abolition of private property, we are left with a major difficulty. For
although property is a source or form of power, a means of controlling
others and not merely things, it is, in the Marxist schema, preceded by
the power which derives from the occupation of strategic positions –
positions of control – in the productive system. As Marx wrote in *The
Critique of Political Economy*: 'There is no property anterior to the
relations of domination and subjection which obtain in production, and
which are far more concrete relations.'[90] The elimination of property
does not itself destroy domination in the productive process, and it
cannot be simply assumed that such domination will not produce the
same consequences as before, even in conditions of material abundance.

Marx's remarks about abolishing the division of labour bear intimately
on the question of power and property. The division of labour, inequality
of power, property and classes are connected evils, and must all disappear, or the battle has been lost. The definitional manoeuvre of linking classes with private property and classlessness with its absence
leaves the prophecy as wishful thinking underpinned by an unsophisticated economic reductionism. Moreover, Marx's account of the structural transformation involved in the transition from capitalism to communism does seem to leave some of the original sources of social conflict and misery intact. The discussion of alienation, for example, raises
the crucial question – the origin of man's alienation – but does not
answer it. Marx not only denied that private property was its cause, but
treated private property as a product of alienation – though later the
relationship becomes reciprocal.[91] The gaps and the difficulties, which
reflect Marx's inability to tie up all the parts of a very complex theory,
also represent concessions to, or a disguised recognition of, social realities. Others arise from his philosophically proper refusal to try to state,
or settle, the problems of the future in advance, though one wonders
how he was able to say as much about the basic features of communism
as he did. These problems concern, especially, the nature of authority
and its possible form and extent, the possibility of dissatisfaction and
alienation, and the form and content of future change. Engels insisted
that there were no perfect societies, that 'all successive historical systems
are only transitory stages in the endless course of development of human
society from the lower to the higher'.[92] We can assume the fact of
future change and the continuing development of productive forces. If
productive relationships continue to exist, and some people to occupy

more significant economic and social positions than others, might not this movement and change provoke its own characteristic conflicts and inequalities, which will need to be fought in their turn? The invocation of metaphysical or mythical conceptions, or arbitrary redefinitions of the contradictions under socialism,[93] hardly remove the difficulties.

Marx believed that the social structure of gentile communities, with their absence of hierarchy, political institutions, problems of power, and structural conflict, could be repeated, but even within his own theory the sources of the old evils are not satisfactorily excluded, while outside it there are many social facts which make the realisation of his vision seem, at least *prima facie*, unlikely.

II

The way to communism, Marx frequently argued in the stirring aftermath of the great French Revolution, lay through a process of revolutionary violence and revolutionary dictatorship. His faith in proletarian revolution as a source of purification and a means to freedom is one for which the history of revolutions provides little ground.

Most revolutions have taken place in circumstances of administrative collapse, social fragmentation and financial chaos. The leaders of the assertive forces have generally promised a great deal – the destruction of power and power-hunger, the emergence of true freedom and justice or 'liberty with bread without terror', in Castro's phrase. Particular revolutions may have been justifiable or they may have been inescapable, and may have added to the sum total of human goods, but each has failed to realise much of its dream. Each – Robespierre's or Lenin's or Mao's or Castro's – has resulted in the replacement of the old, crumbling authority by a new and centralised state apparatus, and by the use of coercion – though to varying degrees – against dissenters, opponents and doubters. The new authority has often been more stringent than its predecessor – a prediction which Marx's anarchist opponents made in relation to the proletarian dictatorship. Franz Borkenau referred to the 'law of the twofold development of revolution', by which he meant that they 'begin as anarchistic movements against the bureaucratic state organisation, which they inevitably destroy; they continue by setting in its place another, and in most cases stronger, bureaucratic organisation, which suppresses all free mass movements'.[94] The inability of revolutionaries to achieve their proclaimed ends was pointed out, in general terms, by the most eloquent conservative opponent of rapid change. Edmund Burke argued against the French Revolutionaries, who were in his view the champions of objective total overturning, that they were driven madly forward by presumptuous speculations. They were bad citizens, for, 'considering their speculative designs as of infinite value, and the actual arrangement of the state as of no estimation, they are at best indifferent about it'.[95] He brings out the unintended consequences of their actions, their inability to build a society according to plan. While Burke's account of the French Revolution as a whole seems to me to be extremely misleading, he has laid his finger on two of the important factors which help explain the 'betrayal' of revolutions – the fact that on the whole revolutionaries lack the integrity and the knowledge that they ascribe to themselves, and that they exaggerate the plasticity of their environment. Burke asserted that because they destroy the public affections, which are great and necessary aids to the law, they are driven ultimately to seek to order their society through the gallows. While the explanation is inadequate, the gallows have certainly loomed large in post-revolutionary societies.[96]

My argument is touched by the pessimism about the possible achievements of revolutionaries and radicals which is so deep-rooted in Western society today. Experience of the ruthless internal logic of revolutions, along with belief in the possibilities of quieter, less catastrophic methods of change, or mere preference for the *status quo*, have made the Marxist hope seem empty and dangerous to many, and have led commonly to a complete misunderstanding of what Marx was at. But it does seem to me that, insofar as Marx asserted the creative power of revolution or, more broadly, the vast content and depth of possible change, his confidence can reasonably be questioned. This statement has no bearing on the matter of the legitimacy of any particular revolution, nor do the exaggerated expectations of some revolutionaries mean that they should not have acted as they did. The question that I am raising concerns the grounds, from past history and present tendencies, for believing that revolution could inaugurate a truly new and human social order. It may, of course, be denied that there is any evidence relevant to Marx's prophecy, and particularly to the occurrence and outcome of the proletarian revolution. And it is clear that there is a philosophically suspect escape-route available to the Marxist. He can argue that the new man emerges only in the proletarian revolution, of which there have not been any yet, or that if any have taken place they have been subject to such special difficulties – war or counter-revolutionary plots or 'capitalist encirclement' – that they do not constitute a fair test. The proof of Marx's prophecy is the communist revolution. There are no possible disproofs. The Marxian proletarian revolution leads to communism: the appropriate criticism is not that Russia after 1917 demolished Marx's notion of communism, but concerns whether revolutionary (or any other) means could ever inaugurate a communist society, even if all the objective conditions were just right.

My argument was not designed to terminate at this unsatisfactory point, though I do wish to stress that theories which predict or advocate a radical transformation of human nature may be forced to this position, and that they are not entirely to blame. Too often such theories are simply met with summaries of existing experience, generalisations from the habits and qualities which they are seeking to alter. Existing social reality, which may itself be misinterpreted, is simply taken as data from which social possibilities can be read off. Yet the human nature which is thrown against them may be limited to a particular society or a particular period of human history. The inescapable facts of life are sometimes too easily invoked. Nevertheless, the experience that we have of revolutions hardly provides any ground at all for a belief that they can usher in a communist society, even if they have sometimes improved the societies in which they occurred. The actual history of revolutions (and this is a matter of experience hitherto – men *may* one day behave differently) is one of chaos, mingling or alternating with clinging government, political violence, and sharp inequalities of power and resources. Occasionally a powerful new force may emerge, and promote massive reconstruction, as in China, but in general experience of revolution does not reveal conscious planning of a really new order by men who hold all the necessary strings in their hands.

III

Marx and Engels believed that in a communist society there would be no more political activities and no more relations of conflict, and of domination and subordination, between men. In these circumstances political safeguards, for individuals and for groups, would not be necessary. Despite the admission of difficulties during the transitional period, and the redefinition of certain political activities so that they no longer bear that odious name, Marxism does greatly diverge from typical liberal assumptions in relation to the possibility of an harmonious communist society. The divergence derives from different assumptions about human nature and, related to these but not confined to them, conflicting views about the institutional arrangements necessary to society. The question is one which is normally set in advanced industrial societies rather than in 'society in general'. How much freedom, equality and creativity is compatible with industrialism and social order – and, indeed, how much is desirable? Are bureaucracy and oligarchy inescapable features of modern societies, whether capitalist or socialist? If so, does the problem of political regulation of rulers remain crucial? For many social theorists

Marx remains, despite the more restrained vision of the latter parts of *Capital*, an obvious utopian, a romantic anarchist, blind to the limitations which the 'system' and men's own urges place on social development. His conceptions of the reconciliation of man and nature, of the end of alienation, of the transcendence of the state and so on, lie beyond the terms of classical liberal and conservative discussion and, in relation to that tradition, tend to appear as parts of a millenial fantasy.

There is a whole range of problems and questions, which have not merely bothered economists but have given them a *raison d'être*, which were hardly touched on by Marx in his discussions of communism. How were resources to be allocated? Which goods were to be produced? Mightn't serious conflicts over this issue emerge even in a wealthy and egalitarian society? What was the relationship between investment and consumption to be? How were the rewards of labour to be distributed? How was work to be organised? How was labour to be found for dirty or unpopular jobs? What of the perennial problems of technological progress, unemployment and redundancy? It is reasonable to reply that detailed answers are not yet possible because conditions constantly change,[97] and something of an explanation is offered in the claim that all needs will be satisfied in conditions of material abundance, and that men will cease to want useless luxuries, and that as a result the traditional concern of economics – the scarcity of goods – will have disappeared. The old political economy is presented as a science of scarcity, which will naturally be transcended when society moves beyond scarcity. But, of course, this claim itself is very much in dispute, and Marx did assume rather too readily that he was speaking of real economic and political possibilities, that these traditional problems would not arise in the future, and that the self-regulating communist society would therefore be free of the stresses and conflicts which had characterised and undermined its predecessors.

While Marx did not seriously examine the sphere of managerial decisions, he does seem to have assumed that the managers or supervisors of the communist economy would not constitute a class, in the Marxist sense. This was because of the linkage of class with private ownership of the means of production, which enabled even such a critic of Bolshevik Russia as Trotsky to inflate public ownership as the great undeniable achievement of the revolution, preventing the emergence of new classes. The weakness of this thesis is that, however plausible it may have been in 1850, it had become quite clear by the end of the century, with the increasing separation of ownership and control, that it ascribed far too narrow basis to class. Classes based on different distinguishing characteristics emerged. Writing in the 1930's, Burnham, in a work which enjoyed a brief influence, although its revelations were hardly new, identified a new managerial class as the distinctive and significant force of his time. That class had acquired two crucial rights – 'control over the access to the instruments of production' and 'preferential treatment in the distribution of the products of those instruments'.[98] Marx foresaw much of this development, but failed to relate it to his broad vision of the communist future. For the argument holds that profound social stratification and inequalities of power can and do exist in societies in which private property in the means of production has been abolished. Control of the instruments of production without ownership proved to be a source of effective power for, as M. Djilas stressed in *The New Class*, power is a general category of which ownership is one case only. Similarly, class conflict is only a special, though crucial, case of group conflict, which is itself only one, though the crucial, case of social conflict. As far as the distribution of power is concerned, it seems clear that new classes may derive privileges from political power itself, and could in fact establish vast economic inequalities without property ownership and inheritance. Again, one can also envisage a ruthless government of self-mortifying ascetics or philosopher kings who exercise power without seeking economic advantages from their position. Bakunin, for example, saw Marx's ideal as essentially one of intellectual tyranny by socialist professors and intellectuals, a 'pedantocracy' which would be decidely anti-democratic in character.[99] This view misrepresents Marx's goal, but does draw attention to the possible significance of (non-economic) drives to power. Finally the problem of bureaucracy was not confronted with any great seriousness by Marx. He described and condemned the growing race of parasites, but did not present any convincing reasons as to why their days were numbered – and, as later history has shown, bureaucracy is a key feature of advanced and complex industrial societies, whatever their label.

The common and appropriate criticism of Marx's ideal focusses upon the variety of divisions and conflicts between men, the diversity of sources and kinds of power, and the tenacity of conflict and forms of power. The central claims of these rather pessimistic theories are that inequality, division and conflict are not traceable to capitalism alone, nor are they simply the results of private property – though one must avoid abstracting any single institution out of Marxism as *the cause* – but are permanent characteristics of social organisation, whatever its particular economic form. These claims are quite compatible with the views that these features of social life should be fought at all times, that some forms of them are preferable to others, and that in some special historical circumstances, or in small associations, they may be substantially diminished. These problems – if they are regarded as problems – may be peculiarly pressing in large industrial capitalist states, but they are not confined to them. The generality of bureaucracy and oligarchy was affirmed by R. Michels in his study of the distribution of power in political parties. Although he failed to define precisely his famous iron law of oligarchy, the general point is fairly clear. 'It is organisation which gives birth to the dominance of the elected over the electors, of the mandatories over the mandators, of the delegates over the delegators. Who says organisation, says oligarchy.'[100] Elsewhere he made the additional and stronger claim that those in authority develop interests peculiar to themselves, which necessarily conflict with the interests of the collectivity. Michels offers two explanations for the emergence of oligarchies – a psychological and a technical one. The first assumes the 'perennial incompetence of the masses', who require direction and guidance and also reveal a tendency to hero-worship. Whether or not this was a fair description of the existing state of affairs, and whether or not it represents a permanent state of affairs, is questionable, but must be left on the side at this stage. It is clear, however, that we cannot use this generalisation as a means of invalidating the ideals of Marx – or, for that matter, Mill – unless it can be shown that the incompetence of the masses is irremediable. The second reason advanced by Michels to explain the fact of oligarchy is that when organisations reach a certain size[101] and a certain degree of complexity it is no longer possible for the members regularly to gather together and to personally participate in decision-making. To cope with the complex and heavy organisational duties a class of professionals is necessary. A natural division of labour develops.

These sociological theories constitute a new 'dismal science', whose laws – 'neutral', 'objective', 'inevitable' and 'universal' – restrict the utopian vision, especially as it relates to complex industrial societies. The common assumption is that there will always be small groups, elites, minorities, controlling the business of society. The argument was often developed explicitly to destroy the Marxist notion of a classless society of equals, and the classical democratic picture of rule by the people. Mosca, for instance, wrote that in the world in which we are living 'socialism will be arrested only if a realistic political science succeeds in demolishing the metaphysical and optimistic methods that prevail at present in social studies'.[102] These 'realistic' theories commonly deride the anarchist thread in European political thought, with its detestation of compulsion, artificiality and government by clerks, and its yearning for more warmth and substance in individual lives. The 'unrealistic' claims of the individual against the institutions, habits and men which were confining him, were most elegantly and clearly put by Rousseau, a thinker with whom Marx has striking affinities.

Rousseau attacked the 'slothful and idle life of the bourgeoisie', the false and soft life of the cities, the 'gilt and tinsel of the courtier' and the remoteness and impersonalism of large bureaucratic societies. 'When, among the happiest people in the world, bands of peasants are seen regulating affairs of State under an oak, and always acting wisely, can we help scorning the ingenious methods of other nations, which make themselves illustrious and wretched with so much art and mystery.'[103] This is a dream or myth, not a serious programme for social reorganisation. However, it is possible to recognise the necessary conditions for the organisation of life in complex societies and to seek as much satisfaction of human needs and yearnings as is compatible with their existence. It may not be possible to release men from all of their chains, but it is not hard to conceive how some of them may be removed. The division of labour of the kind condemned by Marx can, for example, have its ill-effects reduced by something more than the introduction of muzak to the factories. The comments of Marx, or Fourier, on vocational training, on increased responsibility for the worker and on the use of leisure time, might serve as the starting point of a large-scale assault on the system.

This will not, however, achieve the general goal of Marxism. For this goal is the abolition of the political system and not merely the more successful pursuit of human satisfactions within and through it. It is the anti-political drive of Marxism that is in question – the preoccupation with spontaneous social processes leading to desirable consequences which marked the laissez-faire analysis of capitalism and which Marx projected into the future. Small societies, in a condition of creative and intense mutuality – Rousseau's ideal, or Kibbutzim, or monasteries, or even communities of scholars – may emerge within advanced industrial societies, and there may be times of heightened companionship within the larger society, but neither the small society nor exceptional times are relevant as models for the general and continuing structure of relationships of the modern nation. That Marx's transformation of politics into administration is less substantive than it seems, being partly a matter of redefinition, and that he speaks of the need for management under communism, is not being denied. But there remain a whole series of unanswered questions relating to the nature of the decisions in industrial society, how they are to be reached, and how, given the inescapable importance of specialist knowledge and the probable emergence of new ruling groups, the mass of the people are to ensure their responsibility to them. It is not necessary to assume the extensive tyranny of planners imagined by Hayek,[104] but merely to recognise that, even if the knowledge and participation of the bulk of the people can be mightily increased, there will still remain differentiations of power, hierarchy and, related to this, social conflict and the problem of restraining those in authority for making a bad use of it.

It is here that liberal criticisms of Marx's ideal have focussed. Robert Tucker, for example, attacks the notion of a 'unitary or classless society that would be devoid of inner antagonisms', claiming that it fails utterly to embrace the necessary conditions of social freedom. 'Here freedom presupposes a structure of relatively autonomous smaller societies within the larger social framework, and political, legal and other arrangements providing orderly and open outlet for the manifold tensions and conflicts that are inseparable from the social condition.'[105] Tucker's attack on Marx rests upon a particular view of Marx's illusion and a particular view of 'the social condition'. He traces Marx's dangerous view of social freedom to a supposed confusion of 'the search for unity of a divided self with the search for unity of a divided society'.[106] Marx's error is allegedly that of basing his image of both social division and social harmony upon an analogy with division and harmony within the individual person. But whereas it may make perfectly good sense to subordinate the conflicting desires of the disintegrated or schizophrenic man to some overall or unifying pattern, such a goal is inappropriate and dangerous when applied to societies, which are healthy only when significant conflicts take place. However, it seems to me that there is very little evidence to show that Marx's view of society rested upon an analogy, false or otherwise, with the individual person – nor, incidentally, does it seem to me that the notion of the stability and harmony of the individual, which underlies Tucker's argument, is itself always appropriate or desirable. But the main issue is not the origins of Marx's 'error', but the particular view of 'the social condition' which he advanced, and the liberal view which is normally counterposed to it.

This liberal-pluralist theory, which remains suspicious of man's potentialities, has been especially popular in America, where it underlay the constitutional debates and the Federal Constitution. It assumes that diversities naturally arise in society and are to be valued, and that men want power and will abuse it, given the chance. Mason, at the Federal Convention, expressed the prevailing view when he said: 'From the nature of man, we may be sure that those who have power in their hands...will always, when they can...increase it.'[107] The essential protections are both social and political, and Marx is condemned for his failure on both counts. He did not provide for the marshalling of the productive diversities of society against the persistent dangers of tyranny, but assumed the disappearance of the main sources of social differentiation, and he contemptuously dismissed political safeguards against power and the powerful in such terms as 'the hackneyed forms of routine parliamentary democracy'. He believed that in a society free of conflicts there would be no power-hungry rulers, and hence no need for constitutional checks on those in positions of authority. The liberal rejection of Marxism focusses upon the undesirability of harmony as a social goal, and on the impossibility of eliminating hierarchy and conflict, which is regarded as much more than the product of classes or private property or scarcity. Clinton Rossiter, one of Marx's American critics, has contrasted in detail the Marxist and the American views of society. 'To place either the laws or commands in the hands of any man or class or party appears to us a total denial of individual liberty.'[108] 'Our aim has always been to institutionalise the uses of political power, that of the Marxists to personalize it, and their aim is a direct legacy from Marx and Engels.'[109] It is clear, claims Rossiter, that 'Marx's perfectibilitarianism [*sic*] removes him almost completely from the area of political reality, and that anyone who chooses to follow him must abandon belief in the necessity of checks on political power'.[110]

In terms of such interpretations of classical Marxism – that it contains no understanding of the will-to-power, and of the continuing need to restrain and discipline rulers and people – critics sometimes present the Russian Revolution as a demonstration of Marx's theory in action: 'the main features of the Russian experiment appear to be the necessary consequences of that theory'.[111] However, the circumstances in Russia were in important respects different from those required for the proletarian revolution, and hence the events there cannot provide a direct practical refutation of Marx's faith, in the senses either of showing communism to be impossible, or Bolshevik authoritarianism to be the realisation of Marx's prophecy.[112] Marx did not envisage a barracks or factory state, and it was in recognition of his declared ideal that the liberal wing of Marxism has attacked the Soviet experiment. On the showing of his disciples, there is more to Marx than some of his Western critics dream.

But much liberal criticism of Marx's account of communism seems justifiable, in that his ultimate vision appears to be unrealisable in its fullness, despite the frequent claims that in some capitalist societies the political realm is actually withering away. The need for political mechanisms with the goal of restraining rulers is likely to persist for a long time yet. But the view that Marx provides an opening for the totalitarian state, that behind his dream of the united fraternal society there lies the nightmare of brutal tyranny, is not at all acceptable. Marx is sometimes portrayed as the spiritual father of Stalin, as Rousseau was that of Robespierre, according to this story. But here an illegitimate step has been taken. Stalin's Russia was obviously profoundly different from Marx's imagined future, even though there were aspects of Marx's thought which were congenial to or utilisable by Stalin.[113] Marx was not advocating a regime based on terroristic police control, elitist domination and enforced conformity. He claimed that, in certain broadly specified conditions, basic disagreement, partiality and conflict would disappear. He assumed the disappearance of the historical sources of evil, and did not justify the behaviour of élites whose violence testified to the persistence of the old Adam, in themselves and their subjects. The persistence of violence, conflict and politics was a sure indication that the objective conditions for the new society were not present. We may properly deny that harmony, rationality, or moral unanimity are realisable or desirable social goals, and hold that power and conflict will always demand political and social regulation. Marx, despite his tough empirical analysis, was hardly more realistic than the socialists he condemned, but he was not the advocate, conscious or unconscious, of a particularly onerous and distinctively twentieth century political order. Too much criticism of his communist utopia confronts the perverted Marxism of some of his disciples with a liberal myth, according to which stability, equality and individual self-realisation have been achieved, and manipulation and concentrations of power have been ended, in modern capitalist states.

PART 3   MILL

6   *Ideas, classes and social change*

John Stuart Mill stood in the forefront of such typical liberal causes as the extension of the franchise and of education, parliamentary reform, the protection of civil liberties and the emancipation of women. He was the major formulator of the doctrine to which the bulk of the emerging liberal intelligentsia adhered. His writings reveal clearly the hesitations and dilemmas of the improving liberal at a time when demands for far-reaching political and social change challenged liberal values and the partially established framework of liberal institutions. Popular aspirations – or, at least, the aspirations of tribunes and agitators who deemed themselves popular – and the conditions of the populace, influenced and threatened liberalism before it had come into its own. The tensions and uncertainties into which it was forced are highlighted in the complex body of Mill's doctrine, with its tendency to disintegrate, under pressure, into separate parts with possibilities of widely divergent development.

The (misleading) image of Mill as a muddled eclectic gains some support from his own stated conception of his task. He took it upon himself to act as a creative synthesiser of the valuable parts of the various doctrines with which he came into contact. However we characterise his intellectual achievement and the open and the subterranean influences upon it, he consciously chose 'practical eclecticism' as a methodological principle, assuming that there was likely to be some truth in every doctrine, and that the most useful task of the philosopher was to discern that part, and combine it with the true portions of other doctrines. In the preface to the first edition of A *System of Logic* his declared intention was 'to harmonize the true portions of discordant theories'.[1] But this oversimplifies and intellectualises the process, which was more complex and unnoticed than this, and was certainly less grand and clearly defined than that of marrying the eighteenth and the nineteenth centuries, the Enlightenment and Romanticism, or Bentham and Coleridge – vast, artificial enterprises and summaries of his achievement. We find in Mill, in addition to his acknowledged eclecticism, subjection to many diverse influences, and to conflicting forces within himself. He learnt from many teachers – the classical political economists and the utilitarians, John Austin, de Tocqueville, Saint-Simon and Comte, and the English Germanic school, especially Wordsworth, Carlyle, Coleridge, Maurice and Sterling. The doctrines which influenced him were not themselves frozen, but changed and contained divergent threads, and they tie up and overlap with each other, so that it becomes difficult, at times, to distinguish the precise influence upon Mill's own arguments.[2] The English Romantics helped strengthen his emotional and spiritual side, and his interest in the 'internal culture' of the individual. This interest arose out of that process of self-doubt and self-discovery which culminated in his emotional crisis in early manhood, which seemed such a devastating judgement on the thin rationalism of his upbringing.[3] Despite this crisis, however, Mill remained subject to 'reason', fearful of passion and not particularly imaginative, and dry and cool towards the instincts and weaknesses of others. In much of his writing on social problems and the plight of the labouring class, the discussion is somewhat remote and bookish, lacking precision and immediacy. Often, as John Vincent suggests, doctrine did the work of information and experience.[4]

Divided, with conflicting sympathies and goals, and with such a mass of doctrine and experience to harmonise, Mill found it a hard and constant struggle to maintain a coherent and internally consistent doctrine. In the *Autobiography* he characterised his approach, stating that, after taking in any new idea, 'I could not rest until I had adjusted its relation to my old opinions, and ascertained exactly how far its effect ought to extend in modifying or superseding them'.[5] Again, commenting on his reaction against Benthamite orthodoxy, he said, 'I found the fabric of my old and taught opinions giving away in many fresh places, and I never allowed it to fall to pieces, but was incessantly occupied in weaving it anew.'[6] This constant rethinking, which seemed to be his natural cast of mind or intellectual style, but was also justified as a methodological principle, made him unpopular among the single-minded. To them he appeared as a trimmer or fence-sitter, excessively concerned with compromise, and full of complications and equivocations. This foreshadows a common line of attack upon Mill as the uncommitted or incoherent eclectic, within whose work lie undigested and incompatible impulses and doctrines. But we should note also that, as Mill perceived it, synthesis and systematisation were creative and commanding activities, and that, especially during his aggressive radical phase, he seemed fanatical and doctrinaire to many.[7]

Mill remained uncertain and apprehensive about future social developments. He continued to worry about contemporary trends, and about the nature of the most desirable future for all men. His hesitations, his compromises and his changes of opinion, which he himself sometimes exaggeraté̄d, make his liberalism appear something of a patchwork – as would be the case with any vital and pragmatic liberalism – so that a judicious selection of his ideas can produce a portrait of the communitarian or the individualist, of the advocate of a rational unanimity (or 'moral totalitarian', even) or the committed libertarian, of the welfare statist or socialist or the laissez-faire philosopher, of the democrat or the elitist. But although each of these labels draws attention to some aspect of Mill's thought, they are labels attached by us and not by Mill, and the dichotomies which they imply give a false impression of being exhaustive and mutually exclusive, and both they and the labels are too precise and constricting to catch the full range and variety of Mill's thought, and the various levels at which he worked.

It is necessary at this point to confront the view of Mill, who stated that he was a man of 'no system',[8] and who insisted on the necessity and the value of 'a catholic spirit in philosophy',[9] as either a muddled eclectic, or a philosopher who embraced several incompatible philosophies simultaneously. Mill's own account of his eclecticism cannot be taken to mean that he was a passive recipient of various doctrines, or that he tried to root about disinterestedly amongst the prevailing philosophies in a quest for some notional wholeness or harmony. Eclecticism was not a fundamental value, but a supposedly fruitful approach. His basic intellectual enterprise was that of establishing a sociological and moral science of human behaviour, and this in turn had a crucial practical dimension – that of improving the human lot, which meant primarily increasing and developing the general human capacity for self-determination. Intellectually, eclecticism means that truth may be found in many places, though the philosopher must scrutinise whatever he discovers in terms of his existing theoretical framework, at once removing all elements of prejudice, obscurity and mere assertion from it, and adjusting it, rather than simply adding it, to that framework; practically, it means examining all available modes of living and social experiments to see what possible contributions they can make to the realisation of the basic goals. Naturally, experience led him to imagine different conditions for, and institutional forms of, the goods he valued. We find that Mill accepted, often provisionally, certain ideas and proposals that lead beyond liberal individualism. But the appropriate question then is not whether Mill was a liberal or a socialist, or a democrat or an elitist, but how far he succeeded in elaborating a convincing image of society and social change, in relation to the abilities and concerns that he deemed important. For these apparent opposites are parts of different continuums, and can be connected and combined in a number of reasonable ways. I am suggesting that Mill's writings can be considered most fairly in relation to his central ideals – methodological,

moral and practical – and what he made of diverse argument, information and experience in relation to them. I am not suggesting that his
liberalism cannot be seen as liberalism in an age of transition, or that
his doctrine does not contain diverse and conflicting elements, though
undue concentration on these aspects may lead us away from his view
of man, his confidence, and the definiteness with which he conceived
and pursued his improving mission.

In deciding whether or not a certain view or position of Mill's is
incompatible, or hard to reconcile, with others that he held, one would
have to consider its historical place in his writings – whether one
emphasis is made rather than another because of the particular conditions and problems at the time, or whether a genuine change of belief
occurs, and also its logical status within his system – whether it is intended as a description or a prediction or a recommendation.[10] There is
often a difference between the form which a value was to take in his
own society at that time, and how it would appear and be judged in the
imagined future. In some cases Mill avoided ambivalence or contradiction by projecting desired states of affairs into a hypothetical future in
which the various goods clashed neither with each other nor with the
propected social order, while limiting present radical demands and
goals – which might challenge basic values – with the argument that
they were not truths for the present time. Concentration upon what
was appropriate and feasible in the present, along with a persisting
anxiety about future possibilities, encouraged Mill to deny the imminence of the rational or the democratic or the socialist utopia, and to
insist upon a whole series of preconditions before they came within
historical reach. However, some inconsistencies remain even when we
take account of Mill's historical shifts and the varying proximity of
his goals. His battle against the philosopher's evil of one-sidedness,
combined with his flexibility, his receptiveness and his humanitarianism, led him to equivocate, or to avoid laying down one firm line, on
vital issues. But this was as much a source of strength as a revelation of
weakness.

THE MOVEMENT OF IDEAS

Mill's analysis of the sources of social influence and social change ascribed the major but not the sole role to intellectual forces. In his general study of this question, in *A System of Logic*, he sought one prime
agent of social change in what he recognised to be a complex and
dynamic process. His answer was that 'the state of the speculative
faculties of mankind' was this predominant element.

> Every considerable advance in material civilization has been pre-
> ceded by an advance in knowledge: and when any great social

change has come to pass, either in the way of gradual development or of sudden conflict, it has had for its precursor a great change in the opinions and modes of thinking of society. Polytheism, Judaism, Christianity, Protestantism, the critical philosophy of modern Europe, and its positive science – each of these has been a primary agent in making society what it was at each successive period, while society was but secondarily instrumental in making them, each of them (so far as causes can be assigned for its existence) being mainly an emanation not from the practical life of the period, but from the previous state of belief and thought.[11]

In *Representative Government*, in the course of a brief and general account of the forms of types of power, he distinguished muscular power, property, intelligence, organisation and government, and chose intelligence, revealed in knowledge and opinion, as the most important force in social life. He cited Luther's influence, the end of the Negro slave trade from Africa, and the rule of the enlightened despots, to show the predominance of beliefs over interests and physical and economic power.[12] 'It is how men think that determines how they act, and though the persuasions and the convictions of average men are in a much greater degree determined by their personal position than their reason, no little power is exercised over them by the persuasions, and the convictions of those whose personal position is different, and by the united authority of the instructed.'[13]

Although these general assertions about the most significant causal factors might seem to conflict with his inductivist approach, Mill made them confidently. As far as he was concerned, the state of man's speculative activities was the almost paramount agent of social progress. Progress depended upon 'the law of the successive transformations of human opinions'.[14] He held, not only that opinions, belief and knowledge were the prime determinants of social change, but that the continuous transformation of opinions, which was the essence of history, was a progressive movement. 'It is my belief indeed that the general tendency is, and will continue to be, saving occasional and temporary exceptions, one of improvement; a tendency towards a better and happier state. This, however, is not a question of the method of the social science, but a theorem of the science itself.'[15] He believed that a great forward march of intellect was actually taking place, with educated public opinion becoming a force of increasing significance in Western society, and with institutions necessarily being brought into conformity with it. Not only were rulers or potential rulers becoming wiser: their wisdom was percolating through to a more instructed audience, whose quality might be improved much further. Hence he attached great importance to educated minorities, and to devising institutions and arrangements which would ensure that their beliefs, or acceptance of their beliefs, would spread widely throughout society, thereby repeating in the individual the progress of civilisation itself, with knowledge and rationality supplanting passion and prejudice. Hence, also, an exaggeration of the power and the single-facedness of reason. Inspired by intellectualist and optimistic assumptions, he was to dispose far too easily of those sinister interests which utilitarianism had regarded as deep-rooted, and which he himself had stressed in his denunciations of aristocratic power, when deference was given to ignorant and selfish rulers. Largely because of his high estimate of the social significance and the cleansing power of ideas, Mill inflated the power of rational men, and often neglected the power of institutions to hold back reasonable change.

While giving this crucial though not exclusive causal role to ideas, Mill believed that much needed to be done before society would become rational. In the common manner of social theorists, he emphasised the intellectual anarchy or spiritual travail of his own times. He was much impressed by Saint-Simon's distinction between 'critical' and 'organic' periods. Critical periods, which Mill presented less pejoratively than did Saint-Simon, were unstable, disorderly, atomistic and ruled by egoism, while organic periods were stable, harmonious, ruled more by feelings of association, common conceptions of social duty, and widely accepted intellectual authorities. Mill thought his a critical period. He believed himself to be surrounded by the ruins of the old established doctrines, which could not be artificially maintained. He stressed that he lived in an age of transition, 'in a kind of confusion of many standards',[16] 'in an age of weak beliefs'.[17] In 'The Spirit of the Age' he referred to the common conviction of his generation, which he shared, that 'the times are pregnant with change; and that the nineteenth century will be known to posterity as the era of one of the greatest revolutions of which history has preserved the remembrance, in the human mind, and in the whole constitution of human society'.[18] The fundamental transformation of English social and intellectual life had hitherto been primarily destructive, in that the established framework, the old ties and attachments, had been destroyed without new philosophic truths emerging to take their place. Destruction, however, had to precede regeneration, and Mill was confident that he lived, not during a period of mere demolition but one of the general reconstruction of the opinions of the civilised world. Feudal, aristocratic and ecclesiastical beliefs and institutions were vacating their place, leaving the way clear for more elevated successors. Diversities, anarchy and conflict were necessary preludes to the emergence of new authorities and the discovery of doctrines appropriate to the new age. Mill believed that intellectual conflict had costs and dangers, in that it left the people without clear and agreed guides and directions, but that it was both inescapable and fruitful in certain periods. He does not provide any account of why the mind moves in its mysterious way, why ancient doctrines break up, and conflict and crisis emerge, at particular times, and why, at other times, intellectual leaders come to accept the same basic beliefs and the people to accept their authority. It is, very much, pure intellectual history. There is a strong positivist element in his argument, in that competition of ideas was to lead to closer approximations to the truth, and hopefully, to the repetition, in the moral and political sciences, of the 'imposing unanimity' of the physical sciences. Intellectual and social dislocation were temporary, and certainly did not constitute an ideal state of affairs. Free competition between individuals in pursuit of the truth was not unending, but was to be supplanted, in the natural course of things, by united – though self-critical – authority. Free intellectual enterprise leads to a community of intellectual beliefs, and to change within a stable framework of shared beliefs. In these circumstances the masses, who only fall away from their natural guides when these guides dispute amongst themselves, would once more rely upon the newly unanimous learned class. 'Any doctrines which come recommended by the nearly universal verdict of instructed minds will no doubt continue to be, as they have hitherto been, accepted without misgiving by the rest.'[19] In developing these views, Mill frequently declared his anger at the intellectual backwardness of the English, at their vulgarity, and their hostility to general ideas, though elsewhere, for example in his repudiation of socialism, he welcomed their pragmatism and readiness to compromise. Anti-intellectualism might protect them against bad social doctrines, but it also made them immune to what was good and constructive. As an ideologist of Philosophical Radicalism, dedicated to the rule of right reason, Mill deplored this characteristic. However, he expected that the overwhelming present need to stimulate mental regeneration would diminish with time, as the English returned to intellectual and social homogeneity under the leadership of the wise.

Mill's view of the role of ideas and reason in social life can now be presented in a very broad and abstract frame, leaving out complexities. Ideas, from wherever they may come, are the most significant sources of social change. Mental change precedes, and presumably causes, social change. The historical development of men's ideas about society and themselves is progressive – the body of truths steadily increases and spreads more widely. However, according to Mill's rather vague philosophy of history, progression occurs – presumably at very different rates – in unstable or transitional periods and in stable and settled periods, which arise out of the former. Mill saw himself as an intellectual participant in a transitional period, with the role, along with others, of encouraging mental regeneration, by defining its conditions and, as far as possible, its vital beliefs. The new order which emerges from the transitional period is characterised by the steady narrowing of the area of reasonable conflict and diversity, or the uncoerced growth of intellectual and moral cohesion. Looked at from this side, his central political concepts are 'progress', 'reason', 'unanimity' and 'intellectual leaders', and the immediate task becomes that of establishing the authority of the wise.

This view of history and of the place of his own society in it led into a sharp and critical analysis of the existing distribution of power. The period of transition was a period of intellectual dissension in which those fittest to rule were excluded from political power. The gulf between political power and capacity meant that government was no longer productive or legitimate. Mill meant by an age of transition one in which society

> contains other persons fitter for wordly power and moral influence than those who have hitherto enjoyed them: when worldly power, and the greatest existing capacity for worldly affairs, are no longer united, but severed; and when the authority which sets the opinions and forms the feelings of those who are not accustomed to think for themselves, does not exist at all, or, existing, resides anywhere but in the most cultivated intellects, and the most exalted characters, of the age.[20]

This discrepancy would be overcome when society returned to a natural state, in which 'worldly power, and moral influence, are habitually and undisputably exercised by the fittest persons whom the existing state of society affords'.[21] In these circumstances, 'real' and 'constitutional' power would be exercised by the same people. Mill took it to be an elementary political truth that 'whatever is the growing power in society will force its way into the government by fair means or foul. The distribution of constitutional power cannot long continue very different from that of real power, without a convulsion.'[22] At times constitutions or governmental rules were out of phase with the 'real political strength' in society, and in such circumstances rulers were unlikely to survive, or to act effectually or morally. For Mill, forms of government were futile contrivances if they were not adapted to powerful intellectual forces. His view that the tide of new ideas and knowledge would erode and eventually sweep away the established regime was brought firmly to earth, and given a class dimension and a radical anti-aristocratic thrust, in the claims that the middle class was intellectually and economically, but not politically, dominant, and that its political exclusion was a source of instability and wastage of resources. Persons belonging chiefly to the middle class were, he believed, 'the ascendant power in the present social and political condition of the kingdom'.[23] Constitutional recognition of this fact, involving especially extensions of the franchise, was necessary for the wise government as well as for the good order of the kingdom. The general doctrine of the power and value of ideas in social life is thus given direct political relevance and a clear class content. The conflict of ideas was matched, though not exactly, by a conflict of social forces, and was to be ended, properly, by the predominance of one of these social forces, and the spread of its characteristic abilities and virtues.

THE CONFLICT OF CLASSES

The basic category in utilitarian social theory was interest, and it was here that the main problems of the theory naturally emerged. The theory, which Mill modified considerably, rested upon an extremely simple view of man's appetites and drives. Man is portrayed as a self-interested pursuer of pleasure and avoider of pain, which are 'homogeneous real entities', and only man thus conceived – narrowly and abstractly – is the proper subject of political theory and scientific legislation. The political problem facing the utilitarians can be put, in general terms, as that of ensuring that the individual appetites which they perceived, and which they did not condemn, never became strong enough to tear society apart. Bentham believed that jealousies, clashes of interest, hatreds and rivalries would always characterise human life, and Mill attacked him for presenting the world as 'a collection of persons pursuing each his separate interest or pleasure, and the prevention of whom from jostling one another more than is unavoidable, may be attempted by hopes and fears derived from three sources – the law, religion, and public opinion'.[24] But he believed that personal interests could be made to coincide with duty, and with the general interests of the community, and consequently he was not forced to a Hobbesian solution. His main fear, like that of both Mills, was not that anarchy might prevail, but that the calculating egotists would exercise political power for private or sectional advantage, and it was therefore natural that all three should try to devise 'securities' for good government, which would curb or control the dangerous desires which they associated with man's existing nature, while differing about the extent to which they sprang from removable social sources.

The conflict between the egoistic individual of utilitarian theory and the general social goals which it prescribed – the greatest happiness of the greatest number – was met, within that increasingly protean body of thought, in three main ways. Between them, the broadening of the psychological theory, the natural harmonisation of interests, and the provision of checking and elevating devices, explained why conflict rarely reached a devastating intensity, and made available instruments of social control where necessary. The crudity and severity of the psychological doctrine was reduced by incorporation of the 'social feelings', which made self-interest less pure and more complex, though the social feelings could be interpreted as themselves sources of private pleasure. Bentham himself widened the basic or natural drives to include altruism and fellow-feeling. He stressed the importance of 'sympathetic bias' and argued in *The Introduction to the Principles of Morals and Legislation* that utility was equivalent to the most extensive and enlightened benevolence. Secondly, in certain areas, and specifically in the sphere of economic life, conflicting ends were held to harmonise unconsciously or naturally, as described in the classical political economy. Diverse and clashing individual interests, guided by rational wills, interacted to produce a complex, intricate system of interdependence. Finally, and linking up directly again with the psychological doctrine, man could be both checked and elevated by educational and political devices, including constitutions. Even if man's natural or basic drives were held to be self-regarding and ineliminable, they were clearly subject to manipulation, and might be enlarged, and developed in fruitful directions. Mill emphasised that altruism and fraternal and other social feelings were strengthened in the normal course of civilisation, and might be encouraged and drawn forth by political and educational means. Thus the grounds for an optimistic theory of social order were at hand. Depending upon one's original psychological premises, and the allowance made for such historical and social factors as training and education, habit, rules, incentives, promises and fear of authorities and opinions, the need for political and legal controls and sanctions will be more or less pressing and extensive. The artificial identification of interests certainly remained a primary concern of the ultilitarians, particularly in relation to the likely behaviour of governors. James Mill was within the mainstream when he presented the means of checking the powerful as the central question in political inquiry. In his words: 'All the difficult questions of government relate to the means of restraining those, in whose hands are lodged the powers necessary for the protection of all, from making a bad use of it.'[25] The dogma that man is motivated perpetually by self-interest could be employed with especial severity against certain rulers, past or present, though it might also be subtly withdrawn, or half-forgotten, in relation to other possible masters. The proposed utilitarian answers to James Mill's problem were often superficial or evasive,[26] and bore something of a class bias when the middle ranks, or sections of them, were seen as the best possible rulers.

J. S. Mill's analysis of class and class interest sprang directly from this utilitarian background. When he was writing *Representative Government*, *The Times* indicated how pejorative a term 'class' was. The writer referred to the terms 'class prejudices' and 'class legislation' – classic and appropriate Chartist phrases of the thirties and forties – and concluded that we 'inveigh against the selfishness of class interest'.[27] For Mill, classes or groups smaller than the society itself, characteristically revealed sinister interest. He was extremely concerned at the strength of class interests, which were major obstacles to the realisation of the common good. Class and class conflict were great social evils, especially when the members of the class were ignorant and aggressive. He defined classes loosely and pejoratively as 'any number of persons who have the same sinister interest...whose direct and apparent interest points towards the same description of bad measures'.[28] A sinister interest is one that is partial and selfish, opposed to the permanent, shared interests of a community, whatever these might be. On this criterion virtually any organised or distinct body or group could be seen as having its class interests, its own particular prejudices. Mill used the term 'class' to refer not only to landlords, great manufacturers, skilled labourers and unskilled labourers, but to Spartans and helots, planters and negroes, princes and subjects, nobles, and men and women.[29] His primary concern was with the landlords, the capitalists and the labouring class,[30] although he sternly condemned the unchecked domination of women by men. As time passed, the conflict between the workers and the middle ranks became the vital, consuming one, but for the young Mill, as for his father and for Bentham, the key conflict was that between the aristocrats, who clung to their power and privilege, and the rising middle class, which was determined to win political dominance.

Bentham and the Mills believed that the self-preference principle had run rampant in non-representative governments, in which the rulers utterly ignored the general happiness. In his preface to the second edition of *The Fragment on Government* Bentham wrote that he had not realised, when the work first appeared, that governments were 'the elaborately organised and anxiously cherished and guarded products of sinister interest and artifice'. James Mill was much more vehement. He argued that monarchy and aristocracy would always defeat the ends of government, which were to advance and safeguard the interest of all. Monarchs and aristocrats constantly sought property and power, forcing their subjects down to the subsistence level and inflicting endless cruelty to secure their absolute subservience of will.[31] J. S. Mill followed his father in asserting the strongly class character of most governments and claimed, in a generally sober text, that it is the interest of a king or a ruling aristocracy to 'possess and exercise, unlimited power over the people; to enforce, on their part, complete conformity to the will and the preference of the rulers...and to assume to themselves an endless variety of unjust privileges...to degrade others below themselves... unless a sufficiently strong counter-interest is provoked by the fear of provoking resistance'.[32] In such conditions, the people were normally forced into one mould by repression and indoctrination, as in Marx's stable class societies. Non-representative governments are portrayed, then, as tyrannous and brutal class governments, serving the interests of the rulers, who were controlled only by revolution, or the fear of provoking it. In Mill's view such last-resort sanctions against misrule were quite inadequate, partly because people, naturally indolent, were prepared to endure a tremendous amount of misrule before being moved to act.

The utilitarian psychological doctrine was wielded with most force against the aristocracy, which became a clear embodiment of human nature at its worst. Mill swore 'enmity to the aristocratical principle'[33] on behalf of the Philosophical Radicals, whom he presented as a party of the universal interest. He held that aristocratic leaders were avaricious and venal and, supported by such corrupting institutions as the church, were responsible for most of the evils of the existing society. The assault on the selfish groups – in the first instance, monarchs and aristocrats – rested on assumptions about the effects of power which was unlimited in a formal or political sense, e.g. by constitutional checks. The possession of power normally blinded men to realities, as it was then blinding the English rulers of Ireland. It encouraged in its holders, such as Louis XVIII, a lack of moderation, an unwillingness to compromise. Mirabeau and others knew, Mill said, 'that it is next to impossible for a monarch, used to absolute power, to accommodate himself to limitations'.[34] In England the king and the lords would overthrow the constitution, which did not restrict them sufficiently, if they had the chance. Misleading histories, full of aristocratic myths, aided their designs. Depictions of the age of chivalry as one in which power was exercised discreetly by those most fitted to rule were far from reality. 'The age of chivalry was the age of aristocracy, in its most gigantic strength and wide-extending sway; and the illusions of chivalry are to this hour the great stronghold of aristocratic prejudices.'[35] Mill praised the muckraking French historians, such as Dulaire, who were engaged in 'the toilsome and thankless service of dragging into light the vices and crimes of former days'.[36] Because of his assumptions about the effects of unrestricted power, and his actual study of aristocratic governments, especially in England, he rejected appeals to the good character of the existing rulers, declaring that 'we cannot be forced back to the times when rulers were thought not to be made like human beings, but to be free from all the passions and appetites by which other men are misled'.[37] There were rare and accidental cases of capable and disinterested aristocracies. Mill described the Prussian aristocracy as 'a most highly and skilfully organised aristocracy of all the most highly educated men in the kingdom'.[38] The representatives of the British Government in India were, despite some differences, of the same character. But Mill did not analyse the conditions favouring the emergence of an educated and public-spirited aristocracy, apart from the suggestion that in Prussia the popularity of the government was almost a necessary condition of its existence. Presumably this dependence on public opinion would bring it close to representative government. The East India Company in India remained disinterested because it did not have much chance to profit from misgovernment – as a result 'it can be kept entirely clear of bias from the individual or class interests of anyone else'.[39] But these conditions – an alert and demanding public opinion and the lack of opportunities for exploitation – did not operate in the English case. Mill did not expect any moral or intellectual growth on the part of the landed, hereditary aristocrats of England, who showed little initiative or urge for self-improvement, and who, more precisely, failed to undertake any serious study of legislation. Such students were rare, and the examples provided by Mill revealed the social sector in which he was to seek salvation. Because of the scarcity of students of politics, he claimed, 'the man who has spared some one or two hours a day from his counting-house or his chambers for reading and reflecting on public questions, must meet with joyful acceptance'.[40] The excluded or underprivileged middle class, spearheaded by the Radicals, developed valuable social qualities as they made their way in the world. But the landed class had none of this constructive experience. Mill not only condemned it for its moral failings, but dismissed its economic contribution as negligible. Its members were inactive, constituting a class in the community 'whom the natural course of things progressively enriches, consistently with complete passiveness on their own part...They grow richer, as it were, in their sleep, without working, risking, or economizing.'[41] Naturally conservative, the enemies of reform and improvement, they lacked sympathy for the people and all sense of social duty. In opposing the repeal of the Corn Laws they revealed their selfish class interests, which were naturally very different from the 'public' interest represented by the assertively bourgeois Anti-Corn Law League. The varied complaints of the reformers were directed, essentially, against 'the sinister interest of some portion of those whom Grattan emphatically called "the proprietors of Parliament" '.[42] In fighting against the Corn Laws, against the whole untidy and irrational English legal system, with its partisan magistrates and packed juries, in seeking the extension of the franchise and the end of corruption and intimidation in the constituencies,[43] the reformers came up against their entrenched power. They would not retire gracefully before the new wave of enlightenment. Moreover, their influence was deep-rooted and could not be suddenly removed, and the reformers would have to contend with it for some time to come. The evils of centuries were not to be remedied in a day. The obstacles to representative government created by aristocratic power and influence would survive aristocratic government itself. For aristocratic government had been exclusive government, and capable outsiders had been given no chance of gaining the political experience necessary to successfully run the government. It would take time until there was sufficient experience available to fill all positions of authority. Moreover, the ascendancy of priest and aristocrat had been accepted by the people, who remained subject to laws and morality emanating from that corrupt class. In 1830 Mill condemned the people, not for their self-assertiveness but for their deference to their traditional governors. In his words, 'the fault of the multitude has never been distrust of the rich, but too habitual and implicit a confidence in them'.[44] The multitude had been left as it had been found, or as it had easily become – superstitious, prejudiced and apathetic. It was to be rescued, and the irresponsible and moribund ruling caste replaced, by the rising power in the kingdom – the enterprising, educated middle class. The first task of that class was to annihilate aristocratic institutions and their underlying values, which powerfully supported primitive and irrational social attitudes. Mill was proclaiming a doctrine for a post-aristocratic world, and it was a clear part of his purpose to replace the ascendancy of the reactionary landed oligarchy by a new ascendancy of progressive elements.[45]

Mill believed that the radicals, or the disqualified classes, would naturally come to the top with the 'progress of civilisation'. His view of the middle section as both the developing power and the source of virtue in society was a popular one at the time, particularly among those who saw themselves as parts of it – though to outsiders, this must have seemed so much gratuitous self-compliment. In 1826 Sir James Graham happily described the middle ranks as the seat of public opinion, and referred to them as 'that numerous class, removed from the wants of labour and the cravings of ambition, enjoying the advantages of leisure, and possessing intelligence sufficient for the formation of a sound judgment, neither warped by interest nor obscured by passion'.[46] It is not at all surprising that the middle class or the middle ranks should be given a special and elevated role in nineteenth-century English social theory, given the place which they were seeking and gradually winning. Nor is it surprising that explanations of their rise were full of moral recommendation. Both Mills explained – while exaggerating – the intellectual hegemony of the middle class in terms of the readiness of all groups to accept the lead given by the intelligent and the disinterested. There is little perception of the interest which underlay its ideas, or of the illusory elements in them. James Mill's neat and complacent thought on representative government had ended with a eulogy to the middle class, which he expected to dominate because of its wisdom. 'There can be no doubt that the middle rank, which gives to science, to art and to legislation itself, their most distinguished ornaments, the chief source of all that has exalted and refined human nature, is that portion of the community of which, if the basis of Representation were ever so far extended, the opinion would ultimately decide.'[47] J. S. Mill, who attempted much more detailed social and class analysis than his liberal and utilitarian predecessors, identified the progressive, enlightened forces with 'the Disqualified Classes', which felt oppressed and unjustly treated by the existing rulers. Their spearhead was the manufacturing and mercantile classes. The 'natural' radicals comprised a number of overlapping groups, including the ten pound electors, skilled employees, the working class, dissenters and church reformers, and such rural elements as small proprietors or yeomen, the prosperous farmers and the owners and occupiers of land connected with towns. Mill wrote that 'the men of active and inspiring talent, indeed, in all classes except the highest, are radicals everywhere; for what is radicalism, but the claim for pre-eminence for personal qualities above conventional or accidental advantages'.[48] The radicals are portrayed generously in this profoundly moral version of English history and its present conflicts, which fit into the long struggle between liberty and truth on the one hand and prejudice and obstructiveness on the other. It is the moral quality imputed to the radicals which takes the breath away – they are the thinking men, the men of aspiration and enterprise, of virtue, education and personal endowment. On the other side were the privileged classes, cherishing their unearned distinctions, and safeguarding their narrow and selfish interests within the existing order.

This highly tendentious and proselytising social analysis, which belongs primarily to the simple and crusading decade of the thirties, exaggerates both the homogeneity of the radical forces or 'the people', much of whose radicalism remained latent and had to be brought to the surface, and the clarity of the confrontation between the two great groups, people and aristocracy. The over-sharp drawing of the social conflict, which underrated the strength, resilience and persisting influence of the aristocracy, is accompanied by an equally simple, equally sharp perception of the moral conflict. But general interest rarely faces sinister interest so unambiguously. The people, conceived abstractly and idealistically at this stage, are presented as principled and democratic battlers against a self-regarding and irresponsible enemy, which would be swept away in the normal development of civilisation. But the people, conceived here in a common character as citizens, and not in the real diversity of their economic interests, beliefs and so on, are not presented as equal: they engage in a valorous common enterprise under the leadership of the best and wisest. At this stage, it was the task of the Radicals to adequately define the principles and the social forces, and to push the conflict to extremes, encouraging organised action against the vicious constitution of the legislature, and not simply against particular grievances, such as the Corn Laws. The roots of evil, and not its various symptoms or expressions, had to be destroyed. However, Mill's ebullient and emphatic Radicalism was later to disappear as 'the people' broke up into distinct and conflicting groups, which obviously could not all be enlightened champions of virtue. During the thirties group conflict seemed legitimate, as it was directed against the old and the selfish, but it soon lost its legitimacy when the exponents of virtue themselves were challenged, and their claims rejected, by dangerous and ignorant proletarian forces. It then became a matter of denying the existence of valid class conflict, and seeking to close the actual gaps between classes, rather than of opening up and crystallising social and political divisions. Mill's conception of class, and of social change and social conflict, became deeper when class confronted him as a dangerous social force, for which he could find no objective or rational ground.

Mill portrayed the natural leaders of society, many of whom were left unenfranchised in 1832, as energetic, studious and cultivated. Below the rank of gentlemen, they were yet above the people, particularly with respect to those qualities necessary for political leadership – knowledge, calmness and freedom from prejudice. Mill, in the course of his efforts to organise a genuine Radical party, held that Radical candidates must be free from sinister interest, 'sufficiently accessible to motives of a more generous kind, to prefer the good of the whole above the separate interest of the rich'.[49] He did not envisage plutocratic government. The kind of person that he had in mind was probably a member of the dissenting, or lapsed dissenting, middle class – austere, just, independent men like his father, rather than such paragons of the new commercial morality as Hudson the railway king, or wealthy exhibi-

tionists of the kind later portrayed by Trollope. The very wealthy were
suspect. Mill wrote in 1835: 'the middle classes...if freed from the
coercive power of the rich, have an interest absolutely indentical with
that of the community on all the questions likely to engage much of
the attention of parliament for many years to come'.[50] Such claims
may seem the products of blind faith, or at least of parochialism, and
one's doubts are supported by Mill's own tart criticisms of commercial
civilisation and of many of the middle class or 'shopocracy'. Mill often
condemned the bourgeoisie for money grubbing, servility – 'open-
mouthed and besotted admiration' for their superiors,[51] philistinism,
mediocrity, mean and contracted minds and dispositions, and lack of
vision. This suggested the need for substantial change before they
would become rational persons, conscious of their social obligations and
capable of constructive political leadership. His Radicals were the
superior elements of the class: he had no absurd trust in the class as a
whole. Furthermore, while he was generally optimistic both about
the unity of the Radicals and about their moral and intellectual qualities, he expressed frequent doubts about their political organisation and
the stature of their leaders. He never succeeded in finding a Radical
leader who could have used parliament as 'a rostra or a teacher's chair
for instructing and impelling the public mind'.[52] It became a frequent
cry that there are 'no men of talent among us'.[53] He lamented
the absence of heroism and greatness in such hopeful times, when
public opinion, led by discriminating guides, was becoming so powerful
a force. 'Circumstances cannot always continue to do what men will
not, or are not capable of. Circumstances are blind guides. The use
of intellect is never with impunity abandoned in the affairs of
nations.'[54]

While Mill was often concerned at the shortcomings of the rising
power in England, he became much more troubled by the strength and
assertiveness of the labouring class, whose process of growth had been
entangled with but different from that of the middle class. But long
before a clear middle class ascendancy was established, the two classes
were facing each other with some hostility. The political claims of a
class generally conceived to be incompetent and violent, troubled liberal
reformers, who feared both social conflict between the property-owners
and the propertyless, and extensions of the franchise which could lead
to working-class power. Matthew Arnold, in many respects a kindred
spirit to Mill, complained of the growth of the populace, that vast portion of the working class, which, 'raw and half-developed, has long lain
half-hidden amongst its poverty and squalor, and now is issuing from
its hiding-place to assert an Englishman's heaven-born privilege of
doing as he likes, and is beginning to perplex us by marching where it

likes, meeting where it likes, bawling what it likes, breaking what it likes'.[55] Its demands far outran its capacities.

However, Mill sympathised with – and desired to improve – those whom, following Saint-Simon, he called the poorest and most numerous class. The working-class leader, Holyoake, praised him for his concern with public justice and his defence of the friendless. 'His sentences were fortified defences of the interests of the low. With him philosophy was not the mere pride of the scholar, but the protection of the public.'[56] Mill anticipated and worked towards the moral and intellectual improvement of the workers, but did not rate their existing abilities highly. He recorded in the *Autobiography* how, given the wretchedly imperfect state of education, he and Harriet dreaded 'the ignorance and especially the selfishness and brutality of the mass'.[57] He added that socialism presupposed a change in the character of 'the uncultivated herd who now compose the labouring masses, and in the immense majority of their employers'.[58] 'Brutal ignorance' and 'obstinate prejudice' were widespread. In general, the workers were immature, uninstructed, unreflective, irrational and selfish – a condition which was not, in the long run, irremediable, and which was in part the heritage of aristocratic misgovernment. There were, however, stirring exceptions, which indicated the nature of things to come. Mill praised some of the working-class leaders, e.g. in 1839 describing the politicians of the class as 'almost universally its most respectable and well-conducted men'.[59] Earlier he had waxed eloquent over the actions of the Parisians in 1830 – swayed by that strange exhilaration which sometimes grips even the cautious Englishman when he surveys his more unsettled and revolutionary neighbours. 'The inconceivable purity and singleness of purpose, almost amounting to naivety, which they all show in speaking of these events, has given me a greater love for them than I thought myself capable of feeling for so large a collection of human beings, and the more exhilarating views which it opens of human nature will have a beneficial effect on the whole of my future life.'[60] But such disinterestedness and concern were rare, and Mill did not retain such faith in the French, and remained suspicious of the English working class, which easily fell under the sway of such demagogues as the Tory Radical Stephens. His view of the likely quality of an ascendant working class – as well as his harsh feelings towards the existing parliament – are revealed in his comment that such a class would become prey to 'base adventurers in the character of professional politicians', who would encourage them to think their own crude notions better than 'the theories and refinements of thinking people'.[61]

Poverty and ignorance could easily lead to destructive class conflict. Mill was extremely conscious of the dangers set by poverty – which he generally blamed on to overpopulation – to a democracy, or indeed to any society. In discussing respect for property in America he wrote: 'When, indeed, the poor are so poor that they can scarcely be worse off, respect on their parts for rights of property which they cannot hope to share, are never safely to be calculated upon.'[62] But when the labouring class was very poor, it was probable that it would remain a subject class, passively accepting its fate. 'Universal suffrage is never likely to exist and to maintain itself where the majority are prolétaires; and we are not unwilling to believe that a labouring class in abject poverty ...may be kept politically in subjection.'[63] In such circumstances they would have little opportunity of developing the characteristic human excellences, which were essential to both individual self-realisation and social stability.

Moreover, class conflict could prove disastrous, even without leading to a revolutionary clash of the kind sometimes envisaged by Marx. During the Chartist decade, when middle-class leadership was denounced and rejected by many of the labourers, thereby exploding the pretension of a united people, Mill became deeply worried by the condition of England question – that division of the country into two nations which so agitated contemporary social reformers. He described the working classes as 'classes deeply and increasingly discontented, and whose discontent now speaks out in a voice which will not be unheard'.[64] Chartism was 'the first open separation of interest, feeling and opinion, between the labouring portion of the commonwealth and all above them'.[65] The absence of the personal qualities that produce co-operation led to concealed enmity, 'that sourde enmity which is universal in this country towards the whole class of employers, in the whole class of employed'.[66] In his *Principles of Political Economy* Mill made it clear that he regarded class hostility as the responsibility of both sides – though the form in which he put the criticism at that stage suggests that the prima facie case against employers was stronger than that against the employed. 'The total absence of regard for justice or fairness in the relations between the two, is as marked on the side of the employed as on that of the employers.'[67] Their unreasoning hatreds were especially objectionable and unfortunate when set against the widespread prosperity and achievement which association would have made possible.

Mill's view of the strength and nature of class antagonisms altered historically, but there remains, after his euphoric accounts of 'the people' in the thirties, a firm and fairly consistent notion of the dangers set by class conflict and class aspirations to his basic objectives. In the late thirties he could point still to the wisdom of the working class leaders in London, who 'have shaken off, within the last few years, many crude notions, and have made quite progress enough not to see any benefit to their class in a general conflagration, nor look to agrarian laws, or taxes on machinery, or a compulsory minimum of wages, as the means of improving its condition'.[68] But the working-class agitation, and the spread of what he regarded as fallacious views, during the forties left a deep impression on him. In 1859 he wrote: 'The non-represented classes, as a body, are just now, to all appearances, peaceful and acquiescent. But they were not always so; we are not far from the days of Chartist insurrections, and monster petitions signed by millions of men.'[69] That experience led him to doubt that the working class would remain within the confines of rational, middle-class politics, and to his major fear – not of revolution by the labourers, but of a legislative class tyranny, through their premature admission to the franchise. 'One of the greatest dangers. . .of democracy, as of all other forms of government, lies in the sinister interest of the holders of power: it is the danger of class legislation; of government intended for (whether really effecting it or not) the immediate benefit of the dominant class, to the lasting detriment of the whole.'[70] His fear of the spread of governmental power was lesser or greater depending on the class which was to wield political power, for this would determine the content of legislation. Sometimes he was worried that the middle class might be dominated by sinister interest,[71] but he was primarily concerned at the use which the poorest and most numerous class might make of political power. If previous ruling classes had used their position to advance their own rather than the general interest, why should the uninstructed industrial masses be different? They, too, would govern for their own ends if there were insufficient barriers against class domination. Directed by their immediate and apparent interest rather than their real ultimate interest, and hence unaware of the actual consequences of their programmes, they would choose tyranny and conflict rather than collaboration. A purely democratic suffrage would be likely to produce 'a legislature reflecting exclusively the opinions and preferences of the most ignorant class'.[72] In the middle decades of the century that class appeared to him to be obsessed by the relations between labour and capital, and to be demanding the vote as a means of ensuring a just distribution of resources. 'They believe that they are ground down by the capitalist. They believe that his superiority of means, and power of holding out longer than they can, enables him virtually to fix their wages. They ascribe the lowness of those wages, not as is the truth, to the overcompetition produced by their own excessive numbers, but to competition itself.'[73] Hence, although working-class leaders were shaking off many crude notions, Mill was almost as much concerned as were such anti-democrats as John Austin and Robert Lowe[74] at the probable consequences of the immediate extension of the vote to all. In his comment on *Democracy in America* he wrote that, as it was, the labouring class would be likely to interfere with contracts, introducing 'unenlightened legislation for the supposed interests of the many; laws founded on mistakes in political economy. A minimum of wages, or a tax on machinery, might be attempted.'[75]

THE PROBLEMS AND THE POINTS OF CHANGE

Working-class aspirations and demands faced liberal philosophers with an urgent and fundamental dilemma. The liberal-democratic creed which they expounded, and which had been focussed with revolutionary effect against traditional rulers, had dangerous implications when applied to mankind at large. The new danger was the mass, demanding the right to participate in political life and power, and using the radical elements in the liberal democratic ideology to support that demand. Liberalism therefore tended to face two ways at once, and to maintain a deep-seated ambivalence towards democracy. On the one hand it was forward-looking, wielding democracy as a weapon against the old order, while on the other it was conservative, seeking to protect the new masters against the menaces inherent in radical interpretations of democratic claims and ideals. In effect it became the normative theory of a new form of inequality, which was, allegedly, more rational and legitimate than that which it was supplanting. Liberal philosophers were compelled to seek modifications of the democratic principle, at least 'for the time being', to prevent it from destroying aspects of the existing society – private property or free enterprise or culture or privilege – which they valued highly. Hence a number of conservative political devices were invented to protect freedom and merit. In the circumstances, the liberal ideal of the self-realising and self-sufficient man, with his energy, creativity, vitality and love of diversity, seemed a fiction and an impossible dream when applied to most men. It was a reasonable ideal for the cultured and prosperous. But, for nearly all the rest, liberal rhetoric ran far beyond its concrete realisations, and became a façade for the achievements and the power of a small minority. In Mill, the clash between the promise and the dynamic of the liberal doctrine on the one side, and the actual institutional prescriptions which supposedly embodied the ideal on the other, is clear. So is the socialist interpretation and reduction of his theory. Mill wanted to protect wisdom, skill and individuality against the possible invasions of the uninformed mass; to his critics the arguments seemed a transparent defence of a new ruling class against its democratic opponents.

Mill's interpretation and resolution of the class problem was quite different from those of his socialist critics, and coheres with his general views of the importance of ideas and the possibility of a rational social order. Class conflict had real, concrete causes but could be eliminated by a mixture of intellectual perception and moral choice. Mill recognised that classes had some solidarity and strength, but he never conceived them as having a real identity of interests, or a natural process of development. His prolétaires are those of Lammenais, not those of Marx. He rejected the notion that class divisions were natural and beyond man's control, commenting in 1834 that writers on society

> revolve in their eternal circle of landlords, capitalists and labourers, until they seem to think of the distinction of society into those three classes as if it were one of God's ordinances, not man's, and as little under human control as the division of day or night. Scarcely any one of them seems to have proposed to himself as a subject of inquiry, what changes the relation of those classes to one another are likely to undergo in the progress of society.[76]

Even when he viewed the impact of class as deep and discouraging, he continued to insist that men could be liberated from class by reason, by perceiving the world correctly, and he felt that the tendency for this to happen was increasing with the progress of civilisation, which meant largely the diffusion of intelligence. The notion of the general interest which enlightened men would accept had, of course, a partisan political content of which its opponents were quite aware. But for Mill the basic propositions of classical political economy seemed to be predominantly true, and to indicate what was in the common interest – despite occasional appearances to the contrary and despite socialist attacks, whose factual warrant lay only in exceptional circumstances. Class conflict was irrational. Hence, unlike Marx, Mill strongly denied that there was any objective or real clash of interests between working class and middle class and argued that, as political economy itself revealed, the union of classes was both desirable and, given right thinking, possible. Thus social cohesion or community depended upon, and would follow from, rational political attitudes. It was in this connection that Mill stressed the difference between 'real' and 'apparent' interests, equating real interests with distant and unselfish interests, which tended towards harmony, and apparent with immediate and selfish interests, which tended toward disharmony.[77] As most people were then not rational, not dominated by their real ultimate interests, it followed that the best political decisions would not emerge from majority choice.

Mill's vision of a liberal democratic society, his normative theory, thus clashed sharply and obviously with the reality – the irrationality, prejudice, authoritarianism and division - which he saw about him. He was quite conscious of the rift, and struggled to end it. He saw social conflict, potential tyranny and the willing renunciation of freedom in large societies with increasing population problems: he desired to draw people together in intelligent communal activity in a world in which all had sufficient material resources. If this was to be done, the political power of the ignorant and selfish would have to remain limited as long as they were ignorant and selfish. He feared, not merely a mass electorate but the whole broad movement towards what de Tocqueville called 'equality of condition', and what he himself called the general tendency of modern civilisation. The mass society which he envisaged would be likely to destroy eccentricity, individuality and genius, thus crushing the minorities which he took to be the major source of antagonism and improvement. As a result, it could well become mediocre, conformist and intellectually stagnant, lacking vitality, movement and fruitful competition, and without the means of realising the public interest. Hence the universal franchise was a possible instrument of destruction. Its immediate introduction seemed an extremely dangerous step, which Mill never supported. The English working class needed guidance during its phase of immaturity, until its errors and prejudices were removed. Prudence, justice and vision demanded the gradual, progressive extension of the suffrage. But in Mill's view it was still a question of laying foundations. Universal suffrage was not on the immediate political agenda. He wrote in 1835:

> Happily there is no need for a speedy decision of the question. Many important things are yet to be done, before universal suffrage can even be brought seriously into discussion: and it will probably never be introduced, unless preceded by such improvements in popular education as will greatly weaken the apprehensions at present entertained of it. . .no one is disposed to deny that we ought cautiously to feel our way, and watch well the consequences of each extension of the suffrage before venturing upon another.[78]

In 1839 he wrote in similar vein, 'let Universal Suffrage be ever so desirable, let it even be ever so practicable when the minds of the other classes have been for some time gradually prepared for it by intermediate measures, it cannot be either good or practicable now'.[79] In *Representative Government* restrictions and variations on universal suffrage remained a paramount concern, and he continued to stress the dangers of class legislation and the necessary safeguards to the weak side of democracy.

The problem might seem to have a simple solution. If possible, exclude the workers from political power, or, at least, give them a very restricted political role, and build safeguards into the political system so that the enlightened and virtuous occupy strategic positions, thereby increasing their natural influence. However, the moral development of individuals – all individuals – was, to Mill, the central concern of politics and political institutions. Given a fundamental commitment to human self-realisation or autonomy, the elevation of the labouring class was an essential part of his ideal – despite his assertion of the need for temporary limitations upon its power. He was anti-paternalist, indicating, for example, that a benevolent and virtuous despot would create greater obstacles to general improvement than a bad one, for his good laws and orderly and efficient government would put no pressure on the people, nor antagonise them, and they would be left passive and stunted, with their latent resources untapped. His arguments against over-solicitous government and against socialism similarly assume the vital importance of developing individual faculties and thereby enabling people to become self-determining. Governments had to conduct their business in the existing circumstances, with the people as they were, but Mill was not content to devise a political system simply to protect the enlightened and the emancipated from the masses. He wanted ability and virtue to be extended, and this sometimes demanded action from above and outside, in order to develop capacities for self-management. Like British rule in India, which was to be judged according to the extent to which it provided good government in the present and laid the foundations for free institutions, liberal government was to be evaluated in terms of its contribution to the eventual elimination of the paternalism and the restrictiveness which existing human nature made necessary. Governments should contain the best individuals available at the time and act to improve the general standards of the people, developing their active capacities – intelligence, self-reliance, moderation, and the habit of innovation – and strengthening their social instincts, thereby building permanent and profound protections against tyranny and against class warfare. This theory certainly poses substantial problems, concerning especially how the stage of development or the degree of maturity of a people, class, or group is to be determined, what mixture of self-activity and restraint best allows for the development of their capacities, and how the skill and probity of rulers and guides can be ensured, particularly given the desires imputed to all men in classical utilitarian theory.[80] However, the fact that we may be dissatisfied with Mill's treatment of these issues by no means suggests that his ideal of general human autonomy is mere window dressing or hypocrisy.

Mill's discussion of the grounds for representative government brings out clearly the genuineness of his concern with autonomy. He develops two main arguments for representation, which lead in different directions. The first and characteristically utilitarian one is often taken as characteristically liberal, because of its congruence with a market theory of society. The argument holds that each man is the best judge and guardian of his own interests, and needs political rights to promote those interests, and to protect himself against the misgovernment which, given the assumption of sinister interest, seemed the inevitable result of unrepresentative systems. Mill's self-defence argument assumes that rulers, who lack sympathetic understanding rather than goodwill – though his attacks on monarchs and aristocrats were normally far stronger than this – are generally unable to appreciate fully the claims and demands of different sections of the community, unless these have their acknowledged spokesmen. Hence extensions of the vote and civil liberties were necessary to ensure that people, who normally understand their own interests best, could put their case, thereby producing fairer and more just political decisions.[81] According to this argument, political participation is necessary in order that the various interests within society can be defined adequately and their conflicting claims considered and adjudicated. In the light of this criterion alone, a good society would be one in which all interests were accommodated and given due weight. It would be competitive and stable, but it would not – as such – value self-realisation or diverse individual achievements and ends.

Mill's second argument is that to which he attached most importance. It is concerned with the citizen's self-development, to which democratic or participatory processes were vital. Political participation has a creative role as a source of moral and intellectual improvement. It was to draw forth capacities, to lift men to concern for the larger community and a conciliatory attitude towards the other members of society, thus strengthening the faculties which representative government required. The political system was to be evaluated, not simply in terms of the wisdom of public policy but also of the quality of the citizens themselves, though obviously the wisdom of many public policies is determined largely by the degree to which they contribute to the elevation of the citizens. Public policy and the political system itself must be evaluated in terms of their contribution to self-government by the individual citizens: in the end, good government must include self-government. In this sense, the link between progress and the growth of autonomy is not empirical but conceptual, for the growth of autonomy is the primary constituent of progress.

Thus Mill's social and political theory contains impulses towards both élitism and a wider distribution of rights and resources. The élitist element arose from his concern with the quality of political decisions, his desire to see the public interest realised in state policy, and his beliefs about the present distribution of virtue and intelligence. Given persisting doubts about the political powers of the ordinary man, majority rule seemed unlikely, at least 'for the time being', to produce skilled and disinterested government. Consequently, while accepting the general principle of representative government or majority rule, Mill introduced qualifications and checks to reduce popular influence on governmental decisions. He supported democracy restricted in both the size of the adult voting public and in the powers of the elected assembly. Yet he did not regard the intellectual and moral condition of the masses as fixed. They were not passive, inert stuff, to be manipulated forever by élites, no matter how moral. The development of their capabilities was conceived both as a source of stability and as the major constitutive element in progress. But as their development presupposed both restraint, against their destructive desires and fantasies, and participation in managing the social destiny, a vital tension built up in Mill's thought. His own resolution of the problem was to insist that the threat which they posed to liberty, culture and government in the public interest was in 'the present stage of things', and that substantial changes would and must occur.

Mill envisaged a slow but genuine transformation. Wise politicians, recognising the tenacity of existing sentiments and the gradual seepage of new ideas, would build on what existed, whether in overseas dependencies or in their own societies. 'Great changes should not be made at the first moment when a bare majority can be attained for them. The idlest fears, the most unfounded dislikes, must have some time allowed them to wear off. Nothing which can be gained from a slight acceleration of the improvement of institutions, is an equivalent for the danger incurred when they improve faster than the minds of a large and powerful part of the nation.'[82] Mill emphasised that social problems were many-sided, in specific cases and in general terms, as in his rejection of the narrow premises of the geometric method, which based its abstract theory of society upon a single force or a single property of human nature.[83] The roots of evil were tangled, and their removal necessitated an experimental, complex and gradualist approach. Replying to a request to contribute to a dissertation on the remedies for the economic and social evils of the country, he wrote:

> The causes of existing evils, it seems to me, lie too deep, to be within the reach of any one remedy, or set of remedies; nor would any remedial measure, which is at present practicable, amount to more than a slight palliative for those evils; their removal, I conceive, can only be accomplished by slow degrees, and through many successive efforts, each having its own particular end in view, and so various in their nature that a dissertation which attempted to em-

brace them all must be so general as to be very little available for the practical guidance of any.[84]

Mill was the determined advocate of a particular method of change, now labelled 'piecemeal engineering' – meeting particular grievances within the established system and not trying to change the world overnight (although, in his case, particular reforms were conceived in relation to a larger vision). This he took to be England's characteristic method of political change. Because of the adaption of its institutions and processes to the pressures which naturally emerged in society, sudden, dramatic and violent change had been avoided, and changing values, interests and beliefs had been incorporated into the system. Commenting on the ideas of the revolutionary socialists, who wanted rapid change and economic management from the centre, Mill wrote that their ideals would fail disastrously, and that

> its apostles could have only the consolation that the order of society as it now exists would have perished first, and all who benefit by it would be involved in the common ruin – a consolation which to some of them would probably be real, for if appearances can be trusted the animating principle of too many of the revolutionary Socialists is hate; a very excusable hatred of existing evils, which would vent itself by putting an end to the present system at all costs even to those who suffer by it, in the hope that out of chaos would arise a better Kosmos, and in the impatience of desperation respecting any more gradual improvement. They are unaware that chaos is the very most unfavourable position for setting out in the construction of a Kosmos, and that many ages of conflict, violence and tyrannical oppression of the weak by the strong must intervene.[85]

Unfortunately, rational change – the steady and continuous absorption of new groups and new claims – sometimes proved impossible, because of the extent of the evil confronted and the inflexibility of the prevailing political institutions. Grievances in France had not been remedied when there was time, and as a result a great, destructive convulsion had occurred.[86] Mill feared that the lack of concessions to the Irish would similarly produce a dramatic historical retribution. On the other hand – and, for Mill, there was always an other hand – revolutionary demands characteristically went beyond the capacities of the people and brought on conflict unnecessarily. 'Unquestionably it is possible to do mischief by striving for a larger measure of political reform than the national mind is ripe for and so forcing on prematurely a struggle between elements, which, by a more gradual progress, might have been brought to harmonize.'[87] For Mill, political institutions were not simply the natural products of history beyond conscious change. He cited the examples of Solon, Lycurgus, Frederick of Prussia and Bonaparte as political leaders who planned political institutions, though not in the abstract. They adjusted their plans to the conditions of the time.[88] Recognising, in general terms, the limits imposed upon change by the traditions, habits and intellectual capacities of particular peoples, Mill was ready to limit the utopian or abstract imagination to the actual conditions in which men found themselves. As he emphasised in his dull but decent paragraphs on the organic theory of government, institutional change was not a free process, but had to be adapted to time, place and circumstance. States were not works of art, and the secular heaven was not immediately at hand – though counterposing the other general point, societies could be substantially improved as a result of deliberate policy.[89] Political rulers could alter social conditions and provide means whereby the values and standards of the people become higher, so that they become conscious participants in community life and are not left an alienated and potentially destructive mass outside it. Mill envisaged large-scale changes to 'human nature' and to social organisation, and criticised those who regarded existing human nature, and the existing relations between men, as universal and inescapable. The error was that of reading off as human nature the behaviour of one's contemporaries and fellows. This was an error with which Mill charged the classical political economists:

> the principal error of narrowness with which they are frequently chargeable, is that of regarding not any economical doctrine, but their present experience of mankind, as of universal validity; mistaking temporary or local phases of human character for human nature itself; having no faith in the wonderful pliability of the human mind; deeming it impossible, in spite of the strongest evidence, that the earth can produce human beings of a different type from that which is familiar to them in their own age, or even, perhaps, in their own country.[90]

In the course of his last analysis of socialism, which was published posthumously, Mill indicated how the opinions of mankind 'have always tended to consecrate existing facts, and to declare what did not yet exist, either pernicious or impracticable'.[91] The defenders of the existing order normally protested, unfairly, against socialist attacks on particular, historical institutions, holding that 'the evils complained of are inherent in Man and Society, and are such as no arrangements can remedy'.[92]

Mill remained uncertain of the ultimate possible dimensions of social change. He suggested, vaguely, that in a future state of enlightenment and virtue many, if not all, of the disagreeable aspects of his own society might disappear. He dreamt of a society in which a substantial growth in wisdom, altruism and the power of individual self-management has occurred, and which is characterised by widespread, unforced agreement over moral values, with a corresponding diminution in the role of force in social life. In the meantime, he fought changes which went beyond the revealed capacities of the people. Because of the ordinary level of development, he elaborated a series of prescriptions which were defensive – to prevent bad government in the short term, and reforming – to raise the people's capacities in the longer run. But in the end, his vision of the ultimate social state is in some respects like that of Marx, and unlike that condition of 'perpetual and never resolved crisis' whose acceptance Talmon takes to be typically liberal.

7 *The elevation of mankind*

Mill believed that social and political problems were manageable and, more optimistically, that men could create a rational, harmonious polity. Conflict and misery could be substantially removed. 'Poverty, in any sense implying suffering, may be completely extinguished by the wisdom of society, combined with the good sense and providence of individuals...All the grand sources in short, of human suffering are in great degree, many of them almost entirely, conquerable by human care and effort.'[1] Moreover, given a sound economic base and proper perceptions, democracy could be made compatible with liberal values, skilled government and social justice. Despite the dangers of mediocrity, conformism and ignorant rule, Mill believed that certain dominant tendencies supported his hopes, as the democratic prospect depended upon 'the natural laws of the progress of wealth, upon the diffusion of reading, and the increase of the facilities of human intercourse'.[2] Enlightened men thus acted in a favourable setting, in which high wages and the spread of reading, amongst other things, were ensuring intellectual and moral growth. Political design could ensure that social arrangements encouraged the political virtues – intelligence, conciliation, and respect for the rights and interests of others. An active, informed and generous-minded citizenry was the only true protection against sinister interest. Mill praised those working-class leaders who sought to elevate the workers and did not simply assert their rights, regardless of their existing capacities. William Lovett, for example, wisely made 'the improvement of the working classes as much an object as their emancipation'.[3] Mill strongly condemned the soft-headed, middle-class reformers whose answer to social problems was mere 'pseudo-philanthropy', which asserted men's right without stressing their own degree of responsibility for their plight, and thus left the sources of social evil untouched, and the people remained as they were. For him, the central means to the elevation of the masses and their integration into society were improvements in the economic situation, good popular education, and facilities for increasing popular participation in social and political life. Thus the environment in which men acted – and clashed – was to change, and selfish and ignorant men were to be drawn progressively into society. Violent and insatiable demands would disappear, and the major sources of conflict would wither away peacefully. In this change of circumstances, of which the major cause was a change in men's perceptions and values, educated and rational men were, naturally, to play a crucial part.

THE ECONOMIC FOUNDATIONS

In Mill's view, political economy was not a purely factual study confined to economic phenomena. He recognised the interaction of political, moral and psychological forces with economic factors, and sought to connect his economic analysis with other branches of social philosophy and with 'the best social ideas' of his own time. The task of political economy thus went beyond analysis of the conditions of prosperity to the maximisation of happiness. He had to consider 'how far the particular nature of those commodities [i.e. those described in the science], and the manner in which they are distributed among the different members of the community, are conducive to human happiness in the largest sense and upon the most extended scale'.[4] It was a recommending prescriptive discipline, with an important part to play in the achievement of a rational and harmonious society. Such a conception of the largeness of political economy was not new. But although there was nothing stunning or revolutionary about Mill's conception of the role of economics, or about his specific analysis of economic phenomena, his efforts to reconcile the dismal science with hopes of improvement, and to soften and elevate the competitive system to which he remained committed, were striking and influential. He was quick to point out the element of vested interest and the lack of historical imagination in many defences of the free economy, and inveighed constantly against egoism. Appeals to public-spiritedness are as pronounced in his economic as in his political works.

The basic economic facts with which Mill began were man's improvidence and the niggardliness of nature. The major source of poverty, ignorance and social conflict was, according to his uncompromising Malthusianism, the pressure of population on resources – on land and on the supply of capital. Man's plight was the result neither of unjust social arrangements nor of technological progress. It was a consequence of the facts that resources were more or less fixed, while man's power of reproduction was infinite or indefinite, so that the doubling of population in one generation was commonplace. Mill constantly pointed his finger at the ignorant poor, reminding them and their shallow champions that blind submission to their animal instincts was the true cause of their poverty. Their heedless procreation overstocked the labour market, thus lowering wages, and if their economic position did temporarily improve, the gain was squandered frequently in large families. 'From the habits of the population in regard to marriage, the poor have remained poor.'[5] This problem was naturally more intense and immediate in 'old and fully peopled' countries than in new ones, rapidly increasing in wealth and population. America, for example, could tolerate a population explosion much more easily than could England. Commenting on the general advantages of the Americans, Mill wrote: 'The Americans are a democratic people: granted; but they are also a people without poor; with a "far west" behind them. . .with boundless facilities to all classes for "raising themselves in the world"; and where a large family is a fortune.'[6] To some extent the more crowded countries could relieve their population problems in the short run without seeking to limit the normal increase. Emigration, and especially colonisation, could act as a safety valve as long as it was able to keep pace with the increase of population. But ultimately colonialism, emigration and the expansion of productivity would be unable to absorb the increase of numbers.[7] The natural barriers would finally be met.

Mill stressed the fact that economic productivity was limited. 'But however much we may succeed in making for ourselves more space within the limits set by the constitution of things, we know that there must be limits. We cannot alter the ultimate properties either of matter or mind.'[8] The economy was not open-ended, and economic or technological expansion could not be relied upon to solve the problems set primarily by the imbalance between population and resources. But, while claiming that there were ultimate limits or final barriers to productivity, and that this was something which must be regarded by policymakers, not as a distant theoretical point, but as a matter of urgency, Mill did not indicate the limits with any precision. In relation to the land, he rejected the image of the final barrier as a wall, likening it to 'a highly elastic and extensible band, which is hardly ever so violently stretched that it could not possibly be stretched any more, yet the presure of which is felt long before the final limit is reached, and felt the most severely the nearer that limit is approached'.[9] He also stressed the flexibility of capital. 'The expansion of capital would soon reach its ultimate boundary, if the boundary itself did not continually open and leave more room.'[10] The general limits to the increase of capital were set by the tendency of the rate of profit to fall, owing to the saturation of fields of investment. The falling rate of profit, which featured significantly in contemporary theories of capitalist society, was traced back to the declining quantity of fertile land. The increasing use of inferior lands led to a rise in subsistence costs and thus to a rise in wages. Mill stressed the fact that he was speaking of a tendency only, and pointed to significant countertrends – 'commercial revulsions' or overtrading, leading to the destruction of capital, the importation of cheap commodities, the flow of capital to higher profits abroad[11] and improvements in the productive arts. In addition, low profits on large capitals were often sufficient to satisfy investors. Nonetheless, profits were approaching the minimum, at which the incentives to saving would disappear, and the stationary state, that phobia of the classical economics, would come into being.[12] In the old countries it was very close at hand. Men needed to recognise that 'we are always on the verge of it, and that if we have not reached it long ago, it is because the goal itself flies before us'.[13] Thus, in the case of capital as of land, the gap between the existing and the complete utilisation of resources was gradually closing, but it was hard to predict the point at which it would finally be closed. Man approached more and more the limits of his world and the problem was merely evaded in theories which blamed social inequality or injustice rather than the relative scarcity of resources. 'The niggardliness of nature, not the injustice of society, is the cause of the penalty attached to over-population.'[14] That problem would have to be faced no matter how radically institutional arrangements were altered. Mill had no fear of nature's niggardliness as long as overpopulation was avoided. The stationary state, which he did not depict as necessarily static or mediocre or conflict-ridden, could be characterised by a civilised and comfortable life for all.

Mill therefore rejected those theories which placed the blame for existing social evils on capitalism or industrialism or industrialisation. While believing that the labourers could suffer temporarily from the introduction of machinery, he argued that, as a matter of fact, 'there is probably no country whose fixed capital increases in a ratio more than proportional to its circulating'.[15] If there were temporary changes for the worse, they were nothing when set against the ultimate benefit to the labourers. Should some combination of circumstances lead to a too rapid diversion of capital to machinery, however, 'it would be incumbent on legislators to take measures for moderating its rapidity...there cannot be a more legitimate object of the legislator's care than the interests of those who are thus sacrificed to the gains of their fellow-citizens and of posterity'.[16] But as a general explanation of low wages the mechanisation hypothesis was a quite inadequate one.

The basic source of economic stabilisation was restriction on population increase, which could produce a happy relationship between men and resources. Where the population problem was serious, Mill felt it proper to demand either 'prudent or conscientious self-restraint',[17] as practised in some countries, or legislative sanctions where the people remained lax. Prudential motives and social affections already seemed to operate amongst the middle classes and the skilled artisans. Restraint was encouraged particularly by the fear of losing 'the decencies of their situation in life'[18] or the 'moral minimum'[19] to which they had become accustomed, or by the desire to raise the normal level even higher. They were tied to prudential habits – and to the social order generally – by existing or anticipated standards of living. Mill hoped that the labourers might be moved eventually by similar interests, and suggested that, after improvement of a signal character has occurred, as in France after the Revolution, and 'a generation grows up which has always been used to an improved scale of comfort, the habits of this new generation in respect to population become formed upon a higher minimum, and the improvement in their condition becomes permanent'.[20] Such a process was actually taking place. 'Every advance they made in education, civilization and social improvement, tends to raise this standard; and there is no doubt that it is gradually, though slowly rising in the more advanced countries of Western Europe.'[21] But the weight of the population problem was so great, and the ignorance of the poor so impervious, that Mill sought to justify laws against improvident marriages when the people refused to restrain themselves voluntarily. Compulsion was legitimate where the problem was extreme. As he stated in *On Liberty:*

> In a country either over-populated, or threatened with being so, to produce children, beyond a very small number, with the effect of reducing the reward of labour by their competition, is a serious offence against all who live by the remuneration of their labour. The laws which, in many countries on the Continent, forbid marriage unless the parties can show that they have the means of supporting a family, do not exceed the legitimate powers of the State.[22]

He berated those sentimental humanitarians who offered the workers privileges without stressing their duties – 'not to have more children than they could support'. They not only failed to face the Malthusian problem seriously, but they acquiesced in a cruel sexual tyranny against women and in the continuing dominance of brute instinct. He sharply condemned sentimental attacks on 'hard-hearted Malthusianism': 'as if it were not a thousand times more hardhearted to tell human beings that they may, than that they may not, call into existence swarms of creatures who are sure to be miserable, and most likely to be depraved; and forgetting that the conduct, which it is reckoned so cruel to disapprove, is a degrading slavery to a brute instinct in one of the persons involved, and most commonly in the other, helpless submission to a revolting abuse of power'.[23] His advocacy of the industrial and social independence of women rested in part on its likely effects on over-population, in that 'breeding dollar-hunters' would cease to be their sole preoccupation, and the 'animal instinct' of both sexes would become weaker. Female emancipation would help reduce the brute in man. For the rather ethereal Mill, the diminution of passion in its various forms was a central component of the growth of civilisation. He shared the popular view that reason and cultivation were the enemies of instinct and, more especially, sensuality, and aspired to the general weakening and withering of the degrading appetites.[24]

Assuming self-discipline or, failing that, external discipline, Mill rejected the pessimistic interpretation of Malthusianism, which had been used as an argument against the indefinite improvability of human affairs, regarding it instead 'as indicating the sole means of realizing that improvability by securing population through a voluntary restriction of the increase of their numbers'.[25] Poverty, misery and conflict were thereby removable. The material needs of all could be satisfied without the utter transformation of the economic system.

Although Mill refused to place the primary and direct responsibility for misery and strife upon existing social arrangements or technological innovation, and although he thought that existing shortcomings and frictions were remediable within capitalism, he strongly condemned the industrial market society in terms of its values and the passivity and the self-enclosed existence of the bulk of its members. Sheer economic growth gave him little pleasure. He hated the level of English political life, the domination of the commercial spirit, the selfishness, the ascendancy of mere wealth.[26] He complained of the drudgery and narrowness of the lives of the industrial labourers, subjected to the division of labour. In his discussion of Comte's ideas, he indicated the ill effects of extreme specialisation:

> The increasing specialization of all employments; the division of mankind into innumerable small fractions, each engrossed by an extremely minute fragment of the business of society, is not without inconveniences, as well moral as intellectual, which, if they could not be remedied, would be a serious abatement from the benefits of advanced civilization. The interests of the whole – the bearing of things on the ends of the social union – are less and less present to the minds of men who have so contracted a sphere of activity. The insignificant detail which forms their whole occupation – the infinitely minute wheel they help to turn in the machinery of society – does not arouse or gratify any feeling of public spirit, or unity with their fellow-men. Their work is a mere tribute to physical necessity, not the glad performance of a social office.[27]

This was a statement made in passing, and, characteristically, it is rather ponderous and evasive, with its double negative – specialisation is 'not without inconveniences'. It has none of the directness and power of Marx's indictment of man's plight under the existing division of labour. But while Mill did not pay much attention to those features of industrial life which were comprehended by Marx in the theory of alienation, his mild criticism connects closely with his view of the rational and productive man, who is many-sided and not confined to particular occupations and interests. Explicitly, however, his criticisms of capitalist industrialism are concerned much more with the system of distribution, which he found extremely unjust but manipulable, than with the deficiencies of the one-sided labourer. While the laws of production were of the nature of physical truths, distribution was a matter of human institution solely, being dependent upon customs, laws and standards, and subject to change at man's discretion. Moreover, the problem of production seemed to be largely solved – abundance was at least within reach – but that of distribution persisted, and was subject to widespread and often highly critical discussion because of its inequalities and injustices which, in Mill's view, distorted the free enterprise system, especially in old societies. It was high time to settle the issue consciously in terms of standards of justice, prudence and sound economic theory – and, in the process, to destroy simple redistributivist myths. Mill agreed that men were rewarded almost in inverse proportion to their labour. Those who never worked at all gained most, while 'the most fatiguing and exhausting bodily labour cannot count with certainty on being able to earn even the necessaries of life'.[28] If the choice were between the existing inequality, injustice, drudgery and virtual slavery, which were the products of the self-adjusting economic system, and communism, with all its chances, Mill said, 'all the difficulties, great or small, of communism would be as dust in the balance'.[29] But he did not see this as the choice. The ideal socialist or communist[30] society was to be compared properly with a private property system purged of its too obvious weaknesses, and the comparison would be largely concerned with the economic efficiency, the effect on population growth, the distributive arrangements and the freedom and individualism of these different social and economic orders. While Mill's discussion of communism was quite sympathetic, especially in relation to the economic objections normally brought against it, he did not become in any serious sense a socialist.[31] He condemned unjust distributive arrangements, and stressed that existing institutions were provisional, and needed to be critically evaluated. But he did not claim that socialism was feasible or unequivocally desirable. He advised people to wait and see, and meanwhile advocated improvements to the private property system, and experimentation with the more appealing forms of socialist or communist enterprise.

Mill's analysis of communism is particularly interesting in view of the clash between his conception of the most desirable social order and what he regarded as practical possibilities in the present. He indicated, in almost aristocratic terms, his displeasure with the competitive ideal – the ideal of those who thought that 'the normal state of human beings is that of struggling to get on; that the trampling, crushing, elbowing, and treading on each other's heels, which form the existing type of social life, are the most desirable lot of human kind, or anything but the disagreeable symptoms of one of the phases of industrial progress'.[32] But his psychological assumptions made it seem unlikely that a cooperative order could be quickly introduced. For the kind of order envisaged by the communists presupposed higher capacities, higher moral and intellectual standards, than were possessed by most people. Like democracy, communism was an ideal currently within reach of the élite only. Industrial efficiency and progressiveness required a competitive free enterprise system, which offered the strongest available incentives to the individual to improve himself. Communism rested too heavily on virtues – especially public-spiritedness – that were in short supply. In his *Chapters on Socialism* Mill suggested that, if the desire to improve one's own economic condition could not be satisfied, people would compete in more destructive ways. People naturally aspire, and compete with each other, and they may clash in socially dangerous areas.

> When selfish ambition is excluded from the field in which, with most men, it chiefly exercises itself, that of riches and pecuniary interest, it would betake itself with greater intensity to the domain still open to it, and we may expect that the struggles for preeminence and for influence in the management would be of great bitterness when the personal passions, diverted from their ordinary channel, are driven to seek their principal gratification in that other direction.[33]

Consequently he expected communist societies to be undermined by appetites whose strength their exponents had underrated or ignored. The lust for power would supplant the less harmful economic desires – selfish ambition may be channelled into more or less damaging areas – while most people would revert to mankind's natural indolence. In addition, Mill saw poor prospects for liberty and individualism, economic flexibility and adventurousness, and occupational specialisation, in communist societies. He also rejected the economic doctrine underlying revolutionary communist theory, that is, the doctrine that working-class wages and conditions were deteriorating. Despite some vicissitudes, he believed that 'permanent causes' were working towards an improvement in the mode of living of the European working-classes, and that the evils of the existing society were slowly diminishing.[34]

Mill continued to support private ownership of economic resources. He stressed the need to publicly defend private property – 'that primary and fundamental institution'[35] – in view of increasing working-class attacks upon it and, while declaring that communism could conceivably be practised in some future state of general enlightenment and virtue – a prophecy in which he was never forceful – he concluded that, in that meantime:

> We may, without attempting to limit the ultimate capabilities of human nature, affirm, that the political economist, for a considerable time to come, will be chiefly concerned with the conditions of existence and progress belonging to a society founded on private property and individual competition; and that the object to be principally aimed at in the present stage of human improvement, is not the subversion of the system of individual property, but the improvement of it, and the full participation of every member of the community in its benefits.[36]

The vast inequalities existing at that time prevented a fair trial of the free enterprise system, as rewards were still largely determined by pre-existing advantages. Because of the large accumulations of wealth Mill fought to limit rights of inheritance and bequest, which preserved or even accentuated substantial inequality. The institution of property, which in fact varied widely in different societies, could be improved, and should be improved for prudential and for moral reasons, particularly through a wider diffusion of economic resources. The prospect of gaining property was a great incentive to labour and to progress, as Mill had argued in relation to the Irish peasants. In economic matters, self-interest and individualism remained central: the social principle had not yet penetrated that sphere.

But it had touched it, and Mill stressed the significance and the value of workers' co-operatives and profit-sharing schemes, operating within the competitive system. In this connection he revealed considerable sympathy for socialism – a socialism of small, competing co-operative associations, whose relations with each other he never seriously considered. This socialism was syndicalist, far from the centralised state socialism of the twentieth century. Mill felt that such associations, many of which had been established in Paris, would give the workers a much greater personal interest in their work by rewarding them proportionately to their contributions. They would be better, happier, more dignified, more enthusiastic and involved and hence more productive, when working under self-imposed rules than they would working for some external person or group. In addition, these moralising entitites would undermine class divisions and bring about an association rather than a conflict of interests. They could revolutionise society through

> the healing of the standing feud between capital and labour; the transformation of human life, from a conflict of classes struggling for opposite interests, to a friendly rivalry in the pursuit of good common to all; the elevation of the dignity of labour, a new sense of security and independence in the labouring class, and the conversion of each human being's daily occupation into a school of the social sympathies and the practical intelligence.[37]

Mill had great hopes for co-operative production, which, with the emancipation of women, he described as 'the two great changes that will regenerate society'.[38] He foresaw, with mankind's improvement, the eventual predominance of one form of association, 'not that which can exist between a capitalist as chief, and work people without a voice in the management, but the association of the labourers themselves on terms of equality, collectively owning the capital with which they carry on their operations, and working under managers elected and removable by themselves'.[39] But even assuming that labourers become citizens within their own enterprises, the question of the relationship between these enterprises and the larger society remains to be determined. Mill sometimes slid a little too easily into the assumption that in the associations they would have the public good in mind, rather than the good of their own particular association. Why should participation within co-operative bodies tie their members to the community rather than isolate and divide from it? Do participatory institutions necessarily feed and support each other within the total society – whose predominant arrangements may be themselves non-participatory? It seems possible that generosity, enthusiasm and feelings of mutuality may end, or sharply diminish, at the boundaries of the co-operative, especially if it exists within a larger community which is indifferent to it, or which is organised according to significantly different principles. Mill's assumption – it is not quite an argument – does have an immediate plausibility, however. He believed that co-operatives would themselves constitute spheres of citizenship, in which rationality, disinterestedness and social affection would grow and become preponderant, and that generous feelings for the whole community would spread from them, and would in turn be sustained by other participatory institutions within the society. He also assumed that the associations, along with industrial partnership schemes, could gradually transform the capitalist system from within, successfully competing with the purer capitalist enterprises, and showing the way to a better future. This assumption enabled him to accept the vital importance of private property at that stage, whilst envisaging its steady and peaceful transcendance in the future. He had, once more, the best of both world.

POLITICAL PARTICIPATION

Mill's belief in the value of participation by men in their own enterprises, which underlay his recommendation of co-operatives, is revealed even more clearly in his defence of the gradual extension of political self-government. He felt that self-government would increase men's rationality and social sympathy and develop their active, self-reliant capacities, thereby bringing them to the highest level of which they were capable. Actual social changes convinced him that it was impossible to keep the working class in a position of dependence. Unacceptable as he found radical claims for the political dominance of the workers, he could not accept the view that all their affairs should be regulated for them. 'The poor have come out of leading strings, and cannot any longer be governed or treated like children...the theory of dependence and protection will be more and more intolerable to them, and they will require that their conduct and condition shall be essentially self-governed.'[40] Cheap newspapers, dissenting preachers, large-scale production, railways, trades unions, popular lectures and political agitation had contributed to a growth in reflectiveness, political concern and public spirit. Even the struggle to determine their own political future, which was often only conceived as a means of protecting class interests, could have elevating effects, despite the errors which the labourers frequently made. 'Although the too early attainment of political franchises by the least educated class might retard, instead of promoting their improvement, there can be little doubt that it has been greatly stimulated by the attempt to acquire them.'[41] Mill believed in the right of individuals to make mistakes and fall, but also held that making one's own mistakes was far more likely to have constructive effects than would continuous coercion and restriction of the many by the enlightened. He had a great deal of faith in the effects of political participation itself. He described the franchise as 'a potent instrument of mental improvement', and was deeply influenced by de Tocqueville's explanation of the conscientious citizenship of the Americans in terms of their democratic institutions.[42] In de Tocqueville's view, the small self-governing New England townships taught social principles and initiated political activity, as well as providing – along with other local institutions – a check against the dangers of a democratic despotism, by which he meant 'the absolute rule of the head of the executive over a congregation of isolated individuals, all equals but all slaves'.[43] The diffusion of intelligence, activity and public spirit amongst the governed was the only security against political slavery, and was particularly important when members of the government were intelligent and talented.

It is therefore of supreme importance that all classes of the community, down to the lowest, should have much to do for themselves; that as great a demand should be made upon their intelligence and virtue as it is in any respect equal to; that the government should not only leave as far as possible to their own faculties the conduct of whatever concerns themselves alone, but should suffer them, or rather encourage them, to manage as many as possible of their joint concerns by voluntary co-operation; since this discussion and management of collective interests is the great school of that public spirit, and the great source of that intelligence of public affairs which are always regarded as the distinctive character of the public of free countries.[44]

Thus – a good liberal in this – Mill emphasised the importance of society rather than the state,[45] and the value of action initiated and shared by free individuals. Voluntary participation in community affairs, especially in local associations, was itself vital for the growth of individual faculties: if the people had much to do for themselves they would learn to walk on their own feet. Local bodies 'stand nearer to the merits as well as the defects which belong to the spontaneous energies of the private citizen'.[46] Municipal and provincial institutions helped transform subjects into citizens, and were thus crucial to man's public education. Popular local institutions were 'a school of political capacity and general intelligence',[47] 'the most efficient of all instruments for training the people in the proper use of representative government'.[48] They were of particular value to the less-educated sections of the community, who required such indirect schooling. As in more formal schooling, good teachers were necessary, to influence beneficially their moral and intellectual inferiors, 'inspiring them with a portion of their own more enlarged ideas, and higher and more enlightened purposes'.[49] The usefulness of local representative bodies depended on their 'bringing inferior minds into contact with superior, a contact which in the ordinary course of life is altogether exceptional, and the want of which contributes more than anything else to keep the generality of mankind on one level of contented ignorance'.[50] In addition to free and popular local and municipal institutions, Mill supported trade unions and co-operatives as counters to selfishness and ignorance. Jury service was a further means of developing the active faculties of the individual. As he wrote in an important passage in *On Liberty*, voluntary activity in these various organisations and enterprises furnished 'the peculiar training of the citizen, the practical part of the political education of a free people, taking them out of the narrow circle of personal and family selfishness, and accustoming them to the comprehension of joint interests, the management of joint concerns – habituating them to act from public and semi-public motives, and guide their conduct by aims which unite instead of isolating them from one another'.[51]

Mill envisaged continuous public activity in a network of voluntary associations and in certain governmental institutions, which would ensure a democratic and participatory foundation for political life. At the local level the issues were close and concrete, if not necessarily clear, and hence highly motivated participation could be expected there. Mill does not tell us much about the internal structure of these various institutions – for example, whether they are organised democratically themselves, or whether they are replicas, in miniature, of his élitist model of representative government – nor does he indicate the limits of their power. Are people to exercise themselves on local issues whilst remaining cut off from the centres of public policy-making? However, at the level of feelings, preferences and capacities, the imagined flow of connection – local participation to the wider society and the state – is clear. Continuous activity is conceived as educational and transforming. It not only increases people's self-reliance, but it strengthens the ties between them and thus knits a firmer community. Mill believed that increasing experience in managing their own affairs and increasing co-operation with others would lift men beyond their narrow private interests and their exclusive private circles, especially the family, and encourage them to seek the public interest. In particular, they would learn good sense, forbearance, prudence and impartiality, and in this way political participation would help eradicate class conflict, and thereby strengthen social cohesion. The political order becomes self-sustaining, as the people, through actually working their own institutions, develop the capacities and gain the values which are necessary for creative action within the democratic system.[52]

EDUCATION

Education, in which participation in economic and political enterprises and associations forms a crucial part, was the essential support of a stable and progressive society. Mill placed enormous weight on it, treating it as an instrument and, more broadly, a body of influences, which was capable of undermining the related evils of ignorance, indolence, and class conflict. He blamed ignorance for much destructive social behaviour, claiming, for example, that 'in England, it would hardly be believed to what a degree all that is morally objectionable in the lowest class of the working people is nourished, if not engendered, by the low state of their understandings'.[53] Because of ignorance men could not discern the nature of their true interests, and selfish and hostile attitudes developed. They failed to see that it was in their interest to behave prudently and morally, that what was in the public interest, as defined by Mill, was also in their interest. Moral exhortation was pointless to the uneducated – 'like preaching to the worm who crawls on the ground how much better it would be for him if he were an eagle'.[54] Mill made many scathing attacks on the educational system of his time, allowing few exceptions to the general badness. One exception was the Scottish parochial school, which he praised for its part in producing a reflecting, observant and self-governing peasantry. In his *Autobiography* he lamented the 'wretched waste' of precious early years.[55] As a consequence he strongly supported the establishment of a national system of education. The matter was so important, the people so stunted and private agencies so inadequate, that education seemed a necessary sphere of state action. In this area the uninformed consumers were not competent judges of the commodity, as they had erroneous conceptions 'of what they want'. They did not know what was good for them, while tolerably civilised government recognised the need for education, and ought both to give financial support to elementary schools, and to compel elementary instruction for all children. Mill treated as almost a self-evident maxim that 'the State should require and compel the education up to a certain standard, of every human being who is born its citizen'.[56] But he inserted a liberal proviso, deriving from his hostility to a single, uniform educational system, charged with the task of establishing public virtue. State schools should be only one amongst competing options and experiments. Governments should not have a monopoly of education, as this would enable them to mould opinion, and do with the people what they pleased.[57]

The severity of Mill's criticisms of existing educational practice is closely connected with his assumption of the extraordinary power of a well-designed educational system – an assumption so extreme that he could claim that there was nothing at all surprising about his own educational progress,[58] although the broadness of his notion of 'education' reduces the apparent absurdity of his claim. For Mill asserted, not only that human nature changed significantly, and that consequently one could not build universal theories on the basis of its form in any particular, historical society, but that it could be shaped deliberately. This optimistic assumption underlay his science of character formation, or ethology, which was to contribute powerfully to moral progress. In explaining how women had been suppressed and stunted by arbitrary social arrangements, which had made the ideal of woman the submissive female, the embodiment of merely domestic virtue, Mill referred to the lesson of history in showing 'the extraordinary susceptibility of human nature to external influences, and the extreme variableness of those of its manifestations which are supposed to be most universal and uniform'.[59] Human nature is made by circumstance. Following the associationist David Hartley, Mill described the raw material with which the educator had to deal as amazingly pliable. Associationism taught him to believe in 'the formation of all human character by circumstance, through the universal Principle of Association, and the consequent unlimited possibility of improving the moral and intellectual condition of mankind by education'.[60] Consequently he could write that 'the power of education is almost boundless'[61] – although his notion of education is such a broad one, comprising so much more than schooling, that the problem diminishes at this point, to reappear elsewhere. Sometimes Mill presents the pristine, innocent mind as a blank sheet, without any predispositions or tendencies any way, simply awaiting the impress of society, but at other times he suggested that the educator and the corruptor did not start off equal, because children had a natural tendency towards goodness. Natural motives or drives, which are good, provide a positive foundation for the educator. As Mill told the students at St Andrews:

> If you take the average human mind while still young, before the objects it has chosen in life have given it a turn in any bad direction, you will generally find it desiring what is good, right, for the benefit of all; and if that season is properly used to implant the knowledge and give the training which shall render rectitude of judgement more habitual than sophistry, a serious barrier will have been erected against the inroads of selfishness and falsehood.[62]

Given at worst neutral and at best promising material with which to work, the educator and the legislator should be able to produce a rational and harmonious society. Consequently religion did not seem necessary for the child's moralisation, although Mill conceded that appeals to revelation, which provided strong sanctions for legal systems and moral codes, had probably been required by some ancient peoples.[63] But he felt that religion had virtually had its day as a social instrument, and that the power which it had once exercised by virtue of clerical control over the young could and should pass to more advanced bodies of doctrine.[64] Given access to young minds, these new beliefs could do far more to create a good society than traditional religion, with its appeals to selfishness, had ever done.

What, for Mill, was the object of education, which included not

merely formal training in schools and universities, but the entire network of social institutions which moulded and formed the individual?[65]
In general terms, the purpose of formal education was to transform
people, and especially the labouring masses, into rational beings, 'beings
capable of foresight, accessible to reason and motives addressed to their
understanding'.[66] It would enable them to pursue intelligently their
own interests and those of their group. By increasing man's knowledge
of necessity in its various forms, it would destroy persistent economic
fallacies and prevent the emergence of absurd and destructive aspirations. It would encourage the ability to reflect, enabling more and more
to reach the ideal of being able to form 'a rational conviction on great
questions of legislation and internal policy'.[67]

This brings us to the centre of Mill's ideological assumptions, which
arise directly in his account of the path which the rational, educated
man would follow. For education is conceived as a strengthener of the
social feelings, as a source of harmony in societies which, largely because
of its influence, are elevated and free. The ignorant man is far less
attached to his fellows than is the educated individual.

> Further, as the strongest propensities of uncultivated or half-
> cultivated human nature (being the purely selfish ones, and those
> of a sympathetic character which partake most of the nature of
> selfishness) evidently tend in themselves to disunite mankind, not
> to unite them – to make them rivals, not confederates; social
> existence is only possible by a disciplining of those more powerful
> propensities, which consists in subordinating them to a common
> system of opinions.[68]

Given Mill's close linkage of knowledge, virtue and social cohesion,
whatever undermined ignorance strengthened social bonds. By inculcat-
ing a sense of social obligation and encouraging feelings of disinterestedness and altruism, the dangers of social conflict – highlighted
in utilitarian social theory and apparently confirmed by much of Mill's
own observation – would be reduced sharply. Mill thought that these
feelings were already becoming more powerful with the growth of
civilisation. In an improving, or morally progressive, state of society,
feelings of unity grew anyhow. And already, without assuming the
widespread impact of education, Mill had rejected Bentham's psychological theory on the ground that its account of the influences on
human behaviour was too narrow, and that in particular it underrated
the disinterested feelings, of which the social feeling were part.[69] Hence,
when he wrestled with this problem in *Utilitarianism*, he could find self-
sacrifice for the general good a perfectly natural human capacity. For one
who recognised that some men disinterestedly pursued public goals, and

that fraternal feelings were already strong, men did not seem to be dangerously or permanently set apart from each other. As a consequence social peace is not seen as dependent upon curbing and coercive political devices, or upon the external inducements offered by Christianity for duty to one's otherwise separate fellows. There is, according to this view, a powerful natural foundation for social solidarity, which militates against dangerous conflict. The psychological basis of utilitarian morality is 'the social feelings of mankind; the desire to be unity with our fellows'.[70] 'The deeply rooted conception which every individual even now has of himself as a social being, tends to make him feel it one of his natural wants that there should be harmony between his feelings and aims and those of his fellow-creatures.'[71] Laws and social arrangements were to add to this existing foundation of sociality, by placing 'the happiness...or the interest of every individual, as nearly as possible in harmony with the interests of the whole'.[72] In the end it would be possible to destroy permanently all 'the selfish propensities, the self-worship, the unjust self-preference, which exist among mankind'.[73]

Where ignorance is linked so intimately with vice and social division, education could be credited with great transforming power – that of undermining selfishness, prejudice and class interest and encouraging the duties of citizenship, political participation and the feeling of belonging to the community. It was the primary and deliberate agent of socialisation, which could reduce egoism, lead the individual to associate individual happiness with the good of the whole and hence, by marrying private interests and public goals, resolve the political dilemma of utilitarianism. Indeed, Mill went as far as to suggest that education could help furnish man with a new, rational religion. He had learned from Comte's *Traité de Politique Positive*, from which he in the main dissented, how the service of humanity could be given 'the psychological power and social efficacy of a religion'.[74] The strength of secular social morality in ancient Greece was impressive and could be repeated. Education, drawing out deep-rooted human feelings, could encourage devotion to the common good and establish the paramountcy of the general interest. Virtue would become habitual. Mill even suggested that elevated feelings, such as those expressed in the Spartan's devotion to his state, could be extended to the whole world, so that men would identify themselves with 'the entire life of the human race'.[75] Its general interest would become a source of emotion and a chief motive of conduct. The cultivation of an altruism which embraces everybody is thus the chief – and feasible – goal of education. 'No efforts should be spared to associate the pupil's self-respect, and his desire of the respect of others, with service rendered to Humanity.'[76] In his essay on 'The Utility of Religion', Mill hopefully wrote that 'the sense of unity with mankind, and a deep feeling for the general good, may be cultivated into a sentiment and a principle capable of fulfilling every important function of religion and itself justly entitled to the name'.[77]

In discussing these things, Mill recruited public opinion as a support of morality or moralisation. He assumed, like Adam Smith, that men could not bear the contempt or disesteem of their fellows, that they wanted approval and respect. If public opinion was not in a perverted state, their readiness to conform would reduce anti-social behaviour. Thus public opinion, working particularly on man's sense of shame and fear of isolation, could be used to discipline men, so that they would take account of the social good. Individual rectitude was to be maintained through the coercive use of social norms – though through habit and moral development they would gradually lose their external character. Some rules, Mill argued, 'must be imposed, by law in the first place, and by opinion on many things which are not fit subjects for the operation of law'.[78] Public disapprobation, as a sanction, was to be directed against socially damaging or harmful practices, but not against mere objects of dislike. Public scrutiny and public disesteem, attached to elevated moral standards which are developed largely through education and example, helps maintain the rational content of action, and ensures that men fulfil their basic social obligations, even where these are non-legal in character. In a rational society certain courses of action will be excluded effectively through the weight of moral consensus. Men are not free to do all legally permitted things, indiscriminately. For example, public opinion could be mobilised against poor couples with large families. Malthusians deter the selfish from intemperance 'by stamping it as disgraceful'.[79] The open ballot was to ensure disinterested voting by keeping potential egoists under the watchful eye of the general public, and therefore ashamed to pursue their selfish interests. Political choices had to be defensible as independent and rational acts. One of the possible strengths of communism was that public opinion could be expected to declare itself strongly against indolence and intemperance.[80]

It is clear that this argument forms a significant part of Mill's theory of liberty, and drives it in an unexpected direction. The discussion of education and the social religion pictures a society very different from the individualistic and contractual society which conservative philosophers have traditionally condemned as the ideal and the fruit of liberalism. Social discipline and a sense of community are invoked against some of the potential excesses of individualism, whereas the essence of *On Liberty* is the defence of diversity and independence against possible invasions by society. In the latter case Mill was troubled by the immense, intrusive and dangerous power of social sanctions which were destined to create an inferior state. The creative individual is threatened by a mediocre and encompassing social conformity, by 'a hostile and dreaded censorship'. But in other cases social order and progress were threatened by independence of an anti-social kind, and in these circumstances it seemed fitting to Mill that an elevated or enlight-ened public opinion, partly created by the educational system, should act as a restraining and positive force, to both check and improve men. Certain choices and certain modes of existence were inferior and socially dangerous, and in such cases the heavy weight of moral opinion could properly fall upon them. This was Mill's somewhat uncertain and ambiguous response to what has been a common liberal fear – that a liberal society, lacking social solidarity and permitting a great range of belief and action, would break apart, or at best be seriously weakened or threatened by the variety it encouraged. The collective opinion, which may not be the actually existing opinion of the people, but one yet to be established, has been introduced frequently to create or sustain the liberal society. And that is a two-edged weapon, liable to threaten liberal values because of its very unwieldiness and intrusive-ness. It is true that Mill was opposed utterly to a tyranny of virtue, but his fear of irrational and irresponsible – hence socially harmful – action led him to concede too much to an elevated and elevating public opinion.

Mill's account of education as a means towards social union is hardly satisfying in other respects. It is all very well to claim that edu-cational improvement will ultimately make the 'feeling of unity with our fellow-creatures' part of our nature, and that genuine public affec-tions and a sincere interest in the public good are possible to every 'rightly-brought up human being'. But Mill did not consider seriously such vital issues as how these powerful feelings emerge, how – especially given the assumptions of associationism and utilitarianism – one can ascribe an initial advantage to virtuous tendencies, and how the 'natural social feelings' connect with and modify social conflict. He simply assumed that man's ordinary and basic feelings contributed to social order and had to be reinforced, rather than overcome or repressed, and that the needs and interests of social groups could be harmonised readily as a result of reforms. We also need to know precisely the kind of education that was proposed, the precise points at which it was to meet and improve existing human nature, and its relationship to the competitive economic order within which it worked. Was Mill pro-posing the spread of the general education plus specialist training that he advocated in his inaugural address at St Andrews? To whom would such an education be accessible? He wanted a system that would pro-duce rational, questioning, self-critical individuals. Would they necessarily feel solidarity with their fellows? How is the educational system to inculcate brotherly love or a love of humanity – abstract concepts which seem to have little directive power over conduct? The national community, let alone mankind at large, is too big and remote to act as a concrete symbol for common action, except on rare occasions. And not any solidarity would do – the effective training for national citizenship (compliance, a blind sense of duty, stereotypes of outsiders), which existed most strikingly in Nazi Germany and Stalinist Russia, was obviously far from Mill's ideal. Finally, in conditions of economic scarcity the sense of community is unlikely to develop to anything near the required degree. Mill's ideal presupposes, not only good men, but a systematic and extremely creative educational system operating in optimum social conditions. When advocating his own ideal he tended to exaggerate the power of education, while against his more radical opponents he was far more conservative, stressing the difficulties of creating a new man through education. He agreed with the communists when they traced the weakness of the 'public and social feelings' to imperfect education, but added that much time would be required before the qualities of the few rational and disinterested individuals spread to the majority, as the education of men is 'one of the most difficult of all arts, and this is one of the points in which it has hitherto been least successful; moreover improvements in general education are necessarily very gradual, because the future generation is educated by the present, and the imperfections of the teachers set an invincible limit to the degree in which they can train their pupils to be better than themselves'.[81] Mill thus faced a common dilemma. How could education – an integral part of a complex society – be detached and made an instrument of radical reform? From what Archimedean point could the enlightened liberal – he who would educate the educators – train and legislate for general improvement? And how was social power to be redistributed so that all men are placed under 'an enlightened direction of social and educational influences'?[82]

8 The élite and liberal politics

Mill's concrete political and institutional recomendations are now to be considered against an assumption of his reforming zeal – his efforts to elevate society at large – and in the light of his reputation as a leading liberal and classical democratic theorist. The question, put brutally, is whether or not his recommendations amount to a case for the middle class of his own day. Does his justification of authority and of the political institutions necessary for authority to be exercised properly, and for its influence to spread easily, amount to an argument for élite predominance? And does his élite, when his own general and rationalist phrases are stripped away, reveal the features of the middle class, or of its superior elements?

Mill wanted knowledge to be powerful, and he crusaded for an end to the existing turbulence and a return, at a higher level, to a rational state of intellectual and social harmony. He wanted a government both moral and skilled, and naturally emphasised the role of the educated. The authority which he supported did not, as far as his own argument ran, derive its claim from wealth or birth, but from intellect.[1] It was, on the face of it, a cultural and intellectual élite, with far greater political competence than the mass of men and therefore specially equipped to govern and to lead. His critics – and occasionally Mill himself – saw its actual social content. In addition to his explicit élitism, with its disguised class bias, it is commonly suggested that his general doctrine – the style, drift and substance of his liberalism – was above all relevant to the few, that it took little account of the actual resources, economic and otherwise, of the bulk of mankind. The cultural and intellectual and even the economic pursuits which he praised were beyond their means and often beyond their comprehension. The final element in this picture of the bourgeois Mill is the particular kind of popular government that he recommended. Classical democracy, which is associated normally with popular rule, the sovereignty of the people or equal participation in political life,[2] seems a larger ideal than Mill's. Under Mill's kind of popular government, which did not necessarily mean a government chosen on a universal franchise, political questions were to be decided by 'the deliberately-formed opinions of a comparatively few, specially educated for the task'.³ To the natural influence of the wise, which was exercised in a variety of subtle ways, was to be added a series of 'correctives or 'counteractives' to bad – especially popular – tendencies. These were to prevent public policy being placed 'at the mercy of public ignorance, and the presumptuous vanity of political men'.⁴ The leaders of mankind were not merely to tell the truth and show the way, in the manner of Coleridge's rational and cultured clerisy, but they were to be over-represented and, if possible, dominant in the institutions of government, through such devices as a limited franchise, plural voting, a second house, a legislative commission and the abolition of pledges. The effort to protect minorities, which at the time seemed to be the most advanced sections of the community, led Mill to define and curtail representative government in terms of existing differentiations, which were largely economic. However, while Mill did limit democratic principles to accord with the skills and virtues of élites and the ignorance of ordinary men, there were powerful elements in his thought questioning élite dominance – anti-paternalism, the firm utilitarian assumption that each man is the best judge of his own interests and the specific acceptance of political restrictions on the ruling minority. He made it clear to Bain, in discussing *On Liberty*, that 'the notion of an intellectual aristocracy of *lumières* while the rest of the world remains in darkness' fulfilled none of his aspirations, which were 'to make the many more accessible to all truth by making them more open-minded'.⁵ He envisaged a fruitful and productive relationship, in conditions of intellectual freedom, between the morally and intellectually advanced members of the community, and the ordinary people. Everybody could not develop to the same degree, exercise the same powers and undertake the same responsibilities, but each should be encouraged and aided to develop to the pitch of which he was capable. Mill's doubts about the rectitude and integrity of even wise leaders were combined with a desire to improve all men, and the result was an untidy and unsuccessful compromise which can best be labelled democratic – or even bourgeois democratic – Platonism. Mill did more than put a democratic façade over capitalistic inequality, but he cannot be characterised as unequivocally democratic even according to his own lights. He was not a democrat of whom it could be said that he genuinely wanted democracy but failed to see the large social changes which would be needed if it was to become a reality.

ÉLITE, MASS, AND REPRESENTATIVE GOVERNMENT

In Mill's major writings the few occupy a crucial position – as leaders of taste, as social and political guides and authorities, and as sources of initiative. In *On Liberty,* for example, he argued that the many could only escape mediocrity if they were guided 'by the counsels and influence of a more highly gifted and instructed One or Few'.[6] He assumed that there were superior persons, persons with political skill and insight who were free from sinister – or mean and partial– interest. They were learned, impartial, moderate, concerned with the good of the whole, and loving virtue for its own sake. Their minds were reforming, 'cultivated' and 'instructed', capable of guiding and improving public opinion on the greater concerns of practical life'.[7] In addition, they were characterised by what Locke called 'indifferency', which involved a willingness to 'assert. . .liberty of thought [and] discard all authority'.[8] Thus they were free-thinking, critical and detached, following their own reason and their own nature without submitting to custom or authority. They were experts who were also, in Mannheim's sense, pure intellectuals, with autonomous values and conduct, neither representing a class nor embodying its aspirations. Unmoved by the passions of the men about them, they were supremely capable of undermining the class basis of existing conflicts, and of drawing all men closer to truth and justice.

Mill portrays the elevated few as selfless, skilled and thinking for themselves. He refers to them as 'the tribunal of the specially instructed', and the 'intellectual benefactors of humanity'. On the other hand most men were incapable of freeing themselves from the trammels of custom and tradition, of separating themselves from their personal and class interests, and of mastering the technical complexities of politics. They needed leadership, primarily because of their limited understandings, their ignorance of moral principles and their inability to make free and informed moral choices. The traditional liberal view of each man as his own guide and authority thereby collapses on the ordinary man's incapacity. Under the influence of such conservative thinkers as Wordsworth and Coleridge, Mill praised the speculative Tories for their awareness that it was good for men to be ruled by a higher intelligence and virtue.

> It [speculative Toryism] is therefore the direct antithesis of liberalism, which is for making every man his own guide and sovereign master, and letting him think for himself, and do exactly as he judges best for himself, giving other men leave to persuade him if they can by evidence, but forbidding him to give way to authority; and still less allowing them to constrain him more than the existence and tolerable security of every man's person and property renders indispensably necessary. It is difficult to conceive a more thorough ignorance of man's nature, and what is

necessary for his happiness or what degree of happiness and virtue
he is capable of attaining than this system implies.[9]

He also referred to the 'narrow views' and 'mischievous heresies' of
liberalism. His differences from a more complacent and superficial
liberalism and utilitarianism emerge in various contexts and at various
times. His philosophy of history does not depict the man of the transitional period as the man whose human nature was being fulfilled. In
one major respect the transitional period was unnatural, as it threw men
heavily upon their own resources at a time when most of them were
not rational individualists. Incapable of wisely exercising their freedom,
at least during this stage, they needed an orthodoxy and a sensible
deference to the enlightened. One of the major worries of *On Liberty*
is the willingness of the ordinary man to renounce liberty, and to
renounce it by accepting and strengthening the suffocating conformities
and the shallow constricting leadership which were quite disastrous in
a critical period, which was distinguished precisely by a genuine and
fundamental clash of ideas. It was thus necessary to defend cultured
and civilised minorities, dedicated to the processes of intellectual argu-
mentation and discovery, against an antagonistic society.

Mill did not present mass deference to the few, actually or ideally,
as the result of psychological need, of a yearning for salvation or submission arising out of insecurity, loss or loneliness. It is the submission,
non-coercive in character, of the ignorant people to 'their own natural
leaders in the path of progress'.[10] It is a proper and voluntary deference,
quite distinct from 'mental slavery' and from subservience to rulers as
such, and compatible with wide popular liberty and individuality. But
the line is drawn in the area of political competence. Mill held that it
was neither desirable, necessary nor possible that everybody should
have a detailed knowledge and understanding of the major political
issues confronting their society. What was required was an ability to
recognise those who were capable of making reasoned and expert political judgments. 'It is not necessary that the Many should themselves
be perfectly wise; it is sufficient, if they be duly sensible of the value
of superior wisdom...They would then select as their representatives
those whom the general voice of the instructed pointed out as the most
instructed.'[11] Mill ordinarily argued that the correct notion of popular
representation was that the people choose their governors, and not that
they themselves judge in detail on public questions, though presumably
they would need some knowledge of the questions, as well as sufficient
moral insight, to choose their representatives wisely. The people judge
the candidates: the free-floating representatives judge the measures. Mill
often used a typical Platonic analogy between legislator and physician

– the people may be qualified to judge 'the merits of different physicians, whether for the body political or natural, but it is utterly impossible that they should be competent judges of the different modes of treatment.'[12] He therefore rejected pledges, because they inhibited rational decision-taking, and advocated government by the few for the benefit of the many. Political leaders were accountable to the electorate and morally bound to pursue the general interest. Mill's suggestion that legislators are the physicians of the body politic implies that politics is a cognitive science – satisfying the needs rather than the demands of the people, and seeking the popular good rather than the popular will – and denies the long-term significance of conflict over values in political life. The experts would agree, ultimately, on what constituted health for the body politic. However, in medicine the concept of health is fairly clear-cut – it does embody valuations – and thus disputes about ends are not central, and there are accepted and agreed procedures for reaching proper conclusions, whereas with the 'body politic' it is not at all clear what constitutes good health or, alternatively, ends are not given and fundamental conflict persists.

At present I am concerned primarily with the political implications of Mill's association of knowledge with an enlightened minority. But the epistemological problem, to which his positivism and his theory of history offered a solution, must at least be indicated firmly, in passing. The ignorant and the immature are encouraged to defer to the united authority of the wise. But upon what assumptions does the expected unity of the wise rest? Mill assumed that moral and political beliefs could gain, and were gaining gradually, the same degree of confirmation and the same degree of common acceptance as the truths of natural science. He explained the existing differences between moral and natural science, not as the result of different methods or content, or of a radically different relationship to human interests and prejudices, but as the result of the fact that moral science was not yet sufficiently advanced. In principle, present divisions and conflicts could be ended rationally. As John Austin had argued, linking agreement between experts and popular acceptance of their conclusions, 'the adepts in ethics...would commonly agree in their results, and...a body of doctrine and authority, to which the multitude might trust, would emerge from the existing chaos'.[13] Indifference or impartiality would produce unanimous agreement and thereby provide a good ground for common acceptance – something which Mill saw occurring historically, as error and division were overcome in the continuing process of free and critical enquiry.

Mill could hardly justify unequal political participation and political power in terms of the, as yet unrealised, prospect of a shared moral and political science. But he did favour political institutions in which the educated and disinterested – if temporarily divided – sections of the community were over-represented in relation to their numerical support. Consequently, his democratic credentials are thrown strongly into question. The thrust of much of his argument for political participation is democratic, but his actual political prescriptions fall well short of democracy. His well-known comment on participation in *Representative Government* can serve as a starting point:

> the only government which can fully satisfy all the exigencies of the social state is one in which the whole people participate; that any participation, even in the smallest public function, is useful; that the participation should everywhere be as great as the general degree of improvement of the community will allow, and that nothing less can be ultimately desirable than the admission of all to share in the sovereign power of the State.[14]

This statement contains important qualifications, especially concerning the general degree of improvement of the community – it may be, as yet, in an extremely backward state, or an 'early stage of improvement' – and the 'ultimate desirability' of a general share in sovereign power. The concrete relationship between the temporary limitations and the ultimate realisation needs to be probed, and if the gap lasts long enough, or if inadequate provision is made for its removal, we may question the author's commitment to the final ideal or aspiration. This is not to query the empirical basis of Mill's claim. It was not wrong for him to argue that England was unready for universal participation then, especially given his notion of what participation involved, nor would a democrat be compelled to deny his argument. It is common and proper procedure to specify the empirical conditions which need to be satisfied for a programme to become relevant or for an ideal to be realised. In so far as Mill's time-scale is concerned, it is less fruitful to say that he was a worse democrat than someone who advocated immediate universal franchise than it is to say that representative government seemed to him to be feasible only when further social changes had taken place. A further problem concerns the nature of the 'representative government' which he praised. What is the precise meaning given to 'participation' and a 'share in sovereign power'? It may be that Mill held, not merely that England was unready – in the present state of civilization – for representative government, but that he built restrictions or safeguards into representative government itself, so that when it finally became practicable it would not be representative in a strong sense, and the stress would be on citizen participation in community life rather than in decision-making at the most significant points. If this were true, it might be objected that Mill's democracy permits citizens to participate and agitate on the fringes of power, while major political decisions are taken by an unrestrained élite. And if, for Mill, participation is supported simply for its supposed educative or moralising effects, it could remain compatible with a quite inegalitarian distribution of power, and a continuing lack of self-determination, on the part of the ordinary man, in large areas of his life. There is a vast difference between participation which satisfies and elevates individuals, and that which involves equal power in the determination of public policy, or control over what affects one most profoundly.

The representative government favoured by Mill was distinguished by a variety of protective devices designed to restrict popular power or, what is the same thing, to maintain and even strengthen the position of qualitatively superior minorities. Representative government or rational democracy combined skill and popular government, but the two elements existed in tension, with the element of popularity being eroded constantly by the requirements of skill. The extraordinary influence of virtue and wisdom on public policy was presented by Mill as an essential and distinctive feature of representative government. 'A representative constitution is a means of bringing the general standard of intelligence and honesty existing in the community, and the individual intellect and virtue of its wisest members, more directly to bear upon the government, and investing them with greater influence in it, than they would in general have under any other mode of organisation.'[15] Mill's justification of his specific proposals for reform assumes that the primary danger to political life arises from the growing power of the masses, which challenged minorities and variety. Conflict or antagonism as such are treated as vital to social progress. Public opinion needed to be balanced, and its tyrannous possibilities counteracted, by 'a great social support for opinions and sentiments differing from those of the mass'.[16] At one stage he suggested, following Coleridge, that a leisured and a landed interest – though certainly not the leisured and the landed interest of existing English society – might act as alternative centres of power to the predominant class or classes.[17] At times mere difference seemed to be the decisive recommendation, but generally the alternative power is presented as a crusading and elevating classless power, which plays a dynamic part in bringing about social regeneration.

The key institutional innovation supported by Mill was the scheme of personal or proportional representation which had been elaborated by Thomas Hare. Mill could think of no arrangement 'better adapted to keep popular opinion within reason and justice, and to guard it from the various deteriorating influences which assail the weak side of democracy'.[18] The arguments in its support were three. It was just, it provided for the representation of high intellectual and moral capacities, and it maintained diversity within society. In the first place, Mill rejected the existing electoral system on the grounds that it represented merely local majorities, and that instructed and independent individuals, who were diffused throughout the country with no particular area of concentration, tended to be systematically under-represented at the national level. The proposed reform would bring representation into a fair relationship with support in the country. Similar demands are, of course, still commonly made on behalf of evenly distributed minorities, and are often accompanied by assaults on the tightly organised party systems of modern democracies, on behalf of free, thinking, individualistic candidates. Mill had no love for the party system, though in his time political parties were much looser bodies than they have since become.[19] The second argument for proportional representation was that, in providing for the representation of intellectual qualities, it would ensure that class representatives did not have things all their own way. Knowledge and virtue would have their spokesmen. In Mill's words, 'so much should I hope from the natural influence of truth and reason, if only secured a hearing and a competent advocacy, that I should not despair of the operation even of equal and universal suffrage, if made real by the proportional representation of all minorities, on Mr Hare's principles'.[20] Assuming that the selfish class forces were roughly equal – an assumption which he often made, though it was not always based on empirical study – Mill hoped that the instructed minority would have a casting vote as well as a moral voice. Finally, he stressed the importance of an alternative centre of power to the predominant class or classes. Antagonism or conflict of ideas is a condition of social progress, and it is primarily threatened by the democratic majority, which easily destroys all sources of initiative and opposition.

Mill's tentative arguments for a second chamber also stress the need for a centre of resistance to the predominant power in the constitution. An upper house is a safeguard against the dangers of undivided power, though additional checks are required. In some of his writings Mill expressed the hope that the second chamber might be something like the Roman senate, where officers of state and other notables could bring their skill and experience to bear upon political problems. Once again freedom from class interest is an overriding concern, and one of the grounds of its popular acceptance. 'It would disarm jealousy, by its freedom from any class interest.'[21] The best constituted second chamber was, characteristically, one which embodied 'the greatest number of elements exempt from the class interests and prejudices of the majority, but having in themselves nothing offensive to democratic feeling'.[22] Majority, 'class' power was to be limited by further devices, which would also, presumably, be inoffensive to democratic feeling – the destruction of pledges, so that constituents could not bind their representatives, who would become free-floaters,[23] plural voting, and the limitation of the primary role of the legislature to the endorsement of the decisions of a meritocracy of professional rulers.

Mill's account of the proper powers of the legislature is pervaded by the same internal schism – the skilled few against the aggressive, class-interested but improvable mass – as is the bulk of his political discussion. In his review of 'Democracy in America', he suggested limiting the role of the lower house to discussion, the control of expenditure and the like, while the task of framing and altering laws is given to a skilled senate or council of legislation. In *Representative Government* he argued that the people should have, through the representative assembly, the 'ultimate controlling power', but that the assembly lacked the skill to actually carry out the business of government. A numerous assembly is not fit for the tasks of administration or legislation, but it can properly discuss and debate legislation which is drafted elsewhere. At this point the emphasis is upon the greater proficiency of a smaller body, though occasionally Mill expressed fears of bias and self-interest in the representative assembly. The assembly was to have the power of passing or rejecting draft laws from the commission of legislation, which was composed of professional legislators. This would, in Mill's view, combine skilled and democratic government. It is not always clear, however, whether it is professionalism (skill) or goodwill and rationality that are the relevant criteria in limiting the scope of the democratic principle. What is clear is that Mill introduced layer upon layer of safeguards against ignorance and self-interest, and that the problem was far more than an administrative one. He remained hopeful that his plans would work and would not provoke democratic censure.

> By such arrangements as these, legislation would assume its proper place as a work of skilled labour and special study and experience; while the most important liberty of the nation, that of being governed only by laws assented to by its elected representatives, would be fully preserved, and made more valuable by being detached from the serious, but by no means unavoidable, drawbacks which now accompany it in the form of ignorant and ill-considered legislation.[24]

But the assumption that it was possible to devise institutions dominated by minorities which were nonetheless inoffensive to democratic – quite apart from proletarian – feeling, was taken too easily, and his own doubts were not allowed to disrupt the general body of his recommendations.

They were the troubled second thoughts of a man committed to something else, whereas in other minds they were sufficient to blow the liberal system apart.

THE POLITICAL PROCESS

Mill envisaged parliament as an institution within which the instructed few played a creative role, not simply in terms of influencing particular decisions, but by elevating the class representatives so that class rivalry and prejudices would play a decreasing part in political life. Parliament, rather than the streets or the battlefield, was the natural and appropriate centre for political conflict or antagonism, and it was a centre where conflict should not merely be institutionalised, but overcome. Mill's optimism was encouraged by his belief that selfish interests were normally divided. He claimed that justice and the general interest normally prevail in any tolerably constituted society because of the division of selfish interests, which is certainly a doubtful empirical statement, though 'tolerably constituted' may be defined in a special and perhaps tautologous way. Mill does seem to have assumed – falsely – that the opposing class forces in nineteenth-century England were roughly balanced, allowing to classless individuals a strategic importance which political engineering might enhance.[25] He ended his general justification of representative government by claiming that it 'ought not to allow any of the various sectional interests to be so powerful as to be capable of prevailing against truth and justice and the other sectional interests combined'.[26] Any sectional interest should be 'dependent for its successes on carrying with it at least a large proportion of those who act on higher motives and more comprehensive and distant views'.[27] Mill speaks often in terms of neat balances, guarding the common good. Groups should have strength enough to make reason prevail but not enough to prevail against it. The actual political process which he favoured was that in which – in a 'tolerably constituted' society – classless intellectuals, the champions of truth and justice, were so placed that any sectional interest required their support, as well as that of the more reasonable and disinterested members of the class groups, whose detachment from their more selfish fellows was one of his constant objectives. Rational forces would increase steadily as the political institutions took root. Mill defined the goal of parliament, in strikingly un-Marxist terms, as that of bringing together 'the best members of both classes, under such a tenure as shall induce them to lay aside their class preferences, and pursue jointly the path traced by the common interest'.[28]

In practical terms, Mill envisaged two roughly balanced class groups requiring, for the realisation of their goals, the support of disinterested and rational individuals, who would exact some tribute for the general interest as the price of their support. Their function is both mediating and educative. As such, it seems most plausible in bargaining situations, for example, where the distribution of economic rewards is in question, and where the parties have an interest in reaching a settlement. In the case of disputes over wage increases mediators sometimes reach settlements or compromises which are regarded by the competing parties as reasonable. However, such solutions are far more likely in the case of conflicts of interests – as over the division of the national product – than in the case of decisions which largely involve principles or rights and perhaps clashes of 'objective truth'. In many questions of foreign policy – as, for example, whether or not to declare war – there may be no point of compromise between opponents and defenders of the policies in question, nor, indeed, may the parties which compete on other issues compete on this one. The bourgeoisie and the proletariat may equally delight in the oppression of Ireland or war against Russia, and, in such cases, Mill's leaders of opinion would have no strategic position within the parliament. It is only in some cases a matter of giving conflicting parties their due: in other cases, the champions of virtue may be alone against a united and vicious community.

At times their mediating role was played down, and the emphasis placed on the objective standards of which they were aware. Mill brought out the difference in his distinction between conciliation by compromise and conciliation by justice, between 'the vulgar *juste-milieu* of mere time-savers, and that which aims at contenting all parties by being just to all'.[29] The latter is conciliation not by compromise but by justice – 'by giving to everybody, not the half of what he asks, but the whole of what he ought to have'.[30] In these circumstances the leaders would not be mediating between the claims of competing groups – in the tone of the Mill of the thirties, they would not be 'trimmers', seeking easy and shallow compromises – but would be measuring them against the general interest. In Mill's aggressive words: 'The only interest which we wish to be consulted is the general interest, and that, therefore, is the only one which we desire to see represented.'[31] Clearly, Mill did not want the mere hodge-podge, the incessant bargaining without principle, which is accepted both descriptively and normatively in contemporary pluralist theory. The proper resolutions were just ones, which might lie outside the conflicting claims altogether; for example, in a dispute over wage increases the leaders may suggest a wage decrease and a reduction or freezing of prices, and in such circumstances they may antagonise both of the parties, and presumably lose all influence into the bargain. I do not mean to suggest that in cases of arbitration or bargaining there is nothing outside the claims themselves within the sphere of discussion – there are appeals to, and explanations in terms of, the general interest, taking the form perhaps of 'what the economy can afford'. But there is in general an element of compromise as well, as in most circumstances there must be. If 'settlements' lay outside the disputed area or corresponded to the claims of one of the groups only, they would be unlikely to find widespread acceptance, though they might be just in terms of some standard or other.

While Mill insists upon the paramountcy of the general interest in particular decisions and as the goal of public policy, and requires remarkable capacities on the part of his disinterested political leaders, who must know what the people need and deserve, he accepts the necessity of compromise and habitual and customary acceptance of relationships and connections in describing the conditions of a stable political order. Society would not survive if it was subjected to a desperate battle for principle or efforts to impose justice. Polarisation and disintegration would follow from open ideological warfare. As I argued in the previous chapter, Mill believed that, in the process of being absorbed into the community, men would learn the principles of constitutional morality, which were vital to social solidarity. These principles included acceptance of the right of opponents to exist, an attitude of trust towards them, and a readiness to moderate extreme demands so that satisfactory compromises could be worked out – apparently through a moral and moralising evaluation of conflicting claims. Political conflict was to be gradually civilised through the extension of these values, which were essential to free government. 'One of the most indispensable requisites in the practical conduct of politics, especially in the management of free institutions, is conciliation: a readiness to compromise, a willingness to concede something to opponents, and to shape good measures so as to be as little offensive as possible to persons of opposite views.'[32]

Mill's belief in the importance of consensus and compromise emerges also in his more general discussion, in the essay on Coleridge, of the necessary framework or the necessary conditions of social life. He offers some unexceptionable observations on the importance of social unity, fraternity and homogeneity – what he called the elements of social union. He rejected certain simple views which are normally associated with the Enlightenment. The highly critical *philosophes* often forgot the role of the institutions and creeds which they condemned for being outmoded or false, and wrongly depicted their sudden abolition as sheer gain. They forgot that they 'still filled a place in the human mind, and in the arrangements of society, which could not without great peril be left vacant'.[33] Mill identified three essential empirical conditions of civil society – a system of education, the existence of feelings of allegiance or loyalty, and a strong principle of cohesion among the members of the community. In discussing his second condition Mill raised the major issue, which was that though there had never been a society 'in which collisions did not occur between the immediate interests and passions of powerful sections of the people',[34] many societies had nonetheless hung together. His explanation was that in all lasting political societies there has been 'something which men agreed in holding sacred', which was 'in the common estimation placed beyond discussion' – though presumably such fundamental beliefs could be called into question in the uncommon estimation. These basic principles of social union varied in different societies, and whilst it was unjustifiable to condemn those of past societies from the vantage-point of the nineteenth century, Mill naturally believed that those developing in his own society were superior. The shared beliefs could be religious, the feeling of loyalty could be attached to certain persons or laws or ordinances, or it may attach itself, as seemed likely in Mill's future, to distinctively liberal principles, 'to the principles of individual freedom and political and social equality, as realised in institutions which as yet exist nowhere, or exist only in a rudimentary state'.[35] These principles, then, set the limits within which the free play of opinion and argument normally occurs. When the people disagree about fundamentals, the society is in danger of collapse. Mill's third essential condition of stability was a psychological one, of the kind which he envisaged in *Utilitarianism*: 'a strong and active principle of cohesion among the members of the same community or state. . .a principle of sympathy, not of hostility; of union, not of separation. . .a feeling of common interest. . .one part of the community do not consider themselves as foreigners with regard to another part.'[36]

There is an obvious interaction between these three conditions, and it is one of the weaknesses of Mill's discussion that he did not closely analyse the relations between them. His ideal educational system, which was to provide a 'restraining discipline' for men, would clearly do a lot to inculcate the shared values and to increase sympathy, while a feeling of common interest presupposes agreement on certain general principles or beliefs. Recent discussions of consensus have frequently stressed the fact that political conflict in liberal democratic societies is set within a wider framework of political agreements. Robert Dahl, for example, has suggested that, in a sense:

> What we ordinarily describe as 'democratic politics' is merely the chaff. It is the surface manifestation, representing superficial conflicts. Prior to politics, beneath it, enveloping it, restricting it, conditioning it, is the underlying consensus on policy that usually

exists in the society amongst a predominant proportion of the politically active members. Without such a consensus no democratic system would long survive the endless irritations and frustrations of elections and party competition.[37]

Such claims, of course, need a great deal of further analysis and supporting argument, especially to determine the nature and content of the consensus, the groups which fall within it and how they do so, and its causes. It is not clear, for example, that consensus is prior to politics, as politics contributes to it and reinforces it, and sometimes transforms it, so that a particular consensus may emerge from preceding political conflict. Mill, who certainly had little of Dahl's enthusiasm for party and interest group competition, did believe strongly that continuous participation in political life, even by men who were initially selfish and short-sighted, would bring about greater agreement and closer community ties than had previously existed. He saw feelings of common interest and loyalty gradually strengthening in modern societies, especially in England and France, though the choice of France seems strange in view of the turbulent history of that country. Perhaps Mill's historical grasp was twisted by the grand visions of Saint-Simonians and Comteans.

The values which Mill thought essential to free institutions could not exist when the inhabitants of a country were not, and did not feel themselves to be, members of the same public. Where there were different nationalities within a country, or where there were mutually exclusive and deeply held views, as in the United States over slavery, the conditions of political union were not present. As Mill wrote in his discussion of nationality: 'Free institutions are next to impossible in a country made up of different nationalities. Among a people without fellow-feeling, especially if they read and speak different languages, the united public opinion, necessary to the working of representative government, cannot exist.'[38] In such societies, competing leaders were backed by unyielding, homogeneous forces.

The relevance of this to Mill's conception of class, and to his political prescriptions for England, is clear. He wished to break down solid class groups and to gradually establish a society of closely connected individuals, who are moved by concern for the common good. A rigid cleavage into classes or parties was socially dangerous and misrepresented the divisions and desires of the community. In Mill's words: 'We know that the constitution does not exist for the benefit of parties, but of citizens; and we do not choose that all the opinions, feelings, and interests of all the members of the community should be merged in the single consideration of which party shall predominate.'[39] Flexible coalitions, shifting with the issues under discussion, were therefore much preferable to tightly organised class parties which could not sensitively register the richness and diversity of the community, and which undermined the unity of the people. Class organisations misrepresented – as they intensified – actual social divisions, and imposed false choices on the representatives. A properly constituted democratic parliament would not be the undeviating exponent of particular class or party interests, but a centre of wide-ranging, free discussion. Mill commented on the dangers of clearly defining and representing separate interests in relation to so-called progressive and permanent forces. 'In this as in every other case, it is not separating classes of persons and organising them apart, but fusing them with other classes very different from themselves which eliminates class interests and class feelings.'[40] Once again he assumed the creativeness of rational argument, given flexible, rational and imaginative leadership. He hoped and expected that classes would crumble and that adherents of classes would be transformed into citizens. Politics was to be no longer the clash of harsh, uncompromising entities. He praised Hare's scheme as 'a healing, a reconciling measure, softening all political transitions, securing that every opinion, instead of conquering or being conquered by starts and shocks, and passing suddenly from having no power at all in Parliament to having too much, on the contrary, should wax or wane in political power in exact proportion to its growth or decline in the general mind of the country'.[41] Political activity, as he defined it, was to be a key means of healing the divisions within the community.

LIBERAL SOCIETY AND THE END OF CONFLICT

Mill preferred a particular kind of social union, and thought that it was emerging gradually. His economic and historico-moral writings, as well as his more overtly polemical pieces, underlay and supported his moral ideal. And Mill's account of the general form of a good society – he does not discuss much its precise institutional characteristics – makes it quite clear that one common presentation of his thought, as the epitome of extreme individualism, ignores some of his basic themes and concerns.

Mill is often presented as a philosopher of the *Gesellschaft*, as one who had an ideal of the self-determining individual, unrestricted by the community except in a narrow sphere of anti-social acts. His defence of a sphere of self-regarding actions, with firm boundaries distinguishing and separating individuals from each other, and his attacks on the dangerous and limiting power of public opinion, feature prominently in this picture of the pristine liberal. Thus, for example, D. G. Ritchie

attacked Mill's view of the individual as abstract and negative. His own
view is that the more we learn of human society, 'the more we discover
that there is no absolute division, but that every atom influences and
is influenced by every other'.[42] Mill has suffered from the common
image of liberalism – arising from what has been, historically, one of its
obsessions – as a creed which was concerned primarily with legal constraints on the 'free' individual, and which fought to liberate man, in
theory, in definition and ostensibly in fact, from the complex of relations
in which he had previously existed, and in which he was both located
and defined. Liberalism as a whole is presented commonly as a political
theory which treats people as atoms and stresses diversity and competition rather than likeness and community, and is thus seen as an idealised and political version of the free enterprise society. Allegedly, it
reduces society to a collection of separate individuals, temporarily united
for private purposes, and fencing themselves off as protection against
the depredations of other, hostile men. From a conservative viewpoint,
the liberal seriously undervalues authority and conformity, and thereby
threatens the social order and the common man. He tears apart stabilising and humanising customs and traditions, encourages abrasiveness and
conflict, and fails to perceive the dangerous political implications of the
endless pursuit of individual ends, including the Romantic goal of self-
realisation. Working on false and pernicious assumptions about man,
the liberal seeks a form of society which, given actual human nature,
would produce anarchy, or the amorphous, disintegrated mass of modern
society. Socialist attacks on liberalism, from quite anti-conservative
assumptions about human and social potentialities, similarly portray it
as a disintegrating, demolishing, laissez-faire philosophy. Thus Robert
Paul Wolff utilises the insights of a conservative sociology in a typical
attack on Mill. According to Wolff's Mill

> other persons are obstacles to be overcome or resources to be ex-
> ploited – always means, that is to say, and never ends in them-
> selves...society continues to be viewed as a system of independent
> centres of consciousness, each pursuing its own gratification and
> confronting the others as beings standing-over-against the self,
> which is to say, as objects. The condition of the individual in such
> a state of affairs is what a different tradition of social philosophy
> would call 'alienation'.[43]

My own account of Mill has emphasised his conception of man as an
essentially social animal, to whose natural and customary attachment to
his fellows is added, as civilisation develops, rational perceptions of his
actual and necessary links with them. Mill's autonomous man has a
character which is 'self-reliant, rational in its assessment of the world,

tolerant, wide-ranging in its interest, and spontaneous in its sympathies'.[44] He has a deep concern for others, and a deep attachment to the social norms and institutions which symbolise and guarantee their common development. Mill's hostility to whips and scourges as means of persuasion cannot be read as a warrant for 'selfish indifference' towards other lives and, indeed, liberty is interpreted by him as a source of social duty and common enterprise.[45] Mill's version of society may seem, at times, to be thin – and certainly, I find that he did not grasp sufficiently the social limitations on free action and rational choice – but he had no notion of the free individual striding alone, without any sense of social obligation and concern. He is pre-eminently the servant of others, which may force him to oppose their demands and passions strongly. He is not merely accountable to them, when in political office, but is linked by training, inclination and sympathy, which arises out of common membership of social organisations and from wider human need.

Mill was extremely critical of the economic and social – as well as the ideological – conflict that he saw about him, and sharply attacked market notions of human society. He was repelled by much of liberal culture and by the idea of 'a society only held together by the relations and feelings arising out of pecuniary interests'.[46] Selfish and destructive characteristics – egoism creating social war, an opposition and not a harmony of interests – could be traced to present moral standards and existing social institutions. As privilege was eroded, natural sympathies were bound to become stronger, and the objective grounds of social conflict to diminish. A more integrated community, which required the eradication of many of the present distinctions between men, seemed increasingly close. 'Every step in political improvement renders it more so, by removing the sources of opposition of interest, and levelling those inequalities of legal privilege between individuals or classes, owing to which there are large portions of mankind whose happiness it is still practical to disregard.'[47] Wise legislation, individual prudence, fair opportunity, education, political participation and the diffuse and various influence of the enlightened were to cut away offensive and socially divisive forms of differentiation between individuals and to establish a stable, harmonious and progressive order, which in terms of class would be similar to the state recommended by Aristotle – 'where the middle part is strong and the extremes weak'. Mill felt that social mobility within a broadly egalitarian framework already existed in America, and that a similar tendency was observable in England. The middle class was constantly increasing in size with the general growth of prosperity, and its position and power worked against social conflict. Mill found that 'though the distance between the two extremes of society may not be much diminshed, there is a rapid multi-plication of those who occupy the intermediate positions. There may be princes at one end of the scale and paupers at the other; but between them there will be a respectable and well-paid class of artisans, and a middle-class who combine property and industry'.[48] In his comments on the stationary state he declared that 'the next state for human nature is that in which while no one is poor, no one desires to be richer, nor has any reason to fear being thrust back, by the efforts of others to push themselves forward'.[49] Mill, following his obsession with the problem of population, felt that if only England could use its 'temporary breathing-time' – created primarily by emigration – to introduce 'moral and intellectual improvements' which would hold population at a stable level,[50] then a state of virtual economic stagnation would be compatible with the maximum development of all men. Of course, he very much underrated the productive potential of the new industrial system but, given an unnecessarily grim view of the ceiling to economic possibilities, it is striking how he nonetheless felt that a most desirable form of society was realisable. 'It is scarcely necessary to remark that a stationary condition of capital and population implies no stationary state of human improvement.'[51] In such circumstances, class and economic differentiation would decrease sharply, and society would be marked by the widespread pursuit of the higher pleasures, as mere drudgery disappeared. The art of living would continually improve. In Mill's words, society would be characterised by 'a well-paid and affluent body of labourers; no enormous fortunes, except what were earned and accumulated during a single life-time; but a much larger body of persons than at present, not only exempt from the coarser toils, but with sufficient leisure, both physical and mental, from mechanical details, to cultivate freely the graces of life, and afford examples of them to the classes less favourably circumstanced for their growth'.[52] Leisure would become more important, and creative, and the art of getting on would play a decreasing part in human life. In this benign and harmon-ious condition, unmarred by the furies of avarice and self-aggrandise-ment, parliament would no longer be a meeting place of 'the attorneys of certain small knots and confederacies of men',[53] each pursuing parti-cular interests, but a gathering of classless individuals, perceiving the general interest and recognising human solidarity. There would be no distinct labouring class[54] and class prejudice and hostility would fade away, though competition would not (yet) be abandoned. A purified capitalism would be egalitarian and classless.

Mill's attitude towards social and intellectual conflict and diversity is thus a complex one. While making a highly significant distinction between the character of the present, transitional age and a later settled time, and hence between present and future practicalities, he failed to tie together his general philosophy of history and his specific analyses of his own times. Many things then seemed to him abhorrent but – for the time being – inescapable, while many desirable outcomes are presented only in the most vague outlines. But it seems clear that Mill did not regard significant intellectual conflict as a permanent feature of human society, and that his ultimate vision of society is one in which partial interests and the distinctions between men based upon their membership of associations or groups within the state, are very seriously eroded. Mill was not, in the long term, a pluralist in relation to either the political or the intellectual worlds. The community which adheres to the Religion of Humanity is not characterised by significant diversities. It is one in which the old selfish instincts, those which had hitherto led man to conflict with his fellows, have died away. The social and political structure necessitated by division, conflict, jealousy and selfishness would disappear along with its causes. Mill wrote, in 1835, in a rather speculative passage, that where deceit on the part of rulers is rendered virtually impossible by popular enlightenment, the people could almost do without government altogether – 'at least, without force, and penal sanctions, not (of course) without guidance, and organized co-operation'.[55] Such a vision would be immensely reinforced by the optimistic theory of a pervasive Religion of Humanity, tying people together in a much more rational, unselfish and genuine community than had existed hitherto. Their harmony, which presumably rests upon economic and legal achievements, is rational in character, resting upon agreement between the enlightened and the deference of the less enlightened to them – as the end-result of a long process of questioning, criticism and argument. The harmony which Mill anticipated and sought to foster is also, by implication, more lasting in character than in earlier periods, for it is marked by a higher state of intellectual insight, and by a clear awareness of the economic necessity which made persisting conflict so dangerous.

The warmth for intellectual homogeneity or agreement which Mill sometimes revealed has led to vehement rejection of his liberal or libertarian credentials. He is occasionally portrayed as the founder of a new and intolerant secular faith, according to which liberty was a useful means of corroding and battering down established loyalties and institutions, but was neither an end nor a permanent need of human society. The liberal becomes the proselytiser for a thoroughly rational authority, with whose establishment the need and the justification for liberty will disappear. Fitzjames Stephen presented the rudiments of this estimate of Mill,[56] which is elaborated in Maurice Cowling's recent book, *Mill and Liberalism*, which contains an energetic, peevish and one-sided assault on Mill in these terms, although it can be argued in Cowling's favour that he has taken hold of part of his subject and that he is trying to demolish a perhaps too secure reputation. Cowling accuses Mill of 'moral totalitarianism'. His desire for a moral or spiritual consensus and his attempt to provide a received doctrine to fill the vacuum which had existed in the age of transition since medieval times, are thrown into prominence.

> Mill, like Plato, Marx and some others, implies that men do really (or would in practice if they could be educated to) agree about the character of the means suitable to determining the content of right action, and that education ought ideally to remove all those blinkers which prejudice, interest, ignorance and animal passion impose on the motives of rational men, so long as account is taken of the circumstances: that, if only men will submit their actions to critical examination, a moral, social and intellectual consensus will eventually supersede the miscellaneity of the age in which he lived. Agreement must not be imposed: about that Mill is certain.[57]

Despite the various qualifications, Cowling's argument is fairly clear. Mill desired and envisaged the eventual disappearance of serious moral and intellectual conflict. Mill's libertarianism becomes a means towards the achievement of a particular kind of character, and to rational agreement amongst educated men. In Cowling's words again, 'there is beyond the libertarian character of the means an assumption of the fundamental homogeneity of all rational judgment'.[58] According to this view of Mill, liberty was to produce a new orthodoxy and a tightly integrated social order, founded upon shared beliefs.

Certain of Mill's comments and assumptions, to some of which I have referred already, support such an interpretation. One main purpose of *A System of Logic* was to investigate the possibility of forming a body of received opinion in moral and political science. He wrote in the preface to the first edition that the final book was

> an attempt to contribute towards the solution of a question, which the decay of old opinions, and the agitation that disturbs European society to its inmost depths, render as important in the present day to the practical interests of human life, as it must at all times be to the completeness of our speculative knowledge: viz. Whether moral and social phenomena are really exceptions to the general certainty and uniformity of the course of nature; and how far the methods, by which so many of the laws of the physical world have been numbered among truths irrevocably acquired and universally asserted to, can be made instrumental to the formation of a similar body of received doctrine in moral and political science.[59]

He often suggested the likelihood of agreement between learned men on major issues. He wrote of unanimity amongst the instructed on all the great points of moral and political knowledge, and referred several times to 'the united authority of the instructed'. In *On Liberty* he spoke of the increase of agreed doctrines with the improvement of mankind, 'a gradual narrowing of the bounds of diversity of opinion'.[60] But he believed that diversity of opinion would prove advantageous 'until mankind shall have entered a stage of intellectual advancement which at present seems at an incalculable distance',[61] and that it was a good, not an evil, 'until mankind are much more capable than at present of recognising all sides of the truth'.[62] He felt that diversity of opinion was natural and useful in an age of transition. In the 'Essay on Coleridge' he wrote of 'the importance in the present imperfect state of mental and social science, of antagonistic modes of thought'.[63]

Mill assumed that ultimately reason speaks in only one voice, and that at an incalculable distance in the future rational men would agree, and obscurantism, superstition, prejudice and mere custom would be driven out. Free discussion and free, wide-ranging experience were to lead to a gradual withering of the area of conflict and the growth of the body of universally accepted doctrines. But whilst this is a significant strand in Mill's thought, Cowling's crude polemic against liberal crusaders ignores a number of basic distinctions and subtleties, acknowledgement of which is necessary if Mill's thought is not to be distorted. To treat liberty as a means to some other good, or a genuinely liberal society as the eventual father of a society which agrees freely and rationally on fundamentals, is not to urge the removal of liberty and diversity, though it is to weaken their long-term status. Various other means towards rational consensus could have been adopted – élite monopoly of education, censorship, the indoctrination or incarceration of irrational dissenters or deviants, forcing to be free, and so on – but these were all opposed deeply by Mill. He was not committed, either directly or by implication, to the coercive establishment of reason – which was a contradiction in terms to him, anyhow. If conflict and experimentation were to diminish it would be because men voluntarily agreed with each other, not because they imposed their will on others – something which, in Mill's view, would destroy the liberty of the subjected groups and would corrupt those imposing their will. The transitional period would last as long as there was substantial disagreement, and then, by definition, it would be over. At virtually all times the weight of Mill's argument and of his emotional commitment was on the importance of intellectual vitality, originality and diversity, and against the dormancy and slumber of opinion with which they normally conflicted. To take one characteristic statement, in the essay on 'Centralization', which was published in 1862, Mill declared his support for liberty and his doubts about unity. Unity, he wrote, 'stands for the negation of the main determining principle of improvement, and even of the permanence of civilisation, which depends on diversity, not unity'.[64] He added that the effort to cut the affairs of mankind to a single pattern led to an irresistible tendency to subject all of them to a single will. In his reactions to Comte his view of liberty emerges clearly. He accepted, in general terms, what he took to be Comte's ideal of spontaneous rational agreement between the intellectual leaders of mankind. But when he became aware of the true character of the Comtean dream – that rationality was to be the result of authoritative imposition by the enlightened, and not the result of free inquiry – he sharply attacked his erstwhile mentor. The second part of his critique of Comte contains a withering castigation of the later Comte, who 'came forth transfigured as the High Priest of the Religion of Humanity', who saw himself as 'the supreme moral legislator and religious pontiff of the human race', who was, in short, 'a morality-intoxicated man'.[65] He attacked Comte's preoccupation with harmony and unity, his desire to systematise and his fear of independent thought.

> May it not be the fact that mankind, who after all are made up of single human beings, obtain a greater sum of happiness when each pursues his own, under the rules and conditions required by the good of the rest, than when each makes the good of the rest his only object, and allows himself no personal pleasures not indispensable to the preservation of his faculties? The regimen of a blockaded town should be cheerfully submitted to when high purposes require it, but is it the ideal perfection of human existence?[66]

Mill recognised the two-sidedness of liberal ideals – intellectual diversity was from another viewpoint chaos, and economic competition easily became destructive conflict. In both respects he expected and desired the diminution and, ultimately, the disappearance of fundamental clashes. But he remained a firm believer in the voluntariness of beliefs and in the legitimacy of existing intellectual diversities. He stressed, against Comte, the remoteness of any future homogeneous order, as he did in relation to socialism or communism.

> A time such as M. Comte reckoned upon may come; unless something stops the progress of human improvement, it is sure to come: but after an unknown duration of hard thought and violent controversy...the hope of such accordance of opinion among sociological inquirers as would obtain, in mere deference to their authority, the universal assent which M. Comte's scheme of society requires, must be adjourned to an indefinite distance.[67]

Mill's image of the homogeneous community – and the extent and the area or content of that homogeneity are hardly examined at all – was vague and not at all a matter of immediate concern for him. If it came into being it would be as a result of a lengthy and peaceful historical process, and not at the instigation of moral tyrants or philosopher kings. Mill's portrayal of that distant future state reads more as a pathetic hope and a pious wish than as a serious expectation. To elevate this, along with his scattered statements in support of a clerisy or a rational dominant group, and his justifications of a unifying educational system and a religion of humanity, into the central theme in his writings, does violence to his continuing and powerful espousal of liberal values of free discussion and argument. He was not prepared to sacrifice these to a dream of unity. That vision did create problems and difficulties, of course. For example, how would man's critical self-awareness remain strong and active if the spur of clashing ideas were removed? Is the long struggle for truth completed, or is the next phase of intellectual agreement merely an interlude before creative and fundamental conflict breaks out again? Does the defence of rights become less crucial because men voluntarily refrain from exercising them? But although these are difficult questions, and not ones to which Mill gave serious attention, they do not suggest that Mill was a moral totalitarian or worse.[68] However, he was optimistic about human improvement, and his concern with social cohesion and with rational agreement between free men, and his belief that good ends and enlightened men and groups would harmonise in the end, blur simple contrasts between his social vision and that of Marx. Mill was not committed, empirically or morally, to permanent and fundamental evaluative diversity.

CLASS AND LIBERAL POLITICS

While Mill's liberal credentials have recently come under close scrutiny, the hidden and at times overt class bias of his warnings and recommendations has been submitted to more continuous and more probing examination. The question to be faced now is the ambiguous and even hostile relationships between the political virtue defined and discerned by Mill, and the actual or likely class interests of those whom he wished to see in authority. That Mill himself was uneasily aware of the conflict does not remove it.

Mill made out a case for political inequality in terms of the skills and the virtue possessed by certain members of society. He never regarded himself as the defender of particular class power, but spoke always in the more elevated language of rationality, disinterestedness, impartiality and integrity. He was seeking certain qualities, not the ascendancy of a class. But in seeking the closest possible approximations to these qualities in his own imperfect times, he was bound to diminish them, and to find them in tainted or biased quarters. Occasionally he recognised the class character – rather than the sheer rationality – of the bourgeois rule which was the natural fruit of his political proposals. Comforting himself on the prospects of democracy, he wrote: 'In every country where there are rich and poor, the administration of public affairs would, even under the most democratic constitution, be mainly in the hands of the rich...Political power will generally be the rich man's privilege, as heretofore.'[69] This recognition of the significance of economic differentiation conflicts with and undermines the frequent claims on behalf of the 'united authority of the instructed', and constitutes one of the basic problems in Mill's social theory. For, while the rich may sometimes be instructed, and would probably constitute the majority of those who were instructed, Mill gave no good reason why they should reveal the powers of constructive enterprise, knowledge and especially freedom from class prejudice.

The shortcomings of Mill's doctrine of classless élites, and Mill's own uncertainty, emerge most clearly in his discussion of plural voting. Additional votes were to be given to the mentally superior, but because of the weaknesses of the prevailing educational system, another and temporary ground of differentiation was required. This approximate test, which involved no property qualification *per se*, was 'superior function' or occupation, which meant that employers, manufacturers, merchants, bankers and suchlike would have voting privileges. The division between educated and uneducated roughly corresponded to that between rich and poor, with the result that what from one angle seemed a protection of superior merit was from another a defence of property. Mill generally assumed that those with superior knowledge would be concerned with the general interests of society, yet they were precisely those with major stakes in the existing order, and they could hardly be expected to share Mill's view that the order itself should be called into question and regarded as provisional. In a passage which reveals his doubts, Mill wrote that the distinction in favour of education, 'right in itself, is further and strongly recommended by its preserving the educated from the class legislation of the uneducated; but it must stop short of enabling them to practise class legislation on their own account'.[70] This is a fatal concession to Marx – the educated bourgeoisie may itself have class interests, which would presumably conflict with the common good. Given extremely optimistic assumptions about the power of education, it may seem that liberalism, though a doctrine associated especially with the cultivated middle classes, is essentially a classless ideal, but it was quite evident that class allegiances and prejudices were not always destroyed by education, nor could the beautiful appearance of 'reason' altogether hide the grosser class realities behind it. Marx might have argued in relation to Mill as Engels did, wrongly, in relation to Rousseau – that the rational state was the idealised kingdom of the bourgeoisie. Mill was occasionally, if fleetingly, troubled by the problem, and conscious that the linkage of the general interest and the middle class, or sections of it, was not altogether convincing. At this point democratic institutions, involving checks against power-hunger or class interest, and ensuring the responsiveness of leaders to the people, became of crucial importance once more. The anchorage in reason was not sufficiently secure.

In terms of the psychological views which he wielded against the privileged and powerful generally, Mill's assumption of rational bourgeois rulers seems excessively optimistic. He wrote in *Principles of Political Economy*:

> All privileged and powerful classes, as such, have used their power in the interest of their own selfishness, and have indulged their self-importance in despising, and not in lovingly caring for, those who were, in their estimation, degraded, by being under the necessity of working for their benefit. I do not affirm that what has always been must always be, or that human improvement has no tendency to correct the intensely selfish feelings engendered by power; but though the evil may be lessened, it cannot be eradicated, until the power itself is withdrawn.[71]

In this passage he specifically rejected the ascription of disinterestedness and imagination to ruling classes. 'It is an idealisation, grounded on the conduct and character of here and there an individual.' It is clear that, other things being equal, the same must be said of Mill's models of disinterested rulership.

But were other things equal? In the first place, Mill reduced the problem somewhat by modifying the psychological theory which he inherited, though even his softened psychological doctrine seemed to apply unevenly. The bad tendencies in human nature seemed to operate pre-eminently in those social groups for whom he had least time. In these cases, however, he usually found that the lack of accountability was a strong encouragement to selfish action. In his general revision of Benthamite psychology – and here we taken no account of class and historical variations – Mill argued that it exaggerated man's domination by his worldly interests and the self-interestedness of rulers. He denied that these assumptions were universally true, and emphasised the importance of duty and philanthropy, 'habitual sentiments and feelings', 'the general mode of thinking and acting', tradition and public opinion. Many forces or influences swayed men. The problem of political power was reduced because of the strength of non-interested motives in human nature, and the fudging of naked interests by other forces. The Benthamite philosophy, according to which interest always determined man's actions, either worked with a loose notion of interest, which made the claim uninformative, or with a narrow one, which provided no adequate basis for human action.[72] However, the quandary remained. Mill's psychological theory, supported by the study of past and present, led to a profound distrust of ruling classes, which were subject to the passions and appetites of other men. Yet, against the claims of the potential ruling mass, of whose defects he was well aware, he was compelled to elevate a particular social and intellectual group, though by no means a fixed élite, and to assert its claims as the saviour of social values. But why should the lust for power and the deep-rooted selfishness of previous rulers have disappeared in their case, and what explanation is offered as to why this might be the case? It is possible to argue that a properly designed educational system could do the job, but Mill's England was, as he often despairingly wrote, poorly equipped in this respect. Consequently, there is a peculiar mixture of fantasy and realism in his descriptions of the instructed – their presumed virtues may not be sufficiently widespread or strong, and he is driven back to seeking to control them by regular and widely based elections. They could not be simply excluded from the operations of the laws of human nature. Hence, in the second place, Mill had to emphasise accountability, the provision of constitutional checks to the selfish interests which inspired much human behaviour. In England and the other nations of modern Europe – and the statement is muted, in contrast with its anti-aristocratic formulation – 'responsibility to the governed is the only means practically available to create a feeling of identity of interests, in the cases, and on the points, where that feeling does not sufficiently exist'.[73]

Mill faced the same major problems concerning impartial leaders as had Rousseau. Rousseau sought both to have his enlightened and creative legislator accepted by the people, and to provide checks against him, where necessary. At one stage Rousseau's legislator is advised to use divine authority to deceive the people and gain their consent, while Mill is uncertain just how his wise legislators could gain positions of power. It is not at all obvious that ordinary men would accept their credentials, particularly if their 'truths' concerned matters about which the classes conflicted. Mill commented sceptically on the Saint-Simonian ideal of a directing body with the duty of dispensing distributive justice to every member of society. He held that even with the necessary knowledge, the directors would be unlikely to satisfy everybody. He suggested that they would either have to use force, or be 'believed to be more than men, and backed by supernatural terrors'.[74] Because of the quality of the people, virtue must sometimes sneak in. Yet does virtue remain secure? In discussing the legislator, Rousseau could not, because of his psychological assumptions, concede complete impartiality to the great creative figure, so he turned again to the people, previously rejected because of their ignorance, as the appropriate judges of fundamental policy.[75] Moreover, Mill's middle-class leaders, unlike Plato's guardians or Rousseau's legislator, may have a direct economic interest in selfish legislation. There are no safeguards (apart from elections) written into the theory to prevent them from enjoying the ordinary rewards of power, and in these circumstances appeal to their 'moral trust' or their 'severe responsibility' may be inadequate.

Mill was driven into a corner by his conscientious pursuit of virtuous leaders and a residual realism which warned him against granting them everything. The internal restraints on the intelligent may not always be strong enough. And yet Mill's hopefulness persisted. Perhaps this hopefulness reflected his own social background and position as an intelligent aspirant for influence who was unused to political or economic power. As Maurice Cowling puts it:

> Mill's situation, as a highly articulate, intellectually ambitious member of a middle-class, literary intelligentsia with little opportunity to exercise open, conventional political power, made it likely that his claims to political authority would be based, if based on authority they were, on intellectual rather than social superiority. Looked at from one point of view, that is what his moral and political writings are – claims to supersede leadership based on social, by leadership based on intellectual, superiority.[76]

But the people he wanted to trust were bourgeois as well as instructed, and it was highly questionable whether the disinterested rationality which he valued would emerge in these circumstances.

Of course, even if we assume good intentions and political intelligence on the part of Mill's rulers, the notion of the general interest still raises many difficulties. What are the permanent and joint interests of the community? We might take, as such an interest, 'the improvement of man himself, as a moral and intellectual being'. Assuming that we can state fairly clearly what this means, there remain immense problems in determining the way or ways in which it might be realised. It could, depending upon particular visions and accounts of the facts, involve a commitment to socialism or to extreme laissez-faire individualism. Similarly, if we define the general interest in terms of some value or values, such as justice, liberty, equality and security, the problems mount, and divisions increase, as soon as attempts are made to press the definition more specifically. People commit themselves readily to general values precisely because they can mean so many different things, and find concrete realisation in such diverse institutions. Moreover, having class-less politicians would not resolve the problem of determining what the general interest is, in actual social contexts. Class is not the sole cause of limited or selective vision. Particular philosophic or economic schools may produce doctrines which are just as narrow and one-sided as those created by more sordid interests. And, as with Mill, the crust of reason may be deceptive, in that what is held to be rational – the sound political and economic principles which are to guide all men – is itself thoroughly ideological, and not necessarily binding on the rational men of that, or later, ages. Thus the 'fallacies of political economy' of one generation may become truths or acknowledged necessities for those who come afterwards, as the doctrine of a minimum wage has become in many parts of the Western world. From the truism that the rational – or any other – man occupies a particular historical and a particular social place, it follows that reason is permeated by contin-gency or chance, and that it cannot – at least as long as these diversities persist – speak in one clear voice to all men.

PART 4   CONCLUSIONS

9   Marx, Mill and modern society

The doctrines of Marx and Mill, and movements and ways of thinking and acting which they inspired, or helped inspire, have played a significant part in social change during the past century. But, while the theories are themselves historical events, they have decomposed and large parts of them have withered, as the situation which they sought to describe and to alter has changed. Liberalism has become, in many modern hands, a banal and conservative theory, offering uplifting rhetoric and excessively and obsessively careful and neat advice, where tough, concrete analysis and far-reaching social change seem necessary, even to achieve its own declared goals. Emptied of the vitality and energy which had made it a formidable and destructive force in its heyday, it has become in its turn idle and fanciful, disguising and myth-making rather than exposing and challenging. Marxism, as has often been pointed out, has succeeded to the position to which it assigned its predecessors. It has become, as a total system, an ideological reflection of a past era. It comprehended, though imperfectly, the age of bourgeois capitalism. The owl of Minerva may in fact spread its wings before the dusk falls, but the world cannot be endlessly rejuvenated by any one philosophy, nor held still in any one man's terms.

In the writings of Marx and Mill we see what are, from very different angles, crystallised and incomplete representations of the reality of their own times. Their analyses, prescriptions, programmes and predictions are naturally deeply marked by the impress of their own institutions and general social environment. They took some things for granted, and could not grasp fully the extent, the forms and the implications of the unprecedented changes which occurred during their lifetimes. Naturally they arbitrarily froze the historical process at certain points. But it is possible to salvage more than discrete hypotheses from the wreckage of the great systems. To claim that their perspectives and analyses are clearly inadequate to a changed social reality – which is no more than they would have expected – and that their followers have often wriggled and evaded when they should have considered societies with some flexibility and freshness, is not to write off the theories *in toto* as historical curiosity pieces. While they throw features of their own societies into sharp relief, they are more than idealised and stylised reproductions of them – their force and imaginative power, the survival of dangers they feared and enemies they fought, the positive and optimistic accounts of man which they elaborated, and the critical attitude which they took toward social reality enable them to stimulate enthusiasm, and to act as (incomplete) guides to change, against the easy conformities, complacencies and fatalisms of the present. Certain themes and threads have been developed sensitively and creatively. But, unfortunate and natural as it may be, liberalism and Marxism have been used as dogmatic supports of current interests, as doctrines to celebrate and justify the achievements of particular societies – and to remove their astringent, unsettling, critical character, especially in the case of Marxism, is to violate them as much as does their mechanical repetition as sources of critique in the present. Marxism is an unfinished philosophy, and Marx must be rescued constantly from his professed disciples.

Before looking more closely at certain aspects of contemporary societies and contemporary social theories which bear upon the classical liberal and Marxist doctrines, it is necessary to present a brief but systematic contrast of them. The differences between Marx and Mill are not simple differences about determinable matters of fact, though we naturally seek to independently assess history and social conditions to discover the relevance and appropriateness of their claims and expectations – and these assessments must in turn be justified – and to discover both the empirical consequences of the pursuit of the ideals in question, and what form their incarnation would be likely to take, as perceived from our present, and certainly limited, standpoints.

Marx and Mill differed significantly, both over the interlocking moral evaluations and abstracted descriptions of their societies, and over a great variety of specific issues, which fit more or less easily into the general theories. These theories were not coherent and unchanging, but contain amendments, qualifications, uncertainties and unassimilated – and perhaps unassimilable – 'raw' hypothesis and fact, which were never thoroughly incorporated into what can be called the general or central doctrines. At the same time, different parts of those doctrines relate complexly to each other, and to the broader conceptual systems. So it is at the risk of some vulgarisation that I try to isolate the most important differences between them. These differences of view are real, and in many cases it is proper to decide which are superior, or closer to the evidence. They are not merely subject to elucidation. The major differences relevant to this study concern the operative forces in social change and the intensity with which they act, the degree and the sources of stability and conflict – most significantly, class conflict –

within societies, and the nature and the proximity of the more communal or cohesive future society. Each saw capitalist society as subject to pressures for far-reaching change. Neither was conservative. But generally, in broad or abstract statements and summaries of their central beliefs, and also in particular cases, they identified different dynamic factors, and different forces holding men together in societies, and as a result their predictions and prescriptions diverge considerably.

Marx tried to catch the essence of his materialist theory in the statement that life is not determined by consciousness, but consciousness by life. This means that the forces, mode and relations of production, which together constitute the economic substructure of society, rather than intellect or reason or conscious choice, are the decisive elements in social change. The relationship between the different elements of society is, of course, not mechanical but dialectical, so that the less significant elements have independent characteristics and independent causal force, playing back on and helping mould the more distinctively economic phenomena, and anachronisms may clutter up and confuse the historical process. Societies are seen as closely integrated, with the parts forming a totality – ideas, legal systems and institutions, classes, economic enterprises and practices, technology and so on, are recognisable and tightly knit parts of the general society, though they recurrently fall out of phase and separate, to be drawn together again as the result of radical and often violent change. The practical implications of this view of society – which may turn out to be very conservative – is that particular problems or institutions, such as distribution, cannot be isolated from society as a whole and treated as subject to reform or transformation independently. It made no sense to Marx to treat educational or political institutions as levers of change, for they existed within and were minor parts of the determining or controlling structure. This is not to say, however, that it is impossible to locate areas of society which are crucial to the process of change, or peculiarly vulnerable to political penetration. The location and exploitation of these areas has been the essence of Marxism's revolutionary enterprise.

From another perspective, this account of society becomes a theory of human nature – a theory, that is, of how man makes social change and is made by it, and of the shortcomings of man and society in relation to Marx's own standards or values. Subjected to this total system, whose parts formed and influenced him in various ways, man was the victim of history, which was the unintended product of human actions. He put his stamp upon the world and made himself, but in an alienated and inadequate way. Marx denied the ability of pre-communist man – subordinated, under capitalism, to the external and coercive law of the market and to supporting beliefs and institutions – consciously to control and manage his own environment. Men could not be free or human as long as they lived within that overbearing structure, which tainted all that it touched. The incapacity and the mutilation of man made the claims and prescriptions of liberalism meaningless, and constituted the main ground for denouncing the existing society. Nonetheless, the existing inabilities of, and restrictions upon man, were also sources of his ultimate emancipation. Life does not merely determine consciousness, but determines or shapes it in specific directions, and awakens some men and drives others into uncalculated but radical and educative political action. The broken creatures of capitalist industrialisation, educated by suffering, conflict and revolutionary theory, merge into a more and more clear-cut class, which develops homogeneity and self-consciousness in conflict with others. In part, the conflict arises out of the pursuit of scarce resources which are unevenly distributed and wastefully exploited, but the suppressed class also struggles, half-comprehendingly, for a humane and rational social order. Such an order can emerge only with the destruction, root and branch, of existing social institutions. For although Marx stressed the profound technological continuity, and the less profound but still significant organisational continuity, he emphasised the sharp conceptual and historical distinctions between old and new order – between unfree and free labour, alienation and objectification, commodities and useful objects, class man and socialised individual. The extent of the leap, even if it is made slowly, accounts for an element of paradox in Marxism that is altogether lacking in liberalism. Marx implied clearly that, on the other side of the historical divide, man would be rational and co-operative, the conscious master of natural and social forces, no longer controlled from outside by political institutions, religious fictions, commodities and so on. The antithesis between man and society would dissolve with the transformation of its elements. The communist revolution was a revolution to end all revolutions, all hostile conflict, all politics and all fantasy. It was to mark, for each man, the liberation of diverse capacities and the satisfaction of diverse needs, and it was to make social relations intelligible and transparent. Communist society was to be far different from a society of contented, brainwashed sheep.

Marx depicted societies as prey to powerful distintegrating forces, which in the case of capitalism were eventually to produce a free, classless, genuine community. He gave short shrift to the various counteracting forces, which helped maintain consensus or acquiescence or brute passivity, although their strength was explained often as a function of economic development. When capitalism was immature, the proletariat could hardly be expected to be other than submissive. The forces which helped maintain social stability, or which kept class conflict latent or muddled, included economic interdependence via the division of labour and the market, which ensured the satisfaction of the material needs of at least some sections of the proletariat; political coercion, which was of particular significance when the system was threatened directly; ideology, which legitimised coercion and exploitation by disguising the brutality of capitalism and creating false notions of its achievements and possibilities, and which contained myths about the unity of people and nation; and a number of particular historical factors, such as emigration, which acted as a safety-valve by drawing off the surplus population of the more crowded states, thus reducing their social problems and tensions in the short term. These forces blurred class conflict, the sharpening of which was, within the Marxian theory, necessary for the eventual abolition of classes. The theory assumes the objective roots of class conflict and itself strives, as the ruthless and disinterested science which harmonises with the interests and aspirations of the workers, to aid the process of class maturation and hence class war. Consequently Marx's evaluation of 'cross pressures' differs fundamentally from that of such a political scientist as Lipset, for whom cross-pressuring serves as a valuable integrator into a system which, in his view, will always be characterised by class conflict and the clash of interest, and which is, moreover, worthy of preservation.

Social institutions and the capitalist system have far less weight and oppressiveness in Mill's theory than they do in Marx's, where they enter man's very pores. Mill's conception of society – and of social constraint – is altogether looser and less holistic than Marx's, in that its different levels or parts are not seen as closely integrated or interrelated. It is not a totality in the Marxian sense. And those aspects of society which Mill emphatically identified as the most generally significant ones – thereby deviating from the distinctive belief of Hume and the empiricists that there was no basic cause – were ideas and rational decision. Mill's vocabulary and his moral doctrine focus on the free, choosing individual – on progressive beings, intellect and virtue, altruism, personal endowments, the good of the whole, teachers or mentors, enlightened minorities. Change grows from moral and intellectual roots. Mill confidently asserted the primary role of ideas, and of those capable of formulating and developing ideas, and found the progress of intellect strongly confirmed in his own time. Wisdom was filtering increasingly through society, and prejudice was becoming a diminishing force in social life. Speaking broadly, then, it is how men think that determines how they act. The men of ideas make history though, admittedly, not from the whole cloth. This slightly disembodied history and social analysis, with its assertion that the hated sinister interests were weakening, naturally seemed to Marxists to underrate the formative influences and restraints on man in capitalist society, and simply to invent the true consciousness and autonomy of the rational man. Mill believed that men could choose their institutions, within large areas, and could certainly – to cite an important case – determine the laws of distribution. Given such a high estimate of ideas and conscious choice, Mill focussed upon the peaceful, controlled transformation of political and educational institutions and forces as the levers of change and improvement. Societies were amenable to political manipulation. Mill was generally critical of revolutionary action, believing that in England at least all necessary changes could come peacefully through meeting practical grievances as they arose. The English political system did not exist everywhere, however, and Mill did hold that in some circumstances the extent of the evil confronted, and the inadequacy of facilities for change, made peaceful transitions impossible. But this would be a rare case, especially in advanced and flexible states. Rational appeals and rational social devices, acting upon groups whose natural feelings, according to this reformed utilitarian psychology, disposed them towards fellowship but whose supposed group interests, defined in ignorance, opposed them to others, were to gradually undermine the bases of group conflict and to establish an harmonious community, unbedevilled and undivided by separate interests and by selfishness. Political institutions worked on reconcilable interests, in a situation in which class conflict appeared absurd and irresponsible. In relation to capitalism, Mill had no conception of a genuine and systematic conflict of interests, arising out of different roles or positions, and hence could not conceive of true consciousness as consciousness of a basic cleavage or rift within the ranks of 'the people'. While it was possible to provoke violent conflict – which was both artificial and unproductive – it was also possible, and far more sensible, to reach accommodations through the moderate and peaceful expression of conflicting views and interests. However, the desired reconciliations were not simply those of competing selfish interests, but those in which considerations of the common good played a formative part. Mill's desired future was one in which unreasonable social groups, given wise government and adequate perception of their own and the general interest, including recognition of the need for population restraint, would be absorbed into society, thereby removing the dangers and the costs of class conflict. Intellectual development and economic advance would crumble the foundations of class – though Mill never conceived the threatening labourers as being nearly as radical or unified as they were by Marx. Mill believed that profound institutional, mental and moral changes might occur in the distant future, and found some present warrant for his hopes, but he remained uncertain and shifting about the precise point in human progress that had been reached already, and every utopian peroration can be matched by a melancholy statement that the times are not yet ripe, and that ignorance will predominate for a long time yet. Whatever changes might come, liberty, individuality and community were compatible with a reformed private property system. Reason and justice accept, indeed dictate, a social order marked by economic and political inequality. Inequalities are probably here to stay though, to ensure stability and wider self-development, they ought to be reduced and placed within a civilising institutional framework.

The conceptual schemes, the social theories and the political strategies of Marx and Mill obviously clash at vital points. There are some affinities between their conceptions of man – autonomy, activity, a true consciousness and sociality loom large in each – and there are surprising elements of utopianism, glimpses of a radically different future, in Mill's social vision. But these affinities may be exaggerated if attention is focussed on words and concepts rather than on the total social theories in which they are set. Such a criticism can be levelled appropriately at Oppenheim's claim that Marx and Mill essentially shared the same commitment to freedom, 'the same ultimate goal of society "in which the free development of each would be the condition of the free development of all" ',[1] and, less sharply, at Kaufman's suggestion that 'Mill's ideal of the good life is more like Marx's conception of unalienated man than it is like Bentham's happy man'.[2] I agree with the general drift – rather than the precise content – of these statements, which is that we are not faced by a clash absolute and overall between Marx and Mill. Mill was not defending liberal bourgeois society against a Marxist challenge, and was himself highly critical of liberal orthodoxy, while Marx's revolutionary theory was penetrated by some of the bourgeois conceptions which, he thought, misrepresented existing social realities. But we must be wary of assigning great significance to those similarities of language which we discover. Ideals can only be understood adequately in relation to a thinker's analysis of existing institutional structures and norms, and to his imagined and valued alternative states. They can be further elucidated through knowledge of the social background and focus of a theory, and of its particular intellectual heritage. Marx was outside and estranged from the dominant traditions of his adopted land; he was heavily influenced by a dramatic social theory built around antitheses and conflict, and friendly to prophecy; and he saw himself as the champion of the most suppressed class, the substance and context of whose lives he drew vividly and powerfully. Mill was the proud member of a civilisation which he thought capable of steady expansion; his prescriptions were gradualist and rated moral and political factors, conducive to harmony, very highly; and he was the champion of creative minorities, though he wished also to improve the conditions and raise the capacities of the labourers. Industrial life lay at the edges of his interest. For Marx, proletarian uprising was a portent of the true and constructive consciousness of the class: to Mill, the great reconciler, it was a serious and unnecessary danger to civilised achievement. Mill's goals of freedom, rationality and human development could be realised within social arrangements which were thoroughly incompatible with the fulfilment of Marxian man. Marx focussed on different constraints and limitations on man but, more significantly, human liberation – the vast change from total deprivation to total emancipation – implied far more to him than Mill's improvement of a tolerable society. He may have understood what Mill was at, but Mill seemed to him caught within the confines of bourgeois political economy, bourgeois rationality and bourgeois liberty.

In his few comments on his liberal contemporary, Marx presented him as a fumbling, superficial, confused and unoriginal – though honest – eclectic, who did not deserve the scathing contempt which could properly be showered on a Bentham.[3] Marx's central criticism of Mill was that he was attempting to do the impossible, to reconcile the irreconcilables – capitalist political economy and the claims of the proletariat. In Marx's words, 'although men like John Stuart Mill are to blame for the contradiction between their traditional economic dogmas and their modern tendencies, it would be very wrong to class them with the herd of vulgar economic apologists'.[4] Mill, of course, continued to work within the limits of bourgeois society, which he did not challenge as vigorously and rabidly as did Marx. From a Marxist viewpoint he was a figure of compromise, akin to those revisionists who were later to earn the wrath of those who saw themselves as full-fledged revolutionaries, standing firmly for the proletarian cause. Lukacs put the criticism as follows: 'Revisionism is always eclectic. Even at a theoretical level it tends to blur and blunt class differences, and to make a unity of classes – an upside-down unity which exists only in its own head – the criterion for judging events.'[5] Given a picture of things according to which social division must be provoked and brought into the open before progress can be made, those who value a common heritage, and treat all men as brothers, who sit on fences and bridge gaps, must be condemned as anti-revolutionary. They are. But whether their notions of unity are confused and purely theoretical, as Lukacs alleges, or whether they fairly represent social realities, and whether or not their perceptions and goals are morally satisfactory, are questions which are generally ignored, or dismissed dogmatically, by the angry enemies of revisionism.

In presenting this kind of attack on 'the liberal compromise' – for, to the liberal, it may have been no compromise at all – Marx was trying to show the liberal's inability to attain his own stated goals, because of the shortcomings of his theories of social causation and human relationships. Marx put the fine words and decent hopes of liberalism up against a very different social theory – or conception of social reality – and thereby sought to show their utopian character. For example, Mill's view of the general interest as a genuine community interest, at once ascertainable and objective, and of classless calculators who can perceive it, rests upon a non-recognition of the profound social, class and ideological conditioning of supposedly free men. For Marx, the general interest in class society could mean only the interest of the progressive class, as against those of decrepit and decaying classes. But class interest was not an error to be overcome by a dose of education, or by fantasies about common human nature and Man as Such. Mill's programme left the pillars of the capitalist class structure standing, and hence, whatever merely constitutional changes took place, ruling classes, inequality and exploitation would persist, preventing the general emergence of the autonomous, sovereign individual of liberal theory. The argument is that, in a social order of the kind characteristically envisaged by liberals, the major liberal values could not be embodied or realised. Liberalism reflects and idealises, without transforming, the evil reality of capitalist society, which must be transformed if genuine individualism is to come into being. In its application to Mill, the charge is not hypocrisy, but that his vision of life, if it is assumed to have any relevance to the generality of the people, would require much more far-reaching structural change, especially to the property and the class system, than those which he actually advocated.

At this stage it is necessary to separate two points of attack. The first concerns what we actually understand by such liberal goals as individualism, self-determination, moral autonomy and the flowering of personality. Are they morally adequate notions or goals? What important values and considerations do they exclude or overlook? For example, does the close linkage between property and liberty in liberal theory mean that the liberal vision is narrowly selfish, idealising a society which is little more than a collection of self-absorbed calculators? According to this criticism, which is developed particularly by C. B. Macpherson – following Marx – the individual is the proprietor of himself, his powers and capacities, and political society becomes an instrumental device – to ensure personal satisfactions through the maintenance of free exchange and contract.[6] Individuals in society are perceived as externally related, and fraternity – the notion of a solid, conscious and vital community – is undervalued, if considered at all. The second criticism concerns the actual form of social organisation which would be required to implement the ideal in question. The recommended liberal economic and social order, because of the inequalities, biases, frustrations and emptinesses which are integral to it, is seen as incapable of embodying liberalism's own aspiration. The hopes remain empty, and are caricatured by a destructive reality. Marxism thus, along with the bulk of socialist theory, rejects the characteristic liberal account of the resources of the individual in a competitive, free enterprise, class society, arguing that the competitive system necessarily destroys masses of people while encouraging and praising the diversity and achievements of a few. Only a few men have the resources and capacities to develop themselves. The results of the spontaneous operation of social forces are thus perceived in very different ways. Liberalism becomes a formalistic class doctrine, and its sovereign individual a figment or abstraction. Real class man is a eunuch, castrated by his society, and liberalism leaves him weak, incomplete and isolated, as it found him. Hence socialists may be deeply attached to liberal values, but hostile to the institutional structures advocated by liberals, and may, indeed, claim to be implementing or completing liberal principles, by giving concrete and democratic content to the liberty and individuality which often remained empty and formal in liberal hands.

Liberalism is, however, a protean doctrine or collection of doctrines, changing historically, and very diverse at any particular time. Criticisms for thinness, lack of both social consciousness and a sense of social complexity, and for blindness or complacent oversight, apply much more to some 'liberals' than to others. Such criticisms apply much more to Bentham or Spencer, for example, than to Mill, or Green and Hobhouse, who socialised liberalism to a considerable degree. Mill was certainly an extremely equivocal philosopher of the market society, and emphasised men's real social obligations, their close connections in the present, and their more satisfying and close relationships in the future. With T. H. Green we find a more conscious and clear-sighted effort to increase the actual powers and capacities of individuals, to assist the underfed denizen of the London yard to share positively in the rights and the common life of Englishmen. But once again, we may respect the insight and the ideal and find that the means recommended for its realisation fall short of what is required, though it is generally difficult to determine *exactly* what is required to realise ideals in the variable, changing and restrictive historical conditions in which men act. It is not only the problems of causality – discovering the levels of change, if there are any – and of determining what would constitute the realisation of particular ideals, but of doing these things within a world which is itself constantly altering and being altered, thereby throwing up new problems and throwing out old solutions.

Marxism rejects the psychologism of much liberal theory – the treatment of the isolated or bare or independent individual as the datum of social analysis or social policy – and instead presents men as shaped or formed by their society, even if they sometimes react back on it as semi-autonomous individuals. As stated, the criticism is too general to be useful. With whatever abstract models they may play, few people these days propose Robinson Crusoe as the basis of concrete social analysis. What is needed now – perhaps from both sides – is more precise understanding of the ways in which men are formed or determined and constrained, and the nature of whatever autonomy or 'dialectical initiative' their formation and their constraints allow to them.

Men come into a world which is already there, solid, weighty and dense, defined and defining, and by the time they act consciously in it or against it, they are formed creatures, already deprived of certain possibilities and capable of seeing only certain things.[7] The very young Marx made the point, rather weakly, when discussing man's inability to choose a vocation. 'Our social relations, to some extent, have already begun to form before we are in a position to determine them.'[8] To this prison called society, with whose particular norms, habits, definitions, structures and taboos – various infringements of human nature and potentiality – they are vitally concerned, radical social critics frequently counterpose an image or standard of human autonomy or authenticity, perhaps underpinned by a story of man's decline in some historical circumstances or other. But if history is a history of loss and degeneration, or if society is a source of frustration and deformity, and if things are to be changed, we need to know the accessible stages and the crucial elements in these processes, so that the problems of desocialisation or resocialisation can be at least faced intelligently. The sources of man's lost innocence, like its badges, are legion. History and society are abstractions, and must be unravelled before we can sensibly consider questions concerning proper and improper, and removable and irremovable, influences and pressures. The influences, pressures and constraints are many and diverse, and range from blatant impediments to human action – walls, chains and bullets – to the most subtle and hidden of persuaders. Although it is common to present society as if it were an organised and coherent body of interventions, intrusions, controls and influences, there is no isolable identity or force which is society. It is pervasive, continuous, changing, internally differentiated, and includes – amongst many other things – languages, governments, laws, commissars and capitalists, schools, families, churches, work-places, interest-groups, newspapers, competition and colleagues. The various subcultures and social forces collide and conflict as well as interact and merge, and they impinge in different ways upon the individual and impinge on different individuals differently. Often radical critics of society have taken very lightly the tasks of sorting out and defining the relevant forms of socialisation, and of discriminating between the contingent and the necessary or the inescapable – indeed, taking such tasks lightly sometimes seems to be a necessary condition of radical optimism. The writings of Herbert Marcuse, and to a lesser extent those of Marx, suffer from a tendency to characterise 'society' in a crude, unitary way, and from a matching tendency to depict 'freedom' in an abstract way. Marx argued in *The German Ideology* that existing individuals had been set a very definite task – that of 'replacing the domination of circumstances and chance over individuals by the domination of individuals over chance and circumstances'.[9] While such a notion of the genuinely free individual – free from personal and social dependency – may be immediately appealing, it needs to be specified in more concrete terms, especially as 'circumstances' mostly are other people, and hence it must be possible that mastering circumstances involves pushing others about. Our actions and our inactions make the world in which everybody acts: the mere existence of other people impinges on our freedom. In the case of Herbert Marcuse, we find a reasonable denial of the present existence of the sovereign, rational individual of liberal theory, a pessimistic account of the destructive effects of different formative influences on the individual, and a handful of vague and hopeful comments on possible, or coming, human self-determination. My objection is that Marcuse fails to specify the circumstances in which free and rational choices might be made, and thus fails to make clear what aspects of socialisation will remain in the non-repressive society which he desires. Does he complain about a bad mode of socialisation, or is he against any socialisation, as presently understood? We are formed by society, but is all the forming – which may go very deep – equivalent to thwarting and mutilation? Is genuine freedom compatible with a social structure at all? A statement by Christian Bay, in *The Structure of Freedom*, seems very much to the point here:

> Human behaviour is restrained by innumerable circumstances, and the great majority of these are not perceived as restraints. Factors in childhood backgrounds, conventions, ...interpersonal relations, aspirations and expectations for the future – all these aspects of life can be said to imply numerous restraints on the individuals, restraints that as a rule either are taken for granted as part of the self or the situation or are unperceived parts of the unconscious.[10]

When we cut out all the diseased tissue, prune away what has been imposed on man by the repressive societies of history, what is left? What is the free, autonomous human being really like? Is the radical dream in one sense a return to the liberalism previously dismissed as hollow, a return – via an extremely hostile and generalised critique of existing society and the illusions of liberalism – to the notion of the sovereign individual as the man freed from society?

These questions, and the social theories from which they arise, lead directly to consideration of the nature of the self or of personal identity. They raise the crucial issue of the relationship between man's historical identity – or identities – and both the contingent features of particular societies, which may be peculiarly clinging, and the common – and perhaps necessary – features of all societies. It must be acknowledged at the outset that conceptions of genuine freedom or autonomy, which are themselves socially constructed, are naturally underlain by their own theories of socialisation and their own views of the limits within which freedom can and should be exercised. The various visions of the essential or authentic self remain visions of man in society, and specify different social conditions for their realisation. They presuppose less constricting social influences, and not the removal of all social influence. For the free self requires, not merely a large range of options but a capacity to choose, to envisage and pursue different courses, and that capacity presumably has to be put there or implanted or encouraged somehow. Mere dead possibility – lots of doors to open if one desires to do so – is not enough. Thus, while the concept of autonomy is counterposed reasonably to much that passes for freedom, its advocates normally build into it their own notions of free or rational activity, and recommend modes of socialisation which seem conducive to it. Mill's autonomous man acts within a framework which Mill deemed rational; Marx's autonomous man requires a different social order from Mill's, but behaves responsibly and socially, and not as a frenzied, self-assertive egoist. while the message of many of the modern champions of spontaneity is roughly: 'Be yourself – but not whatever you like.' But although radical theorists themselves prescribe much of the content, and certainly the limits, of free or autonomous human action, those limits, and the social structures linked with them, are commonly seen as unrealisable or as violently destructive of man as we know him. Those who talk of 'the human condition', rather than of particular and changing human conditions, may be dismissed by the prophets as conservative theologians, but prophets, with their wild denunciations and millennial promises, may have as little grasp of human potentiality and need as those who try to hold them where they supposedly are. R. D. Laing puts a very radical question: 'But if we could strip away all the exigencies and contingencies, and reveal to each other our naked presence?'[11] He wants authentic human relationships – without clothes, disguises, crutches, masks, roles, lies, defences, anxieties, props, games and greasepaint. But could such freedom mean that men are emptied, degutted, like Burke's naked, shivering creatures, rather than becoming self-reliant and loving, with settled and individual identities? Might not rules, defences, definitions, even predefinitions, be necessary to identity, authenticity and autonomy? David Martin admits – as is obvious – that they may be very costly, but sees them as the necessary ground of social existence. He argues that they 'admit an amelioration in the way they operate, and total reciprocity, absolute openness and lack of demarcation are neither possible nor desirable'.[12] In addition, the efforts of social thinkers to free men from all their chains, real and imagined, removable and irremovable, may lead to contempt for the traditional – and sometimes ineffective or inadequate – means of protecting liberties and choices, and to hostility and arrogance towards ordinary men. Socialisation creates capacities for freedom, and societies create conditions for their exercise: the profound limitations and biases of all known societies and all known processes of socialisation sometimes lead to attempts to throw out the lot indiscriminately.

However difficult to apply, the comparative testing of Marx and Mill should be attempted. In what senses have their conflicting accounts of, and predictions for, capitalist society been confirmed or disconfirmed by events this century? And how telling are present confirmations and disconfirmations?

It is assumed commonly that human relations, whether of conflict or harmony, are related closely to the amount, quality and distribution of the resources available to men. On the whole, conservative – and some liberal – writers have stressed the shortage of resources which, together with man's nature, call for a spartan, suppressive regime. Some emphasise economic scarcity, others human rapacity, for what is important may be, not the simple lack of material goods, but the alleged need to control or channel human desires, lest they tear society apart.[13] But while conservative thinkers generally assume both scarcity and the persisting lowness of men, radical and optimistic philosophers have usually envisaged a condition of economic plenty which will facilitate human liberation and remove some of the major causes of social disharmony.

Mill and Marx both believed that scarcity would have drastic political consequences. Marx assumed that collaboration and co-operation were unusual under capitalism, where class conflict was the norm. Despite its technological power, the capitalist system must eventually restrict production. Scarcity, and a growing knowledge that the system perpetuated scarcity, made it inconceivable that class interests would be reconciled within capitalism. The economy, more and more disastrously chaotic, could satisfy neither basic human needs nor the various demands made upon it – demands which the system encouraged by its competitive ethos. The failure was inherent in capitalism, and could not be removed by political regulation, or by any imaginable distribution of such limited and uneven supplies as capitalism could produce. As the Duchess put it in *Alice in Wonderland*, 'the more there is of yours, the less there is of mine'.

Prima facie it may seem that conflict is likely to be intense in stationary societies, or in societies in which many people are in a condition of constant or increasing poverty. In such societies, where whole hecatombs of workers may perish from want, the marginal utility of income in extremely high, as a relatively small increment may make the difference between starvation and survival. The marginal utility of social progress, for example, in the field of working conditions, or working hours, is also extremely high where conditions are bad and hours long – a decrease in the working day from ten or twelve hours to eight is in an important sense more urgent than is its fall from eight to six hours.[14] However, situations of extreme poverty do not always or necessarily engender revolutionary action. The causal link between material suffering and violent political activity is an extremely uncertain one, and cannot be taken for granted – as it often is by economists, amongst others. For example, Kenneth Boulding claims that, in a stationary society,

> the conflict is perceived as an acute one. If one gets more then, automatically, the rest of the people must get less. The luxuries of the rich are literally paid for by the destitution of the poor. It is little wonder that such societies tend to generate acute class conflicts that occasionally burst forth into violent revolution. In a stagnant society, the only road to relieve the poverty of the poor seems to be to expropriate the rich and divide up the proceeds.[15]

This thesis immediately raises the crucial question of the links between social structure, social and economic conditions, and consciousness. One cannot simply assume that poverty – or, more broadly, economic conditions – are single and isolated variables, as men's psychology, nature and perceptions are also involved. It is easy to say from outside how the road to salvation must, or should, seem, but from inside, the social order may seem unassailable, neither made by man nor subject to him. As a matter of historical fact, the very poor are often conservative, demoralised and escapist, worshipping and serving existing rulers, or dreaming of heavenly or some other distant happiness. They may be like Marx's lumpenproletariat, or the Warsaw unemployed of the 1920s, as described by Zawadski and Lazarsfeld: 'The masses cease to exist as such when the social bond – the consciousness of belonging together –

does not bind any longer. There remain only scattered, loose, perplexed and hopeless individuals. The unemployed are a mass only numerically, not socially.'[16] In such cases of atomisation, or where widespread poverty is accompanied by a conservative and other-worldly religion and a rigid social hierarchy, as it has been in India, radical mass movements may never arise or, if arising, may not take a positive or a political form. Rather, outbursts and assertiveness remain wild and aimless.[17] But while conditions of chronic poverty are often associated with political conservatism and ignorance, economic improvements, with advances in education, communications and so on, generally create rising expectations, which frequently lead to questioning of what was hitherto accepted as natural, and to a restlessness, an insatiability in demands, which is not present in extremely poverty-stricken communities. New wants and needs are not compared with traditional ones, but emerge in relation to a sudden increase of presumed possibilities. The horizon of desire widens, established titles and standards of legitimacy are rejected, and disaffection grows. In some cases revolutions have occurred when rising expectations, attendant upon economic advance, are met by economic difficulty or decline.[18]

Whatever the eventual consequences of downward economic trends would have been, advanced capitalist societies have not had to face the precise pressures anticipated by Marx. Whatever harsh comments he made about the capitalist's motivation, his failure was far less a failure of psychological theory than a failure at the level of economic theory. His prediction of inevitable breakdown failed, not because capitalists were nicer or more intelligent than he imagined, but because neither they nor anyone else were subjected to the economic imperatives, to the confining and rigid economic system, which he had assumed. The screws were never tightened. Mill also underrated the productive possibilities of capitalism, but he did have a more accurate view of the moral, habitual and psychological factors linking men even to imperfect systems. Capitalist societies, partly because of their unsuspected productive capacity and partly because of regulation and the development of more sophisticated economic techniques, have proved capable of satisfying many of the most pressing working-class claims, at least in the countries with which Marx was most concerned.[19] This has been largely the result of a vast increase in goods rather than through redistribution, of which the extent has often been exaggerated.[20] To take the English case, there have been only minor changes in the distribution of income since 1860, but wages have retained a roughly constant share of a continually expanding national income. The spread of social services has also had a significant impact on the general standard of living, and has helped reduce potential sources of conflict. Of course, many demands upon the system have not been satisfied, or have been only partially satisfied, but the continuous process of adjustment and absorption generally keeps tension below boiling level.

The normal absence of intense class conflict in Western industrial societies is not traceable solely to increased productivity and whatever redistribution has taken place. The increase of what is available in general, and for specific social groups, is part of the story. But groups have been satisfied, or have been willing to act peacefully within the system, because of the growth of political and judicial institutions which appear to give their claims reasonable attention. Social conflict itself has provoked the search for new means of negotiation and interaction, with the aim and effect of channelling and controlling antagonisms and hostilities, and diminishing unpredictable, threatening and dramatic sallies on 'the system' by the discontented. In the course of this process of socialisation, class claims and demands have been modified, and their character altered. However, this is not to say that the economic institutions of capitalism have been changed profoundly or that conflict has withered away. A high degree of inequality and of concentration of economic ownership and control exists, as do antagonism and conflict, but capitalism has a more civilised and friendly countenance, or mask. There is general acceptance of, or acquiescence in, the broad features of the institutional system within which conflict and change occur. Even where particular decisions have been rejected, the dissatisfied groups have normally preferred, where possible, to work for more acceptable settlements through parliaments, pressure groups and arbitration courts, while seeking in some cases to reduce their bias, rather than to reject the whole system of negotiation, or the whole society of which these institutions are an integral part. A brief and generalised consideration of the way in which trades unions and labour parties have come to accept the institutionalisation of conflict will make it clear why the workers have not acted upon what Marx took to be their objective interests, why they have taken the broad and corrupting road of revisionism despite the anguished warnings of the communist fathers.

In several advanced capitalist countries the extension of the franchise has enabled the absorption of most excluded and potentially disaffected groups into the political order. Parliaments have become, as Mill believed they could, arenas in which different interests compete and make their claims articulate, though their decisions are far less influenced by 'the public interest' than he hoped they would be. His disinterested reason is nowhere in the ascendant. But in the course of pressing their claims, the nature of the disputants has changed. Whether we describe the process as one of moralisation or civilisation or one of betrayal and cowardly capitulation, the point remains that interests and morals are closely connected. They are not totally distinct, with the latter cloaking the former. Interests are normative – what they are, what one conceives them to be, depends heavily on values. The existence of procedures for discussion, negotiation and compromise are likely to alter their character. In a system where interests can be pursued in a relatively free and open way, and where the procedures for reaching settlements at least appear to take account of the claims of all parties – although that appearance may be utterly misleading – interest groups will try to avoid making, or seeming to make, absurd and irresponsible or patently selfish demands, and in doing this they will be affected by general views of what is reasonable. Interests have the sharp edges taken off them, and are given a moral component, in parliamentary institutions, partly by the need to win friends, partly by the recognition that progress through existing institutions can only be gradual – while the costs of going outside them are likely to be extreme, and the rewards uncertain.

The proletariat, Marx's 'universal class', which was to play the major role in social transformation, did not act in the expected and necessary way. We cannot say whether it would have done so if subjected to the wage pressures anticipated by Marx, but for whatever reason it has lacked the radicalism and the homogeneity which he expected. This failure shattered the Marxian system at its very centre and lay behind the theoretical divergences and conflicts which have multiplied amongst the disciples. Revisionist[21] interpretations of Marxism accept that failure. Bernstein, who altered the inherited Marxist categories to accord with what seemed to him to be existing facts, believed that capitalist societies were becoming increasingly prosperous and stable, that democratic institutions were making it possible for the proletariat to share in the new-found wealth and that, as a result, the misery and the class division which were to precede the Marxist revolution were in fact diminishing. The consumption of the workers was increasing, real income was rising and there was no sign of capitalist crisis. The class structure was becoming more complex, especially with the growth of the white-collar or bureaucratic-managerial class, and the emergence of 'troops of shareholders', who also became the troops of capitalism, while small and middle-sized properties were holding their own and even increasing.[22] Bernstein believed capitalism and liberal-democratic institutions to be much more flexible than had Marx who, perhaps, had derived his image of social change from the rigidities of feudalism.

Feudalism, with its inflexible organisations and corporations, had to be destroyed almost everywhere by violence. The liberal organisations of modern society are distinguished from those of feudalism precisely in being flexible, and capable of change and development. They need, not to be destroyed, but only to be further developed. For this we need organisation and energetic action, but not necessarily a revolutionary dictatorship.[23]

He found the late nineteenth-century working class a far cry from Marx's alienated, class-conscious proletarians. They were no longer outcasts, but had become citizens, participating members of the national community, which educated and protected them, and whose leaders they helped elect. As the material position of important sections of the working class improved, and as they were absorbed into the community and the nation, the grounds of radical social conflict increasingly withered away. Citizenship spread, along with the virtue of the citizen – civility. As Edward Shils has said in a somewhat abstract passage, civility is

> acceptance of the tasks of the management of public affairs in collaboration with others and with a regard to the interests, individual, sectional and collective, of the entire society. The sense of responsibility for and to the whole, and a general acceptance of the rules which are valid within it, are integral to civility. Civil politics is the politics of effective compromise within an institutonal system accepted as of inherent legitimacy.[24]

It is difficult to generalise about the relative stability of early and advanced capitalist societies. For those imprisoned within the dominant picture of American society, the present extent of, and past increases in, social stability in the Western world are apt to be exaggerated. Stability in contemporary Germany or Italy is hardly greater than it was in Marx's day, and in capitalist countries where there has been no notable increase in stability, there have been sharp increases in productivity and increases in real income, while education and social services have become more widespread and ample. But economic and institutional changes have contributed strongly to existing stability. These include the growth of productivity and the extension of social services, governmental regulation of the economy and institutional arrangements for the representation of different claims, including especially the political enfranchisement of the working class. The different elements support each other. Rapid increases in production and the existence of political institutions which they have helped manage, have enabled workers to make undoubted material advances, and naturally this has affected their consciousness and their feelings. Mill had hoped – reasonably, it seems – that improving economic circumstances and participation in political life would bring about the spread of constitutional morality, or what have been called the political virtues – conciliation, compromise, moderation and adaptability. For it seems that the rules of the game – biased and imperfect as they may be – are accepted widely, or at least, that their modification is pursued, in general, by political and legal means. The change or limitation of consciousness, which has brought so much anger and sorrow to Marxist theorists, seems to be a result of more than economic improvements. Condemned by Marcuse and his followers for his passivity and his happy consciousness, condemned for a lack of rationality and imagination, the modern worker can nonetheless offer reasonable grounds for his present preferences and for his inactivity. He can point to his powerlessness, for drastic social change is simply not available to him. His own skills and organisations may have become more sophisticated, but the ruling class (or the plural élites, or 'the system') has also gained in strength, skill and elusiveness. Meanwhile the worker becomes disillusioned about the possibility and the rewards of drastic social change – his own organisations are subject to bureaucratic and oligarchic tendencies, public economic enterprises suffer from 'the dead hand of government', and the actual performance of socialist states shows little of the spectacular productive advantages and the widespread liberation of men which were promised. The alternatives to capitalism thus seem greyer than they were painted and, while their shortcomings are exaggerated by much of the mass media, they are not simply invented by them. Marcuse focusses too sharply on the element of brainwashing and the lack of moral and imaginative power in the worker-subjects, and underrates the extent to which they sit passively, enjoying what material consolations they can, because they realise the nature of their intractable situation. Marcuse says, 'It is intolerable, and only slaves would bear it', while the workers are saying, 'It is unbeatable, and there seems nothing better, so adapt to it.' The mass of people do not embrace the system with the mindless, brainwashed, shallow complacency which Marcuse sometimes imputes to them.

A form of liberalism which is less imaginative and critical – more down-to-earth and self-satisfied – than that of Mill is strong in Western society today, and has lately been especially rampant in American sociology and political science. It denies or redescribes what others present as the oppressiveness of contemporary social life, seeing it as neither radically tainted nor destructive, and it rejects the Marxist conflict picture of capitalism. Focussing on the stability of affluent democratic societies, its major images are conservative in character – 'integration', 'equilibrium', 'organism', 'consensus' and 'function' – and represent society as capable of absorbing or accommodating conflict and danger. The organism slowly adjusts and evolves. The primary political concern of this body of theory is the survival of the constitutional order in advanced capitalist states, which are held to be increasingly invulnerable to damaging class conflict of the traditional kind.[25] Social life does not polarise around classes, and while they, or segments of them, may battle at times, it is in a muted, confused and discontinuous way. Consensus plays a major part in the theory, as it allegedly prevents the development of fundamental conflict over the system itself, or at least diverts such (potential) conflict into peaceful channels. However, while it seems true that many modern liberal-democratic states are characterised by a considerable degree of stability, with almost everybody accepting or acquiescing in the structure of institutions, rights and powers which constitute the democratic polity, consensus theories are often imprecise and sometimes circular, which makes them inadequate tools for understanding social stability. Does consensus involve agreement or something weaker, and if it does involve agreement, what counts as evidence of its existence? Continued use of the highways and by-ways? If agreement, agreement on what? On the legitimacy of the social order? Or on the hopelessness of ever, in practice, beating the system? Is consensus the fundamental, framework value, the 'central value system', within whose confines lesser conflicts are properly fought out? Does it mean the same thing to different people? Agreement amongst whom – all the people, or most of them, or the political activists, or the key interest groups? What explains consensus itself? Is consensus supposedly an active force – and, if so, what are the assumptions about human psychology upon which it rests? The belief that the existence of society is a daily plebiscite exaggerates the rational, choosing element in compliance, and may lead to an exaggerated idea of the moral claims of the society in question. Even if we can distinguish usefully between conflict within the system and conflict about the system, we cannot condemn the latter until we have evaluated the society and adequately defined the grounds of allegiance to it. Many consensus theorists reveal a great deal of complacency about their own social system, and fear dissent and conflict inordinately. Like latter-day Burkes, they exaggerate both the unity and virtue of stable societies and the terrible consequences of rapid modification and change.

In structural terms, modern democratic societies are presented, in many of these sociological theories, as fluid, flexible and pluralist. The boundaries between classes are not precisely or firmly drawn, partly because there is such a variety of competing groups, merging and overlapping with classes and undermining their sole sway. In fact, class and class antagonism play a diminished role in the predominant theory, with its stress on new élites, the particular and various issues dividing and uniting men, the complexity of human allegiances, ties, doubts, resentments, hopes and goals, the remarkable interdependence of men in modern industrial societies, and the consequent blurredness or opaqueness of the social structure. The sheer weight of the social order limit hope and aspiration. Despite the fact that, for masses of men, the promise of improvement remains illusory, there is rather more social mobility than Marx anticipated – or, at least, social mobility is intelligently selective, and effective in its 'leader-stealing' function – and this, as he feared, has worked against strong class identification and loyalties. He saw how upward mobility could stabilise capitalism, as it had the Catholic Church in the Middle Ages. 'The more a ruling class is able to assimilate the most prominent men of the dominated classes the more stable and dangerous is its rule.'[26] He tended to treat the United States as a singularly mobile society, without clearly defined class conflict. There classes existed but had not yet become fixed – they 'continually change and interchange their elements in constant flux'.[27]

Social pluralist theories stress the stability to which pluralist institutions are a major contributor – they are at once complex and responsive, giving way to the various pressures which play subtly upon them. In a peaceful bargaining situation they steadily appease the dissatisfied and remedy outstanding grievances, thereby nipping conflict in the bud. The political process becomes one of incessant bargaining between diverse interest groups, which avoid large, destructive claims and compete moderately for (normally) economic advantage, and by so doing, they check and balance each other and the government – where the government is credited with an independent existence. The politics of pressure groups becomes a central feature and safeguard of democratic politics in three senses – the groups reduce the rootlessness and isolation of individuals, by drawing them into social life, their autonomy is a protection against excessive state power, and the various shifting lines of division dissipate energy and loyalty, muddle conflict and thus prevent the emergence of one fundamental line of social cleavage. Participation is segmental rather than total. As one typical champion of social pluralism has put it, the cross-cutting solidarities 'help prevent one line of social cleavage from becoming dominant, and they constrain associations to respect the various affiliations of their members lest they alienate them'.[28] However debilitating pluralist theory may be to radical aspiration, it has certainly pointed to real sources of stabilisation. Pluralist theories both perceive and justify a particular manner of political behaviour, and both reflect and contribute to the social realities of their time. Their moral and political thrust is normally clear. Affluence and 'effective' democratic institutions allegedly lead to conservatism or realism, to an acceptance of the legitimacy of the existing system, while doctrinaire politics, ideological enthusiasm and utopianism – rigid, apocalyptic and dangerous – wither, and are condemned as the fruit of psychic disorder. In the Western world today, claimed Daniel Bell, there is 'a rough consensus among intellectuals on political issues; the acceptance of a Welfare State; the desirability of decentralised power; a system of mixed economy and of political pluralism'.[29] This rough consensus is seen as a proper result of the achievements of the democratic welfare state, but it becomes even more attractive when the dangers of radical – and specifically utopian – thinking and action are observed. The democratic welfare state marks a profound transformation of the objective environment of political action and provides continuing access to its members: pursuit of radical goals, now unnecessary, is responsible for the major disasters of the century. The road to the concentration camp is paved with utopias and ideologies. End-of-ideology theory – itself ideological, and an element in the situation it describes, as a lever for inaction – thus presents a picture of growing convergence over general principles, which has reduced the area of social conflict and left room for technical disputes only. Politics is being supplanted, though not in the Marxist manner, by administration. Hannah Arendt – neither behaviouralist nor political scientist – claims that in our mass societies the political realm has to a large extent withered away, and quotes Engels favourably. She comments: 'In a society under the sway of abundance, conflicting group interests need no longer be settled at one another's expense, and the principle of opposition is valid only so long as there exist authentic choices which transcend the objective and demonstrably valid opinions of experts. When government has really become administration, the party system can only result in incompetence and wastefulness.'[30] The Marxist vision has certainly come to earth with a thud.

Pluralistic accounts of how things actually work -- how groups compete and how claims are made and met – are normally pervaded by dubious moral and idealistic assumptions. It is often assumed that legitimate groups naturally gain their appropriate share of power or property – that if all goes well, as a strong critic of pluralist theory has paraphrased the argument, 'every significant interest in the nation will find expression, and to each will go a measure of satisfaction roughly proportional to its size and intensity'.[31] This claim, as presented by Wolff, certainly meets serious difficulties, including the questions of how one measures the intensity of an interest and what it means to say that a group wins satisfaction proportional – even if roughly – to its size and intensity. A rather weaker but still questionable claim is made by Robert Dahl, one of the leading pluralist thinkers. Dahl has written that the normal American political system, with all its defects, does nonetheless 'provide a high probability that any active and legitimate group will make itself heard effectively at some stage in the process of decision'.[32] Yet, if this is to amount to a clear empirical claim and not a mere tautology, we require adequate accounts of the normal system, the legitimate groups, and what it is to be effectively heard. The criteria of legitimacy may be defined very narrowly, so that certain groups – Negroes or poor white Southerners or Puerto Ricans – are left outside the pale, or are for some other reason not effectively heard. It is power and resources, including nuisance-value, and not real need and numbers, which determine how groups do in the political competition. Even a cursory glance reveals the limits to the diffusion of power within the capitalist democracies. The groups that count in the making of major decisions are few and strong. Many groups are not seriously or adequately spoken for. Their lack of power, and the limits and biases of the system, are sufficient to leave them outside and unheard. The scope of decision-making – what is regarded as a legitimate part of politics – is always sharply limited, and always sharply limits certain prospects, although new accumulations of power could enable its scope to be expanded, or its bias to be changed. Schattschneider has commented pertinently on the loading of the pressure-group system. 'All forms of political organisation have a bias in favour of the exploitation of some kinds of conflict and the suppression of others because organisation is the mobilisation of bias. Some issues are organised into politics while others are organised out.'[33] Competition or conflict takes place within an extremely limited segment of the area of possible political conflict, and within that segment particular interests are strongly favoured. The constantly reiterated advice to the angry and the powerless, that they should work through the established processes, makes sense primarily to those who are used to being listened to and taken account of. To the weak it must often sound like a disguised admonition to remain impotent. Yet to most people those processes seem tolerable, partly because their outlooks and perceptions are shaped in conformity with them. Their seemingly free responses to issues and problems have been already structured: their capacity to envisage alternative courses, as well as their capacity to act and their readiness to do so, are diminished sharply by both social experience and social influence. They are not slaves, they do make reasonable choices, and the democratic institutions in which they acquiesce are not mere façades, but they do take the existing system too much for granted, and fail to realise its restrictiveness, and its inaccessibility to some sections of the society.

Those who depart from the narrow path of pluralist virtue are likely to find themselves classed as unacceptable deviants, who need to be treated so that they will accept their fate. In relation to the functioning system, taken as the norm, the deviant will tend to be dismissed on psychological or moral grounds, as unbalanced or wicked, failing to adjust to an order which is not itself to be called seriously into question. The prevalent interest in the psychic sources of individual behaviour, in the pathology rather than the programme of dissent, gives the impression that existing institutions are satisfactory, if not natural. It was not totally absurd for Kuusinen to complain recently[34] that Western workers dissatisfied with capitalism were advised to see a psychiatrist, to be freed of tensions, strains or maladjustment. However, he might have added that in the Soviet Union dissenters are placed in psychiatric clinics to be cured of their individuality. In many societies, radicalism is treated as a medical condition.

The claims of pluralist-consensus theory, as it bears upon the Marxist notion of social conflict, are that pluralism, within a setting of material abundance, restrains rulers, who are not cohesive or homogeneous, from acting in the way envisaged by Marx; that pressing claims are satisfied, perhaps even to precisely the right degree; and that these two factors, combined with the existence of diverse groups which undermine class coherence and loyalty, restrain the lower class from violent political activity, and end ideological, class politics. The complacency and apathy of ordinary men result from the achievements of modern democracies, which do not require widespread political involvement in order to work well. 'Where the rational citizen seems to abdicate, nevertheless angels seem to tread.'[35] In fact, apathy is sometimes seen as a functional requirement of stable democracies in the present circumstances – given the quality of the ordinary man, democracy would be threatened by a barbarian upsurge if he entered decisively into political life. There are clearly affinities between this picture of stable democracy and the concrete and immediate vision of reformed political life presented by Mill, in which common men would choose their leaders from among the politically active and educated minority. Mill, however, while fearing sudden mass intrusions into politics, sought the improvement and development of the ordinary man, so that his latent capacities might be drawn out, releasing him from narrowness and passivity, and making him capable of informed and concerned political activity. Moreover, his desired élite is distinguished by rationality and disinterestedness: it was not characterised by the pursuit or the achievement of economic advantage and privilege. Mill's ideals, while seemingly much more plausible than those of Marx, are far from realisation in contemporary democratic societies.

* * *

311

For the contemporary Marxist, the achievements of democratic societies – whether he dismisses them or not, and however he classifies them – pose serious problems, whose analysis requires some detachment from the incubus of inherited theory. Of course, he can find plenty of shortcomings and conflicts in these societies, which are glossed over by the protecting theories. The 'embourgeoisement' of the working class, and the pacifying consequences of embourgeoisement, are exaggerated frequently. Standards of living are not as uniformly high, nor is class consciousness as emaciated, as is suggested by those comforting claims about the fundamental problems of the industrial revolution being solved, and so on.[36] Placidity and complacency do not of themselves remove social problems and political divisions, which may take new forms and burst out openly at different points. Evils may have become less prodigious, or at least – in some ways – less blatant, and may not be fought by broad-based and distinctive class organisations, but there are powerful and passionate divisions over such crucial matters as foreign policy, racialism, education, the environment, and self-determination in many areas of life. There are telling assaults on liberal-pluralism because of its inability to respond effectively to drastic and urgent social problems – though the suggested answers commonly invoke technocratic élites, unencumbered by the shallow and ignorant popular will, rather than returning to the people. But while the more violent and confused politics of the present does not seem to be the harbinger of new mass or class movements, it is clear that the spread of consensus or non-partisanship have been exaggerated by the premature prophets of a non-political world, though their theories do reflect the fact that economic and political advancement has cut away the roots of some traditional conflicts. Moreover, there are many drab and poverty-stricken areas in these 'affluent', 'post-ideological' societies.[37] But in the first place the divisions do not occur along class lines, and in the second, the poor and discontented lack homogeneity, organisation and political significance. These things complicate, where they do not destroy, the search for a theory which defines, exposes and brings out the conflicts, instabilities and hypocrisies of 'the veiled class society', and make it difficult to find and organise a radical, practical force to battle against the system.

The basic problem, within Marxist theory, arises from the split between the proletariat and the radical criticism of capitalist society, between the practice and the theory, between the heart and the head. Marxist proletariats, which are occasionally invented anew, as a whole exist metaphorically, or in a dream. Yet the absorption of large sections of the proletariat into capitalist society has been recognised, accounted for and explained away by Marxist theorists, as it was in some respects by Marx and Engels in their analyses of opportunism. The main concerns of labour movements in Britain, America and much of Western Europe have been generally bread and butter issues – millenial aspirations have been rare. The workers accepted their golden, and baser, chains without even realising that they were imprisoned, and were unconcerned, if they knew, that security and material comfort did not amount to the independence, creativity and self-realisation which inspired Marx's original theory. It was understandable that Marxists should issue prophetic denunciations of the workers for contenting themselves with a mess of pottage rather than their birthright of freedom, and it was also understandable that the workers would not hear. Marxist critics argue, reasonably, that capitalist power has not been broken, that wealth – still extremely concentrated – and ideological strength are used to determine the acceptable forms and limits of conflict, and that many workers, along with many others, remain either frustrated or with their capacities unrealised. It is reasonable to say that they lack the equipment to make genuine or rational choices, though it is far harder to specify and create the conditions in which such choices might be made generally.

The common gap between ordinary experiences, interests and goals, on the one hand, and revolutionary social theory on the other, raises the crucial issue of consciousness, and how the usual level of working-class consciousness and aspiration are to be raised. There are two obvious and opposed responses, each beginning from a belief that, in the ordinary course of events, proletarian aspiration would remain low. Each is pessimistic about proletarian spontaneity. One drops to the existing level of consciousness, whilst the other seeks to raise it from outside. The Social Democratic path led to electoral politics and working within the system, whilst Lenin, hostile to trade union consciousness and to economism, created a vanguard party to bring enlightenment to the masses – ostensibly for the masses, but certainly despite them and, if necessary, against them. Leninist assumption and practice, above all, have led to charges of intellectual infiltration and even invention of the labour movement. Intellectuals 'verbalized the movement, supplied theories and slogans for it ... made it conscious of itself and so doing changed its meaning.'[38] But these positions, which are in one respect extremes, do not exhaust the possibilities, as the rich history of Marxism has revealed. It was not necessary to follow either Lenin into the authoritarianism of the enlightened or Bernstein into subordination to existing tendencies. It was possible for intellectuals to define and bring out the struggle which was latently or implicitly there, without dominating or creating the movement, on the one hand, or surrendering to its inertia and short-term goals on the other. This was the role Marx and Rosa Luxemburg conceived themselves as playing, as did others with less right to do so.

But history – the result of a mass of conflicting human actions – may come to the aid of the stricken consciousness. To rescue revolutionary social theory and to rescue man, some Marxists postulated an eventual return to capitalist normality, i.e. crisis (after the temporary stabilisers of imperialism and the permanent war economy), and shifted the geographical focus of the theory to colonial society or the Third World, which was, within the communist theory of imperialism, the eventual gravedigger of capitalism. But again, the Third World, as a unified revolutionary force, poised against a common, imperialistic enemy, is – like the proletariat – an intellectual construct rather than a concrete reality. There are many divisions, and rival paths and prospects, within the anti-colonial movement.

Within the advanced capitalist states themselves, the crucial problems posed by stability, the 'happy consciousness' and acquiescence, have provoked ingenious, angry, evasive and perceptive theories of many kinds. In some, Marxism tends to disappear into ethical-literary criticism reminiscent of True Socialism and Young Hegelianism. Words and inflated abstractions rule, with free-floating concepts and formulae taking over from realistic social analysis. Perceived against the simplicities of grand theory, an insistence upon concreteness, precision and the complexity of things is apt to appear less friendly to truth than to authority, less intellectual wisdom than moral cowardice. The unity and the evil of the enemy are exaggerated, and constructive radical forces are built out of nothing more substantial than dreams and wishes, or from a structural analysis which looks less at the consciousness of actual people than at how it ought to be. The vocabulary reeks with dialectic, totality, critique, over-contradiction and liberation. Revolutionary attitudinising is associated often with a romantic and backward-looking aspiration, retreating to Arcadia from cold reason, relentless technology and pervasive bureaucracy – deserting the modern world rather than seeking to seize and master it. Much contemporary radical theory is touched strongly with adventurism, élitism and romanticism. The poignancy of the Marxist position in the stable capitalist world emerges strikingly in the case of Herbert Marcuse, whose writings are instructive not so much for their solutions as for the way in which they embody some of the basic problems of social theory – socialisation, how to break through false consciousness and reach 'utopia', or what is portrayed as utopia, how to combine theory and practice. Assuming the absence of demonstrable agents and agencies of social change – especially the absence of a revolutionary proletariat – and exaggerating the homogeneity and tidiness of the system, he inclines towards a total pessimism, broken only by occasional and uncharacteristic declarations of optimism. How can true theory gain a foothold in consciousness? Comfortable, hollow, one-dimensional men, headpieces stuffed with jingles and platitudes, laugh and jeer at their tutor, or watch him passively on television while he, seeking revolutionary battalions, despairs even of the student-worker 'alliance', and retreats to the tattered army of the misfits and the outcasts, uncontaminated by the system. But neither the self-assertion of the lumpenproletariat nor the authoritarianism of free, educated men seem likely to produce that attractive but opaque future desired by the despairing prophet.

Modern capitalist societies are complex, bureaucratic, powerful and solid, and are marked by diverse overlapping conflicts – on the surface at least – and by widespread attachment to, or at least toleration of, existing institutional structures. Their considerable homogeneity – ironically, a debased version of the active, communitarian visions of Mill and especially Marx – is the result of apathy and complacency rather than the voluntary agreement of rational individuals. A more plausible image of the life of contemporary man - capitalist or communist – than that of the consensualists depicts it as grey and pointless. Kafkaesque prisoners grope about in a bizarre, remote, mocking and meaningless universe. The self-proclaimed socialist states are stolid, repressive and unimaginative bureaucracies. Domination, hierarchy, illusion and acquiescence in evil characterise all large modern societies, which have not been united by the communal ties envisaged by Marx and to a lesser extent by Mill. They have not freed man from his various dependencies, and made a free, creative individual of him. He is still not responsible for his own destiny. The evaluation of the successive forms of social life in terms of conceptions of what man is and what he has it in him to be is an unending enterprise, as are analyses of 'the facts of the case' in the light of such visions, and action in terms of them. The enterprise in unending because, as Marx never tired of affirming, societies constantly change, and as they change so do problems and possibilities, and the goals, values and nature of men, and it therefore becomes necessary to pursue in new ways the complex vision of a free and truly human community. That task becomes more difficult when the liberating ideas of one generation are allowed to become the straight-jackets of another, when serious critique passes into incantation, and serious politics degenerates into empty if defiant gestures.

Notes

INTRODUCTION

1 *Marxism. An Historical and Critical Study* (London, 1961), p. xiii.
2 *Ibid.*, pp. xiii–xiv.
3 *Ibid.*, p. 26. Emphasis mine.
4 Popper misrepresents both Hegel and Marx, and in a similar manner, in volume II of *The Open Society and its Enemies* (London, 1957). Moral positivism (Hegel) is 'the theory that there is no moral standard but the one which exists; that what is, is reasonable and good; and therefore, that might is right'. Moral futurism holds that 'coming might is right' (p. 206) or that 'History will be our judge' – which means that 'success will judge. The worship of success and of future might is the highest standard of many who would never admit that present might is right' (p. 208). In each case Popper ignores the morally impregnated philosophies of history which provide good, i.e. moral, reasons for preferring what Hegel and Marx did prefer.
5 Cf. Charles Taylor's interesting defence of the view that 'a given framework of explanation in political science tends to support an associated value position, secretes its own norms for the assessment of politics and policies'. 'Neutrality in Political Science,' in *Philosophy, Politics and Society*, 3rd series, ed. P. Laslett and W. G. Runciman (Oxford, 1967), p. 48.
6 I. Berlin, 'Does Political Theory Still Exist?'. in *Philosophy, Politics and Society*, 2nd series, P. Laslett and W. G. Runciman (Oxford, 1962), p. 2.
7 Quoted by S. Wolin, *Politics and Vision* (London, 1961), p. 22.
8 *Thought and Action* (London, 1960), pp. 197–8. In 'Vision and Choice in Morality' (*Supplementary Volume of the Aristotelian Society*, 1956), Iris Murdoch presents a similar view of moral disagreements. She treats some moral differences as like differences of vision rather than like differences of choice, given the same facts. 'We differ not only because we select different objects out of the same world but because we see different worlds' (pp. 40–1). Hence moral differences, or at least fundamental moral differences, are held to be conceptual, so that the situation or the facts do not remain the same if the concept is withdrawn.
9 *The Structure of Scientific Revolutions* (Chicago, 1970), p. 7.
10 Initially Kuhn defined paradigms as 'universally recognised scientific achievements that for a time provide model problems and solutions to a community of practitioners', p. viii. In the postscript to the enlarged 1970 edition, he recognises certain difficulties confronting such a view of the paradigm, and suggests instead the term 'disciplinary matrix', confining paradigm to 'shared example'. Supp., pp. 181–91.
11 25 March 1868, *Selected Correspondence*, p. 242.
12 So Professor Gallie discerns the fundamental cleavage between liberal and socialist morality within as well as between individuals. What could be

more natural, he asks, than that 'the main claims and tenets of each of them – and more, the main springs of appeal and inspiration peculiar to each – should have passed into all or most of us, unobtrusively and perhaps even insensibly, in the course of our education, reading, and day-to-day discussion of political and moral issues?' 'Liberal Morality and Socialist Morality', *Philosophy, Politics and Society*, ed. P. Laslett (Oxford, 1956), p. 121. Of course, such a process seems most likely in a liberal society, in which the legitimacy of the competing doctrines is accepted – and when, the sceptic might add, the distance between them is not very great.

13 The one-sidedness characteristic of Burke's account of radical action and aspiration in France also characterises, to take one example, much recent liberal history of anarchism. Chomsky demonstrates how historians gripped by the prevalent liberal ideology were predisposed against the forces of popular revolution in Spain, and looked instinctively to the anarchists as the villains of the piece. *American Power and the New Mandarins* (New York, 1969), pp. 74–124.

14 In 'Epistemology and Politics', *Proceedings of the Aristotelian Society, 1957–8*, J. W. N. Watkins argues that political doctrines may stand in a peculiarly dependent relation to a metaphysical doctrine, so that the latter may be said to 'endorse' or 'sanction' them. As an instance, he cites the relation between Marx's revolutionary programme and his historicist view of history, pp. 80–1. I would not describe this relationship as a peculiarly dependent one, largely because I rate Marx's specific analysis of capitalism and his moral fervour highly, but it is certainly true that the one supports the other.

15 Feuer, 'Karl Marx and the Promethean Complex', *Encounter*, December 1968, p. 16.

16 There are tremendous problems concerning definitions of fantasy and lunacy, which are generally settled, in practice, by reference to a 'community of discourse' or the norms and habits of particular societies, or majorities in particular societies. From other standpoints those norms and habits may seem absurd, even insane, and it must be left open for the critic of society to reject normal practices and assumptions on this ground and perhaps to treat its pathological cases as in fact its most insightful or liberated citizens – as, for example, R. D. Laing tends to do. Recent Russian psychiatry provides blatant examples of political dissent being treated as a form of mental illness. According to one of I. F. Stone's reports, the chief psychiatrist in the Ministry of Health – Dr Andrei Snezhnevsky – has spoken of 'obsessive reformist delusions' as a variety of mental illness requiring hospitalisation. 'Betrayed by Psychiatry', *The New York Review of Books*, 10 February 1972, p. 8.

17 London: Mercury Books, 1962, p. 313.

18 Cf. Freud's distinction between plausible and nonsensical statements. He writes that if 'a person comes along who seriously asserts that the centre of the earth is made of jam', the result will be 'a division of our interests; instead of their being directed on the investigation itself, as to whether the interior of the earth is really made of jam or not, we shall wonder what kind of man it must be who can get such an idea into his head'. *New Introductory Lectures on Psychoanalysis* (New York, 1953), pp. 48–9.

19 Marx himself is sometimes treated in this way, e.g. by Lewis Feuer in 'Karl Marx and the Promethean Complex'. Feuer stresses Marx's aggressiveness, and writes that Marx's spirit 'required struggle à *outrance*, and the Bourgeois order had to be misperceived, if necessary, to justify struggle against each of its parts', p. 28. One gets the general impression that Marx should have sought medical treatment rather than tried to change society – at

least his hostility to society would have diminished if he had not been so hung up. Unfortunately, although Feuer does present a few interesting pieces of information, his evidence is a mere ragbag of anecdote and concrete detail, from which he derives a simple, crude picture of Marx's psychological state, and then leaps – with a minimum of causal link-up – to Marx's social theories, allegedly explained by the psychological substructure, and thereby condemned.

20 For example, Professor Popper finds great dangers in Cartesianism and in Bacon's view of Nature which, he believes, share the epistemological doctrine that truth is manifest. 'The theory that truth is manifest – that it is there for everyone to see, if only he wants to see it – this theory is the basis of almost every kind of fanaticism. For only the most depraved wickedness can refuse to see the manifest truth; only those who have every reason to fear truth can deny it, and conspire to suppress it.' *On the Sources of Knowledge and Ignorance*, reprinted in *Conjectures and Refutations* (London, 1963), p. 8.

21 Kolakowski, *Permanent vs. Transitory Aspects of Marxism* in *Marxism and Beyond* (London, 1971), p. 200.

22 A philosopher revising a theory or tradition – as Aristotle to Plato or Locke to Hobbes – will normally bring out clearly the issues in dispute. In recognised and particular polemics between rival contemporaries, as Marx against the Young Hegelians, or Rosa Luxemburg against the Revisionists, or the Chinese against the Italian Communists, issues in dispute may be accentuated and clarified, or may be confused in the effort to vilify the enemy and improve one's own image. With Marx and Mill conflicting points of view are sometimes only vaguely intimated, and must be guessed at from a variety of scattered statements.

23 Hence the plausible element in Ollman's stress on the centrality of internal relations to Marxism – in the claim that, 'no matter which of Marx's theories we begin with, to draw out all its relations is to present Marxism, through it is the whole observed from a particular angle and expressed in a one-sided way.' B. Ollman, *Alienation. Marx's Conception of Man in Capitalist Society* (Cambridge, 1971) p. 231.

24 J. Salwyn Schapiro. Comment on Lewis Feuer's 'Discussion of John Stuart Mill and Marxian Socialism', *Journal of the History of Ideas*, IV (1943), 304.

25 Marx to Weydemeyer, 2 August 1851. *Marx and Engels: Letters to Americans* (New York, 1953), p. 24.

26 Quoted Feuer, 'Karl Marx and the Promethean Complex', p. 28.

27 Talmon's three-volume work is entitled *The History of Totalitarian Democracy*. The completed volumes are *The Origins of Totalitarian Democracy* (vol. I) and *Political Messianism. The Romantic Phase* (vol. II).

28 Talmon claims to be defining 'the inner logic of political Messianism', and hence pays little attention to misinterpretations of particular theories. As he writes 'The continuity of a tradition matters more than the authenticity of the interpretation of the canon.' *Political Messianism* (London, 1960), p. 8. It may matter more to Talmon and perhaps to us, but such a focus may lead – as in Talmon's case with Rousseau – to gross, ahistorical caricatures of theories in terms of later developments.

29 *The Origins of Totalitarian Democracy* (London, 1961), p. 254.

30 *Ibid.*, p. 2.

31 *Ibid.*, pp. 12, 12, n. 257, 254 and 5.

32 Cohn, *The Pursuit of the Millennium*, pp. 309–10. One important question concerns the preconditions to and the time of the supposed consummation of history or achievement of a unanimous community. Talmon declares that in a totalitarian democracy the state of ideal harmony is 'precisely

defined, and is treated as a matter of immediate urgency, a challenge for direct action, an imminent event'. *Origins*, p. 2. Yet Rousseau, Talmon's first major totalitarian subject, did not predict the coming of a state of harmony, imminent or otherwise, and did not argue its universal relevance. He seems to have remained pessimistic and deeply conscious of the limited validity of his ideal.

33 *Ibid.*, p. 249.
34 *Ibid.*, p. 264.
35 *Ibid.*, p. 2.
36 *Ibid.*, p. 255.
37 *Ibid.*, p. 254.
38 *Ibid.*, p. 254.
39 *Ibid.*, p. 259.
40 *Marxism: The View from America* (New York, 1960), p. 144.

THE BACKGROUND

1 E.g. Hegel: 'A constitution, therefore, was established in harmony with the conception of Right, and on this foundation all future legislation was to be based. Never since the sun had stood still in the firmament and the planets revolved around him had it been perceived that man's existence centres in his head, i.e. in Thought, inspired by which he builds up the world of reality...This was accordingly a glorious mental dawn. All thinking beings shared in the jubilation of the epoch. Emotions of a lofty character stirred men's minds at that time; a spiritual enthusiasm thrilled through the world, as if the reconciliation between the Divine and the Secular was now first accomplished.' *The Philosophy of History* (New York, 1956), p. 447.
2 *An Essay on the Principle of Population*, first edition (reprinted London, 1926), p. 2.
3 *Reflections on the Revolution in France* (London, 1955), p. 73.
4 This issue did not arise suddenly. For example, R. H. Tawney has taken the contraction of the sphere of religion and the assertion of the independence of economics to be a key development in fifteenth- and sixteenth-century Western Europe (although they existed much earlier). 'The isolation of economic aims as a specialized object of concentrated and systematic effort, the erection of economic criteria into an independent and authoritative standard of social expediency, are phenomena which, though familiar enough in classical antiquity, appear, at least on a grand scale, only at a comparatively recent date in the history of later civilizations.' *Religion and the Rise of Capitalism* (London, 1948), p. 272. It often seems that the early nineteenth-century critics of capitalism were fighting a battle which had already been lost.
5 F. Tönnies, *Gemeinschaft und Gesellschaft*, 1887. This general distinction is an old one, in that philosophers and historians have often contrasted family and contractual or market-type societies. The distinction gained particular force with the development of industrial capitalism, and Tönnies himself witnessed the disintegration of his native rural society – Schleswig-Holstein – under the impact of mechanisation and commercialisation. Tönnies regarded pure natural or brotherly relations and pure contractual relations as ideal types. 'What they represent are ideal types, and they should serve as standards by which reality may be recognised and described.' *Community and Society*. Loomis translation (New York, 1963), p. 248.
6 *The Condition of the Working-Class in England in 1844* (London, 1950), p. 24.

7 For a detailed account of various meanings of 'individualism' – in France, Germany, America and England – see Steven Lukes, *Individualism* (Oxford, 1973), pp. 3–42.

8 'The Communist Manifesto', *Selected Works* (Moscow, 1962), I, 55.

9 *The Condition of the Working-Class*, p. 1.

10 The various machines – the lathe, the spinning jenny, the steam engine and so on – had first to be invented, and required certain favourable conditions before they could be widely utilised. But my concern here is not with the first cause of industrial change – a matter which is often discussed in relation to a vulgarised version of historical materialism – but with the impact of technology, when introduced.

11 See Hobsbawm, *Industry and Empire* (London, 1968), pp. 53–4.

12 Deane, Phyllis and Cole, W. A. *British Economic Growth: 1688–1959* (Cambridge, 1964), p. 192. Marx quotes the factory inspector Redgrave on the effects of steam power, 'The steam-engine is the parent of manufacturing towns'. *Capital* (Moscow, 1961), I, 377, n. 3.

13 For a somewhat flat description of the historical debate between pessimists and optimists, see Brian Inglis, 'The Poor Who Were With Us', *Encounter*, September 1971. The leading protagonists at present are Eric Hobsbawm and E. P. Thompson, pessimists, and R. M. Hartwell, optimist. For a defence of capitalism against the strictures and obloquies of radical historians, see F. von Hayek (ed.), *Capitalism and the Historians* (Chicago, 1963).

14 The population of Great Britain and Ireland increased from 16,000,000 in 1800 to 25,000,000 in 1830. In Great Britain alone it grew from less than 11,000,000 in 1801 to over 21,000,000 in 1851.

15 According to Kitson Clark, about one-half of the population of Great Britain still lived in 'rural conditions' in 1851 – up to which time the natural increase was absorbed by the towns. *The Making of Victorian England* (London, 1965), p. 115. Clark suggests that urbanisation, mechanisation and factories 'had not penetrated as deeply into the life of the community as perhaps we are apt to think'. *Ibid.*, p. 118.

16 *Journeys to England and Ireland*, quoted by E. Hobsbawm, *The Age of Revolution* (London, 1962), p. 27.

17 *Philosophy of Manufactures*, quoted by E. P. Thompson, *The Making of the English Working Class* (Harmondsworth, 1968), p. 487.

18 In *The Great Transformation* (Boston, 1957) Karl Polanyi provides an interesting critique of the market economy in terms of its destruction of community. The quoted phrases are from p. 157, where he also complains that man suffered 'lethal injury to the institutions in which his social existence is embodied'.

19 The question is posed because of the crude contrasts that are often made. We must know precisely which periods and which groups are being contrasted with each other, as well as requiring that each is characterised adequately. We cannot talk of the labouring class as a composite mass, but neither can we go through an indefinite number of case-histories, even if we had the evidence. And particular case-histories would normally be set within the context of a general view conceived earlier, or independently.

20 *The Making of the English Working Class*, p. 487.

21 'The Rising Standard of Living in England, 1800–1850', *Economic History Review*, 2nd series, XIII (1961), no. 3. Hartwell bases his argument on an examination of national income and other aggregate statistics, from wage–price data and from analogy; from an analysis of consumption figures; and from the evidence of vital statistics, from a comparison with eighteenth-century living standards, and from details of the expansion after 1800 of social and economic opportunities. Briefly his argument is that 'since

average per capita income increased, since there was no trend in distribution against the workers, since (after 1815) prices fell while money wages remained constant, since per capita consumption of food and other consumer goods increased, and since government increasingly intervened in economic life to protect or raise living standards, then the real wages of the majority of English workers were rising in the years 1800 to 1850'.

22 *Industry and Empire*, p. 74, and *Labouring Men* (London, 1968), p. 124.

23 It is commonly assumed, after Marx, that capitalism required and found a reservoir of exploitable labour, or 'a reserve army of the unemployed'. However, we seem to be ignorant of the overall quantitative significance of unemployment, at least during the early phases of the industrial revolution. Deane and Cole argue that 'in the early part of the century the probability is that unemployment took the form of short time rather than complete idleness, that it was widespread throughout the economy and that it was highly variable from year to year'. *British Economic Growth*, p. 250. The vulnerability of the labour force was increased by its exclusive dependence on wages with the disappearance of traditional side-resources, such as plots of land.

24 *The Christian and Civil Economy of Large Towns* (Glasgow, 1821), I, 27.

25 Census Report of 1851–53 on Religious Worship, quoted by T. R. Tholfsen, 'The Transition to Democracy in Victorian England', *International Review of Social History*, VI, no. 2 (1961), 232.

26 *The Age of Revolution*, p. 209.

27 In the quoted passage, Hobsbawm speaks of the proletariat as if it were an entity – it had the need for permanent mobilisation impressed upon it. It, or some proletarian leaders? On p. 210 he speaks of proletarian class consciousness and social aspirations being present by the 1830s, though feebler than that of the middle class. On p. 211 he speaks, again in relation to the 1830s, of 'the cohesive solidarity and loyalty which were so characteristic of the new proletariat'. He refers on p. 213 to 'the programme and ideology of the proletariat' (after 1815), despite the fact that the industrial and factory working class as yet rarely existed. There is throughout, as with Marx, a tendency to superimpose a mythical proletariat on the actual class, whose divisions and immaturity are often acutely observed.

28 *The Making of the English Working Class*, p. 10.

29 *Ibid.*, p. 11.

30 *Ibid.*, pp. 9–10.

31 *Ibid.*, p. 12.

32 There were a few instances of successful combinations before this time, e.g. the Kent papermakers and the millwrights. See P. Mantoux, *The Industrial Revolution in the Eighteenth Century* (London, 1966), pp. 444–6.

33 *Capital*, I, 429.

34 S. and B. Webb, *History of Trade Unionism* (London, 1902), p. 87.

35 *Labouring Men*, p. 8.

36 *The Making of the English Working Class*, p. 603.

37 *The Condition of the Working Class*, p. 214.

38 G. Rudé, *The Crowd in History 1730–1848* (New York, 1964), p. 183.

39 On 18 March 1852, Engels praised Jones because, enlightened by the Marxist doctrine, he had found out how to widen 'the instinctive class hatred of the workers against the industrial bourgeoisie', while opposing 'the reactionary cravings of the workers and their prejudices'. *Selected Correspondence*, pp. 87–8. In the late fifties Engels complained about Jones's efforts to bring about an alliance with the bourgeoisie – efforts which Engels took to be bound up with the fact that 'the English proletariat is actually becoming more and more bourgeois, so that this most bourgeois of all nations is

apparently aiming ultimately at the possession of a bourgeois aristocracy and a bourgeois proletariat alongside the bourgeoisie'. 8 October 1858. *Selected Correspondence*, pp. 132–3.

40 Chartism's periods of greatest success were from spring 1837 to January 1840, summer 1842 (the 'plug riots') and spring and summer of 1848. Its periods of vitality are in large part traceable to trade depressions.

41 J. Vincent, *Pollbooks: How Victorians Voted* (Cambridge, 1967), p. 20.

42 *Ibid.*, p. 7.

43 Vincent treats class as a mental convenience, as perhaps a weak potentiality but not an actual force. It is not surprising that Thompson describes Dahrendorf's study of class, which impressed Vincent greatly, as 'obsessively concerned with methodology, to the exclusion of the examination of a single real class situation in a real historical context'. *The Making of the English Working Class*, p. 11.

44 Asa Briggs, 'The Language of 'Class' in Early Nineteenth-Century England', *Essays in Labour History*, ed. A. Briggs and J. Saville (London, 1967), p. 69.

45 Quoted Vincent, *Pollbooks*, p. 17.

46 *Studies in the Development of Capitalism* (London, 1963), pp. 265–5.

47 *Address to the Trade Unions*, published by the Manhood Suffrage and Vote by Ballot Association, and written by either Applegarth or George Howell. Quoted by H. Pelling, *A History of British Trade Unionism* (London, 1965), p. 62.

48 The motive is ordinary enough. Seeking to gain class support, Disraeli assumed (falsely) in 1867 that, if the franchise had to go down to the £6 petit-bourgeois, it should go right down to the town workers, whom he envisaged as the natural enemies of their Liberal employers, and hence Tory. In 1884 Gladstone assumed (falsely) that the country labourers, as natural enemies of the Tory squires, would vote Liberal.

49 Quoted Tholfsen, 'Transition', p. 241.

50 *Manchester Guardian*, 14 October 1858.

51 The 1832 Reform Bill did considerably increase the political power of the middle class, though it did not quite amount to what one historian has called 'the Magna Carta of the English middle class, which in the realm of politics crowned the industrial revolution'. Mantoux, *The Industrial Revolution in the Eighteenth Century*, p. 398. The Reform Act increased the representation of the growing industrial cities, though the electorate was not much enlarged—it grew from 650,00 to 800,000, which still left four-fifths of the adult male population without the vote. The repeal of the Corn Laws in 1846 did mark a significant victory for the cities. I do not mean to suggest that the middle classes, which rose to power in some parts of Western Europe through revolution, and in other parts through peaceful pressure, were homogeneous, despite common interests – usually – in curbing the power of monarchs and aristocrats. There were persistent divisions within the bourgeoisie, e.g. in England between the mercantile interests originally centred around the East India Company and the manufacturers and industrialists.

52 Ernest Jones, that one-time seeming Communist, was reported in the *Birmingham Daily Post* (27 November 1867) as saying: 'Back to the land. It is your only safeguard against the assaults of capital. Talk of confiscating wealth. I propose to give it a legion of additional defenders. It is a national regenerator. Give us a million peasant farmers.'

53 Vincent, *Pollbooks*, p. 32.

54 *The Age of Revolution*, p. 236. They were not, in Hobsbawm's view, 'mere special pleaders for the vested interests of businessmen', but 'they were men who believed, with considerable historical justification at this period,

that the way forward for humanity was through capitalism'. *Ibid,.* p. 238.
55 Quoted by J. Viner, *The Long View and the Short* (Glencoe, 1958), p. 233.
56 After 1830, when the bourgeoisie took power, claimed Marx, scientific bourgeois economy passed away. 'In place of disinterested inquirers, there were hired prize-fighters; in place of genuine scientific research the bad conscience and the evil intent of apologetic.' Afterword to the second German edition of *Capital*. *Capital*, I., 15.
57 The policy of Europe, he complained, 'nowhere leaves things at perfect liberty', and thus causes unnecessary inequalities: 'It does this chiefly in the three following ways. First, by restricting the competition in some employments to a smaller number than would otherwise be disposed to enter into them; secondly by increasing it in others beyond what it naturally would be; and thirdly, by obstructing the free circulation of labour and stock, both from employment and from place to place.' *The Wealth of Nations* (London, Everyman), I, 107.
58 *Ibid.*, p. 24.
59 *Lectures*, quoted Viner, p. 215.
60 *Theory of Moral Sentiments*, quoted Wolin, p. 299.
61 These interferences with natural liberty include provision for coinage and public hygiene, usury laws (restricting the maximum rate of interest to 5%), in some cases the regulation of foreign trade, and proposals for differential taxation. These include important policies which would not be carried out by private agency. Hence Smith's approach to government is not doctrinaire, partly because he recognised that in some cases government was wiser than individual merchants.
62 *General Idea of Revolution in the Nineteenth Century*, quoted by Wolin, p. 414.
63 *Lectures*, quoted Viner, *The Long View and the Short*, p. 218. Smith was concerned primarily with the effective sources of behaviour, and did not pay a great deal of attention to motives generally regarded as more noble but, in his view, lacking in efficacy. His self-interest is extensive, as it includes the interest of one's circle, and also, through the doctrine of the impartial spectator ('the man within the breast'), draws in self-esteem, shame and remorse. Thus self-interest becomes enlightened, through education and incentive, and enlarged, through sympathy, fellow-feeling and a desire to avoid the adverse judgment of others.
64 Quoted by J. M. Burrow, *Evolution and Society* (Cambridge, 1966), p. 10.
65 The familiar view of Adam Smith as an extreme optimist who backed his belief in a system of natural liberty by a suspiciously theological *deus ex machina* – an invisible hand guiding and harmonising individual efforts – is rather simplified. There are certainly elements of theism in his *Theory of Moral Sentiments*, where Smith speaks of 'the great Director of nature', 'the author of Nature', 'an invisible hand' and 'the divine being'. Quoted Viner, *The Long View and the Short*, p. 217. In *The Wealth of Nations* Smith's account is completely naturalistic – he was offering economic and sociological explanations of the social order.
66 *The Wealth of Nations*, I 12. Polanyi, *The Great Transformation*, pp. 44, 58 and 276, provides some evidence that such a propensity is not natural, in that it is not a feature of non-market societies. The classical economists seem to have projected backwards, and described as natural, characteristics of their own society.
67 *Ibid.*, p. 11. R. L. Meek quotes J. Harris, *An Essay upon Money and Coins* (1757) as holding that the 'chief cement' holding men together in society was the fact that they lived 'by betaking themselves to particular arts

and employments', and exchanged the various products. *Economics and Ideology and Other Essays* (London, 1967), p. 204.

68 *Ibid.*, p. 13.
69 *Ibid.*, p. 10.
70 Cf. E. Heimann, *History of Economic Doctrines* (Oxford, 1962). Heimann suggests that the free economy was seen 'to constitute an order in which specialised functions interlock as under a plan. In the absence of a visible mechanism for organizing and integrating economic activities, the operation of a hidden, but nonetheless effective, mechanism for this purpose must be assumed' (p. 9). By 'order' Heimann understands simply highly specific arrangements making any kind of life possible.
71 *The Wealth of Nations*, p. 59. Cf. also his remark that 'people of the same trade seldom meet together, even for merriment and diversion, but the conversation ends in a conspiracy against the public, or in some contrivance to raise prices'. *Ibid.*, p. 117.
72 *Ibid.*, p. 230.
73 *Ibid.*, p. 51. Labour, in Smith's view, was 'the real measure of the exchangeable value of all commodities' (p. 26). In the 'early and rude stage of society' undifferentiated labour could function as the determinant of value, but with the advance of society allowances were increasingly made for variations in hardship and in skill. Variations were adjusted, not by accurate measure, but by 'the higgling and bargaining of the market' (p. 27).
74 *Ibid.*, p. 61.
75 *Ibid.*, p. 60.
76 *Ibid.*, p. 65.
77 *Ibid.*, p. 71.
78 *The Poverty of Philosophy*, p. 55. But, with some of Ricardo's successors, Marx assumed that cynicism was also in the writers. As Meek points out, Ricardo did advance on Smith's theory of value, and was 'virtually the first to fashion anything like a consistent theory of value from the notion that it was not the capitalist's expenditure on subsistence goods for his workmen but the expenditure of energy by the workmen themselves which conferred value on commodities'. Meek, *Economics and Ideology*, p. 66.
79 Quoted by E. Cannon, *Introduction to 'The Wealth of Nations'* (London, 1961), p. xxiv.
80 *The Wealth of Nations*, p. 72.
81 *An Essay on the Principle of Population*, seventh edition (London, 1872), p. 421.
82 Quoted Wolin, p. 487, n. 102.
83 A *Essay on the Principle of Population* (1872), p. vii. In the first edition Malthus wrote that the view of human life given by the author has 'a melancholy line; but feels conscious, that he has drawn these dark tints, from a conviction that they are really in the picture; and not from a jaundiced eye, or an inherent spleen of disposition'. 1926 reprint, p. iv. The changes between the first and the second editions were more substantial than Malthus implied, and than many noticed, especially in relation to the increased significance of moral restraint in the latter.
84 1872 edition, p. 9.
85 To many critics, Malthus's advice seemed puerile – a typical parson's misunderstanding of the real passionate world and a piece of inhuman middle-class preaching to the most suffering class. Carlyle lampooned the Malthusians as follows 'Smart Sally in our alley proves all-too-fascinating to brisk Tom in yours: can Tom be called on to make pause, and calculate

the demand for labour in the British Empire first? .... O Wonderful Malthusian prophets! Millenniums are undoubtedly coming, must come one way or the other; but will it be, think you, by twenty millions of working people simultaneously striking work in that department?' Quoted R. Williams, *Culture and Society* (Harmondsworth, 1962), p. 94.

86 1872 edition, p. 478.

87 *Ibid.*, p. 435. Malthus criticised many governments, and admitted the justifiability of relieving distress in instances 'not arising from idle and improvident habits' (p. 470). But these straws were light indeed compared with the weigth of his attack on the common people.

88 *Ibid.*, p. 423.

89 *Ibid.*, p. 481.

90 *Ibid.*, p. 470.

91 *Ibid.*, pp. 440–1.

92 *Ibid.*, p. 477.

93 *Ibid.*, p. 474.

94 *Ibid.*, p. 474.

95 *Ibid.*, p. 480.

96 Letter to Malthus, October 1820, quoted by R. M. Hartwell, *Introduction to 'Principles of Political Economy and Taxation'* (Harmondsworth, 1971), pp. 15–16.

97 Preface to *The Principles of Political Economy and Taxation* (London, 1962), p. 1.

98 Ricardo to Malthus, 9 October 1820, cited by R. M. Hartwell, *The Rising Standard of Living in England, 1800–1850*, p. 401.

99 *An Essay on the Influence of a Low Price of Corn on the Profits of Stock*, 24 February 1815, quoted by Hartwell, *Introduction to 'Principles'*, p.26.

100 *Principles of Political Economy and Taxation*, p. 264.

101 Meek, *Economics and Ideology*, p. 64.

102 'Lectures on Political Economy', 1833, quoted by Meek, *Economics and Ideology*, p. 69. On p. 71 Meek quotes the economist Scrope, recalling in 1873 how inadequate the prevailing political economy – Ricardo, James Mill, Malthus, Maculloch, etc. – seemed when the many (!) were to enter politics after the passing of the first Reform Bill. 'I could not discover in them any answer likely to satisfy the mind of a half-educated man of plain commonsense and honesty who should seek there some justification for the immense disparity of fortunes and circumstances that strike the eye on every side.'

103 Quoted by E. Halevy, *Thomas Hodgskin* (London, 1956), p. 50. The classical economists had also pointed, though less sharply, to the tendency of capitalism to create a mass of idlers (Malthus), and unproductive and unfairly privileged consumers, such as landowners (Ricardo).

104 J. F. Bray, *Labour's Wrongs and Labour's Remedy* (Leeds, 1839), p. 67.

105 Thomas Hodgskin, *Labour Defended Against the Claims of Capital*, first published 1825 (London, 1932), p. 80. He was a Ricardian in the sense that he regarded labour as the producer of all revenue.

106 Hodgskin defended natural ownership against the Communism of Owen and others. 'The use of such things, like the making of them, must be individual, not common, selfish, not general. It is the right of each individual to own for his separate and selfish use whatever he can make.' Halevy, *Thomas Hodgskin*, p. 118. He condemned the interferences of Communists and Socialists, and of governments, with the natural law.

107 Quoted Meek, *Economics and Ideology*, p. 72.

108 *Capital*, I, 616, n. 2.

2 MAN AND COMMUNITY

1 'The Communism of the *Rheinischer Beobachter*, 1847', *On Religion* (Moscow: undated), p. 84.
2 *Contribution to the Critique of Hegel's Philosophy of Right* in *Karl Marx. Early Writings*, trans. and ed. T. B. Bottomore (London, 1963), p. 44.
3 *Ibid.*, p. 52.
4 *Capital*, I, 184. The process is that in which 'man of his own accord starts, regulates, and controls the material re-actions between himself and nature' (p. 177).
5 *Ibid.*, p. 184.
6 *Ibid.*, p. 179.
7 *Ibid.*, p. 178.
8 *Pre-Capitalist Economic Formations*, E. J. Hobsbawn (London, 1964), p. 69. This work consists of a self-contained section of the *Grundrisse*, translated by J. Cohen, and a lengthy introduction by Hobsbawn.
9 *Economic and Philosophical Manuscripts of 1844*, trans. Martin Mulligan (Moscow, 1959), p. 76.
10 *Ibid.*, p. 104. The economic and social conditions under which labour is carried on may permit 'the natural unity of labour with its material prerequisites'. *Pre-Capitalist Economic Formations*, p. 67. They also may not.
11 Quoted by L. D. Easton and K. H. Guddat, *Writings of the Young Marx on Philosophy and Society* (New York, 1967), p. 24.
12 *The Holy Family*, trans. R. Dixon (Moscow, 1956), p. 254.
13 *Critique of Hegel's Dialectic, Early Writings*, p. 198. As Marx put it in the *1844 Manuscripts*, 'Real man and real nature become mere predicates— symbols of this esoteric, unreal man and of this unreal nature. Subject and predicate are therefore related to each other in absolute inversion' (p. 166).
14 *The German Ideology*, trans. S. Ryazanshaya (Moscow, 1964), p. 135.
15 *The Holy Family*, p. 254.
16 While praising Feuerbach, Marx imputed to him the belief that the degrading 'spectre of abstractions' might be destroyed by exposure of the human and social origins of religious beliefs. He ignored completely Feuerbach's references to science and industry as destroying religion.
17 *The Holy Family*, p. 15.
18 *Critique of Hegel's Dialectic, Early Writings*, p. 202.
19 *Capital*, I, 177.
20 *Pre-Capitalist Economic Formations*, p. 93.
21 For an elaboration, see J. O'Malley, 'History and Man's "Nature" in Marx', *The Review of Politics*, XXVIII, (1966). Western commerce was faced at first with large problems in stagnant and unproductive societies, which lacked the needs or wants which fed it, and which it eventually stimulated. 'Absence of wants, and predilection for hereditary modes of dress, are obstacles which civilized commerce has to encounter in all new markets'. 'Trade with China', *New York Tribune*, 3 December 1859. Printed in S. Avineri, ed., *Karl Marx on Colonialism and Modernization* (New York, 1969), p. 396.
22 *Marx's Grundrisse*, selected and translated D. McLellan (London, 1971), p. 125. Marx argued that, in a dialectical process, production produced the material or object of consumption, the mode of consumption, and the need for the object. 'The need felt for the object is induced by the perception of the object. An *object d'art* creates a public that has artistic taste and is able to enjoy beauty – and the same can be said of any other product Production accordingly produces not only an object for the subject, but also a subject for the object'. Introduction to *A Contribution to the*

Critique of Political Economy, trans. S. Ryazanskaya (London, 1971), p. 197.

23 Ibid., p. 197.
24 Pre-capitalist Economic Formations, pp. 84-5.
25 1844 Manuscripts, p. 116.
26 The Poverty of Philosophy, p. 165.
27 The German Ideology, p. 56.
28 Ibid., p. 331.
29 The Communist Manifesto, Selected Works, I, 58.
30 Capital, I, 609, n. 2.
31 Book review, by Marx and Engels, of two of Carlyle's Latter-Day Pamphlets. On Literature, pp. 110-11.
32 Capital, I, 632.
33 To Lassalle, 16 January 1861, Selected Correspondence, p. 151.
34 Engels dismissed the philosophers' rational social order − their kingdom of reason − as 'nothing more than the idealized kingdom of the bourgeoisie'. Socialism Utopian and Scientific, Selected Works, II, 117. The charge is far too generalised. Such a work as Mably's Code de la Nature, for example, is not at all bourgeois in spirit.
35 The German Ideology, p. 62.
36 'Contribution to the Critique of Hegel's Philosophy of Right', On Religion, p. 54.
37 On Religion, p. 26.
38 The Origin of the Family, Private Property and the State, Selected Works, II, 225-6. Cf. also p. 325: 'Every advance in production is at the same time a retrogression in the condition of the oppressed class, that is, of the great majority. What is a boon for the one is necessarily a bane for the other; each new emancipation of one class always means a new oppression for another class.'
39 Marx and Engels did not have any detailed knowledge of primitive societies before the late sixties. They were strongly influenced by George Von Maurer's work, and later and more particularly by Lewis Morgan's Ancient Society (1877).
40 The Origin of the Family, p. 253. Engels does not indicate the nature of the quarrels and disputes that do emerge.
41 S. Avineri, The Social and Political Thought of Karl Marx (Cambridge, 1970), p. 103. Avineri is here paraphrasing the Grundisse.
42 Ibid., p. 255.
44 Ludwig Feuerbach and the End of Classical German Philosophy, Selected Works, II, 382. Between this and the preceding quotation a significant difference is apparent − in the first 'the lowest interests' usher in class society, while in the second 'the wicked passions' have, since the emergence of class antagonisms, served as levers of historical development. In neither case are we told whence the wicked passions came, but in one they are certainly ascribed a more original if not a more important role. Analysis of their origins is certainly relevant to predictions of their disappearance.

Affinities with Rousseau, who also felt tremendous moral revulsion towards inequality and egoism, are clear. Rousseau lamented the events following the appearance of metallurgy, and agriculture. Iron and Corn, he claimed, produced a great revolution, 'which first civilized man, and ruined him' (The Origin of Inequality. Everyman, p. 199). Man's moral structure and the social structure changed together − society was subjected to the rivalry and competition of conflicting interests, and inequality appeared, linked with the development of property, while men lost their sense of compassion and became subject to new, unstabilizing wants. All became slaves. The wealthy revealed a greed as strong as that of Marx's capitalists, with their 'vampire thirst for the living blood of labour' – they were 'like ravenous wolves, which, having once tasted human flesh, despise every other food and thenceforth seek only men to devour' (p. 203). Ultimately, a supreme arbitrating power was introduced to contain civil discord. 'Such was, or may well have been, the origin of society and law, which bound new fetters on the poor, and gave new powers to the rich' (p. 205).

45 *The Origin of the Family*, p. 266.
46 There are numerous difficulties and imprecisions in Engels's account of the appearance of the division of labour, classes and the state. Most of these cannot be pursued here. However, it is worth noting his claim that the old society was 'burst asunder by the division of labour and by its result, the division of society into classes' (*Ibid.*, p. 318). The division of labour explanation of classes is reasonably consistent, but there is some variation in the meaning of the 'classes' which create the need for the state. At some points it appears that the state emerges because of a complex division of labour which produces rival occupational groups (and there were at least separate occupational groups in primitive society) which are not yet classes in the specific Marxian sense, i.e. economic groups defined by the possession or non-possession of property in the means of production. There were two stages in the development of the division of labour – the appearance of economic differentiation, and the utilisation by some persons of their positions to accumulate possessions, control the labour power of others and bequeath their possessions to their children. Only in the second stage were there classes in the Marxian sense. For a fuller discussion, see J. Plamenatz, *Man and Society* (London, 1963), ch. 6.
47 *The German Ideology*, p. 66.
48 *On the Jewish Question, Early Writings*, p. 29.
49 'The Future Results of the British Rule in India', *New York Daily Tribune*, no. 3480, 8 August, 1853. *On Colonialism*, p. 80.
50 *Ibid.*, p. 81.
51 In his discussion of Russian conditions and possibilities after the late fifties, e.g. his letters to Vera Zasulich, he emphasised the strength and vitality of the primitive communes, which could perhaps move peacefully onto a higher historical form. See *Selected Correspondence*, p. 412. The very important drafts and sketches of his letter to Zasulich are printed, as a composite piece, by P. W. Blackstock and B. F. Haselity (eds.), *The Russian Menace to Europe* (London, 1953), pp. 218–26.
52 *New York Daily Tribune*, No. 3804, 25 July, 1853. *On Colonialism*, pp. 36–7.
53 *A Contribution to the Critique of Political Economy*, p. 189.
54 Avineri, *Social and Political Thought*, pp. 113-14.
55 *Capital*, I, 762.
56 *Ibid.*, p. 760.
57 *The Poverty of Philosophy*, p. 36. But consider Auden's lines:
> Money cannot buy
> the fuel of Love,
> but is excellent kindling.
58 In *The Communist Manifesto*, Marx seems to have objected to the abuse – not the use – of the concept of alienation. He criticised the True Socialists for using vague philosophical language as a substitute for empirical social analysis. For a discussion – itself rather flabby – of some loose and flabby ideas of alienation, see Lewis Feuer, 'What is Alienation? The Career of a Concept', *New Politics*, Spring 1962. What is required is a clear specification of the meaning attached to the term, rather than its abandonment.
59 *The German Ideology*, p. 482.

60 Those who, in my view, have exaggerated the conflict between the young and the mature Marx include Lewis Feuer (see n. 58), Sidney Hook (*New introduction to 'From Hegel to Marx'*, Ann Arbor, 1962), Daniel Bell (*The End of Ideology*, New York, 1965, ch. 15. 'Two Roads from Marx'), and L. Althusser, (*For Marx*, London, 1970). On the other hand, Robert Tucker (*Philosophy and Myth in Karl Marx*, Cambridge, 1961) presents an account of Marxism which very much overrates the significance of the early writings. Tucker perceives a metaphysical or religious theory buried in apparently economic analysis. *Capital* becomes a psychical drama rather than a treatise on economics. Marx, according to this interpretation, projected a neurotic process of the individual onto capitalist society as a whole – and this supposed confusion is used to explain the shortcomings of his vision of ultimate social harmony. Avineri's scholarly and sympathetic account of Marx also seems to me to submerge Marx too much in Hegel, and – partly as a consequence of this – to present Marx's Marxism as more coherent and settled, and freer of moral dilemmas, than it actually is.

61 David McLellan, in his introduction to selected passages from the *Grundrisse*, claims too much in treating the *Grundrisse* as 'in a sense, the most fundamental of all Marx's writings' and as 'the high point' of a continuing meditation on central themes broached in 1844 (pp. 2 and 12). There are several high points in Marx's writing – 1844, 1846, and the period of *Capital*'s completion, as well as 1857–8, but McLellan's emphasis is understandable against a background of comparative neglect.

62 *1844 Manuscripts*, p. 75. Cf *Marx's Grundrisse*, p. 126. 'Work is a positive, creative activity'.

63 *1844 Manuscripts*, pp. 72–3.

64 'Wage Labour and Capital', *Selected Works*, I, 82–3.

65 Friedrich Schiller, *On the Aesthetic Education of Man, in a Series of Letters*, trans. E. M. Wilkinson and L. A. Willoughby (Oxford, 1967), p. 35.

66 *The German Ideology*, pp. 64–5.

67 *1844 Manuscripts*, p. 24.

68 *Ibid.*, p. 27.

69 *Capital*, I, 645.

70 *Capital*, I, 360. Cf. also p. 363: 'Some crippling of body and mind is inseparable even from division of labour in society as a whole. Since, however, manufacture carries this social separation of branches of labour much further, and also, by its peculiar division, attacks the individual at the very roots of his life, it is the first to afford the materials for, and to give a start to industrial pathology.'

71 *Ibid.*, p. 484. In one particular sense, the division of labour becomes worse under the factory system. 'The life-long speciality of handling one and the same tool, now becomes the life-long speciality of serving one and the same machine. Machinery is put to a wrong use, with the object of transforming the workman, from his very childhood, into a part of a detail-machine' (*Ibid.*, p. 422).

72 *The German Ideology*, pp. 44–5.

73 *Ibid.*, p. 67.

74 *Capital*, I, 762.

75 *The German Ideology*, p. 44.

76 A misinterpretation to which Miss Hannah Arendt is prone. She claims that Marx had an almost irresistible tendency to look upon all labour as work (to look upon the labour of our bodies as the work of our hands, or servitude as free, creative activity) and hoped all the time 'that only one more step was needed to eliminate labour and necessity altogether'.

She confuses the abolition of labour (*The German Ideology*) with building a realm of freedom – outside labour – on a foundation of necessity (*Capital*). *The Human Condition* (Chicago and London, 1970), p. 87 and p. 87, n.17. I will return to this point in discussing communism.

77   *Marx's Grundrisse*, pp. 124–5.
78   *Ibid.*, p. 124.
79   Marx attacked Hegel for indentifying the very existence of objects with alienation and for treating objectification – hence man's shaping of the world and himself – as illusory, a mere projection of consciousness. Avineri, *Social and Political Thought*, pp. 97–8.
80   *The German Ideology*, p. 265.
81   *The Holy Family*, p. 157.
82   *On The Jewish Question*, *Early Writings*, p. 13. This is a characteristic phrase of Marx's.
83   *The German Ideology*, p. 82.
84   *1844 Manuscripts*, p. 69. The same relationship could be postulated between man and God. Feuerbach, for example, wrote that 'the more empty life is, the fuller, the more concrete is God. The impoverishing of the real world, and the enriching of God, is one act. Only the poor man has a rich God'. *The Essence of Christianity*, quoted Hook, *From Hegel to Marx*, p. 247. Marx, following Feuerbach, wrote that 'the more man puts into God, the less he retains in himself'. *1844 Manuscripts* p. 70.
85   *The German Ideology*, p. 94.
86   'Contribution to the Critique of Hegel's Philosophy of Right', Introduction, *On Religion*, pp. 41-2.
87   *Early Writings*, p. 37.
88   McLellan, *Grundrisse*, p. 71.
89   *1844 Manuscripts*, p. 137. Cf. also *The German Ideology*, p. 433. 'The power of money, the fact that the universal means of exchange become independent in relation both to society and to individuals, reveals most clearly that the relations of production and intercourse as a whole assume an independent existence'.
90   *1844 Manuscripts*, p. 137.
91   *Ibid.* On p. 141 Marx writes that money 'confounds and exchanges all things, it is the general confounding and compounding of all things – the world upside down – the confounding and compounding of all natural and human qualities'. Marx makes many Shakespearean references – money is the 'common whore', the 'bright defiler' and the 'visible god'.
92   *1844 Manuscripts*, p. 119.
93   *Early Writings*, p. 39.
94   *Marx's Grundrisse*, p. 61.
95   *Capital*, I, 71.
96   *Ibid.*, p. 72. In the *1844 Manuscripts* (p. 93) Marx argues that the mercantilists, who worshipped private property in the form of precious metals, saw private property as an objective substance confronting men, and were therefore 'idolators, fetishists, Catholics'. Adam Smith was the Luther of political economy, internalising private property, the object of worship.
97   *Capital*, III, 809.
98   *Marx's Grundrisse*, p. 63.
99   *Capital*, I, 432.
100 *Capital*, III, 86.
101 For example, medieval Europe, characterised by services and payments in kind. 'But for the very reason that personal dependence forms the groundwork of society, there is no necessity for labour and its products to assume a fantastic form different from their reality...No matter, then, what we

may think of the parts played by the different classes of people themselves in this society, the social relations between individuals in the performance of their labour, appear at all events as their own mutual personal relations, and are not disguised under the shape of social relations between the products of labour. *Capital*, I, 77.

102 *Capital*, I, 310. 'In bourgeois society capital is independent and has individuality, while the living person is dependent and has no individuality'. *The Communist Manifesto, Selected Works*, I, 48.

103 'We thus see that the transformation of money into capital presupposes a historic process which separates the objective conditions of labour, and makes them independent of and sets them against the labourers. However, once capital and its processes have come into being, they conquer all production and everywhere bring about and accentuate the separation between labour and property, labour and the objective conditions of labour'. *Pre-Capitalist Economic Formations*, p. 117.

104 'And the abolition of this state of things is called by the bourgeois abolition of individuality and freedom'. *The Communist Manifesto, Selected Works*, I, 48.

105 *On the Jewish Question*, p. 39. Marx was close to Hegel at this stage. Hegel had indicated the circumstances in which the state could appear external to man, so that he would feel estranged from, and unsatisfied by it.

106 *The German Ideology*, p. 46.

107 *Ibid.*, p. 214.

108 *The Holy Family*, pp. 156–7.

109 *The German Ideology*, p. 77.

110 Marx did indicate, at different times, the emptiness of many of the claims made on behalf of feudalism. See especially the essay 'Antithesis of Labour and Capital' in the *1844 Manuscripts*.

111 *On the Jewish Question*, p. 35.

112 *1844 Manuscripts*, p. 77.

113 *On the Jewish Question*, p. 35.

114 *Ibid.*, p. 35. In this and the preceding quotation Marx was paraphrasing Thomas Hamilton's *Men and Manners in North America*.

115 *Ibid.*, p. 15.

116 *Ibid.*, pp. 25–6.

117 *The German Ideology*, p. 249. Vico earlier put forward a similar view, which is now a commonplace in the sociology of knowledge.

118 *Economic Studies from Marx's Notebooks* (1844–5), T. B. Bottomore and M. Rubel, *Karl Marx: Selected Writings in Sociology and Social Philosophy* (London, 1961), p. 171.

119 *On the Jewish Question*, p. 26.

120 *1844 Manuscripts*, pp. 120–1. On p. 121 Marx writes that it stems from the very nature of estrangement that 'each sphere applies to me a different and opposite yardstick – ethics one and political economy another; for each is a specific estrangement of man and focuses attention on a particular round of estranged, essential activity, and each stands in an estranged relation to the other'.

121 *Marx's Grundrisse*, p. 72.

122 *The Poverty of Philosophy*, p. 112.

123 *Marx's Grundrisse*, p. 72.

124 *Capital*, I, 84–5.

125 *Critical Glosses* (1844), Article 2, Bottomore and Rubel, p. 237.

126 Quoted E. Kamenka, *The Ethical Foundations of Marxism* (London, 1962), p. 36,n.1.

127 *The Holy Family*, p. 163. Cf. also: 'Authentic common life arises not

through reflection; rather it comes about from the need and egoism of individuals, that is, immediately from the activation of their very existence'. 'Excerpts – Notes of 1844', *Writtings of the Young Marx*, ed. L. D. Easton and K. H. Guddat, p. 272.

128 *1844 Manuscripts*, p. 139. Money can transform social bonds. 'Money, then, appears as this overturning power both against the individual and against the bonds of society, etc., which claim to be essences in themselves' (p. 141).

129 Thereby forming a system of 'complete interdependence'. The universal principles operative in civil society are the laws of political economy as outlined by Smith, Say, and Ricardo. See especially para. 183 of *The Philosophy of Right*, Knox translation (Oxford, 1958), p. 123.

130 In 1844 Marx regarded citizenship, participation in the state, as an expression of man's species-being. In the state man is regarded as a species-being, 'man is the imaginary member of an imaginary sovereignty, divested of his real, individual life, and infused with an unreal universality'. The dualism between individual life and species-life is that between the life of civil society and the state. *On the Jewish Question*, p. 14. At this stage the state, freed from self-contradictions, is conceived as a realm and a realisation of rational freedom – later Marx envisaged human emancipation in a different way. See below, ch. 5.

131 Though one could argue that this has only been the case hitherto – that only now have impediments or limitations brought substantial change to a close – or that change has only taken place along particular dimensions, and that certain features of society remain nonetheless endemic, e.g. inequality or scarcity. In either case, the argument would be, normally, anti-utopian.

132 Quoted by John Weiss, 'Dialectical Idealism and the Work of Lorenz von Stein', *International Review of Social History*, VIII (1963), 81.

133 p. 109. Also, p. 110 – industry is conceived as 'the exotic revelation of man's essential powers'.

134 *Capital*, I, 488. Marx wrote that the gem of handicraft wisdom, 'let the cobbler stick to his last', became 'sheer nonsense, from the moment the watchmaker Watt invented the steam engine, the barber Arkwright, the throstle, and the working-jeweller Fulton, the steamship' (p. 488). He also cited the case of an ordinary French workman who discovered his various abilities while in America. The workman wrote on his return from San Francisco : 'I never could have believed, that I was capable of working at the various occupations I was employed on in California. I was firmly convinced that I was fit for nothing but letter-press printing . . . Once in the midst of this world of adventurers, who change their occupations as often as they do their shirts, egad, I did as the others. As mining did not turn out remunerative enough, I left it for the town, where in succession I became typographer, slater, plumber, and etc. In consequence of thus finding out that I am fit for any sort of work, I feel less of a mollusk and more of a man' (p. 487, n.2). Here is some empirical support for the communist prediction.

135 *Capital*, I, 484.

136 *The Holy Family*, p. 176.

137 *Early Writings*, p. 176. Cf. also Marx's reference to the communist movement in *The Holy Family*, p, 113. 'One must be acquainted with the studiousness, the craving for knowledge, the moral energy and the unceasing urge for development of the French and English workers to be able to form an idea of the human nobleness of that movement'.

138 Quoted Easton and Guddat, *Writings of The Young Marx*, p. 199.

THE DISINTEGRATION OF CAPITALISM

1 A typical statement by Marx refers to capitalism as 'a definite social production relation, belonging to a definite historical formation of society'. *Capital*, III, 794. A good deal of confusion has been created because of divergences between the abstract analysis of the first volume, in which Marx was trying to reveal the 'internal and disguised essence of things', and the more concrete and historical discussion of the third volume, in which the complexities of the real world emerge again.

2 *Ibid.*, p. 25.

3 *Ibid.*, p. 856.

4 *Ibid.*, p. 267.

5 *The German Ideology*, p. 267.

6 *Ibid.*, p. 267.

7 Engels, Introduction to *The Poverty of Philosophy*, p. 12. Engels suggested, though, that moral criticism can indicate the instability of a system, with popular condemnation revealing that the established order has served its time. Thus, once a system has reached its height, one would expect it to be subjected to increasingly powerful and widespread moral attacks.

8 *Economic and Philosophical Manuscripts*, pp. 67–8.

9 *Ibid.*, p. 26.

10 *Ibid.*, p. 67.

11 *The Holy Family*, p. 165.

12 *Capitalism, Socialism and Democracy* (London, 1957), pp. 9–10.

13 'Hegel's dialectics is the basic form of all dialectics, but only after it has been stripped of its mystical form, and it is precisely this which distinguishes my method'. To Kugelmann, 6 March 1868, *Selected Correspondence*, p. 240.

14 Martin Nicolaus, 'Hegelian Choreography and the Capitalist Dialectic', *Studies on the Left*, VIII, no. 1, 1967.

15 Nicolaus argues that Marx develops, especially in the *Grundrisse* and in *Capital*, doctrines of the surplus product and the surplus class which are much closer to the realities of advanced capitalist societies than the simple 'Hegelian' picture of the 1844 *Manuscripts* and *The Communist Manifesto*. It seems to me that Nicolaus underrates the persisting magic of that simple vision, which still appealed to the old Karl Marx, though it appears less frequently in his last works.

16 Norman Cohn holds that Marx secularised a common religious vision in his depiction of capitalism, and that what he passed on to present day communism 'was not the fruit of his long years of study in the field of economics and sociology but a quasi-apocalyptic phantasy which as a young man, unquestioningly, and almost unconsciously, he had assimilated from a crowd of obscure writers and journalists'. *The Pursuit of the Millennium*, p. 311.

17 *Karl Marx's Capital* (London, 1925). Once again, such a method seems perfectly reasonable, as it does in Schumpeter's case with his view of the necessary trend towards state ownership – if present tendencies continued to act 'as they have been acting in the interval covered by our observation and if no other factors intruded'. Schumpeter, *Capitalism, Socialism and Democracy*, p. 61. The question is whether this was Marx's method.

18 Lindsay, *Karl Marx's Capital*, p. 9.

19 Thus Avineri argues that, for Marx, the period of unfettered capitalism was short, and that the Ten Hours Bill was a post-capitalist encumbrance on free market activity, which revealed the capacity of capitalism to change

internally towards socialism. *Social and Political Thought*, p. 161. Avineri would reject the view that utter laissez faire was Marx's central image or model of capitalism, and that growing state intervention in the capitalist economy was an infringement or deviation.

20 Preface to the first German edition of *Capital*. *Capital*, 1, 8.

21 *Ibid.*, p. 763.

22 *Ibid.*, p. 8.

23 Note by Engels to the 1888 English edition of *The Communist Manifesto*, *Selected Works*, 1, 36, note d. Such a notion, which Marx seems to have shared, makes 'capitalist society' very much an ideal type, in that the characteristic economic, social and political features of capitalism do not seem to coincide in any one society. Things might change, of course. Consider also Marx's early claim that the Germans are 'the philosophical contemporaries of the present day without being its historical contemporaries'. The *Critique of Hegel's Philosophy of Right*, *Early Writings*, p. 49. On p. 51, he adds 'In politics, the Germans have thought what other nations have done'. The problem, which arises at many points, is what a particular political or philosophical or class development presupposes, especially in respect of economic conditions.

24 Marx to the editorial board of the *Otechestvenniye Zapiski*, November 1877, *Selected Correspondence*, p. 377.

25 *Capital*, 1, 9. Cf. also *The Critique of Hegel's Philosophy of Right*. 'The struggle against the political present of the Germans is a struggle against the past of the modern nations, who are still continually importuned by the reminiscences of this past'. *Early Writings*, p. 47.

26 *The Poverty of Philosophy*, p. 50.

27 Here wages, profit and rent entered into the price. Ricardo's simple labour theory was, according to Werner Stark, 'considerably modified by the employment of machinery and other fixed and durable capital'. *The History of Economics* (London, 1944), p. 33.

28 *Capital*, I 39.

29 *The Poverty of Philosophy*, p. 58.

30 *Ibid.*, p. 73. Schumpeter (*Capitalism, Socialism and Democracy*, p. 24) points out that the labour theory of value only operates in the case of perfect competition, and that even there it only works smoothly if labour is the only factor of production and, moreover, if it is all of one kind. In the case of 'natural' differences between, say, an intelligent and an unintelligent workman, recourse may be had to the market mechanism to bring the two into a proper relation (as with Ricardo and Marx), but this is to introduce some degree of circularity into the argument. It is an appeal to market prices, when the prices are themselves set by the labour time incorporated in the various commodities that make up the market system.

31 *The Poverty of Philosophy*, pp. 58–9.

32 *Ibid.*, p. 64.

33 *Capital*, III, 45.

34 *1844 Manuscripts*, p. 21. On p. 85, Marx wrote that the wages of labour thus have 'exactly the same significance as the maintenance and servicing of any other productive instrument, or as the consumption of a capital, required for its reproduction with interest; or as the oil which is applied to wheels to keep them turning'.

35 *The Communist Manifesto, Selected Works*, 1, 47–8.

36 'Beside this mere physical element, the value of labour is in every country determined by a traditional standard of life. It is not mere physical life, but it is the satisfaction of certain wants springing from the social conditions in which people are placed and reared up'. This traditional standard

of life would be, in part, the result of previous class struggles, including the contribution of workers' institutions, e.g. trades unions. Marx added, however, that this element may be expanded or contracted 'or altogether extinguished, so that nothing remains but the physical limit'. *Selected Works*, I, 442. But there is at least a shift from the crude cost of production theory, in that the worker's price may exceed his subsistence costs.

37 P. Sweezy, *The Theory of Capitalist Development* (London, 1943), p. 84.

38 Schumpeter (*Capitalism, Socialism and Democracy*, p. 27), correctly remarks that the labour theory of value cannot be applied to the commodity of labour, as this would imply that workmen, like machines, are being produced according to rational cost calculation. Workers reproducing rapidly during boom periods could hardly be regarded as having made rational cost calculations.

39 *Capital*, I, 309.

40 *Ibid.*, pp. 630–2. More pungently: 'The worshipful capitalist will never want for fresh exploitable flesh and blood, and will let the dead bury their dead'. *Wage Labour and Capital, Selected Works*, I, 103.

41 It is true that in many industries the wages fraction did decline during the nineteenth century, though without the effects anticipated by Marx. In the case of cotton during the second quarter of the century, estimates by Ellison and others 'suggest that the labour cost per unit of output practically halved in spinning and more than halved in weaving'. Deane and Cole, *British Economic Growth*, p. 189.

42 Dobb, *Studies in the Development of Capitalism* (London, 1963), p. 259.

43 *Capital*, I, 638.

44 P. 189.

45 *Capital*, I, 639.

46 *Ibid.*, p. 634.

47 Quoted by M. Dobb, *Capitalism Yesterday and Today* (London, 1961), p. 46.

48 *Capital*, III, pp. 472–3.

49 Pp. 23–5. This does not exhaust proletarian vices. In the 1844 *Manuscripts* and in Engel's *Condition of the Working Class in England in 1844*, many proletarians are portrayed as not merely selfish but utterly demoralised – alcoholic, sexually licentious, etc. – as well. This is one thing which makes the leap to freedom seem truly miraculous.

50 One of the purposes of the First International, in which Marx was the dominant figure, was to organise international labour for mutual support in the case of strikes. On numerous occasions strike-breakers were imported from the Continent into England, thus defeating particular strikes and making it very difficult to establish habits of collective bargaining. For a detailed discussion, see *Karl Marx and the British Labour Movement* by Henry Collins and Chimen Abramsky (London, 1965).

51 The capitalist is only capital personified. 'His soul is the soul of capital. But capital has one single life impulse, the tendency to create value and surplus-value, to make its constant factor, the means of production, absorb the greatest possible amount of surplus-labour. Capital is dead labour, that, vampire-like, only lives by sucking living labour, and lives the more, the more labour it sucks.' *Capital*, I, 233.

Surplus value is created if value-production continues beyond a certain point, i.e. beyond the point of producing the exact equivalent to the value paid by the capitalist for labour power. In technical terms, surplus value is the excess of total net output over the wages bill, and it thus indicates the share of labour in total output. Marx sometimes spoke of the labourer as working part of the time for himself (until the value of his product equalled his wage) and part of the time for others, which period is described as that of 'surplus' or 'unpaid' labour.

The surplus value

$$\text{the rate of which is } \frac{s}{v} \text{ or } \frac{\text{surplus labour}}{\text{necessary labour}}$$

goes to the capitalist, who is conceived as a provider of capital and not as a manager. The creation of surplus value was described by Marx as exploitation, the rate of which is the ratio of surplus value to variable capital or the wages bill. In this sense it becomes possible to speak of exploitation independently of the miserable living conditions and the suffering which are normally associated with it.

52 *Capital*, I, 152. Marx praised McCulloch for writing that the 'inextinguishable passion for gain, the *auri sacra fames* (accursed hunger for gold) will always lead capitalists' (p. 153, n.2).

53 *Essays on Some Unsettled Questions of Political Economy* (London, 1844), p. 149.

54 *Die moralisierende Kritik und die kritisierende Moral.* 1847 in Bottomore and Rubel, p. 202. Yet the secession to the proletariat of educated members of the bourgeoisie is given considerable significance.

55 *Capital*, I, 152–3.

56 *Ibid.*, p. 595.

57 'At any rate I hope the bourgeoisie will remember my carbuncles all the rest of their lives. Here is yet another proof what swine they are'. Marx cites their opposition to the Children Employment Commission. Letters to Engels, 22 June 1867, *Selected Correspondence*, p. 227. Later in the letter they are described as 'curs'.

58 *Capital*, I, 112.

59 *Ibid.*, p. 592.

60 *Ibid.*, p. 10. Others had stressed the lack of personal responsibility on the part of the capitalist, e.g. Buret, who claimed that the master was not responsible for the level or the duration of wages – 'he himself has to submit to the law which he imposes. Poverty is not so much caused by men as by the power of things'. Quoted *1844 Manuscripts*, p. 48.

61 *Capital*, I, 235.

62 *1844 Manuscripts*, p. 126.

63 *Capital*, I 594. For the capitalist, pleasure is subordinated to production, as recuperation. 'Pleasure is therefore subsumed under capital, and the pleasure-taking individual under the capital-accumulating individual, whilst formerly the contrary was the case'. *1844 Manuscripts*, p. 128. In the manuscript of *The German Ideology* – though later crossed out – Marx referred to 'the continuous subordination of pleasure to money making' by the bourgeoisie (p. 459n).

64 *Capital*, I, 592, n.1.

65 The counteracting or delaying influences mentioned by Marx are increasing intensity of exploitation, reduction of wages below their value, cheapening of the elements of constant capital, relative overpopulation (keeping workers employed in relatively backward industries, with a low

organic composition of capital), foreign trade (more profitable fields of investment), and the increase of stock capital. See Capital, III, ch. 14.

66 1844 Manuscripts, p. 68.

67 Wage Labour and Capital, Selected Works, I, 101.

68 Ibid., p. 101. In these circumstances, value is converted into price of production, and the general law of value asserts itself in a complicated and approximate manner – as the general laws of capitalism frequently do in volume III of Capital, where the real world of the market-place is re-introduced.

69 Cf. the figures provided by Thomas Ellison and quoted by E. J. Hobsbawm, The Age of Revolution, p. 41.

70 Capital, III 254. Or again, p. 799: 'It is one of the civilizing aspects of capital that it enforces this surplus-labour in a manner and under conditions which are more advantageous to the development of the productive forces, social relations and the creation of the elements for a new and higher form than under the preceding forms of slavery, serfdom, etc'.

71 Marx's Grundrisse, p. 86.

72 Capital, I, 264–5. Capital celebrated its orgies in the late eighteenth century, when there was 'a violent encroachment like that of an avalanche in its intensity and extent. All bounds of morals and nature, age and sex, day and night, were broken down'. Ibid., p. 278.

73 He claimed that, in proportion 'as the repulsiveness of the work increases, the wage decreases'. The Communist Manifesto, Selected Works, I, 40. And he thought that the repulsiveness of work was increasing. In The Poverty of Philosophy, Marx wrote that wages oscillate now above, now below the subsistence level, so that the worker 'can participate to a certain extent in the development of collective wealth and can also perish from want' (p. 114). In Wages, Price and Profit he claimed that 'the general tendency of capitalistic production is not to raise, but sink the average standard of wages, or to push the value of labour more or less to its minimum limit'. Selected Works, I, 446.

74 Inaugural Address of the Working Men's International Association, 28 September 1864, Selected Works, I, 377. Marx quoted Gladstone as saying that 'this intoxicating augmentation of wealth and power is entirely confined to the classes of property'. Ibid., p. 379.

75 Selected Works, I, 98. Marx was already familiar with this idea in 1844 – see the quotation from Wilhelm Schulz in the 1844 Manuscripts, p. 30. Marx's point is not the same as that of Tocqueville – that economic decline after progress and a rise in expectations is likely to increase the chances of revolution – though it is used as if it were by James C. Davies, 'Towards a Theory of Revolution', American Sociological Review, XXVII, no. 1, February 1962.

76 Quoted Nicolaus, 'Hegelian Choreography and the Capitalist Dialectic', p. 37.

77 For example, Avineri writes (Social and Political Thought, p. 173) that Marx 'never implied that the absolute position of the workers would deteriorate endlessly'. But this is to shift the basis of the normal argument, which is not over 'endless' deterioration – which, logically and ultimately, could lead only to the death of all workers – but over whether Marx said or implied that the position of the workers would deteriorate absolutely.

78 As Engels, for example, looking in 1892 to the East End of London for a genuine renaissance of the proletariat – there, amongst the uncorrupted, the new unionism was emerging. 1892 Preface to The Condition of the Working Class in England, pp. 15–19.

79 The decennial cycle could be interrupted by minor fluctuations. Engels

had believed, on the experience of 1825 to 1842, that crises recurred every five years, but wrote in the 1892 preface to *The Condition of the Working Class in England* that industrial history from 1842 to 1868 had shown that the real period was one of ten years. *Selected Works*, II, 411. One of Marx's contemporary admirers has described the cycle as 'essentially a cycle in the process of capital accumulation, and the periodic breakdown occurs because the continual urge towards the accumulation and investing of capital outruns the conditions that determine what profit the increased capital can earn'. Dobb, *Capitalism Yesterday and Today*, p. 45.

80 *The Poverty of Philosophy*, pp. 75–6. The capitalist is pushed about by the productive forces. 'The actual degree of development of the productive forces compels him to produce on such and such a scale' (p. 45). Marx naturally rejected Say's law – the law of the market – according to which supply automatically creates the necessary demand. Marx advanced several (connected) theories of crisis – a disproportionality theory, an underconsumption theory and a falling rate of profit theory. But here I am concerned only with the supposed effects of crises.

81 *Wage Labour and Capital, Selected Works*, I, 87. Some writers predicted a decline in the intensity of the fluctuations or a state of stagnation, brought about by the destruction of individual initiative due to the falling rate of profit. This condition was referred to by the classical economist as the 'stationary state'. Engels, who during the 1880's expressed some uncertainty about the nature of capitalism's future, came up with a similar suggestion in 1884. 'The period of general prosperity preceding the crisis still fails to appear. It it should fail altogether, then chronic stagnation would necessarily become the normal conditlion of modern industry, with only insignificant fluctuations'. Introduction to *The Poverty of Philosophy*, p. 22. Naturally such a prospect did not encourage expectations of radical change.

82 *Capital*, III, 253.

83 *The Communist Manifesto, Selected Works*, I, 45.

84 *Capital*, I, 503.

85 *Wage Labour and Capital, Selected Works*, I, 99.

86 *Capital*, I, 763.

87 *The Poverty of Philosophy*, p. 68.

88 Cf. N. Bukharin: 'The class war rises out of the conflict of interests between the bourgeoisie and the proletariat. These interests are as essentially irreconcilable as are the respective interests of wolves and sheep. Peace between the classes is as impossible as peace between wolves and sheep. Wolves want to eat sheep, so sheep must defend themselves against wolves. But if this be so (and unquestionably it is so) then we have to ask whether it is possible for wolves and sheep to have a common will. Every intelligent person knows that it is absurd to talk of anything of the kind. There simply cannot be a will common to sheep and wolves.' Bourgeois-proletarian relations are the same. 'Between them there is war to the knife'. N. Bukharin, *The A.B.C. of Communism* (Michigan, 1966), pp. 63 and 168-9.

89 *The German Ideology*, p. 60.

90 *Capital*, III, 772. Marx stressed here that the same economic basis could exhibit endless variations in its appearance, and that these must be studied empirically.

91 *Capital*, III, 863.

92 *Die moralisierende Kritik und die kritisierende Moral*, in Bottomore and Rubel, p. 201.

93 It has been suggested that Marx used other criteria in defining classes. M. M. Bober suggests that a class, to Marx, was 'a group of people who in

a given society, with a given regime of production, are finding themselves in the same position with reference to two things: the ownership or non-ownership of the property essential in the labour processes, and second, the personal freedom enjoyed or deprived of'. *Karl Marx's Interpretation of History* (Cambridge, 1948), p. 96. I am not aware of any passages in which the degree of personal freedom is treated as a general criterion of class. While it would provide a means of distinguishing some classes from others, e.g. slaves from serfs, and each of these from proletarians, it would not distinguish the petit-bourgeoisie from the capitalists, nor the proletariat from the lumpenproletariat, and the manoeuvre of making them species of the same genus would hardly get round the problem.

94 *Eighteenth Brumaire, Selected Works,* I, 334.

95 *The Poverty of Philosophy,* p. 195.

96 *The Holy Family,* p. 53. The workers discover, in their material situation, 'foes to be laid low; measures dictated by the needs of the struggle to be taken; the consequences of its own deeds drive it on. It makes no theoretical inquiries into its own task'. *The Class Struggles in France, Selected Works,* I, 148.

97 19 October 1877, *Selected Correspondence,* p. 376. For another condemnation of Utopian Socialism as sentimental and petit-bourgeois, see *The German Ideology,* p. 457.

98 P. 60. Emphasis mine. This claim naturally raises many difficulties – to take one example, the feudal nobility can hardly be treated as, literally, a ruling *intellectual* force. Nor, given the heterogeneity of bourgeois culture, whose embodiments include Jacobins and unyielding conservatives, as well as Marx and Mill, does the notion of *ruling* ideas seem a very plausible one.

99 *Selected Works,* I, 34.

100 *Capital,* III, 862.

101 Quoted Nicolaus, *Hegelian Choreography and the Capitalist Dialectic,* p. 44. Marx discussed the ideological classes in *Capital,* I, 446–7. In *Theories of Surplus Value* (Moscow, undated) he mocked their belief that they should not be classified, as they were in the existing political economy, with the unproductive classes! 'The great mass of so-called 'higher grade' workers – such as state officials, military people, artists, doctors, priests, judges, lawyers, etc. – some of whom are not only not productive but in essence destructive, but who know how to appropriate to themselves a very great part of the 'material' wealth partly through the sale of their 'immaterial' commodities and partly by forcibly imposing the latter on other people – found it not at all pleasant to be relegated economically to the same class as clowns and menial servants and to appear merely as people partaking in the consumption, parasites on the actual producers (or rather agents of production)' (p. 170). He added (p. 171): 'The dependence of the ideological, etc., classes on the capitalists was in fact proclaimed,' and that with ex-tension of capital's dominion 'those spheres of production not directly related to the production of material wealth became also more and more dependent upon it'.

102 The nine classes are the capitalists, the landowners, the ideological or sur-plus or middle class, the petit bourgeoisie, the proletariat, the lumpenpro-letariat and the peasantry – sub divided by Engels *(Preface to 'The Peasant War in Germany',* p. 24) into feudal peasants, tenant farmers and agri-cultural labourers. The latter class or section were the 'most numerous and most natural allies' of the proletariat (p. 25). There were splits and con-flicts within all of the major classes at times.

103 On the peasant insurrection of 10 December 1848: 'The symbol that

expressed their entry into the revolutionary movement, clumsily cunning, knavishly naive, doltishly sublime, a calculated superstition, a pathetic burlesque, a cleverly stupid anachronism, a world-historic piece of buffoonery and an undecipherable hieroglyphic for the understanding of the civilized – this symbol bore the unmistakable physiognomy of the class that represents barbarism within civilization.' *The Class Struggles in France, Selected Works,* I, 173.

104 Marx's views of the likely peasant attitude to proletarian revolution seem to have altered between 1852 and the early seventies (specifically in relation to France). In 1852 he seems to have believed that the French peasants would possibly back a proletarian revolution, or at least that they would quickly come to support it, whereas by 1874-5, while still hoping for peasant support, he saw that support as the product of a quite long evolutionary process after the revolution. The position was better where the capitalist tenant had ousted the peasant, making the real tiller of the soil a proletarian or wage worker. See Henry Mayer's discussion of Marx on Bakunin in Études de Marxologie (directeur: M. Rubel), no. 91, October 1959 – especially pages 102 and 109.

105 One may very well doubt whether they constitute a unified group at all. M. Holbwachs, who breaks up the lower middle, or intermediate class into artisans and small tradesmen, the salariat of clerical workers and the lower grades of the civil service (*The Psychology of Social Class* (London, 1948), ch. 5, *passim*) claims (p. 113) that there are 'marked differences between the three largest categories of the intermediate class, and each category responds to a particular set of determinants resulting from its particular function in social life'. He does observe common characteristics. Of course, the actual degree of homogeneity must be pursued empirically in each particular case.

106 *The Eighteenth Brumaire, Selected Works,* I, 308.

107 Marx and Engels, in a review of *Die Religion des Neuen Weltalters,* by G. F. Daumer, wrote as follows: 'If the decline of earlier classes, such as the medieval knights, provided the raw material for magnificent and tragic works of art, that of the petit-bourgeoisie characteristically gives rise to nothing but impotent expressions of fanatical illwill and a collection of Sancho Panzaesque saws and maxims'. *Literature and Art,* p. 92.

108 See Isaac Deutscher, *The Prophet Outcast* (Oxford, 1963), ch. 2. As early as 1930 Trotsky was describing Nazism as the movement of the counter-revolutionary despair of the petit-bourgeois. Holbwachs (*The Psychology of Social Class,* p. 109) has written that the members of his lower middle class 'cling tenaciously to their higher social status and will never forget the distinction between them and wage workers'. It must be remembered that we are dealing here with the supposed general (not universal) characteristics of a group, and that a defender of the class may, without denying the generalisation, point to many petit-bourgeois who were equalitarian, in the forefront of revolutionary movements, and so on. Drapers are not always colourless, thrifty and self-seeking.

109 *The Eighteenth Brumaire, Selected Works,* I, 294–5. Louis Napoleon, representing the latent interests of the peasantry, is portrayed, morally, in his 'true character of chief of the Paris lumpenproletariat' (p. 301) and as 'a Bohemian, a princely lumpenproletarian' (p. 303).

110 *The Communist Manifesto, Selected Works,* I, 44.

111 *The Class Struggles in France, Selected Works,* I, 149. At this point religion was an invaluable weapon of the exploiting or usurious class: 'the mortgage that the peasant has on heavenly possessions guarantees the mortgage that the bourgeoisie has on peasant possessions' (p. 188).

Notes to pp. 130–6

112 *Ibid.*, p. 221. Cf. also pp. 191, 193 and 197.
113 17 April 1871, *Letters to Dr Kugelmann* (London, 1941), p. 125.
114 *Capital*, I, 285.
115 *The Poverty of Philosophy*, pp. 137–8.
116 Marx argued that the interests of the manufacturers and the finance aristocracy were directly and seriously in conflict. 'Their (the manufacturers) interest is indubitably reduction of the costs of production and hence reduction of the taxes, which enter into production, and hence reduction of the state debts, the interest on which enters into the taxes, hence the overthrow of the finance aristocracy'. *The Class Struggles in France, Selected Works*, I, 211. Several years earlier he had pointed to a division between the bourgeoisie and the big industrialists, who were a supranational class with a common interest – a class 'which is really rid of all the old world and at the same time stands pitted against it'. *The German Ideology*, p. 76.
117 The interests of the landed proprietors are presented as being closely linked with those of the finance aristocracy. 'In general the combination of large landed property with high finance is a normal fact. Proof England; proof: even Austria'. *Ibid.*, p. 209.
118 *Ibid.*, p. 191.
119 *The Eighteenth Brumaire, Selected Works*, I, 272.
120 *Ibid.*, p. 307.
121 *Ibid.*, p. 320.
122 *Ibid.*, p. 320.
123 *Ibid.*, p. 329. Cf. Engels on the German National Liberals in Parliament in the late 1860s and early 1870s: 'they have been left in the lurch by those who stand behind them, by the mass of the bourgeoisie. This mass does not want to rule. It has 1848 still in its bones'. Preface to *The Peasant War in Germany*, p. 18.
124 *The Eighteenth Brumaire, Selected Works*, I, 319.
125 *Ibid.*, p. 341.
126 *The Class Struggles in France, Selected Works*, I, 179.
127 *The Housing Question, Selected Works*, I, 604.
128 *The Eighteenth Brumaire, Selected Works*, I, 272–3.
129 Marx and Engels were both conscious of the separation between the British 'governing caste', and the middle class, and stressed the complexities of the ruling class in Germany. In relation to the United States, Engels indicated the divergence of interests in the same group, the different fractions and interests within the two big parties, and the presence of representatives of the various sections of the possessing class in each of them. To Sorge, 6 January 1892, *Selected Correspondence*, p. 521.
130 *The Holy Family*, p. 110.
131 *Ibid.*, p. 165.
132 *The Class Struggles in France, Selected Works*, I, 139.
133 *The Origins of the Family, Selected Works*, I, 322.
134 *The Eighteenth Brumaire, Selected Works*, I, 291–2.
135 Marx to Liebknecht, 11 February 1879, *Selected Correspondence* (Moscow, 1965), enlarged, p. 314. He probably had in mind such leaders as Potter and Odger. It is a little beyond my scope to detail Marx's particular estimates of the English trade union and labour movements at different times. It suffices to note that he and Engels were dubious of the traditional and pragmatic character of the labour movement in that country. Engels contrasted the theory-conscious German workers with the well-organised English labour movement, which advanced slowly partly because of its 'indifference towards all theory'. *The Peasant War in Germany*, p. 32. Marx wrote, in a

confidential circular of 16 January 1870, that the labour movement was totally lacking in 'the spirit of generalisation and revolutionary ardour', and he added that only the General Council 'can supply this deficiency'. Quoted H. Collins and C. Abramsky, *Karl Marx and the British Labour Movement* (London, 1965), p. 85. Here is the notion of consciousness being brought from outside. This state of affairs had to be seen against the defeat of 1848, of which the collapse of Chartism was a sign: 'While the rout of their Continental brethren unmanned the English working classes, and broke their faith in their own cause, it restored to the landlord and the money-lord their somewhat shaken confidence. They insolently withdrew concessions already advertised. The discovery of new goldlands led to an immense exodus leaving an irreparable void in the ranks of the British proletariat. Others of its formerly active members were caught by the temporary bribe of greater work and wages, and turned into "political blacks". All the efforts made at keeping up, or remodelling the Chartist movement, failed signally; the press organs of the working class died one by one of the apathy of the masses, and, in point of fact, never before seemed the English working class so thoroughly reconciled to a state of political nullity.' *Inaugural Address of the Working Men's International Association, Selected Works*, I, 382.

136 *Wage Labour and Capital, Selected Works*, I, 98.
137 Marx to S. Meyer and A. Vogt, 9 April 1870, *Selected Correspondence*, p. 286. Ireland occupied an important strategic place in Marx's picture of the world. It was the Achilles heel of England as Poland was that of Russia, and in each case he strongly supported the national struggle of the oppressed. See Collins and Abramsky, *Marx and the British Labour Movement*, pp. 106–7. Engels claimed that one could see in Ireland that 'the so-called liberty of English citizens is based on the oppression of the colonies' (to Marx, 23 May 1856, *Selected Correspondence*, p. 112). Marx held that if the English proletariat did not support a free Ireland (within a federal system), 'the English people will remain tied to the leading-strings of the ruling classes, because it will have to join with them in a common front against Ireland' (to Kugelmann, 29 November 1869, *ibid.*, p. 277). Ireland was a pillar of reaction in two senses – it enriched the ruling class and it divided the working class.

4 POLITICS AND SOCIAL CHANGE

1 P. 22 and 23 of Marx's notebook of 1844–7, *The German Ideology*, p. 655.
2 *Ibid.*, p. 51.
3 *Ibid.*, p. 39.
4 P. 122. Marx also uses this simple, apparently causal language in his letter to Annenkov on 28 December 1846, *Selected Correspondence*, pp. 39–51, and in *The Preface to a Contribution to the Critique of Political Economy, Selected Works*, I, 363.
5 *German Marxism and Russian Communism* (London, 1956), p. 27. Plamenatz argued that such a theory is implicit in *The Preface to a Contribution to the Critique of Political Economy*. Arguing against what he took to be Marx's view, Plamenatz claimed that 'there are no social relations between men determined (and not merely affected) by their methods of production, and which in their turn determine (and not merely affect) the system of property and the class structure of society'. This is, I think, true but it is not an attack on Marx's general position.
6 Quoted Kamenka, *The Ethical Foundations*, p. 135.
7 P. 58.

8 *Ibid.*, pp. 430–1.
9 *Selected Correspondence*, pp. 500–7. Engels claims, for example, that the money market has 'a development of its own, special laws determined by its own nature and separate phases'. The state has relative independence and movement of its own. Law not only corresponds to and expresses economic conditions, but it must be 'internally coherent'. Philosophy 'presupposes certain definite thought material handed down to it by its predecessors, from which it takes its start'. It may be that, even in accepting multi-causality and interaction, the interacting elements described by Engels remain too much distinct entities, still related mechanically rather than organically.
10 Ollman treats the lack of clearly defined, fixed and mutually exclusive categories as a distinctive feature and a strength of Marxism. He holds that Marx 'manipulates the size of his factors, alters his classificational boundaries, to suit his changing purposes...That Marx had to obtain consistent, mutually exclusive categories is simply taken for granted' (B. Ollman, *Alienation. Marx's Conception of Man in Capitalist Society* (Cambridge, 1971), p. 10), i.e. by those who interpret Marx in a fundamentalist manner. Ollman's claim hardly settles the matter.
11 *The Eighteenth Brumaire, Selected Works*, I, 272.
12 *The German Ideology*, p. 37.
13 *Ibid.*, p. 45.
14 *Ibid.*, p. 51.
15 *Preface to a Contribution, Selected Works*, I, 363.
16 *Article in Vorwärts*, 7 August 1844, in *Selected Writings*, ed. Bottomore and Rubel, p. 218.
17 'Capital Punishment', *New York Daily Tribune*, 18 February 1853, in *Selected Writings*, p. 228.
18 Marx attacked the false but politically useful assumption of individual responsibility in his discussion of the Latest Prussian Censorship Instruction, in which the censors rather than the system were blamed. 'Or is it perhaps that the objective mistakes of an institution are to be blamed on individuals so that the semblance of improvement is achieved without a real improvement? It is this kind of pseudo-liberalism which is apt to make concessions under pressure and that sacrifices persons to maintain the institution, the tools, the object'. *Writings of the Young Marx*, ed. Easton and Guddat. p. 69.
19 Avineri, *Social and Political Thought*, p. 203. It might be more accurate to speak of the state expressing or resting on a perpetual tension – it is hard to conceive the state as itself 'a perpetual tension'.
20 *Selected Works*, I, 483.
21 *Selected Works*, II, 319.
22 *Ibid.*, p. 321. Here the balance of the key contending classes gives power to a declining class. For a general comment, see *The German Ideology*, 'The independence of the State is only found nowadays in those countries in which the estates have not yet completely developed into classes, where the estates, done away with in more advanced countries, still have a part to play, and where there exists a mixture; countries, that is to say, in which no one section of the population can achieve dominance over the others'. (p. 78).
23 *The Civil War in France, Selected Works*, I, 518. Marx examined this situation more closely in *The Eighteenth Brumaire*.
24 Engels to Marx, 13 April 1866, *Selected Correspondence*, p. 214.
25 Marx stressed the growth of bureaucracy in France: 'This executive power with its enormous bureaucratic and military organization, with its in-

genious state machinery, embracing wide strata, with a host of officials numbering half a million, besides an army of another half million, this appalling parasitic body, which enmeshes the body of French society like a net and chokes all its pores, sprang up in the days of the absolute monarchy, with the decay of the feudal system which it helped to hasten.' Under the legitimist and the July monarchies state administration grew. 'Every common interest was straightaway severed from society, counterposed to it as a higher, general interest, snatched from the activity of society's members themselves and made an object of government activity...All revolutions perfected this machine instead of smashing it. The parties that contended in turn for domination regarded the possession of this huge state edifice as the principal spoils of the victor'. *The Eighteenth Brumaire, Selected Works*, I, 332–3.

26 *The Origin of the Family, Selected Works*, II, 324–5.
27 *Communist Manifesto, Selected Works*, I, 36.
28 *The Civil War in France, Selected Works*, I, 517.
29 I am thinking here of arguments which claim that Marx and Engels were either unaware of this fact, or that historical materialism seriously underrates these rules, by treating them as secondary rather than primary. Such 'para-technological relationships', as they are called by H. B. Acton, comprise moral, customary, legal and market relations, which interlock. Marx, according to Acton, did not recognise the importance of these necessary conditions of technological activity, which cannot properly be regarded as superstructural, but must be included as elements of the material basis of society. *The Illusion of the Epoch* (London, 1955), p. 164. I have argued earlier that Marx's was not, in fact, a hard technological theory of history. I should add here that Marx's view of the instruments or forces of production was often very extensive – it included, at different times, tools, hands, brains, eyes, land, communications, social cooperation, the state and the revolutionary proletariat. In *The German Ideology* it is stated that 'a certain mode of production, or industrial stage, is always combined with a certain mode of cooperation, or social stage, and this mode of cooperation is itself a productive force' (p. 18). General social knowledge is described as 'a direct force of production'. *Grundrisse, Selected Writings*, ed. Bottomore and Rubel, p. 91.
30 *The Poverty of Philosophy*, p. 45.
31 *Ibid.*, p. 93. English jurisprudence is 'ever the faithful servant of capital'. *Capital*, I, 296, n.3.
32 *The German Ideology*, p. 357.
33 P. 76.
34 1892 Preface, *The Condition of the Working Class*, p. viii. This statement raises the problem of the point at which class divisions crystallise, class manipulation becomes clear-cut, etc. For Marx the class character appears to have been more pronounced in the mature rather than the juvenile state of capitalism.
35 *Ibid.*, p. 292.
36 *Capital*, I, ch. 10 'The Working Day'. See especially pp. 286, 287 and 289.
37 *Ibid.*, p. 300.
38 *The Holy Family*, p. 47. Engels stressed that we must look 'behind the legal curtains, where real life is enacted'. *The Origin of the Family, Selected Works*, II, 231.
39 *Ibid.*, p. 231.
40 *Capital*, I, 176.
41 'Irish Tenant Right', *New York Daily Tribune*, 11 July 1853, p. 53.
42 James Burnham, *The Struggle for the World* (New York, 1947), p. 10. This

is a general critical point, made in different ways by Marx, Michels, Burnham and Schumpeter, for example – each rejects traditional democratic goals and democratic appearances, as empty either within any imaginable social context, or within the particular social and institutional frameworks within which they were normally conceived.

43 1892 Preface, *The Condition of the Working Class*, p. xiv. Engels was here quoting from an article which he published in *The London Commonwealth*, 1 March 1885.

44 *The Poverty of Philosophy*, p. 192.

45 *Capital*, I, 283.

46 Marx, *Inaugural Address of the Working Men's International Association*, *Selected Works*, I, 383.

47 Avineri, *Social and Political Thought*, p. 210. The previous references are to p. 213.

48 *Ibid.*, p. 210.

49 *Ibid.*, p. 213.

50 According to Avineri (p. 218), Marx 'envisions the revolution occurring in the more developed countries through universal suffrage, not because he insists on a democratic form of legitimization, but because he sees in universal suffrage the resolution of the conflict between state and civil society'. It seems to me that where he envisions the revolution in this way, it is because of the strength of the proletariat.

51 *Ibid.*, p. 220.

52 Avineri notes (pp. 213–14) that universal suffrage, as demanded by Lassalle in Bismarck's Prussia, could not 'be wielded to establish communism', that it was no vehicle of revolution, and that the Prussian state did not hesitate to use measures 'repugnant to the spirit of universal suffrage'. There seems to be a crucial ambiguity in his notion of universal suffrage – between universal suffrage as a vehicle of revolution and as itself a resolution of the conflict between state as a civil society – and a tendency to use the second account of it to foreclose discussion of its role in social change, i.e. by treating it as the resolution of conflict rather than a lever for change. If universal suffrage is, itself, the resolution of conflict or the revolution, questions of its contribution to change, as one political institution amongst others, do not arise. It transforms society by definition.

53 Popper, *The Open Society*, II, 153. Popper refers (p. 150) to Marxism's 'historicist tendency to avoid a definite statement about whether or not violence will actually be used in this phase of history', and links this with the 'Hegelian tendency' to avoid rigid definitions. Popper gives the impression that Marx formulated his predictions and recommendations as he did in order to prevent their falsification. This is too much a logician's approach, and underrates the complexity of the historical problems facing Marx.

54 *The Civil War in France*, *Selected Works*, I, 497.

55 *The Class Struggles in France*, *Selected Works*, I, 233.

56 I. Deutscher, *The Prophet Outcast* (Oxford, 1963), p. 136.

57 *The Class Struggles in France*, *Selected Works*, I, 158.

58 Marx and Engels to Bebel, etc. (Circular Letter), 17–18 September 1879, *Selected Correspondence*, p. 395.

59 Marx to J. B. Schweitzer, 13 October 1868, *Selected Correspondence*, p. 259.

60 Engels, *Marx's Capital*, *Selected Works*, I, pp. 466–7.

61 Marx, *The Chartists, Articles on Britain* (Moscow, 1971), p. 119.

62 *Selected Works*, vol. II of the three-volume edition (Moscow, 1969), p. 293.

63 *Selected Correspondence* (Moscow, 1965), enlarged, p. 334.

64 *Marx's Capital*, *Selected Works*, I, 467.

65 *Introduction to the Class Struggles in France* (1895), *Selected Works*, I, 129. Engels also suggested that the vote was useful as a means of gauging the strength of the Party, thus making it easier to work out what constituted reasonable action in the circumstances. Counting heads would avoid the danger of adventurism – reckless attempts at seizing power. Engels found it necessary to deny that he was 'a peaceful worshipper of legality *quand même* [at any price]'. He wrote to Kautsky on 1 April 1895 that an extract of his Introduction had been published, without his knowledge, in *Vorwärts*, and that it had been trimmed to give the impression that he was a peaceful worshipper of legality *quand même*. *Ibid.*, p. 118, n.1.

66 *Ibid.*, p. 135.

67 *The Class Struggles in France, Selected Works*, I, 172. In France proletarian prospects of improvements within the bourgeois order were peculiarly limited. The defeat of the proletariat in June 1848 convinced it that 'the slightest improvement in its position remains a utopia within the bourgeois republic, a utopia that becomes a crime as soon as it wants to become a reality'. *Ibid.*, p. 162.

68 *The Eighteenth Brumaire, Selected Works*, I, 287. Here and in *The Class Struggles in France* the 'treachery' and the vacillations of the bourgeoisie are mentioned constantly.

69 For example, the reaction to the Commune: 'The civilization and justice of bourgeois order comes out in its lurid light whenever the slaves and drudges of that order rise against their masters. Then this civilization and justice stand forth as undisguised savagery and lawless revenge. Each new crisis in the class struggle between the appropriator and the producer brings out this fact more glaringly.' *The Civil War in France, Selected Works*, I, 535.

70 *New York Daily Tribune*, 31 March 1857, *On Colonialism*, pp. 101–2.

71 Preface to the English edition of *Capital*, *Capital*, I, p. 6.

72 *Introduction to the Class Struggles in France* (1895), *Selected Works*, I, 137. In their statements about the violent, vicious, last-ditch resistance of capital to its imminent overthrow, Marx and Engels anticipate some elements of the communists interpretations of Fascism, though naturally they did not foresee its precise form.

73 Quoted by Stanley Moore, *Three Tactics: The Background in Marx* (New York, 1963), p. 89.

74 *Selected Correspondence*, p. 393.

75 *The Communist Manifesto, Selected Works*, I, 61.

76 *The Poverty of Philosophy*, p. 140.

77 Engels had to revise his opinion in this respect. In *The Condition of the Working Class* (p. 297) he had argued that communism is a question of humanity and not of workers alone – it was to save the bourgeoisie as well. 'Communism stands, in principle, above the breach between bourgeoisie and proletariat, recognises only its historic significance for the present, but not its justification for the future: wishes, indeed, to bridge over this chasm, to do away with all class antagonisms'. In his 1892 preface to the book, he said that this notion, while true in the abstract, was absolutely useless, and sometimes worse in practice, as on current trends it seemed that the social revolution would have to be prepared and fought out by the working class alone. To speak of general emancipation was unrealistic, and to preach a classless socialism was dangerous – its advocates are 'either neophytes, who have still to learn a great deal, or they are the worst enemies of the workers – wolves in sheep's clothing'.

78 Hence Marx attacked Bakunin's proposal to abolish inheritance. 'Like all other civil legislation, the laws of inheritance are not the cause, but the

effect, the juridical consequence of the existing economical organization of society, based upon private property in the means of production, that is to say, in land, raw material, machinery, etc. In the same way the right of inheritance in the slave is not the cause of slavery, but, on the contrary, slavery is the cause of inheritance in slaves...The disappearance of the right of inheritance will be the natural result of a social change superseding private property in the means of production; but the abolition of the right of inheritance can never be the starting-point of such a social transformation'. *Report of the General Council on the Right of Inheritance* (written by Marx in August 1869), *Documents of the First International* (Moscow, 1964), pp. 322–3.

79 Engels to A. Bebel, 28 October 1882, *Selected Correspondence*, p. 427.
80 *Lenninism or Marxism* (Michigan, 1961), p. 105.

5 COMMUNISM

1 *1844 Manuscripts*, p. 114. The main Marxist discussions of the future society are provided in the *Manuscripts*, *The German Ideology*, *The Critique of the Gotha Programme*, the *Grundrisse* and *Capital*, especially volume III.
2 Letter to F. Domela-Nieuwenhuis, 22 February 1881, *Selected Correspondence*, p. 410.
3 *The Civil War in France, Selected Works*, I, 523.
4 *1844 Manuscripts*, p. 110.
5 Quoted by A. G. Meyer, *Marxism. The Unity of Theory and Practice* (Michigan, 1963), p. 115.
6 *Capital*, III, 251.
7 *Ibid.*, pp. 427 and 431. Engels suggested that in some cases the joint stock companies were being outgrown – in the great monopolies or trusts. 'In the trusts, freedom of competition changes into its very opposite – into monopoly; and the production without any definite plan of capitalistic society capitulates to the production upon a definite plan of the invading socialistic society'. *Anti-Dühring*, p. 382.
8 *Capital*, III, 431.
9 *Ibid.*, p. 593. In the same paragraph Marx writes that the banking system 'possesses indeed the form of universal book-keeping and distribution of means of production on a social scale, but solely the form'.
10 Marx states *(Ibid.,* p. 593) that the credit system 'will serve as a powerful lever during the transition from the capitalist mode of production to the mode of production of associated labour', though he adds (p. 594) that this will be only 'as one element in connection with other great organic revolutions of the mode of production itself'.
11 *Inaugural Address, Selected Works*, I, 383.
12 *5 March 1852, Selected Correspondence*, p. 86.
13 *Selected Works*, II, 32–3. Marx's other reference to the proletarian dictatorship is in *The Class Struggles in France*, where he writes that 'the proletariat rallies more and more round revolutionary socialism, round communism, for which the bourgeoisie has itself invented the name of Blanqui. This socialism is the declaration of the permanence of the revolution, the class dictatorship of the proletariat as the necessary transit point to the abolition of class distinctions generally, to the abolition of all the relations of production on which they rest, to the abolition of all the social relations that correspond to these relations of production, to the revolutionizing of all the ideas that result from these social relations'. *Selected Works* I, 222–3.

14 Kautsky felt that a new privileged class was emerging in Russia. His general assumption was that 'where the proletariat represents the majority, democracy will be the machinery for its rule. Where it is in the minority, democracy constitutes its most suitable fighting arena in which to assert itself, win concessions, and develop'. *The Dictatorship of the Proletariat* (Michigan, 1964), p. 133. Others, assuming the dehumanisation of the worker under capitalism, have stressed the necessity – and the value – of terror. Sartre, for example, has written : 'Historic experience of the countries in which communists took power has revealed undeniably that the first stage of socialist society in construction – to consider it from the still abstract view of power – cannot be anything else than the indissoluble aggregation of bureaucracy, the Terror, and the cult of personality'. Quoted by S. Hook, *Marxism in the Western World, Encounter* pamphlet 12, p. 8. This was not Marx's view (nor is it Sartre's present view), though it is fair to point out that the Bolsheviks were not acting in the conditions which he had envisaged for proletarian revolution. One can reasonably doubt, on various grounds, that terror, bureaucracy, etc. are likely to produce or allow the birth of a communist society.

15 Letter to F. Domela-Nieuwenhuis, 22 February 1881, *Selected Correspondence*, p. 410.

16 *The Civil War in France, Selected Works*, I, 523.

17 Kamenka, *The Ethical Foundations of Marxism*, p. 9.

18 *Ibid.*, p. 9.

19 According to Robert Tucker, *Philosophy and Myth in Karl Marx* (Cambridge, 1961), pp. 154–5, Marx was influenced at this point by Lorenz von Stein, who spoke of French raw communism as mere undirected upheaval. Tucker summarises Stein's argument – the theorists of raw communism, beginning with Baboeuf, were 'merely the mouthpieces of an untutored tendency present in the dispossessed and brutalized proletarian masses. This was the tendency to put egalitarianism into practice in a wild *mêlée* of expropriation and destruction of property, communization of wealth and wives, etc'. (p. 155).

20 Marx writes that the 'still immature communism', which is distinguished from developed communism, 'seeks an historical proof for itself – a proof in the realm of the existent – amongst disconnected historical phenomena opposed to private property, tearing single phases from the historical process and focussing attention on them as proofs of its historical pedigree (a horse ridden especially hard by Cabet, Villegardelle, etc.). By so doing it simply makes clear that by far the greater part of this process contradicts its claims, and that, if it has once been, precisely its being in the past refutes its pretension to being essential.' *1844 Manuscripts*, p. 102.

21 *Ibid.*, p. 101.

22 *Ibid.*, p. 100.

23 *Ibid.*, p. 100.

24 *Ibid.*, p. 100.

25 *Selected Works*, II, 23. That this represents a common problem of post-revolutionary societies is a point that hardly needs to be laboured. In 1962 we find Fidel Castro recognising the problem. 'In the Communist Manifesto Marx says that capitalism is digging its own grave – but capitalism digs two graves, one for itself and the other for the society which comes after it. What we must do is to fill the hole rapidly so that the legacy of capitalism may not destroy and bury socialism'. Speech delivered in Camaguey in May 1962. Quoted by B. Goldenberg, 'The Cuban Revolution: An Analysis', *Problems of Communism*, XII, no. 5 (September–October 1963), 9. The theories developed around Thermidor – the thermidorean reaction – by

Trotsky and others stress the return to previous forms of government and economic management. The counter-revolution, or the betrayal of the revolution, is never far away. How far can concessions to 'present reality' (which may be misunderstood) go without giving away the essence of the revolution?

26 Selected Works, II, 24.

27 'Marx's description of the first stage of future society in the Critique of the Gotha Programme closely resembles the account given in the Manuscripts, though his language is more restrained and his thought is economically rather than speculatively oriented'. Avineri, p. 225. On p. 192, note 1, Avineri refers again to the Manuscript discussion as containing a criticism of 'the crudity of communism in its first stages', after quoting from The Communist Manifesto, where Marx unequivocally placed crude communism in socialism's intellectual past. He was referring to a situation in which the proletariat was undeveloped, and in which the economic conditions for its emancipation were absent. 'The revolutionary literature that accompanied these first movements of the proletariat had necessarily a reactionary character. It inculcated universal asceticism and social levelling in its crudest form'. Selected Works, I, 61.

28 The German Ideology, p. 660.

29 Ibid., p. 84.

30 Ibid., p. 86. The process of elevation may take longer, and may exclude the present generation. Cf. Marx's comment in 1850: 'The present generation is like the Jews, whom Moses led through the wilderness. It has not only a new world to conquer, it must go under, in order to make room for the men who are fit for a new world'. Quoted by Feuer, Karl Marx and the Promethean Complex, p. 18.

31 Letters to Dr Kugelmann, pp. 123–4.

32 Avineri, Social and Political Thought, pp. 239–49.

33 Engels to Bebel, 18–28 March 1875, Selected Correspondence, p. 357.

34 Introduction to the 1891 (Berlin) edition of The Civil War in France, Selected Works, I, 485.

35 The Civil War in France, Selected Works, I, 519.

36 Ibid., p. 525.

37 Ibid., p. 521.

38 Ibid., p. 520.

39 John Plamenatz in Man and Society, II (London, 1963), 384–5, analyses some of the difficulties involved in such an administrative system, and holds that it could not work in the required way. His argument rests on assumptions about the nature of local bodies (what they discuss), the impossibility of delegates reaching complete spontaneous agreement at the highest level, and the difficulties in the way of the lower bodies retaining their sovereignty – because of the nature of industrial society, because not all will agree with the big decisions (their sovereignty is then infringed) and because it would be too cumbersome to try to secure such agreement in detail. This argument assumes – correctly, in my view – the complexity of administration and the persistence of conflict. Marx's central assumption was, of course, that of unanimity or basic agreement (the absence of disruptive forces). In that case mandates to delegates would not be necessary, as they would not be broken, and disputes about sovereignty would not arise because everyone would agree with everyone else. This is the ultimate case. The Frenchmen of 1871, and the proletarians immediately after 'the revolution' need more restraints, as the new man has not yet been born. And it is doubtful whether, in a complete sense, he ever will.

40 The Civil War in France, Selected Works, I, 522.

41 *Enthüllungen über den Kommunistenprozess zu Köln,* quoted by Hannah Arendt, *On Revolution,* (London, 1963), pp. 322–3. My translation. Miss Arendt apears to me to exaggerate the difference between Marx's 1871 and his 1873 position.
42 To F. Domela-Nieuwenhuis, 22 February 1881. *Selected Correspondence,* p. 410.
43 Letter to P. van Patten, 18 April 1883, *Selected Correspondence,* p. 437.
44 This remained a major problem for Marx and Engles. In his marginal notes on Bakhunin's *Statehood and Anarchy* Marx recognised its importance (especially in France) and wrote that the proletariat, if it wished to succeed, would have to take measures as a government 'which lead to a direct improvement of his (the peasant's) condition, and which, consequently win him over to the side of the revolution. From the very outset these measures must facilitate the transition from private to collective landownership, so that the peasant himself comes to it through economic means; care should, however, be taken not to antagonise him, for example, by proclaiming the abolition of the inheritance right or of his property The latter can be done only where the capitalistic tenant has ousted the peasant, and where the actual cultivator is just as much a proletarian, a wage-worker, as the rural worker'. *Selected Works,* vol. II of the three-volume edition (Moscow, 1969), p. 411.

The peasant problem has remained probably the major problem for Marxists in undeveloped countries. The concessions made by the Bolsheviks to the peasants were attacked by Kautsky and Rosa Luxemburg, amongst others, on the grounds that they had reactionary effects, creating a class opposed to the further development of the revolution. Kautsky wrote that the revolution had made the peasants 'the most energetic defenders of the newly-created private property in land. It has strengthened private property in the means of production...The thirst for land, which always characterises the peasant, has now, after the destruction of the big estates, made him the strongest defender of private property...The interest of the peasant in the revolution therefore dwindles so soon as his new private property is secured...The victory of the proletariat depends upon the extension of wage labour in the country, which is a protracted process'. *The Dictatorship of the Proletariat,* pp. 116–19. There are many instances where the revolutionary leadership has had long-term objectives which either fail to make sense to the peasantry, or which they understand and oppose, e.g. Castro's problems with the Campesina mentality, or the kulak hostility to collectivisation. Peasants do not always recognise what is good for them.

45 *The Peasant Question in France and Germany, Selected Works,* II, 438.
46 Avineri, *Social and Political Thought,* p. 206.
47 *Selected Works,* II, 24.
48 *Capital,* III, 855.
49 *1844 Manuscripts,* p. 102. In these general terms the Marxist myth is very close to the rather more abstract Hegelian one – where Absolute Spirit has returned to itself when its conflicts with brute matter are finally won. The basic question here – why pure and undivided Spirit goes through, and has to go through, a process of alienation – can be reformulated empirically for Marxism. If there was ever a condition of harmony or unity, how and why did it break up and, if reintegration is to come, are the original and historical sources of conflicts and evil removed satisfactorily in terms of the theory? Of course, the theory may be coherent and complete, but wrong.
50 *The German Ideology,* pp. 44–5.

51 *Selected Works*, II, 24.
52 *Capital*, III, 800.
53 Quoted Nicolaus, *Hegelian Choreography and the Capitalist Dialectic*, p. 38.
54 *Marx's Grundrisse*, p. 142.
55 *Capital*, I, 530.
56 *Ibid.*, 530.
57 *Marx's Grundrisse*, p. 148.
58 *The Human Condition* (Chicago and London, 1970), p. 133.
59 *The Communist Manifesto, Selected Works*, I, 54.
60 *Selected Works*, II, 36.
61 These claims are made by Avineri, *Social and Political Thought*, pp. 232–3.
62 *On Authority, Selected Works*, I, 637.
63 Marx scholars sometimes inflate, and give a utopian dimension to, quite ordinary and unexciting observations by Marx, e.g. the comment (*Capital*, III, 376) that labour in which many individuals co-operate needs 'a commanding will to co-ordinate and unify the process, and functions which apply not to partial operations but to the total activity of the workshop, much as that of an orchestra conductor'. Robert Tucker (*Philosophy and Myth*, p. 199) argues that Marx was here suggesting that industry might be regulated in an artistic way. The members of the 'orchestra', thus conceived, do not feel themselves to be subordinate to any external controlling body, and authority within the factory loses its political or repressive character. It seems to me that Tucker's interpretation of this passage is rather forced, in that Marx was simply drawing attention to the necessity of management and supervision (a 'commanding will') and was not claiming that the workers in the factory were or would be engaged in free artistic creation.
64 As does Hannah Arendt, *The Human Condition*, pp. 87, 105 and 118. It is fair to say that in *The German Ideology* Marx tended to see ideal labour as pure pleasure, as satisfying as leisure activities (Arendt, *The Human Condition*, p. 127), but not that this was his lasting view (cf. *Marx's Grundrisse*, p. 148: 'Work cannot become a game, as Fourier would like it to be...'), and certainly not that he saw the 'realm of freedom' supplanting the 'realm of necessity' (Arendt, *The Human Condition*, p. 104). When he uses these two concepts the latter is the foundation of the former.
65 Letter to Marx, 23 October 1846, *Selected Correspondence*, p. 37. The full account of the objectives of communism is as follows: (1) to achieve the interests of the proletariat in opposition to those of the bourgeoisie; (2) to do this through the abolition of private property and its replacement by community of goods; (3) to recognise no means of carrying out these objects other than a democratic revolution by force. The stress is on the communist movement rather than the future communist society.
66 P. 60. Cf. *The Poverty of Philosophy* and Marx's letter to J. B. Schweitzer (14 January 1865), where Proudhon's bourgeois (individual property) horizons are condemned.
67 *Der Volkstribun, redigiert von Herrmann Kriege*, quoted by Lewis Feuer, 'The North American Origins of Marx's Socialism', *The Western Political Quarterly*, XVI (1963), 55.
68 *1844 Manuscripts*, p. 81.
69 *Capital*, III, 757.
70 Marx's view is only put in very general terms, and rarely, and remains rather obscure, as one would expect. In the *Manuscripts* (p. 114) Marx spoke of the transcendence of communism insofar as it embodied a principle of ownership. What will happen, presumably, is that the whole notion of

possession for oneself, against and to the exclusion of others, will disappear, along with the notion of a self opposed to society. The editor of the Moscow edition of the *Manuscripts* claims that Marx's 'communism as such' ('Communism is the necessary pattern and the dynamic principle of the immediate future, but Communism as such is not the goal of human development', p. 114) refers to 'crude, equalitarian communism, such as that propounded by Babeuf and his followers' (note, p. 114). However, Marx's argument makes it quite clear that 'raw communism' and 'communism as such' are quite distinct. Marx also suggested in the *Manuscripts* (p. 64) that man's relationship with the land would change – there would be the re-establishment of 'the intimate ties of man with the earth, for the earth ceases to be an object of huckstering and through free labour and free enjoyment becomes once more a true personal property of man'. We are not justified in concluding, from these broad statements, that there will be no privacy or no locks or no personal property of any kind in the future.

71 Letter to Engels, 5 March 1869, *Selected Correspondence*, p. 266. The phrase to which Marx was here objecting appeared in the programme of the Bakunist Alliance of Social Democracy.

72 Marx to Weydemeyer, 5 March 1852, *Selected Correspondence*, pp. 85-6.

73 *The German Ideology*, p. 416.

74 *Anti-Dühring* (Moscow, 1959), p. 387. Marx and Engels both argued strongly against the position of the anarchists, which they took to be the position that the state was the key element or lever in the social edifice, and that it must first be destroyed, after which other changes (to capitalism) would naturally follow. They found this superficial. 'We, on the contrary, say: Do away with capital, the concentration of all the means of production in the hands of the few, and the state will fall of itself. The difference is an essential one: without a previous revolution the abolition of the state is nonsense; the abolition of capital is precisely the social revolution and involves a change in the whole mode of production'. Engels to T. Cuno, 24 January 1872, *Selected Correspondence*, p. 335. In the course of an attack on Bakunin, Marx and Engels made one of their most extreme anarchist statements. 'All socialists see anarchy as the following programme: once the aim of the proletarian movement, i.e. abolition of classes, is attained the power of the State, which serves to keep the great majority of producers in bondage to a very small exploiter minority, disapears, and the functions of government become simple administrative functions'. 'Fictitious splits in the International', *Documents of the First International*, 1871-2, p. 407.

75 *Selected Works*, II, 32.

76 As they do in Engels's account of the indispensable social functions, *Anti-Dühring*, p. 247.

77 In *The Communist Manifesto*, the utopian socialists are praised for their proposal for 'the conversion of the functions of the state into a mere superintendence of production'. *Selected Works*, I, 63.

78 Marx to Engels, 8 January 1868. *Selected Correspondence*, p. 230.

79 *Capital*, III, 830.

80 The labour theory of value comes into its own in the socialist society. 'Only when production will be under the conscious and prearranged control of society will society establish a direct relation between the quantity of social labour-time employed in the production of definite articles and the quantity of the demand of society for them...The exchange, or sale, of commodities at their value is the rational way, the natural law of their equilibrium'. Quoted by Joan Robinson, *An Essay on Marxian Economics*

(London, 1967), p. 23. This will end capitalism's anarchic separation of production and consumption.

81 Marx attacked the German Worker's Party in 1875 for making the 'free state one of its aims'. He wrote that freedom consists in 'converting the state from an organ superimposed upon society into one completely subordinate to it'. *Critique of the Gotha Programme, Selected Works,* II, 32. The Paris Commune was recommended for making the political officers responsible to society as a whole. In terms of the early writings, man draws back into himself his alienated powers.

82 *The Poverty of Philosophy,* p. 197.

83 To A. Bebel, 18–28 March 1875, *Selected Correspondence,* p. 357. A more significant issue concerns the relative state of development of the various nations of the world. All the dominant people need to become communist at once, lest communism be smothered at its birth, and hence communism presupposes the 'universal development of productive forces' (*The German Ideology,* pp. 46–7). Presumably this means a rough equivalence of standards between the dominant peoples.

84 *Critique of the Gotha Programme, Selected Works,* II, 24.

85 Mill thought it a possible advantage of communism that public opinion would declare itself against the vices of indolence and intemperance. See below, ch. 7.

86 *Towards the Understanding of Karl Marx* (London, 1933), p. 261.

87 Engels held that the dialectical philosophy 'dissolves all conceptions of final, absolute truth and of absolute states of humanity corresponding to it'. History, like knowledge, is unable to reach 'a complete conclusion in a perfect, ideal condition of humanity'; 'a perfect society, a perfect "state"', are things which can only exist in imagination'. *Ludwig Feuerbach and the End of Classical German Philosophy, Selected Works,* II, 362–3. But he does not suggest the sources of change once socialism arrives.

88 P. 196.

89 P. 52.

90 Quoted by R. Dahrendorf, *Class and Class Conflict in Industrial Society* (London, 1959), p. 11.

91 *1844 Manuscripts,* pp. 80–2.

92 *Ludwig Feuerbach, Selected Works,* II, 362.

93 For example, Stalin admitted that there may be economic problems in the socialist phase (which to him, unlike Marx, was the first stage, distinct from communism), and instanced a lag of productive relations behind productive forces, with the former acting as a fetter upon the latter. The advance on capitalism was that this could now be adjusted without 'explosion'. The contradictions under socialism are of a new kind – they are 'non-antagonistic'. *Economic Problems of Socialism.* See H. Marcuse, *Soviet Marxism* (New York, 1958), p. 166.

94 'State and Revolution in the Paris Commune, the Russian Revolution, and the Spanish Civil War', *Sociological Review,* XXIX (1937), 41.

95 *Reflections on the Revolution in France,* p. 61.

96 One can, in most revolutions, point to widespread terror, e.g. by Robespierre in year II of the revolution (1793–4), when 40,000 were executed (many under the Law of Suspects and the Law of the Maximum), by Stalin during the thirties and by Castro, on a far smaller scale, in the early sixties. But while revolutions generally involve social disintegration, this – and the use of widespread and persistent violence – has also characterised pre-revolutionary regimes, and revolutionary regimes have sometimes increased integration, though they do not normally reduce the level of violence, at least immediately. Moreover, Robespierre and Stalin were not employing

the only means that would hold their societies together: they were using terror to suppress rival groups (the objectives of the revolutionaries varied) and because of their own psychological imbalance (fears and sense of persecution). They could have survived with much less violence.

97 Engels suggested to Conrad Schmidt that there was not much value in considering the question of distribution in the future society, as 'the method of distribution essentially depends on how much there is to distribute, and (that) this must surely change with the progress of production and social organisation, so that the method of distribution may also change'. Socialist society will undergo continuous change and progress. One can only try to find the method of distribution used at the beginning and estimate the general tendency of future development. 5 August 1890, *Selected Correspondence*, p. 496. Even this is much more specific than Marx ever allowed himself to be.

98 J. Burnham, *The Managerial Revolution* (London 1962), p. 74.

99 See especially *Marxism, Freedom and the State*, extracts of which are printed in L. I. Krimerman and L. Perry (eds), *Patterns of Anarchy* (New York, 1966), pp. 80–97.

100 *Political Parties* (New York, 1959), p. 401.

101 Michels seems to have assumed that the certain size lay somewhere between 1,000 and 10,000, i.e. this was the lower limit. In those of greater size the division would simply be intensified.

102 Quoted by T. B. Bottomore, *Elites and Society* (London, 1966), p. 17.

103 *Social Contract*, IV, i, 85.

104 On even democratic socialists: 'What our planners demand is a central direction of all economic activity according to a single plan, laying down how the resources of society should be "consciously directed" to serve particular ends in a definite way.' F. A. Hayek questions whether 'a rational utilisation of our resources requires central direction and organisation of all our activities according to some consciously constructed "blueprint"'. *The Road to Serfdom* (London, 1962), p. 26. The argument is exaggerated and crude ('all economic activities', 'all our activities', 'a single plan', etc.). There are many kinds of planning, some of which depend heavily on spontaneous local forces or the autonomy of separate industries or utilities.

105 Tucker, *Philosophy and Myth*, p. 242.

106 *Ibid.*, p. 242.

107 Or Hamilton, succinctly: 'Men love power'. Quoted from Elliot's Debates by Robert Dahl, *A Preface to Democratic Theory* (Chicago, 1963), p. 8.

108 *Marxism: The View from America* (New York, 1960), p. 88.

109 *Ibid.*, p. 188.

110 *Ibid.*, p. 78. Also, more generally: 'If we were to concede the point that a new race of men can be created by conscious manipulation of the social environment, what power could we then properly withhold from those into whose hands have been placed the levers of political control? The assumption of the infinite plasticity of human nature is a major intellectual support of the totalitarian state, and for this reason, if for no other, we cannot admit its validity' (p. 77). This is truly a pragmatist definition of truth. We cannot, however, determine the validity of general beliefs by indicating their supposed practical consequences – and in other hands they may lead to very different conclusions. A belief in the plasticity, i.e. the potentialities, of ordinary human beings may provoke constructive social action, concerned with increasing their power to develop *their* capabilities. An argument against plasticity may well be a defence of present moulds.

111 H. B. Parkes, *Marxism. An Autopsy* (Chicago, 1964), p. 112. This would not apply, claims Parkes, if it was shown in concrete detail 'how a democratic

and libertarian collectivism, free from the tyrannies of the Russian system, could actually be made to function' (p. 112).

112 The Russian case can, however, be used, in a conservative way, to illustrate the problems faced by revolutionaries, perhaps on lines similar to those taken by Burke in his assault on the French Revolution. For example, S. M. Lipset has argued that the history of the Russian Revolution has 'already demonstrated some of the dire consequences of operating with a theory which deals only with non-existent ideal types'. *Political Man* (London, 1963), p. 26. But although Marxism may have been the central component of the thought of the revolutionary leaders, their 'creative developments' or selectiveness has often altered or mutilated Marx's doctrine, e.g. the emphasis of both Lenin and Stalin on political rather than economic forces.

113 The fact that Marx provided no firm defence of liberal rights, and denounced a class of enemies of the proletariat, obviously leaves the individual – and especially' enemies of the people' – vulnerable when dictatorial disciples of Marx are in power, and can use some of his arguments and concepts without sharing much of his vision. Easton and Guddat, *Writings of the Young Marx* (p. 32), suggest that Marx went wrong in abandoning the principle of subjectivity, which left the implications of his thought 'more congenial to totalitarianism than to the emphasis on the individual person and his self-direction which characterises liberal democracy'. Yet Marx was deeply concerned with individual self-direction, though in my view he was wrong as to the conditions required for the ordinary individual to direct himself.

6 IDEAS, CLASSES AND SOCIAL CHANGE

1 *A System of Logic* (London, 1872), p. 5.

2 For example, 'The Spirit of the Age' has been treated commonly as a Saint-Simonian tract breaking with utilitarianism, but Richard Friedman has presented a strong case that Mill's important justification of authority in that tract is traceable primarily to John Austin. 'An Introduction to Mill's Theory of Authority', in *Mill: A Collection of Critical Essays*, ed. J. B. Schneewind (London, 1969), pp. 379–425.

3 Mill suffered a serious nervous illness or crisis. He spoke of 'the dry heavy dejection' which he endured in 'the melancholy winter of 1826–7'. *Autobiography* (London, 1958), p. 118. In a letter to Sterling on 15 April 1829 he referred to the painful states of mind that he had endured during the past three years, one of which was 'something distantly approaching to misanthropy'. *The Early Letters, Collected Works*, XII (Toronto, 1963), 29. He believed that a revolution took place in his mode of thinking between 1826 and 1830.

4 J. Vincent, *The Formation of the British Liberal Party 1857–68.* (London, 1872), p. 188.

5 *Autobiography*, p. 133.

6 *Ibid.*, p. 132.

7 Hamburger cites some of the charges of doctrinairism and fanaticism which were made against Mill when he supported sharp ideological conflict, or what he called the battle of 'principled extremes'. See J. Hamburger, *Intellectuals in Politics, John Stuart Mill and the Philosophical Radicals* (New Haven and London, 1965), pp. 26–7.

8 *Autobiography*, p. 136.

9 To Sterling, 4 November 1839, *Collected Works*, XIII, 411.

10 I am not attempting to trace the development of Mill's ideas, but to consider some of his persisting conceptions and concerns. Whilst I have

acknowledged some of the changes and variations in his beliefs, my account of his social doctrine will strike the intellectual historian as somewhat abstract and gross.

11 *A System of Logic*, vol. II, Bk. VI, X, § 7, p. 527. The crucial sections of this chapter are sections 7 and 8.
12 *Representative Government* (London, 1960), pp. 183–4.
13 *Ibid.*, p. 184. Occasionally, and especially in his earlier writings, Mill made this kind of point quite brazenly. In 1829, for example, he wrote: 'The intellectual classes lead the government, and the government leads the stupid classes'. To Gustave d'Eichtal, 11 March 1829, *Collected Works*, XII, 29.
14 *A System of Logic*, II, 527.
15 *Ibid.*, ch. X, §3, p. 511. His assumption in favour of progress was strengthened greatly by his reading of Comte, who seemed to him to provide a true and scientific account of man's intellectual development.
16 'Nature', in *Three Essays on Religion* (London, 1874), p. 11.
17 *Ibid.*, p. 70. In these statements Mill was referring to the community at large, though he occasionally complained about his own lack of firm belief. He wrote to Carlyle, on 18 May 1833: 'I am often in a state almost of scepticism, and have no theory of Human Life at all, or seem to have conflicting theories, or a theory which does not amount to a Belief'. *Collected Works*, XII, 154.
18 In *Essays on Politics and Culture*, ed. G. Himmelfarb (New York, 1963), p. 2. The articles on 'The Spirit of the Age' appeared in *The Examiner* during the first part of 1831.
19 *August Comte and Positivism* (Ann Arbor, 1961), p. 97.
20 'The Spirit of the Age', in *Essays on Politics and Culture*, pp. 17–18.
21 *Ibid.*, p. 17.
22 'Civilisation', *Dissertations and Discussions*, I (London, 1860), 172–3.
23 *On Liberty* (London, 1960), p. 143.
24 Bentham in *Bentham and Coleridge*, ed. F. R. Leavis (London, 1959), p. 70.
25 *Essay on Government* (Cambridge, 1937), p. 6.
26 Consider, for example, James Mill's definitional trick with 'Community', and his failure to envisage or allow for the diverse and conflicting interests of the various sections of democratic communities: 'The Community cannot have an interest opposed to its interest. To affirm this would be a contradiction in terms. The Community within itself, and with respect to itself, can have no sinister interest. One community may intend the evil of another; never its own...The Community may act wrongly from mistake. To suppose that it could from design, would be to suppose that human beings can wish their own misery'. *Ibid.*, pp. 10–11. And indeed, his specific proposals, such as those for the extension of the franchise and frequent elections, assume that the governing section of the community can definitely intend the evil of other sections of the same community.
27 *The Times*, 10 August 1861.
28 *Representative Government*, pp. 254–5.
29 Even such 'disinterested' bodies as the East India Company have their corporate feelings. 'All services have, more or less, their class prejudices, from which the supreme ruler ought to be exempt'. *Ibid.*, p. 389. Yet how, given the general claim, can the supreme ruler remain exempt?
30 By the 1860s, the major division was between, on the one hand, labourers and 'those smaller employers of labour, who by interests, habits and educational impressions are assimilated in wishes, tastes and objects to the labouring classes, comprehending a large proportion of petty tradesmen', and, on the other, employers of labour, including retired capitalists, posses-

sors of inherited wealth, professional men and highly paid labourers. *Representative Government*, p. 255.

31 *Essay on Government, passim.* James Mill seemed to regard the having of power as itself a source of pleasure, as well as a means to achieving other satisfactions.

32 *Representative Government*, p. 248.

33 'Fonblanque's England under Seven Administrations', *London and Westminster Review*, XXVII, (April 1837), 67.

34 'Review of Scott's Life of Napoleon', *Westminster Review*, IX, (April 1828), 279.

35 'Modern French Historical Works – Age of Chivalry', *Westminster Review*, VI July 1826), 66. On the same page he commented that the age of chivalry 'was equally distinguished by moral depravity and by physical wretchedness'.

36 *Ibid.*, p. 73.

37 'Law of Libel and Liberty of the Press', *Westminster Review*, XXX (July 1835), 293.

38 'The Rationale of Political Representation', *Westminster Review*, XXX (July 1835), 348. Such aristocracies need not be hereditary.

39 *Representative Government*, p. 389. Cf. the quotation from the same page cited in n. 29, which suggests a broader and more realistic notion of bias than the class bias on which Mill normally concentrated – thought it, too, was an extensive notion. Mill assumed that the corporate interests and prejudices of a body such as the East India Company were superior to the interests and prejudices of a Marxist-type class, just as some people now find political imperialism morally superior to economic imperialism. Economic interests seem meaner.

40 'Pledges', *The Examiner*, 1 July 1832, p. 416.

41 *Principles of Political Economy*, V, ii, §4, *Collected Works* (Toronto, 1965), III, 819–20.

42 'Sir John Walsh's Contemporary History – Progress of Reform', *Westminster Review*, XXXV (April 1836), 290.

43 Mill at this time supported the ballot (secret vote) as a means of preventing unfair influence on electors. He argued that it may be good or bad, depending on the circumstances. 'It is good when the voters own interest is to vote right, but he may be bribed or intimidated by persons whose interest it is that he should vote wrong. It is wrong where his own interest is to vote wrong, and where the only means of giving him a sufficient motive to vote right, is responsibility, either to law or to public opinion'. 'Use and Abuse of the Ballot', *The Examiner*, 28 November 1830, p. 755.

44 'The Ballot', *The Examiner*, 5 December 1830, p. 769.

45 Vincent writes that the Liberal answer to the question, what to do when the landowners cannot govern by themselves?, was not 'to replace the old ascendancy by a new one'. *The Formation of the British Liberal Party*, p. 13. In fact Mill's answer was precisely that, to substitute a new – and qualitatively different – ascendancy for the old. This is not to suggest that there was a genuine middle-class alternative to aristocratic government.

46 Quoted Asa Briggs, *Essays in Labour History*, pp. 56–7.

47 *Essay on Government*, p. 72.

48 'Reorganization of the Reform Party' (April 1839), in *Essays on Politics and Culture*, p. 280.

49 'Prospects of France', The Examiner, IV (10 October 1830), 643.

50 'The Rationale of Political Representation', p. 357.

51 Letter to Gustave d'Eichtal, *Collected Works*, XII, 32.

52 *Autobiography*, p. 166. At one stage Mill thought that Lord Durham was

a possible leader of the Radicals. He wrote in 1837 that if 'Radicalism had its Sir Robert Peel, he would be at the head of an administration within two years'. 'Parties and the Ministry', *London and Westminster Review,* XXVIII (October 1837), 25. And Mill did not think much of Peel. While generally believing that the Radicals in the House of Commons – especially Grote, Roebuck and Molesworth – were well-intentioned, he complained that they lacked drive and decisive leadership. They left the leadership of the Radical portion of the House to the old hands, Hume and O'Connell. Mill often overlooked the divisions between the Radicals, and within radical opinion in the country at large. He became increasingly disillusioned about the feasibility of his aim of breathing a living soul into the Radical party, and in 1840 suggested to Macvey Napier, the editor of the *Edinburgh Review,* that there was no room for a fourth party – the three at that stage being the Conservatives, the Whig-Radicals and the Chartists. 22 April 1840, *Collected Works,* XIII, 430. He had hoped to establish a genuine Radical party, clearly distinct from the existing parties, and containing all the enlightened members of the community. The good Whigs would join the new party while the bad (aristocratic) ones would enter a natural alliance with the Tories. As his hopes for a Radical party declined, Mill often complimented the Whigs, e.g. writing to Fonblanque on 17 June 1840 that the Whig Ministry deserved Radical support. *Collected Works,* XIII, 479. He was finally prepared to work through the Whigs, though he had problems with the terms of collaboration.

His account of Radical objectives was not firm and precise. He meant by Radicalism a refusal to falter or compromise with evils, a cutting at the roots of evils (to Bulwer, 23 November 1836, *Collected Works,* XII, 312), a belief in the absolute necessity of the ballot, with or without an extension of the suffrage ('Radical Party in Canada', *London and Westminster Review,* January 1838, p. 506), a belief in change beyond those accepted by Whigs and Tories, and especially widening the basis of the representative system (to J. M. Kemble, 14 October 1839, *Collected Works,* XIII, 410), or belief in a meritocracy or government of talent.

53 Letter to Gustave d'Eichtal, 15 May 1829, *Collected Works,* XII, 33. He wrote to Carlyle (17 July 1832) that it is 'curious that this particular time, in which there are fewer great intellects above ground and in their vigour, than can be remembered for many ages back, should be the precise time at which everybody is cackling about the progress of intelligence and the spread of knowledge'. *Ibid.,* p. 112. Carlyle did tend to bring out Mill's gloomier side. Mill's complaints about lack of leadership sometimes arose from his faulty social analysis – when his too high expectations were dashed, it was easy to blame bad leaders.

54 'The Close of the Session', *Westminster Review,* XXXI (October 1835), 274.

55 *Culture and Anarchy* (London, 1954), p. 66. More succinctly, Arnold spoke of the rough, who 'comes in immense numbers, and is rather rough and raw'. *Ibid.,* p. 42.

56 *John Stuart Mill as Some of the Working Classes Know Him* (London, 1873), p. 28.

57 P. 196.

58 P. 197. In the preface to the third edition (1852) of *Principles of Political Economy* he indicated that his condemnation of socialism in the earlier editions did not apply to it as an ultimate result of human progress. 'The only objection to which any great importance will be found to be attached in the present edition is the unprepared state of mankind in general, and of the labouring classes in particular; their extreme unfitness at present for any order of things, which would make any considerable demand on either

their intellect or their virtue'. *Collected Works*, II, xciii. But as John Vincent points out, Mill seems to have been unacquainted with such examples of disinterested working-class administration as the Rochdale Pioneers or the A.E.U. *The Formation of the British Liberal Party*, p. 187, n. 30. Familiarity might have reduced his general castigations of the class.

59 'Reorganization of the Reform Party', in *Essays on Politics and Culture*, p. 291. In this article, which was drafted in late 1837 and published in 1839, Mill looked to the Working Men's Association in London, which framed the People's Charter, for 'the best and most enlightened aspect of working-class Radicalism' (p. 291).

60 Letters to James Mill, 20 August 1830, *Collected Works*, XII, 56. He also wrote (p. 62) that there appeared among the victors of the three days 'no personal feeling, nothing but a desire to manifest to the world the justice of their cause, to prove that they have been actuated by no sinister interests, but were led on solely, first to defend themselves, and then to rid themselves of an evil which was no longer supportable'.

61 To J. S. Kinnear, 25 September 1865, in *The Letters of John Stuart Mill*, ed. S. R. Elliott (London, 1910) II, 45.

62 'Democracy in America', *Dissertations and Discussions*, II, 37.

63 *Ibid.*, p. 20.

64 'Reorganization of the Reform Party', p. 282.

65 'Claims of Labour', (April 1845), *Dissertations and Discussions*, II, 188.

66 *Ibid.*, pp. 206–7.

67 IV, vii, § 4, p. 767.

68 'Reorganization of the Reform Party', p. 292.

69 'Recent Writers on Reform' (April 1859), in *Essays on Politics and Culture*, p. 341.

70 *Representative Government*, p. 254. Cf. his letter to William Lovett on 27 June 1842. 'The same horror which you yourself entertain of class legislation, makes me object, in the present state of civilisation at least, if not on principle, to a legislature absolutely controlled by one class, even when that class numerically exceeds all others taken together'. *Collected Works*, XIII, 533.

71 Speaking of situations of diversity of interest, where the law may be used improperly by the dominant party, Mill instanced 'the laws against combinations of workmen, and the laws which have existed at some periods of our history, fixing a maximum of wages'. 'The Rationale of Political Representation', p. 354.

72 'Recent Writers on Reform', in *Essays on Politics and Culture*, p. 359.

73 'Reorganization of the Reform Party', p. 292.

74 Mill quoted Austin (*A Plea for the Constitution*) on the nature of a House of Commons returned by universal suffrage. It would 'ruin our finances, and destroy our economic prosperity, by insensate interferences with the natural arrangements of society, which would not be the less pernicious for not being inspired by theory...We might, therefore, expect from a House of Commons representing the prejudices of the non-proprietary class, a minimum rate of wages, a maximum price of provisions and other necessaries of life, with numberless other restrictions on the actual freedom of contracting'. 'Recent Writers on Reform', p. 342. Robert Lowe, perhaps the most fervent and unrelenting anti-democrat of Mill's time, declared: 'Once give working men the votes, and the machinery is ready to launch those votes in one compact mass upon the institutions and property of this country', and again 'It is impossible for universal suffrage to continue where there are so many poor who will want to divide or destroy property', quoted Asa Briggs, *Victorian People* (Harmondsworth, 1965), pp. 250 and 254.

75 'Democracy in America', p. 31. A generation later, in Representative Government, he cited a law to equalise earnings as a likely piece of bad working-class legislation.

76 'On Miss Martineau's Summary of Political Economy', Monthly Repository, VIII, May 1834, p. 320.

77 Improvement naturally involved the dominance of real interests, which should suppress illusory and selfish interests. In 'Nature' Mill defined self-control, which he found rare amongst the poor and the strong, as 'the power of sacrificing a present desire to a distant object or a general purpose'. Three Essays on Religion, p. 50. The general distinction is a rather loose one, as it ignores calculating egoism just as it does those interests which may be real and immediate. There is, of course, a long tradition of political theory which speaks about real interests (or goals or purposes or even desires) in such a way, normally linking the 'real' with some particular state or community, actual or imagined. Mill cannot be saddled with the dangers associated with some of these doctrines, but, like their expounders, he is sometimes vague and inflated in discussions of what is real and true.

78 'The Rationale of Political Representation', p. 357.

79 'Reorganization of the Reform Party', p. 287. On the same page Mill suggested that the government of the middle classes might be tempered with 'a partial admixture of representatives elected chiefly by the working men'. In his comments on 'Democracy in America' (pp. 20–1) he pointed out some of the distinctions within the working class, with some members already capable of exercising democratic rights. His statements about the gradual extension of the franchise are normally fairly general, and do not provide clear-cut practical guidance.

80 Mill justified paternalism where it was constructive (thus tending towards its own eventual disappearance) and where those in authority were disinterested, or had no stake in profiteering, nepotism and so on. In relation to India, he thought that efficient outside control could provide the conditions for self-government, and that it was preferable in this and other respects to native rule. But he also thought that the process of selection by merit for the East India Company provided some check against possible misgovernment, and that the freedom of that bureaucracy from aristocratic connection and party control made it a prime example of disinterestedness. For a fuller discussion, see Alan Ryan, 'Utilitarianism and Bureaucracy, in Studies in the Growth of Nineteenth-Century Government, ed. Gillian Sutherland (London, 1972), pp. 33–62.

81 Each class, with its special interests, knows some things better than others do, and hence can provide valuable information to legislators. A properly constituted democratic parliament would be 'an arena in which not only the general opinion of the nation, but that of every section of it, and as far as possible every eminent individual whom it contains, can produce itself in full light and challenge discussion; where every person in the country may count upon finding somebody who speaks his mind, as well or better than he could speak it himself'. Representative Government, p. 239.

82 'State of the Parties in France', The Examiner, 28 August 1831, pp. 545–6.

83 A System of Logic, Book VI, chs. 7 and 8.

84 Letter to J. Whiting, 15 October 1842, Collected Works, XIII, 550.

85 'Chapters on Socialism', Fortnightly Review, XXV, n.s. (1879), 525.

86 Cf. Article III, 'The Prospects of France', The Examiner, 3 October 1830, p. 627. 'When justice and the public interest demand the concession of a foot, it is wretched policy to refuse the people an inch lest they should take an ell'.

87 'A Few Observations on the French Revolution', *Dissertations and Discussions*, I, 59.
88 'The Rationale of Political Representation', p. 369.
89 *Representative Government*, ch. 1. Mill contrasted the mechanistic view of government – the typically enlightenment conception of constitutions as similar to steam ploughs or other instruments – with the organic or historical view, according to which governments are not made, but grow. Mill holds that there is some truth in each of these conceptions and that the question cannot be answered in the abstract. His position is misdescribed by M. Oakeshott, who associates Mill with an insidious current misunderstanding of political activity – that 'in which institutions and procedures appear as pieces of machinery designed to achieve a purpose settled in advance, instead of as manners of behaviour which are meaningless when separated from their context, the misunderstanding, for example, in which Mill convinced himself that something called "Representative Government" was a "form" of politics which could be regarded as proper to any society which had reached a certain level of what he called "civilisation", in short, the misunderstanding in which we regard our arrangements and institutions as something more significant than the footprints of thinkers and statesmen who knew which way to turn their feet without knowing anything about a final destination'. *Rationalism in Politics and Other Essays* (London, 1962), pp. 130–1. But though Mill did not regard institutions as pieces of machinery, and though much of his prescriptive writing is the abridgement of traditions, and the following out of their intimations, he did think in terms of politics as the pursuit of ideals or the solution of problems, and this, in terms of Oakeshott's conception of politics, is unadulterated and absurd rationalism.
90 *Auguste Comte and Positivism*, pp. 82–3. The theories which he attacked were, despite their realistic appearance, abstract theories, which failed to take account of the diversities of society. Subject to such abstract notions, the English failed to recognise the peculiarities of Ireland, but treated it as if it were England, and continued to look upon their own political economy as if it were universally valid. 'So far from being a set of maxims and rules to be applied without regard to times, places and circumstances, the function of political economy is to enable us to find the rules which ought to govern any state of circumstances which are never the same in any two cases'. *Mr Maguire's Motion on the State of Ireland, 12 March 1868, Chapters and Speeches on the Irish Land Question* (London, 1870), p. 118. While we may agree with Mill's attack on the arrogance of the English – 'there is no other civilized nation which is so conceited in its own institutions, and of all its modes of public action, as England is', *England and Ireland*, p. 9 – it is also true that something of that conceit, and a good deal of its insularity, pervades Mill's own writings.
91 *Chapters on Socialism*, p. 222.
92 *Ibid.*, p. 224.

7 THE ELEVATION OF MANKIND

1 *Utilitarianism*, p. 14.
2 'Civilization', *Dissertations and Discussions*, I, 172.
3 Letter to J. F. Mollett, December 1847, *Collected Works*, XIII, 727.
4 'The Quarterly Review on the Political Economists', *The Examiner*, 30 January 1831.
5 'Democracy in America', pp. 64–5. The habits of many agricultural labourers were reckless. 'They generally marry as early, and have as many

children to a marriage, as they would or could do if they were settlers in the United States'. *Principles of Political Economy*, II, xi, §3, p. 346.

6 'State of Society in America', *Westminster Review*, XXXI (January 1836), 371. In the 1848 edition of *Principles of Political Economy* he wrote, in relation to the Americans, that 'the proportion of population to land and capital is such as to ensure abundance to every able-bodied member of the community who does not forfeit it by misconduct. They have the six points of Chartism, and they have no poverty; and all that these advantages do for them is that the life of the whole of one sex is devoted to dollar-hunting, and of the other to breeding dollar-hunters'. Note in Book IV, vi, §2, p. 754. Economic abundance does not necessarily raise the quality of life.

7 These were sometimes significant but not always adequate means of reducing the population problem. The 'natural checks' – war, disease and starvation – persisted in some areas. Importation of food could help, as could the substitution of maize or Indian corn for wheat as the staple food of the poor. Emigration was especially important in the case of Ireland, where it had, by the mid-nineteenth century, reduced the population 'down to the number for which the existing agricultural system can find employment and support'. The Irish peasantry saw the terrestrial paradise across the sea as 'a sure refuge both from the oppression of the Saxon and from the tyranny of nature'. *Principles of Political Economy*, II, x, §1, p. 325. In a series of leading articles in *The Morning Chronicle* (October – December 1846) Mill argued that emigration was not the appropriate solution to Ireland's population problem, as there was ample wastelands remaining in Ireland itself. It was necessary to give the peasant a motive for hard work, and this could be provided by a system of peasant proprietorship. 'Make it his interest to be industrious and prudent.' 19 November 1846, p. 4. The indolence of the Irish peasant was 'the result of a social condition in which they can seldom benefit themselves by exertion...The faults of the Irish peasantry are the result of their circumstances.' 17 December 1846, p. 4.

8 *Principles of Political Economy*, II, i, §1, p. 199.

9 *Ibid.*, I, xii, §2, pp. 173–4.

10 *Ibid.*, IV, iv, §4, p. 739.

11 In Mill's words: 'As long as there are old countries where capital increases very rapidly, and new countries where profit is still high, profits in the old countries will not sink to the rate which would put a stop to accumulation; the fall is stopped at the point which sends capital abroad'. *Ibid.*, IV, iv, §8, p. 746.

12 'But though the minimum rate of profit is thus liable to vary, and though to specify exactly what it is would at any given time be impossible, such a minimum always exists; and whether it be high or low, when once it is reached, no further increase of capital can for the present take place. The country has then attained what is known to political economists under the name of the stationary state'. *Ibid.*, IV, iv, §3, p. 738.

13 *Ibid.*, IV, vi, §1, p. 752.

14 *Ibid.*, I, xiii, §2, p. 188.

15 *Ibid.*, I, vi, §3, p. 97.

16 *Ibid.*, p. 99.

17 *Ibid*, I, x, §3, p. 157.

18 *Ibid.*

19 *Ibid.*, II, xi, §2, p. 341.

20 *Ibid.*, p. 342.

21 *Ibid.*, I, x, 3, p. 159.

22 P. 163.

23 *Principles of Political Economy*, II, x, §6, p. 352.

24 This was an old rationalist view, which was shared in Mill's time by such champions of the cultivated man as Arnold and Jowett.

25 *Autobiography*, p. 89.

26 In a letter to Gustave d'Eichtal on 15 May 1829, Mill complained of the English system, 'under which everything is accessible to wealth and scarcely anything to poverty', and of the worst point in the English national character – 'the disposition to sacrifice everything to accumulation, and that exclusive and engrossing selfishness which accompanies it'. *Collected Works*, XIII, 31.

27 *August Comte and Positivism*, pp. 94–5. Mill found the British workman more efficient but less happy than his Continental counterpart. If the Continental workman was to catch up, 'he must become as patient, as conscientious, but also as careworn, as anxious, as joyless, as dull, as exclusively intent upon the main chance, as his British compeer. He will long be of inferior value as a machine, because happily for him, he cares for pleasure as well as gain'. Mill on 'Torrens Letter to Sir Robert Peel', *Spectator*, 28 January 1843, p. 85.

28 *Principles of Political Economy*, II, i, §3, p. 207.

29 *Ibid.*

30 Mill distinguished between communism – a Continental notion implying 'the entire abolition of property', and 'absolute equality in the distribution of the physical means of life' and enjoyment – from socialism, by which he meant a system in which ownership of land and the instruments of production belonged to communities, associations or governments rather than private individuals. It admitted inequality of distribution, grounded on 'some principle, or supposed principle, of justice or general expediency'. Owen, Blanc and Cabet were his communists, and Saint-Simon and Fourier his typical socialists. *Principles of Political Economy*, II, i, §2, p. 203.

31 This is a question which has aroused a good deal of controversy. Mill had close contacts with some of the Saint-Simonian leaders, especially Gustave d'Eichtal, whom he met in 1828, and corresponded with at length. He met Bazard and Enfantin in 1830. Mill praised the Saint-Simonian teachings, while believing them to be too far in advance of existing moral and intellectual standards. His recollection in the *Autobiography* underrates somewhat the enthusiasm of his youth. He wrote: 'I neither believed in the practicability, nor in the beneficial operation of their social machinery' (pp. 141–2). Mill discussed socialism especially in the chapters 'On property' and 'On the Probable Futurity of the Labouring Class' in *Principles of Political Economy*, and in the *Chapters on Socialism* (*Fortnightly Review*, XXV, February, March and April 1879). These latter articles, which were all that Mill had completed of a planned major work on socialism, were published posthumously by Helen Taylor. As for *Principles of Political Economy*, there were some changes, favourable to socialism, in the second edition (1849) but especially in the third edition (1852). By this stage Harriet Taylor had become an extremely powerful influence on Mill. The addition of the chapter 'On the Probable Futurity of the Labouring Class', which did not exist in the first draft, was, Mill said, entirely due to Harriet. 'She pointed out the need of such a chapter, and the extreme imperfection of the book without it: she was the cause of my writing it' (*Autobiography*, p. 208). It does not seem to me that Mill became more socialistic in his later years, as the posthumous *Chapters on Socialism* seem to be rather more sceptical about the claims of socialism than was the 1852 edition of *Principles of Political Economy*. When he wrote the *Chapters on Socialism* he believed

that, because of the increasing electoral strength of the working class, it was exceedingly important to explain and improve existing institutions, which could help forestall premature attempts to establish a socialist state.

32 *Principles of Political Economy*, IV, vi, §2, p. 754.
33 *Fortnightly Review*, April 1879, p. 521.
34 See especially the third *Chapter on Socialism, Fortnightly Review*, April 1879.
35 *Principles of Political Economy*, II, i, § 1, p. 200.
36 *Ibid.*, II, i, §4, p. 214.
37 *Ibid.*, IV, vii, §2, p. 763.
38 Letter to Parker Godwin, 1 January 1869, *Letters of John Stuart Mill*, II, 172.
39 *Principles of Political Economy*, IV, vii, §6, p. 775.
40 *Ibid.*, IV, vii, §2, p. 763.
41 *Ibid.*, p. 764. They may make mistakes, Mill said in the 1848 edition, but that did not matter. 'It is of little importance that some of them may, at a certain stage of their progress, adopt mistaken opinions'. *Ibid.*, note.
42 De Tocqueville viewed this practical political activity of the individual citizen as 'one of the most effectual means of training the social feelings and practical intelligence of the people, so important in themselves and so indispensable to good government' as well as a means of protection (via pluralism) against despotism. Mill, *Autobiography*, p. 163.
43 *Ibid.*, p. 163.
44 *Principles of Political Economy*, v, xi, §6, p. 944.
45 Although Mill believed that the business of society was performed best by private and voluntary agency, he was neither opposed to the state on principle, nor an advocate of the absentee state. Government could act in a variety of spheres. It had certain necessary functions, including the raising of public revenue by taxation and borrowing; the provision of judicature and police; the definition of the substance of property, including inheritance; enforcement of contracts and determination of proper contracts; and provision of public works and facilities. Its optional functions were authoritarian (prohibiting private actions and agencies) and non-authoritarian (side by side with and competing with private agencies). Exceptions to laissez-faire were justified in a variety of cases, e.g. interference to protect the weak (children) and factory legislation – for instance the Nine Hours Bill, in which the poorer classes gave effect to their 'deliberate collective opinion of their own interest'. *Principles of Political Economy*, v, xi, §12, p. 958. But presumably they could be mistaken.
46 'Centralization', *Edinburgh Review*, CXV (April 1862), 342.
47 *Representative Government*, p. 351.
48 'Commencement of the Session – Progress of Reform', *London and Westminster Review*, XXV (April 1836), 274.
49 *Representative Government*, p. 352. Cf. also: 'It is but a poor education that associates ignorance with ignorance, and leaves them, if they care for knowledge, to grope their way to it without help, and to do without it if they do not'. *Ibid.*, p. 359.
50 *Ibid.*, pp. 351–2.
51 *On Liberty*, p. 164.
52 Cf. S. M. Lipset, *Political Man* (London, 1963), pp. 46–7. 'Once established, a democratic political system "gathers momentum" and creates social supports (institutions) to ensure its continued existence. Thus a "premature" democracy which survives will do so by (among other things) facilitating the growth of other conditions conducive to democracy, such as universal literacy, or autonomous private organizations'. In discussions of the means

whereby individuals can be integrated into larger societies, e.g. the nation (from villages or tribes, for example), there has naturally been considerable emphasis on the kinds of measures favoured by Mill. It can be fairly argued that universal suffrage, even where the prerequisites (education, communications, some degree of toleration) are not present, is a means of waking men up, increasing their political energy and associating them with an otherwise remote government. Discussion, Mill said, has 'a necessary tendency to remedy its own evils'. 'Law of Libel and Liberty of the Press', *Westminster Review*, III (April 1825), 295. But Mill was not prepared to take a chance on the interim – the universal vote was not put on the immediate agenda because of his fear of ignorant class rule.

53 'The Claims of Labour', *Dissertations and Discussions*, II, 202.
54 *Representative Government*, p. 252.
55 P. 25.
56 *On Liberty*, p. 160.
57 See *Principles of Political Economy*, V, xi, §8.
58 The details of Mill's remarkable educational training are well known. He made the surprising claim that he was not specially gifted: 'What I could do, could assuredly be done by any boy or girl of average capacity and healthy physical constitution: and if I have accomplished anything, I owe it, among other fortunate circumstances, to the fact that through the early training bestowed upon me by my father, I started, I may fairly say, with an advantage of a quarter of a century over my contemporaries'. *Autobiography*, pp. 25–6.
59 *The Subjection of Women* (Cambridge, Mass., 1970), p. 23.
60 *Autobiography*, p. 91.
61 'Utility of Religion', in *Three Essays on Religion*, p. 82.
62 *Inaugural Address at St Andrews University*, 1 February 1867 (London, 1867), p. 96. Hartley wrote in his *Observations on Man* (1749): 'It is of the utmost importance to morality and religion that the affections and passions should be analysed into their simple compounding parts, by reversing the steps of the associations which concur to form them. For then we can learn to cherish and improve good ones, and check and root out such as are mischievous and immoral'. Quoted by J. W. Burrow, *Evolution and Society*, p. 22.
63 Mill rejected last-resort appeal to supernatural sanctions for human laws or practices – the appeal, for example, of Plato to the foundation myth, or of Rousseau's legislator who, faced with the recalcitrance of the 'blind multitude', uses divine authority, the pretence that the laws are ordained by God, to secure their popular acceptance (*Social Contract*, II, vii). Mill's attitude to traditional religion did not, however, remain constant. In the essay on 'The Utility of Religion', written during the fifties, he judged it extremely harshly, whereas in 'Theism' (written in 1869 and 1870) his historical relativism was much more generous, and he described hopes for the divine government of the world, and the future life as 'legitimate and philosophically defensible' (*Three Essays on Religion*, p. 249). Moreover, he suggested that supernatural hope may aid the ascendancy of the Religion of Humanity (p. 255). Our devotion to our fellow-creatures may be intensified by the feeling that 'we may be cooperating with the unseen Being to whom we owe all that is enjoyable in life' (p. 256).
64 *Inaugural Address at St. Andrews*, pp. 75–6.
65 Education meant, to Mill, 'whatever helps to shape the human being: to make the individual what he is, or hinder him from being what he is not' (*ibid.*, p. 4). Mill included even such factors as climate as educational influences. But most important were the schools, laws and institutions. 'The

real effective education of a people is given them by the circumstances by which they are surrounded. The laws are the schoolmaster, as the ancient statesmen and philosophers well knew, and it is time we should again learn the lesson. What shapes the character is not what is purposely taught, so much as the unintentional teaching of institutions and social relations.' *The Morning Chronicle*, 19 November 1846, unheaded article, p. 4.

66 'The Claims of Labour', *Dissertations and Discussions*, II, 204.
67 *Inaugural Address at St. Andrews*, p. 43.
68 *A System of Logic*, VI, x, §7, p. 524.
69 See especially Mill on *Bentham and Coleridge*, pp. 68–74, and the comments in his *System of Logic*, discussed in the next chapter.
70 *Utilitarianism*, p. 29.
71 *Ibid.*, p. 31.
72 *Ibid.*, p. 16.
73 *The Subjection of Women*, p. 80. Mill was referring here to the results of introducing just relations between men and women, but he assumed – more plausibly – the same results from wider educational and institutional changes.
74 *Utilitarianism*, p. 31.
75 'The Utility of Religion', *Three Essays on Religion*, p. 106. Mill did not suggest how such feelings would be related to, or how they would triumph over, nationalist prejudices. He also suggested that men should model themselves on, and believe themselves to be in the company of, benefactors or noble figures of the past. This would also strengthen their disinterested feelings.
76 *Auguste Comte and Positivism*, pp. 146–7. Such feelings could even improve individual hygiene, as poor health reduced a man's ability to serve his fellow men.
77 'The Utility of Religion', p. 110. On p. 109 Mill states that the Religion of Humanity is a real religion, the essence of a religion being 'the strong and earnest direction of the emotions and desires towards an ideal object, recognised as of the highest excellence, and as rightfully paramount over all selfish objects of desire'.
78 *On Liberty*, p. 69. For a lucid analysis of Mill's distinction between those actions which are subject to social enforcement, whether by law or opinion, and those over which there is no legitimate right of control – though there may be rights and even duties to advise, exhort and persuade – see Alan Ryan, *The Philosophy of John Stuart Mill* (London, 1970), pp. 233–56.
79 'Newman's Political Economy', *Westminster Review*, LVI (October 1851), 92.
80 *Principles of Political Economy*, II, i, §3, p. 206.
81 *Chapters on Socialism*, Fortnightly Review, April 1879, p. 516. In a letter to Harriet Taylor on 21 March 1849, Mill suggested that she exaggerated the ease of making people unselfish, and commented that to speak of making people perfect by education presupposed having perfect people to teach them. 'I must say I think that if we had absolute power tomorrow, though we could do much to improve people by good laws, and could even give them a very much better education than they have ever had yet, still, for effecting in our lives anything like what we aim at, all our plans would fail from the impossibility of finding fit instruments'. Self-flattery, vanity, irritability and that family of vices almost always warped the moral judgments of the very cleverest people. *Collected Works*, III, p. 1030. These seem to me to be fair comments, but they are certainly much more cautious than Mill's better-known comments on the role of education in social change.
82 *Autobiography*, pp. 151–2.

1 The important questions concern the kind of élite which is recommended, and the specific justification of authority which is offered. As Richard Friedman shows, utilitarianism can offer its own justification of authority. His outline of John Austin's utilitarian justification of intellectual authority, as based on assumptions of mass ignorance and the wisdom of the few, stresses its similarity with Mill's justification, which is not, on Friedman's view, primarily traceable to the influence of the Saint-Simonians. 'A New Exploration of Mill's Essay on Liberty', *Political Studies*, XIV, no. 3 (October 1966), 379–425. Cf. also n.2, p. 355.

2 But of course classical democracy is an extremely complex body of thought, containing divergent and even conflicting traditions and lines of argument. There is no clearly defined and agreed classical democratic theory, any more than there is a generally agreed modern democratic doctrine. Classical democracy tends to evaporate on analysis or, alternatively, when attempts are made to embody its values in concrete programmes or detailed institutional prescriptions, wide divergencies appear.

3 'The Rationale of Political Representation', p. 348.

4 *Representative Government*, p. 335. Here he was referring to the fate of India, when skilled and disinterested administration was supplanted.

5 To Alexander Bain, 6 August 1859, *The Letters of John Stuart Mill*, I, 223.

6 *On Liberty*, p. 124. The glory of the average man is that 'he can respond internally to wise and noble things, and be led to them with his eyes open'. In *Utilitarianism* (p. 8) Mill spoke of leaders of taste who could discriminate between the quality of different pleasures – they are people of higher faculties, who are 'competently acquainted' with the various pleasures.

7 *Autobiography*, p. 225.

8 'The Spirit of the Age', *Essays on Politics and Culture*, p. 15.

9 Letter to John Sterling, 20–22 October 1831, *Collected Works*, XII, 84. Mill added that many conservative writers had serious shortcomings, especially that of chaining themselves 'to the inanimate corpses of dead political and religious systems, never more to be revived' (*ibid.*, p. 84). The strength of Mill's criticism of liberalism may be explained in part by the fact that it is contained in a letter to Sterling, who was very sympathetic to Coleridge and the German School.

10 *Representative Government*, p. 328.

11 'The Rationale of Political Representation', pp. 348–9. In a letter to Gustave d'Eichtal (7 November 1829) Mill wrote that he approved of the idea of a spiritual power, 'a state in which the body of the people, i.e. the uninstructed, shall entertain the same feelings of deference and submission to the authority of the instructed, in morals and politics, as they at present do in the physical sciences'. Quoted by W. M. Simon, *European Positivism in the Nineteenth Century* (Cornell, 1963), p. 178.

12 'The Rationale of Political Representation', p. 365.

13 Quoted by J. S. Mill, Austin's Lectures on Jurisprudence, *Taits*, II, December 1837, pp. 347–8.

14 *Representative Government*, p. 217. Cf. also p. 207, where Mill writes that 'the ideally best form of government is that in which the sovereignty, or supreme controlling power in the last resort, is vested in the entire aggregate of the community; every citizen not only having a voice in the exercise of the ultimate sovereignty, but being, at least occasionally, called on to take an actual part in the government, by the personal discharge of some public function, local or general'.

15 *Representative Government*, p. 195.

16 'Democracy in America', *Dissertations and Discussions*, II, 73. Here Mill suggests that the safeguards were to be found in the existence of an agrarian, a leisured and a learned class.

17 'Coleridge' in *Bentham and Coleridge*.

18 *Representative Government*, p. 269. Mill waxed enthusiatstic over the plan; 'this great practical and philosophical idea, the greatest improvement of which the system of representative government is susceptible.' *Autobiography*, p. 219. The quota necessary to be returned is determined by dividing the total number of votes by the number of seats. Mill hoped to combine local voting with the right to vote for anybody in the country, i.e. a voter would vote locally but could vote for someone on the national slate if none of the local candidates pleased him. He also hoped for a redistribution of preferences to secure the correct proportion of seats to popular support. See his *Speech on Personal Representation*, House of Commons, 29 May 1876 (London, 1867).

19 Mill would have completely supported attacks on the existing English party system in terms of its control over the individual M.P. Mill's ideal M.P. is moved by the issues, which he relates to his own principles, and is not dictated to by bodies outside the parliament, e.g. constituency associations, or by caucuses or party oligarchies inside.

20 *Representative Government*, p. 288.

21 'Democracy in America', *Dissertations and Discussions*, II, 78–83.

22 *Representative Government*, p. 331.

23 Cf. 'Pledges', two articles in *The Examiner*, 1 July and 15 July 1832, and the chapter on 'Pledges' in *Representative Government*. If constituents bound their representatives it would mean, normally, ignorance binding intelligence.

24 *Representative Government*, p. 238.

25 This, at least, was his position in *Representative Government*. In 1859, when he wrote of scales, and groups neutralising each other, his view seems to have been that the balance worked the other way. 'Local interests being divided, the worst portion of the electors, those who are corrupted by money or drunkenness, turn the scale'. 'Thoughts on Parliamentary Reform', *Dissertations and Discussions*, III, 6. This seems, *prima facie*, to be as arbitrary as the assumption in *Representative Government*. The truth of either claim depends, of course, on detailed empirical work, which Mill did not undertake. In the latter case he urged the enlargements of constituencies. 'The Local influence of families and corporations would then have more chance of neutralizing one another'. *Dissertations and Discussions*, III, 10.

26 *Representative Government*, p. 256.

27 *Ibid.*

28 *Ibid.*, p. 310.

29 'Lord Durham's Return', *Westminster Review*, XXIII (December 1838), 251.

30 *Ibid.*, p. 260.

31 Quoted from the *London Review* by J. H. Burns, 'J. S. Mill and Democracy, 1829–61', *Political Studies*, June 1957, p. 166.

32 *Representative Government*, pp. 326–6. The values stressed by Mill are also stressed by Bernard Crick in a rather flabby book, *In Defence of Politics* (London, 1962). Crick's general thesis is that 'politics' is an activity concerned with conciliating the various groups which naturally emerge in societies, rather than destroying them as under totalitarian governments. Crick's political virtues, like Mill's principles of constitutional morality, to which they are so similar, are also held to be necessary for social cohesion.

33 *Bentham and Coleridge*, p. 128.

34 *Ibid.*, p. 123.
35 *Ibid.*, pp. 122–3.
36 *Ibid.*, p. 124.
37 *A Preface to Democratic Theory* (Chicago, 1963), p. 132. It is clear that, on the whole, the principles shared by some (not all – perhaps the 'politically active') members of stable democratic societies are very abstract and do not necessarily mean the same thing to all people. In detailed studies it has been discovered that agreement on values or principles exists only at such a general level (and shared beliefs in God or doing our duty are hardly likely to be powerful cohesive forces – they fragment and divide when analysed and specified), that explicit belief in democratic values, when stated concretely, is high only among political activists, and that most people accept rather than believe in democratic norms and values. See Herbert McClosky, 'Consensus and Ideology in American Politics', *American Political Science Review*, LVIII, no. 2 (June 1964).
38 *Representative Government*, p. 361.
39 *Speech on Personal Representation*, p. 12.
40 *Thoughts on Parliamentary Reform.* Quoted J. Robson, *The Improvement of Mankind: the Social and Political Thought of John Stuart Mill* (Toronto, 1968), p. 225.
41 *Speech on Personal Representation*, p. 15.
42 *The Principles of State Interference* (London, 1891), pp. 96–8.
43 'Beyond Tolerance' in *A Critique of Pure Tolerance* (Boston, 1965), pp. 28–9. Cf. also pp. 32–3: 'Durkheim marshalls statistics to show that where the intensity of the collective life of a community diminishes – as their "freedom", in Mill's sense, increases, therefore – the rate of suicide rises…It seems, if Durkheim is correct, that the very liberty and individuality which Mill celebrates are deadly threats to the integrity and health of the personality.'
44 A. Ryan, *The Philosophy of John Stuart Mill*, pp. 254–5.
45 'But disinterested benevolence can find other instruments to persuade people to their good, than whips and scourges, either of the literal or metaphorical sort.' *On Liberty*, p. 132.
46 *Principles of Political Economy*, IV, vii, §1, p. 760.
47 *Utilitarianism*, p. 30.
48 'Democracy in America', *Dissertations and Discussions*, II 63.
49 *Principles of Political Economy*, IV, vi, §2, p. 754. One of de Tocqueville's remarks on American democracy is relevant in this context. 'The good things and the evils of life are more equally distributed in the world: great wealth tends to disappear, the number of smaller fortunes to increase …The sentiment of ambition is universal, but the scope of ambition is seldom vast…life is not adorned with brilliant trophies, but it is extremely easy and tranquil…Almost all extremes are softened or blunted: all that was most prominent is superseded by some mean term, at once less lofty and less low, less brilliant and less obscure, than what before existed in the world'. *Democracy in America* (Oxford, 1953), pp. 595–6. Here the economic tendencies are linked with broader and less desirable trends.
50 *Principles of Political Economy*, II, xiii, §4, p. 378.
51 *Ibid.*, IV, vi, §2, p. 756.
52 *Ibid.*, vi, §2, p. 755. Mill complained (p. 757) that industrial improvements had 'not yet begun to effect those great changes in human destiny, which it is in their nature and in their futurity to accomplish. Only when, in addition to just institutions, the increase of mankind shall be under the deliberate guidance of judicious foresight, can the conquests made from the

powers of nature by the intellect and energy of scientific discoverers, become the common property of the species, and the means of improving and elevating the universal lot'.

53   'The Rationale of Political Representation', p. 369. Mill was here attacking the theory of class representation.

54   'When I speak of "the labouring classes", or of labourers as a "class", I use those phrases in compliance with custom, and as descriptive of an existing, but by no means a necessary or permanent, state of social relations. I do not recognise as either just or salutary, a state or society in which there is any "class" which is not labouring; any human beings, exempt from bearing their share of the necessary labours of human life, except those unable to labour, or who have fairly earned rest by previous toil. So long, however, as the great social evil exists of a non-labouring class, labourers also constitute a class, and may be spoken of, though only provisionally, in that character'. *Principles of Political Economy*, IV, vii, § 1, p. 758. This hoped-for elimination of class was quite compatible with the continued existence of owners and non-owners.

55   'The Rationale of Political Representation', p. 347.

56   *Liberty, Equality, Fraternity*, ed. R. J. White (Cambridge, 1967), especially ch. 6.

57   *Mill and Liberalism* (Cambridge, 1963), p. 34. There are many points at which Cowling's account is open to serious criticism, e.g. his ignoring of the historical context in which Mill made his various statements and his twisting of quotations, but I am concerned here only with the substance of his general claim.

58   P. 26. On p. 44 Cowling writes that the end of Mill's *Liberty* is 'not of diversity of opinion pure and simple, but of diversity of opinion within the limits of a rationally homogeneous, agreed, social consensus about the method of judging and the right end to be approached'.

59   *A System of Logic*, p. viii.

60   *On Liberty*, p. 103.

61   *Ibid.*, p .105.

62   *Ibid.*, p. 114.

63   *Bentham and Coleridge*, p. 104. In the letter to Sterling he made the point even more strongly: 'In the present age of transition, everything must be subordinate to freedom of inquiry: if your opinions, or mine, are right, they will in time be unanimously adopted by the instructed classes, and then it will be time to found the national creed upon the assumption of their truth'. *Collected Works*, XII, 77.

64   'Centralization', *Edinburgh Review*, CXV (April 1862), 358. Cf. also his comment that, until we are given a society which it is desirable to have stereotyped for perpetual use, 'we must regard as an evil, all restraint put upon the spirit which never yet since society existed has been in excess – that which bids us "try all things" as the only means by which with knowledge and assurance we can "hold fast to that which is good" '. 'Article on Newman's Political Economy', *Westminster Review*, LVI (October 1851), 100.

65   *Auguste Comte and Positivism*, pp. 125, 132 and 139–40.

66   *Ibid.*, pp. 141–2.

67   *Ibid.*, pp. 120–1.

68   At one point (*Mill and Liberalism*, p. 93) Cowling writes that Mill's doctrine is 'a socially cohesive, morally insinuating, proselytizing doctrine. Mill was a proselytizer of genius: the ruthless denigrator of existing positions, the systematic propagator of a new moral posture; a man of sneers and smears and pervading certainty'. Mill had his weaknesses, but they

were less than this tendentious passage suggests. Obviously 'moral totalitarian' means something different to Cowling than it does in ordinary usage. He finds it possible, for example, to describe (p. 117) Mill's general culture, which includes following the argument whithersoever it leads, as 'moral indoctrination'.

69 'The Rationale of Political Representation', p. 347. In a letter to John Pringle Nichol on 10 July 1833, Mill referred to 'the anomaly of a democratic institution in a plutocratically constituted society'. *Collected Works,* XIII, 166. Here he was complaining that the people would choose their representatives from the same class as before. A larger and more interesting interpretation of the comment – though this was not Mill's view – is that democratic institutions will not function where economic differentiation is considerable.

70 *Representative Government,* p. 286. Mill suggested that, in special circumstances, intellectual power could be abused. 'The abuse of intellectual power is only to be dreaded, when society is divided between a few highly cultivated intellects and an ignorant and stupid multitude'. *Auguste Comte and Positivism,* p. 171.

71 *Principles of Political Economy,* IV, vii, §1, p. 760.

72 *A System of Logic,* VI, viii, §3, pp. 482–7. See also III, xiii, §7. He did suggest that one could assume narrow self-interest in creating a model, as in the classical political economy, but that this was by no means equivalent to a complete account of society. See *Essays on Some Unsettled Questions of Political Economy* (London, 1844), p. 149.

73 Quoted by Robson, *The Improvement of Mankind,* p. 43.

74 *Principles of Political Economy,* II, i, §4, p. 211.

75 *The Social Contract,* Book II, ch. 6, p. 31. 'How can a blind multitude, which often does not know what it wills, because it rarely knows what is good for it, carry out for itself so great and difficult an enterprise as a system of legislation? Of itself the people wills always the good, but of itself it by no means always sees it'. Two pages later we read that the laws of the legislator must receive the consent of the people – 'there can be no assurance that a particular will is in conformity with the General Will, until it has been put to the free vote of the people' (II, vii, pp. 33–4). Then doubts about the people lead to the view that the legislator may have to deceive them. The point of similarity is that both Rousseau and Mill shift from the popular power to a minority and back. There are differences, too – Rousseau's problem concerns the validity or quality of the laws, which require, as a necessary procedure, free and rational acceptance by the people, whereas Mill sees the problem as that of restraining a potentially selfish leadership. His equivalent of the general will is not necessarily a popular will, whereas for Rousseau the people are sovereign.

76 *Mill and Liberalism,* p. 136. This is one of Cowling's more reasonable claims.

9 MARX, MILL AND MODERN SOCIETY

1 Felix Oppenheim, *Moral Principles in Political Philosophy* (New York, 1968), p. 54.

2 A. S. Kaufman, 'Wants, Needs, and Liberalism', *Inquiry,* XIV, no. 3 (Autumn 1971), p. 202.

3 Marx referred to Bentham as that arch-Philistine, 'that insipid, pedantic, leather-tongued oracle of the ordinary bourgeois intelligence of the eighteenth century'. *Capital,* I, 609.

4 *Ibid.,* pp. 610–11, n. 2.

5 G. Lukacs, *Lenin, A Study on the Unity of his Thought* (London, 1970), p. 55.
6 Cf. Marx's comments on civil society (ch. 2, above) and C. B. Macpherson in *The Political Theory of Possessive Individualism: Hobbes to Locke* (Oxford, 1962), which is based upon the writings of Hobbes, the Levellers, Harrington and Locke. On p. 3 he defines possessive individualism: 'Society becomes a lot of free equal individuals related to each other as proprietors of their own capacities and of what they have acquired by their exercise. Society consists of relations of exchange between proprietors. Political society becomes a calculated device for the protection of this property and for the maintenance of an orderly relation of exchange'.
7 Genuinely free and equal choice obviously presupposes a transformation of the world. Robert Dahl, writing of the conditions necessary for the realisation, in public policy, of the alternative preferred by the greatest number of people, if we also wish to assign to the preference of each individual an equal value, suggests as one such condition: 'All individuals possess identical information about the alternatives'. Dahl treats this as a limit against which real world achievements can be measured, and adds: 'Moreover, even if the [fifth] condition were to exist in full, voters might choose an alternative they would have rejected if they had possessed more information; the [fifth] condition is no guarantee of cosmic rationality'. A *Preface to Democratic Theory*, p. 70. The discussion indicates clearly that, if many of our ordinary liberal values – free choice, equal opportunities and the like – were taken literally, we would have to flee the inequalities and limitations of the real world, and require a spread of superhuman powers and rationality.
8 *Reflections of a Youth on Choosing an Occupation* (1835), Easton and Guddat, p. 37.
9 *The German Ideology*, p. 482.
10 *The Structure of Freedom* (Stanford, 1958), p. 96.
11 R. D. Laing, *The Politics of Experience* (London, 1969), p. 33. In *Sincerity and Authenticity* (London, 1972), p. 119, Lionel Trilling quotes Wilde's interestingly different view. Wilde said: 'Man is least himself when he talks in his own person. Give him a mask and he will tell you the truth'.
12 'Me Doctor, You Patient', *Encounter*, February 1972, p. 73.
13 Cf. John Dunn's argument, against Macpherson, that Locke was not riveting upon man 'the immemorial shackles of scarcity', but asserting 'the boundless repression demanded by the calling'. *The Political Thought of John Locke* (Cambridge, 1968), pp. 262 and 265.
14 However, men may not in fact be more agitated or rebellious when on a starvation wage or working an extremely long day than they may be in improved circumstances, for reasons discussed in the paragraph. In speaking of greater urgency one is not *ipso facto* speaking of greater felt urgency, but in terms of some general criterion of what is necessary to human beings, as when we describe a man dying of thirst as having a greater need for water that someone who has enough and simply a mild desire for more.
15 *Conflict and Defense* (New York, 1963), p. 191.
16 Quoted by James C. Davies, *Human Nature in Politics* (New York, 1963), p. 17.
17 Indeed – leaving aside the economic background and causes of revolutions – supposedly forward-looking revolutionary movements of the twentieth century have been compared with the atavistic and regressive mass movements of the past, and the element of rational political reconstruction played down sharply. Norman Cohn (*The Pursuit of the Millennium*, pp. vii and xiv) sees close connections between the basic 'phantasies' of Lenin

and Hitler and the revolutionary apocalypse of the forgotten *prophetae* of the Middle Ages.

18 De Tocqueville suggested this in *The Ancien Régime*. The theory can be extended beyond expectations of an economic kind. The East German uprising of 17 June 1953 can be plausibly interpreted as the result of governmental resistance to the rising political – and not merely economic – expectations which emerged after Stalin's death.

19 The growing interest of Marxist theorists in underdeveloped societies, in which the Communist Party was frequently conceived to be a peasant or peasant-proletarian industrialising party led by intellectuals, lies outside my scope. Marx did, of course, pay some attention to backward societies, e.g. China and India, but they were not given the revolutionary significance which they have in some later theories of imperialism. Western Europe remained the centre, practical and theoretical, of Marx's work.

20 In England in 1946–7, 1% of the population owned 50% of all private property, and the position has probably changed little since then. Inequality may have increased during the past two decades, partly through superannuation, tax-free payments on retirement, expense accounts, capital gains and other devices which aid the rich particularly. See T. B. Bottomore, *Classes in Modern Society* (New York, 1966), pp. 38–40. The research of Gabriel Kolko in the United States indicates that between 1910 and 1959 the share in national income of the top income-tenth declined only slightly, and remains about 30%, while the shares of the second and third income-tenths actually increased and the shares of the two poorest income-tenths declined sharply (from 8.3% of national income to only 4%). This excludes the sources of real income mentioned above. Bottomore, *Classes in Modern Society*, p. 53.

21 Revisionism has no precise common meaning, but many meanings, depending on the person using the term. The revisionist controversy became serious and open in the German Social-Democratic Party in 1898, though particular issues had arisen earlier, and revisionism was practised without being acknowledged, especially in south Germany. Revisionism was originally identified with the doctrines of Eduard Bernstein, and meant essentially the revision of Marxism is a non-revolutionary or social-democratic direction. The word was first used in its most common present sense by Bruno Schönlank at the 1895 Breslau S.D.P. Congress. See J. Nettl, *Rosa Luxemburg* (London, 1966), I, 202, n. 1.

22 Joan Robinson has remarked on the reversal of the old process – the destruction of small traders – this century. Capitalism is now spewing them out again. 'The robots of automated industry are eroding the labour force, and small-scale traders and self-employed professionals are proliferating to take its place'. 'Has Capitalism Changed?', *Collected Economic Papers*, III (Oxford, 1965), 171.

23 Quoted by G. D. H. Cole, *A History of Socialist Thought*, III, 1: 'The Second International' (London, 1956), p. 290.

24 'The Theory of Mass Society', *Diogenes*, XXXIX (Fall 1962), 56.

25 They may be more vulnerable to other destructive forces. 'The nihilism of masses tends to be a greater threat to liberal democracy than the antagonism between classes'. W. Kornhauser, *The Politics of Mass Society* (London, 1965), p. 237. Many of the theorists of stability seem unaware of the incidence of violence in political life. According to Eckstein's count, there occurred about 1,200 unequivocal instances of guerrilla war, organised terrorism, mutiny, *coup d'état* and so forth between 1946 and 1959. H. Eckstein (ed.), *Internal War, Problems and Approaches* (New York, 1964), p. 3.

26 *Capital*, III, 587.
27 *The Eighteenth Brumaire, Selected Works*, I, 255.
28 Kornhauser, *The Politics of Mass Society*, p. 80. Cf. also Lewis Coser: 'the interdependence of antagonistic groups and the criss-crossing within such societies of conflicts, which serve to "sew the social system together" by cancelling each other out, thus prevent disintegration along one primary line of cleavage'. *The Function of Social Conflict*, (London, 1968), p. 80.
29 *The End of Ideology* (Glencoe, 1965), pp. 402-3.
30 *On Revolution*, p. 276. In *The Human Condition* (p. 131, n. 82), Miss Arendt, in claiming that Marx's classless and stateless society is not utopian, refers to the fact that modern developments have 'an unmistakable tendency to do away with class distinctions in society and to replace government by that "administration of things" which according to Engels was to be the hallmark of socialist society'.
31 R. Wolff, 'Beyond Tolerance', p. 17. Wolff holds that there are many groups left out in the big balance between labour and business, and that there is 'a very sharp distinction in the public domain between legitimate interests and those which are absolutely beyond the pale'.
32 *A Preface to Democratic Theory*, p. 150. John Plamenatz claims that the influence of pressure groups depends upon the number of people for whom they speak, and that in the established democracies every section of the people is spoken for by some organisation or other. 'Electoral Studies and Democratic Theory. I: A British View', *Political Studies*, VI (1958), no. 1. E. Schattschneider puts the point neatly: 'The flaw in the pluralist heaven is that the heavenly chorus sings with a strong upper-class accent. Probably about 90% of the people cannot get into the pressure system'. *The Semi Sovereign People* (New York, 1961), p. 35.
33 *The Semi-Sovereign People*, p. 71.
34 *The Fundamentals of Marxism-Leninism*, p. 175. Elton Mayo, in *The Social Problems of Industrial Civilization* (London, 1966), puts revolutionary feelings down to unhappy childhood, insecure life, etc. – see especially pp. 23-4.
35 B. R. Berelson, P. Lazarsfeld and W. McPhee, *Voting* (Chicago, 1954), p. 311.
36 Cf. the article by J. H. Goldthorpe and D. Lockwood, 'Affluence and the British Class Structure', *The Sociological Review*, XI (July 1963), 133-63.
37 A great deal of empirical work is now being done on the depressed groups in the 'affluent' societies. Thoughtful and penetrating work has been done in this area by Professor Titmuss and Peter Townsend, amongst others. In America, poverty is concentrated in particular sections of the community (e.g. the old ethnic minorities, especially Negroes), certain occupations (e.g. farm workers), and certain regions (e.g. the southern Appalachians).
38 J. A. Schumpeter, *Capitalism, Socialism and Democracy*, p. 154.

Bibliography

WORKS BY MARKS AND ENGELS

Karl Marx
Capital, 3 vols., Moscow, undated, 1961, 1962.
A Contribution to the Critique of Political Economy, London, 1971.
Early Writings, ed. T. B. Bottomore, London, 1963.
Die Frühschriften, ed. S. Landshut, Stuttgart, 1953.
Economic and Philosophical Manuscripts, Moscow, 1961.
Marx's Grundrisse, selected and translated by D. McLellan, London, 1971.
Letters to Dr Kugelmann, London, 1941.
Pre-capitalist Economic Formations, ed. E. J. Hobsbawm, London, 1964.
The Poverty of Philosophy, Moscow, undated.
Selected Writings in Sociology and Social Philosophy, ed. T. B. Bottomore and M. Rubel, London, 1961.
Theories of Surplus Value, Moscow, undated.
Writings of the Young Marx on Philosophy and Society, ed. L. D. Easton and K. H. Guddat, New York, 1967.

Frederick Engels
Anti-Dühring, Moscow, 1959.
The Condition of the Working Class in England in 1844, London, 1950.
Dialectics of Nature, Moscow, 1954.
The Peasant War in Germany, London, 1957.

Karl Marx and Frederick Engels
The German Ideology, Moscow, 1964.
The Holy Family, Moscow, 1956.
Letters to Americans, New York, 1953.
Literature and Art, Bombay, 1956.
On Colonialism, Moscow, undated.
On Religion, Moscow, undated.
Selected Works, 2 vols., Moscow, 1958.
Selected Correspondence, Moscow, 1956.

WORKS BY MILL
Books
A System of Logic, 2 vols., London, 1872.
Auguste Comte and Positivism, Michigan, 1961.
Autobiography, London, 1958.
Bentham and Coleridge, ed. F. H. Leavis, London, 1959.
Chapters on Socialism (posthumous), *Fortnightly Review*, XXV, n.s., 1879.
England and Ireland, London, 1868.
Essays on Some Unsettled Questions of Political Economy, London, 1844.

Bibliography

On Liberty, Utilitarianism and Representative Government, London, 1960.
Principles of Political Economy, vols. II and III of the Collected Works, Toronto, 1965.
The Subjection of Women, Cambridge, Mass., 1970.
Three Essays on Religion, London, 1874.

Selections

Chapters and Speeches on the Irish Land Question, London, 1870.
Dissertations and Discussions, 4 vols., London, 1860s.
Essays on Politics and Culture, ed. G. Himmelfarb, New York, 1963.

Letters and speeches

The Letters of John Stuart Mill, ed. Hugh S. R. Elliott, 2 vols., London, 1910.
The Early Letters, vols. XII and XIII of the Collected Works, Toronto, 1963.
Inaugural Address at St Andrews, February 1867, London, 1867.
Speech on Personal Representation, House of Commons, 29 May 1867, London, 1867.

Journal articles

Edinburgh Review
  'Duveyrier's Political Views of French Affairs', LXXXIII, April 1846.
  'Centralization', CVX, April 1862.

Monthly Repository
  'On Genius', n.s. VI, October 1832.
  'Writings of Junius Redivivus', VII, April 1833.
  'Comparison of the Tendencies of the French and English Intellect', VII, November 1833.
  'On Miss Martineau's Summary of Political Economy', VIII, May 1834.

Westminster Review and London and Westminster Review
  'Modern French Historical Works – Age of Chivalry', VI, July 1826.
  'Review of Scott's Life of Napoleon', IX, April 1828.
  'The Rationale of Political Representation', XXX, July 1835.
  'Law of Libel and Liberty of the Press', XXX, July 1835.
  'The Close of the Session', XXXI, July 1835.
  'State of Society in America', XXXI, January 1836.
  'Commencement of the Session – Progress of Reform', XXV, April 1836.
  'Sir John Walsh's Contemporary History – Tories, Whigs and Radicals', XXV, July 1836.
  'Fonblanque's England under Seven Administrations', XXVII, April 1837.
  'The French Revolution', XXVII, July 1837.
  'Parties and the Ministry', XXVIII, October 1837.
  'Radical Party in Canada', XXVIII, January 1838.
  'Lord Durham and his Assailants', XXIX, August 1838.
  'Lord Durham's Return', XXXII, December 1838.
  'Reorganisation of the Reform Party', XXXII, April 1839.
  'Newman's Political Economy', LVI, October 1851.

Newspaper articles

Daily News
  Leading article (on Reform), 19 July 1848.
  Leading article (on Electoral Districts), 25 July 1848.
  Leading article (on Californian Constitution), 2 January 1850.

Bibliography

The Examiner
'The French Elections', 18 July 1830.
'Prospects of France', I, 19 September 1830; III, 3 October 1830; IV, 10 October 1830; V, 17 October 1830.
'Use and Abuse of the Ballot', 28 November 1830.
'The Ballot', 5 December 1830.
'The *Quarterley Review* on the Political Economist', 30 January 1831.
'State of the Parties in France', 28 August 1831.
'Pledges', 1 July 1832; 15 July 1832.
'Saint-Simonism' (review), 2 February 1834.
'State of Opinion in France', 30 March 1834.

The Globe
Unheaded articles, 6 January 1835, p. 2; 12 February 1835, p. 2; 22 June 1835, p. 2.
Letter (signed A), 16 October 1835, p. 2.

The Morning Chronicle
Unheaded articles, 19 November 1846, p. 4; 22 November 1846, p. 4; 30 November 1846, p. 4; 17 December 1846, p. 4.

WORKS ON MARX, ENGELS, AND MARXISM

Acton, H. B. *The Illusion of the Epoch*, London, 1955.
Althusser, L. *For Marx*, London, 1970.
Avineri, S. *The Social and Political Thought of Karl Marx*, Cambridge, 1970.
Berlin, I. *Karl Marx*, London, 1952.
Bloom, S. F. 'The Withering Away of the State', *Journal of the History of Ideas*, VI, 1946.
Bober, M. M. *Karl Marx's Interpretation of History*, Cambridge, 1948.
Bukharin, N. *The A.B.C. of Communism*, Michigan, 1966.
Collins, H. and Abramsky, C. *Karl Marx and the British Labour Movement*, London, 1965.
Cowden, M. H. 'Early Marxist Views of British Labour, 1837–1917', *The Western Political Quarterly*, XVI, 1963.
Feuer, L. 'The North American Origins of Marx's Socialism', *The Western Political Quarterly*, XVI, 1963.
Karl Marx and the Promethean Complex', *Encounter*, December 1968.
Giddens, A. *Capitalism and Modern Social Theory*, Cambridge, 1971.
Hook, S. *Marxism in the Western World*, Encounter Pamphlet 12.
 Towards the Understanding of Karl Marx, London, 1933.
 From Hegel to Marx, Michigan, 1962.
Kamenka, E. *The Ethical Foundations of Marxism*, London, 1962.
Kautsky, K. *The Dictatorship of the Proletariat*, Michigan, 1964.
Kolokowski, L. *Marxism and Beyond*, London, 1971.
Lichtheim, G. *Marxism. An Historical and Critical Study*, London, 1961.
Luxemburg, R. *Leninism or Marxism?* Michigan, 1961.
Marcuse, H. *Soviet Marxism*, New York, 1958.
Mayer, H. 'Marx on Bakunin', *Études de Marxologie*, No. 91, October 1959.
McLellan, D. *Marx before Marxism*, London, 1972.
Meek, R. L. *Economics and Ideology and Other Essays*, London, 1967.
Meyer, A. *Marxism. The Unity of Theory and Practice*, Michigan, 1963.
Moore, S. *Three Tactics: The Background in Marx*, New York, 1963.
Nicolaus, M. 'Hegelian Choreography and the Capitalist Dialectic', *Studies on the Left*, VI, no. 1, 1967.

Bibliography

Ollman, B. *Alienation. Marx's Conception of Man in Capitalist Society*, Cambridge, 1971.
O'Malley, J. 'History and Man's "Nature" in Marx', *The Review of Politics*, XXVIII, 1966.
Parkes, H. B. *Marxism: An Autopsy*, Chicago, 1964.
Plamenatz, J. P. *German Marxism and Russian Communism*, London, 1956. *Man and Society*, vol. II, London, 1963.
Popper, K. *The Open Society and its Enemies*, vol. II, London, 1957.
Rossiter, C. *Marxism: The View from America*, New York, 1960.
Schlesinger, R. *Marx. His Time and Ours*, London, 1951.
Sweezy, P. *The Theory of Capitalist Development*, London, 1942.
Tucker, R. *Philosophy and Myth in Karl Marx*, Cambridge, 1961.

WORKS ON MILL

Burns, J. H. 'J. S. Mill and Democracy', *Political Studies*, II (June 1957).
Cowling, M. *Mill and Liberalism*, Cambridge, 1963.
Friedman, R. 'A New Exploration of Mill's Essay on Liberty', *Political Studies*, XIV, no. 3, October 1966.
'An Introduction to Mill's Theory of Authority', in *Mill: A Collection of Critical Essays*, ed. J. B. Schneewind, London, 1969.
Hamburger, J. *Intellectuals in Politics, John Stuart Mill and the Philosophical Radicals*, New Haven and London, 1965.
Holthoon, F. L. *The Road to Utopia. A Study of John Stuart Mill's Social Thought.* Assen, 1971.
Robson, J. *The Improvement of Mankind: The Social and Political Thought of John Stuart Mill*, Toronto, 1968.
Ryan, A. *The Philosophy of John Stuart Mill*, London, 1970.
'Utilitarianism and Bureaucracy', in *Studies in the Growth of Nineteenth Century Government*, ed. Gillian Sutherland, London, 1972.
Simon, W. M. *European Positivism in the Nineteenth Century*, Cornell, 1963.
Stephen, J. F. *Liberty, Equality, Fraternity*, ed. R. J. White, Cambridge, 1967.
Willey, B. *Nineteenth Century Studies*, London, 1964.

OTHER WORKS

Arendt, H. *On Revolution*, London, 1963.
The Human Condition, Chicago and London, 1970.
Arnold, M. *Culture and Anarchy*, London, 1954.
Bell, D. *The End of Ideology*, Glencoe, 1965.
Benedict, R. *Patterns of Culture*, London, 1961.
Berlin, I. 'Does Political Theory Still Exist?', in *Philosophy, Politics and Society*, 2nd Ser., ed. P. Laslett and W. G. Runciman, Oxford, 1967.
Bottomore, T. B. *Classes in Modern Society*, New York, 1966.
Élites and Society, London, 1966.
Briggs, A. *Victorian People*, London, 1965.
'The Language of "Class" in Early Nineteenth-Century England', in *Essays in Labour History*, ed. A. Briggs and J. Saville, London, 1967.
Burnham, J. *The Managerial Revolution*, London, 1962.
Burke, E. *Reflections on the Revolution in France*, London, 1955.
Burrow, J. W. *Evolution and Society*, Cambridge, 1966.
Cohn, N. *The Pursuit of the Millennium*, London, 1962.
Cropsey, J. *Polity and Economy: An Interpretation of the Principles of Adam Smith*, The Hague, 1957.
Dahl, R. *A Preface to Democratic Theory*, Chicago, 1963.

Bibliography

Dahrendorf, R. *Class and Class Conflict in Industrial Society*, London, 1959.

Deane, Phyllis and Cole, W. A. *British Economic Growth: 1688–1959*, Cambridge, 1964.

Dobb, M. *Studies in the Development of Capitalism*, London, 1963.
Capitalism Yesterday and Today, London, 1961.

Halbwachs, M. *The Psychology of Social Class*, London, 1948.

Halevy, E. *Thomas Hodgskin*, London, 1956.

Hampshire, S. *Thought and Action*, London, 1960.

Hartwell, R. M. 'The Standard of Living in England, 1800–1850', *Economic History Review*, 2nd ser., XII, no. 3, 1961.

Hegel, G. W. F. *The Philosophy of History*, New York, 1956.
Philosophy of Right, Oxford, 1958.

Heimann, E. *History of Economic Doctrines*, Oxford, 1962.

Hobsbawn, E. *The Age of Revolution*, London, 1962.
Labouring Men, London, 1968.
Industry and Empire. London, 1968.

Kuhn, T. *The Structure of Scientific Revolutions*, Chicago, 1970.

Lipset, S. M. *Political Man*, London, 1963.

Lukes, S. *Individualism*, Oxford, 1973.

Malthus, T. *Essay on the Principles of Population*, London, 1872.

Mannheim, K. *Ideology and Utopia*, London, 1960.

Mantoux, P. *The Industrial Revolution in the Eighteenth Century*, London, 1966.

Mill, James, *Essay on Government*, ed. Sir E. Barker, Cambridge, 1937.

Pelling, H. *A History of British Trade Unionism*, London, 1965.

Polyani, K. *The Great Transformation*, Boston, 1957.

Ricardo, D. *The Principles of Political Economy and Taxation*, London, 1962.

Rousseau, J. J. *The Social Contract and The Origin of Inequality*, London, 1955.

Rude, G. *The Crowd in History, 1730–1848*, New York, 1964.

Schumpeter, J. *Capitalism, Socialism and Democracy*, London, 1957.

Smith, A. *The Wealth of Nations*, London, 1960.

Stark, W. *The History of Economics*, London, 1964.

Stretton, H. *The Political Sciences*, London, 1969.

Talmon, J. L. *The Origins of Totalitarian Democracy*, London, 1961.

Tawney, R. H. *Religion and the Rise of Capitalism*, London, 1948.

Tholfsen, T. R. 'The Transition to Democracy in Victorian England', *International Review of Social History*, VI, no. 2, 1961.

Thompson, E. *The Making of the English Working Class*, London, 1968.

Tönnies, F. *Community and Society*, New York, 1963.

Vincent, J. *Pollbooks: How Victorians Voted*, Cambridge, 1967.
The Formation of the British Liberal Party, London, 1972.

Index

Index

Marx, K.: Works – cont.
118, 119, 136. *See also* Young Marx
Marx, K. and Engels, F.: Works: Com-
munist Manifesto, 22, 64, 103, 106,
118, 127, 129, 148, 165, 186. The
German Ideology, 59, 63, 65, 70, 73,
78, 79, 81, 82, 85, 98, 132, 141, 142,
143, 149, 175, 183, 189, 298. The Holy
Family, 59, 60, 61, 81, 86, 90, 95, 100,
125, 134, 135, 149, 150, 187, 197.
Letters, to A. Bebel etc., 17/9/1879,
158; Circular letter, 17–18/9/1879, 164
Marxism: contra liberalism, 287f
Mason, J., 205
Macpherson, C. B., 295
Mayer, H., 340
Meek, R. L., 51
Messianism, 15f
Michels, R.: and oligarchy, 203
middle class: fitness to rule, 216; increase of, 275; and class interest, 281
Mill, James, 218f; *Essay on Government*, 218, 220, 223
Mill, J. S.: Works: Auguste Comte and
Positivism, 215, 236, 243, 254, 257,
260, 279. Autobiography, 210, 225,
226, 243, 249, 251, 252. The Ballot,
222; Bentham and Coleridge, 217,
264, 269, 278. Centralization, 249,
275. Chapters on Socialism, 235, 236,
245, 246, 257. Civilization, 216, 238.
Claims of Labour, 227, 251, 253. The
Close of the Session, 225. Commencement of the Session – Progress of Reform, 249. Democracy in America,
227, 229, 240, 264, 265, 275. Essays on
some Unsettled Questions of Political
Economy, 111. A Few Observations
on the French Revolution, 236. Fonblanque's England under Seven
Administrations, 220. Inaugural
Address at St. Andrew's University,
252, 253. Leters, to A. Bain 6/8/1859,
259; to G. d'Eichtal, 225; to his
father 20/8/1830, 226; to Parker
Godwin, 247; to J. S. Kinnear 25/9/
1865, 226; to Mollett 12/1847, 238;
to J. Sterling 20/10/1831, 261; 4/11/
1839, 211; to J. Whiting 15/10/1842,
235. Lord Durham's Return, 268.
Modern French Historical Works –
Age of Chivalry, 220. Nature, 214.
Newman's Political Economy, 255.
On Liberty, 217, 242, 250, 251, 255,
259, 260, 278. On Miss Martineau's

Summary of Political Economy, 230.
Pledges, 221, 266. Principles of Political Economy, 221, 227, 240, 241,
242, 243, 244, 245, 246, 247, 248, 249,
251, 255, 274, 275, 282, 284. Prospects
of France, 224, 235. The Quarterly
Review of the Political Economists,
239. The Rationale of Political Representation, 221, 225, 231, 236, 259,
261, 262, 276, 281. Recent Writers on
Reform, 228. Reorganization of the
Reform Party, 223, 226, 227, 228, 231.
Representative Government, 213, 219,
220, 221, 228, 236, 249, 259, 261, 263,
264, 265, 266, 267, 269, 271. Review of
Scott's Life of Napoleon, 220. Speech
on Personal Representation, 271. Sir
John Walsh's Contemporary History
– Progress of Reform, 221. The Spirit
of the Age, 214, 216, 260. The State
of Society in America, 240. The State
of the Parties in France, 274. Subjection of Women, 252. A System of
Logic, 209, 213, 234, 253, 277, 283.
Thoughts on Parliamentary Reform,
272. Utilitarianism, 238, 251, 254,
274. Utility of Religion, 252, 254, 255
money: Marx on, 82f
morality: and social class, 148
Mosca, G., 203

nature: niggardliness of, 241

objectification: contrasted to alienation,
80, 83
oligarchy, 203
Oppenheim, F., 293
overpopulation: problem of, 241f

Palmerston, H.: and Bonapartism, 161
paradigm, 6, 12
Paris Commune: Marx on, 171, 176
peasantry, French, 124
petit-bourgeoisie, 128f
philosophical radicals, the, 223f
philosophy of history, Mill's, 261
piecemeal engineering, 235
platonism, Mill's, 259
political economy: 38f; and socialists,
52f; and class interest, 230; Mill on
239
political participation, 248
political theory: Marx on, 140f; Mill
on, 262f; and consensus, 270–1;
agreement about, 277

Index

Popper, K., 4; and Marx on revolution, 157, 345
positivism: and J. S. Mill, 215
poverty: abolition of, 238
power: and social forms, 213
pressure groups, 310
primitive societies: and Marx and Engels, 66f
principle of association, 252
private property, 79; Mill on, 246
progress, 216
proletariat: as a class, 124f; conservatism of, 135f; revolution tactics of, 135; and Liberal party, 136; English and Irish, 137; dictatorship of, 170, 176; dictatorship and Jacobin dictatorship, 180; revolution and historical revolutions, 199
Proportional representation: Mill on, 265
Proudhon, P.-J., 41; as reformist, 164, 187
Prussia, 221
psychology: Benthamite, 253, 282; principle of association, 252
public opinion: as a moral force, 255

radicals, philosophical, 215f
Raphael: Marx and Engels on, 141
religion: and Marx, 56, 81f; Mill on, 252f; of Humanity, 276
representative government: Mill on, 232f
revisionism, 304
revolution: French and Industrial, 19f; 1848 in France, 131f; French, 134; proletarian tactics of, 135f; transition period, 170f; conditions for, 198; Russian, 206; Marx's grounds for, 289f; preconditions, 302; need for a new theory for, 313
Ricardo, D., 45f, 50f
Rights of Man, 21
Ritchie, D. G., 272
romanticism, 75
Rossiter, C., 17, 206
Rousseau, J. J.: and bureaucracy, 204; and leaders, 283
Rudé, G., 32
ruling class: Mill on, 282f

Saint-Simon, H., 190
Schiller, F., 77
Schnattschneider, E., 310
Schumpeter, J., 100, 333

science: ideology and, 5f
self-interest: and capitalism, 110
Shils, E., 305
Smith, A., 39f; and naturalism, 43; and values, 45f; and labour, 80; Marx on, 88
social class, 120f; definition of, 121f; intermediate classes, 127f; and faction, 132; J. S. Mill on, 219; and liberal politics, 280f
Social Democratic Party; German, and Engels, 160; and the bourgeoisie, 163
social theory: and values, 3f; and language, 6f; disconfirmation of, 9f; and madness, 11; reductionist versions, 12; Marx and Engels on, 139f
socialisation, 29f, 297–300
socialism, 21–2, 52–4, 273, 295–6
society: post-revolutionary, 167f; vs. state, 40–1, 249; Mill on civil, 269; Marx's theory of, 289; Mill on, 291f
Sorel, G., 172
Spartan State: Mill on, 254
species-being: of man, 74f; Marx and Engels on, 145
Stalin, J., 206
state: alienation and the, 85; and civil society, 91; and class interest, 146f; and the revolutionary transition, 180; withering away of, 189; vs. society, 40–1, 249; and education, 251
steam power: and the transformation of production, 23f
Stephen, F., 276

Talmon, J., 15f, 237
technology: Marx and Engels on, 183f
teleology, Hegelian: and Marxism, 196
Thompson, E. P., 26, 28, 31
Tönnies, F., 21
de Tocqueville, A.: and Manchester, 25; and democracy, 248
totalitarianism, 15f; Mill as an exponent of, 276f
transitional age: J. S. Mill on the, 214, 275
transitional institutions, 168f
Trotsky, L., 158, 201
Tucker, R.: and social freedom, 205

unemployed: reserve army of, 107f
unionism, 33f
universal suffrage; 156f; and the working class movement, 158; and chartism, 159; Mill on, 231

Index

universality: and particularity in the state, 145
Ure, A.: and the factory system, 25, 108
U.S.A., and the classical economists, 46
utilitarianism, 2; and social theory, 217f; and psychological assumptions, 217
utopianism: Marx and Engels on, 167; Mill on, 235f

value: labour theory of, 103f
values: and social theory, 3f; and government, 262
Vincent, J., 33, 37, 210
von Stein, L., 92

wages: theory of, 103f; subsistence level, 105
Webb, B. and S., 30
Whitehead, A., 5
Wolff, R. P., 273
women: and raw communism, 173; Mill on, 252
working class: immiseration, 114f; domestication of, 163; abolition of, 196; Mill on, 226; and democracy, 229; consciousness, 301
Wright, T., 34

Young Hegelians: and Marx, 59–61
young Marx: the question of the, 74

Zawadski, 301